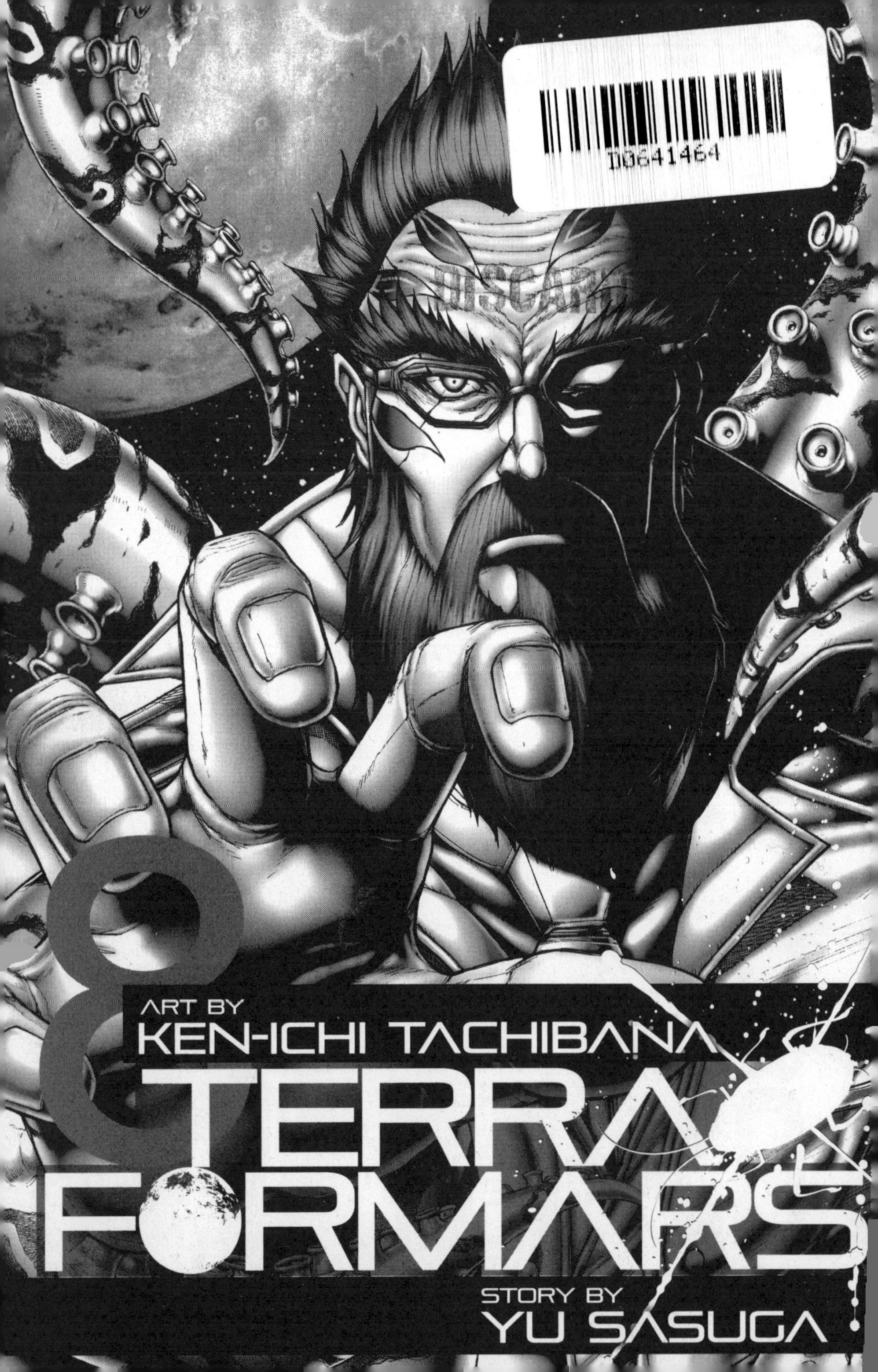
8
ART BY
KEN-ICHI TACHIBANA
TERRA FORMARS
STORY BY
YU SASUGA

TERRA FORMARS 8

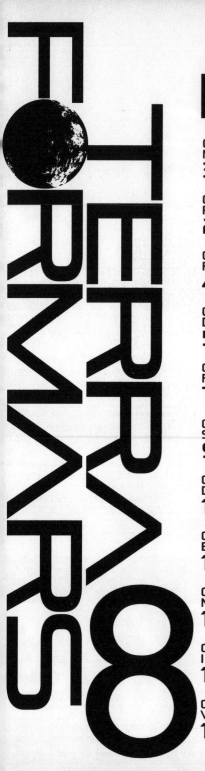

CONTENTS

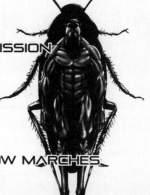

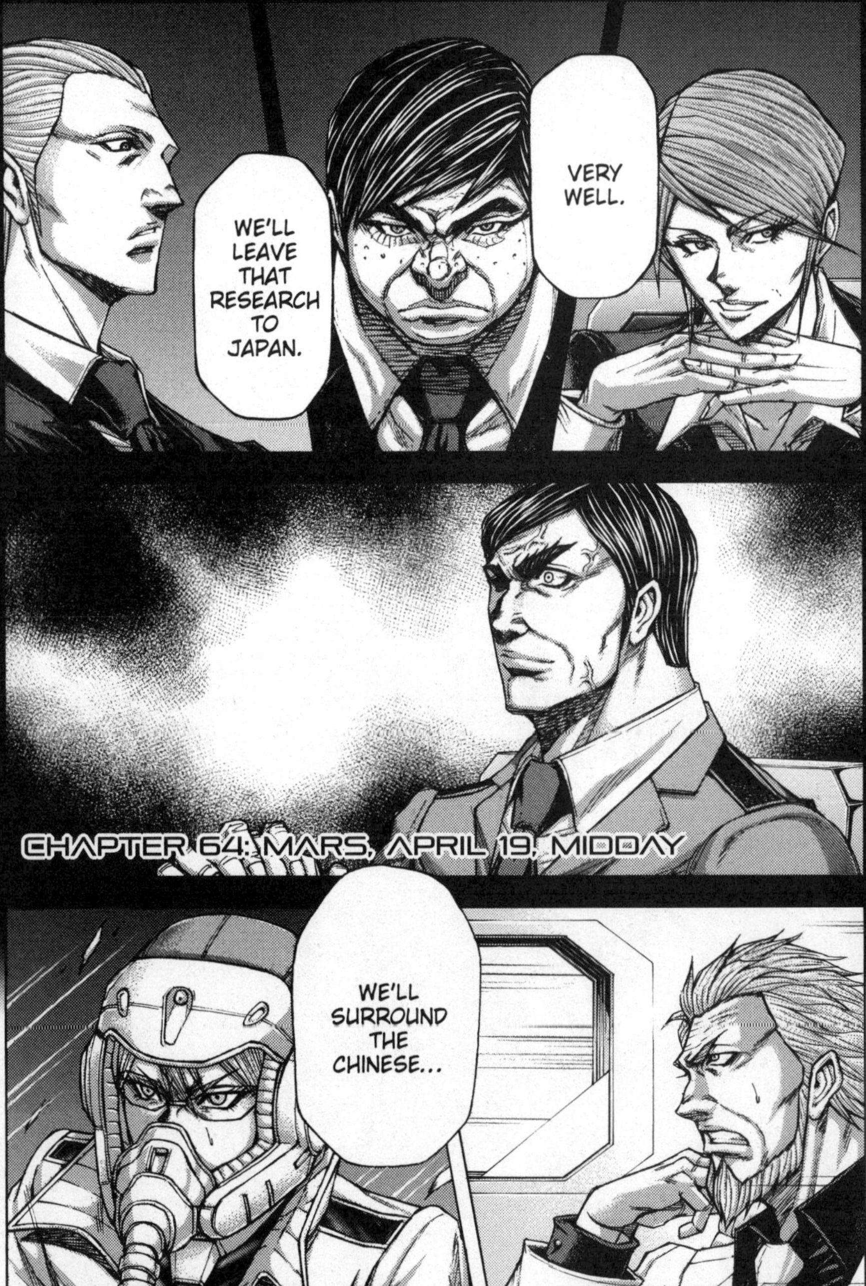
VERY WELL.
WE'LL LEAVE THAT RESEARCH TO JAPAN.
CHAPTER 64: MARS, APRIL 19, MIDDAY
WE'LL SURROUND THE CHINESE...

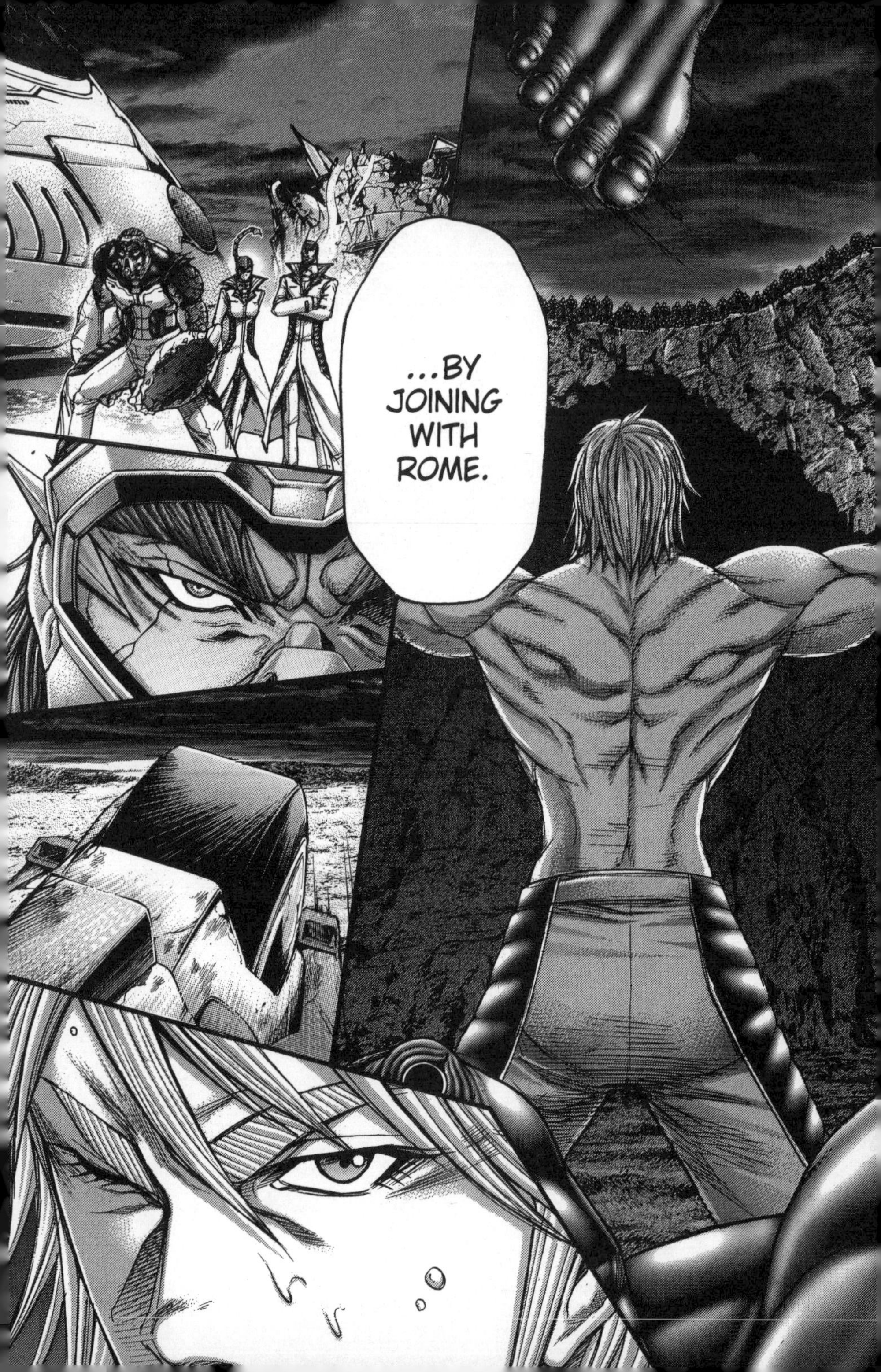
...BY JOINING WITH ROME.

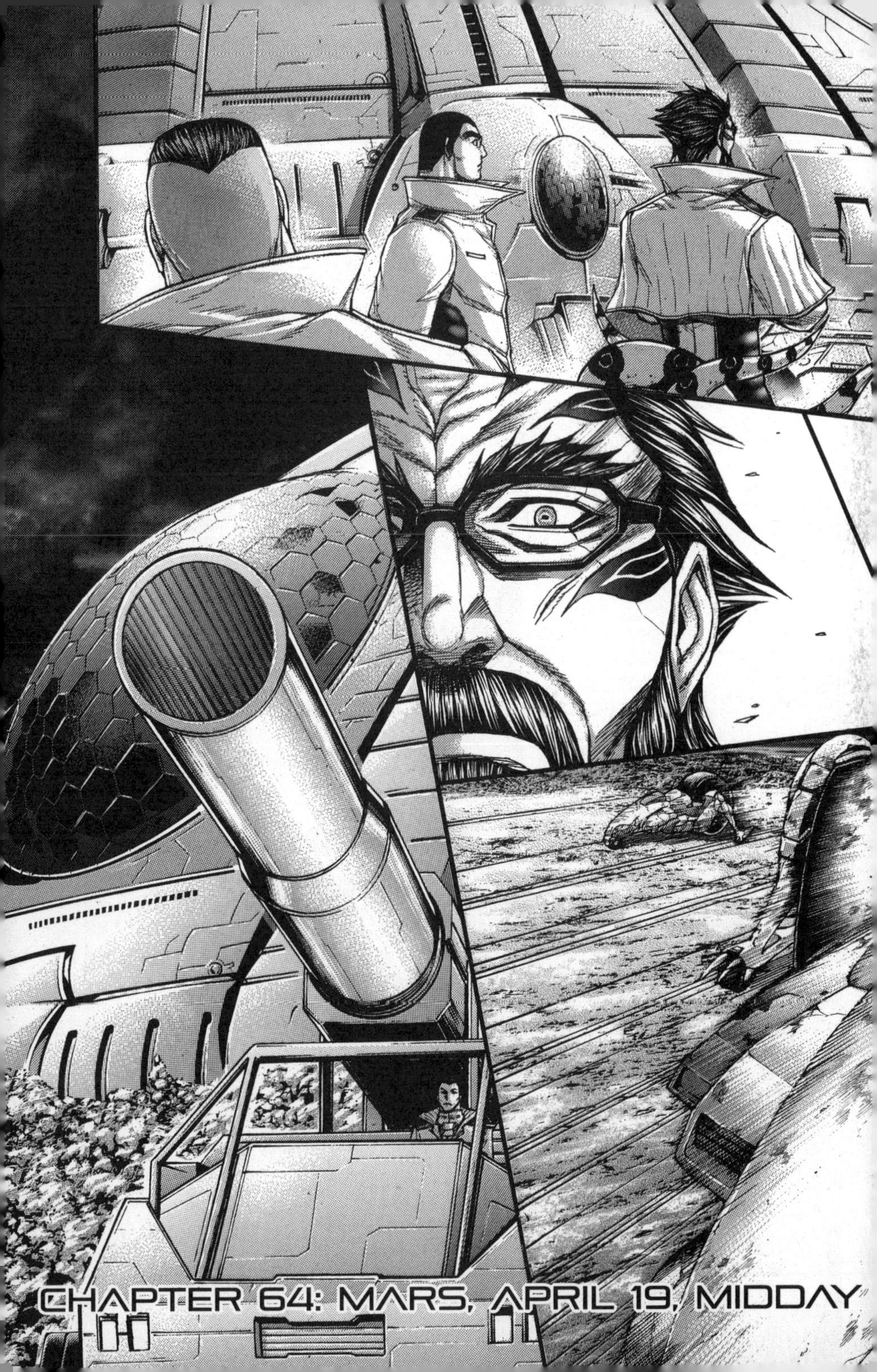
CHAPTER 64: MARS, APRIL 19, MIDDAY

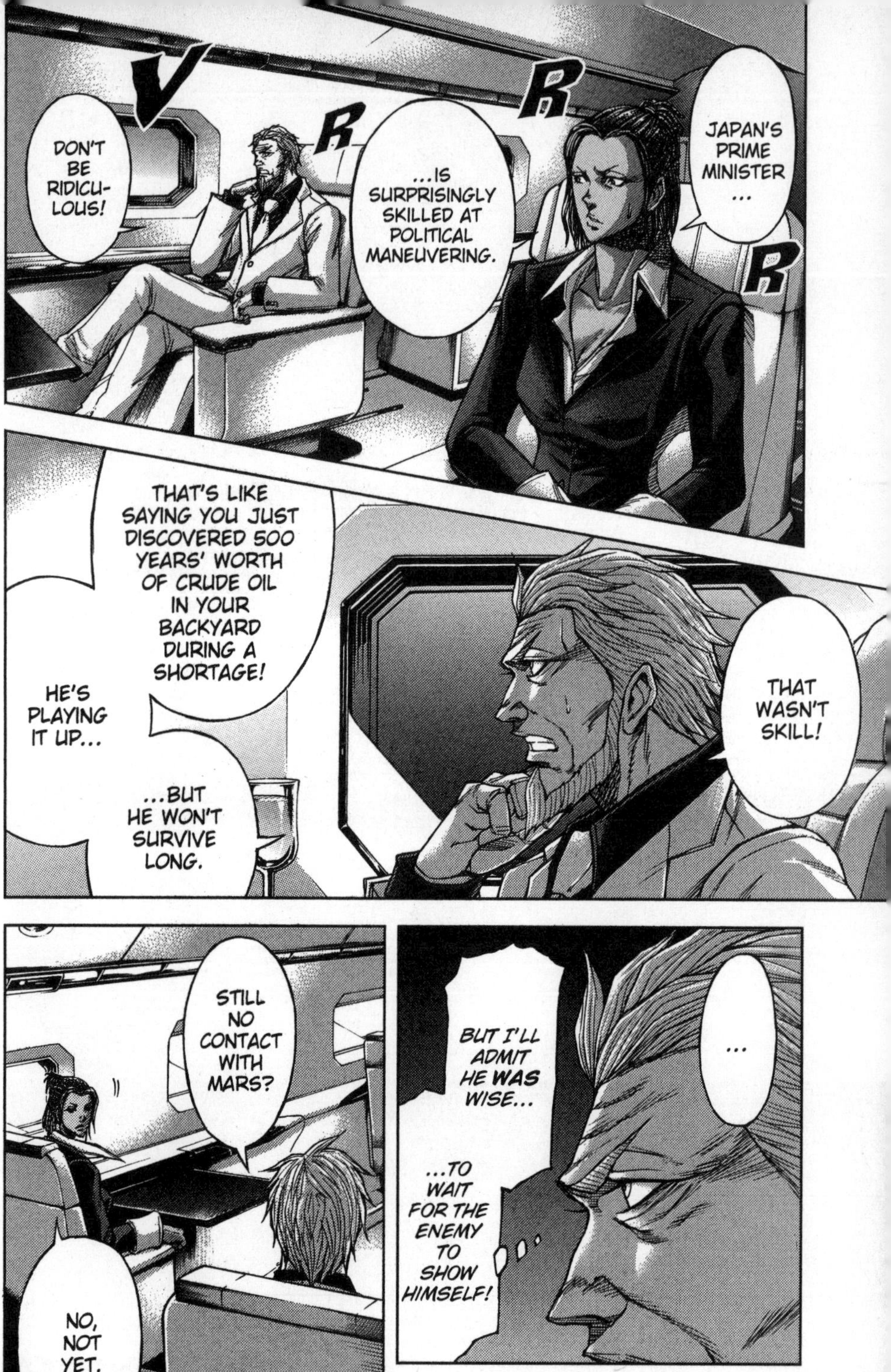
JAPAN'S PRIME MINISTER ...
...IS SURPRISINGLY SKILLED AT POLITICAL MANEUVERING.
VRRR
DON'T BE RIDICU-LOUS!
THAT WASN'T SKILL!
THAT'S LIKE SAYING YOU JUST DISCOVERED 500 YEARS' WORTH OF CRUDE OIL IN YOUR BACKYARD DURING A SHORTAGE!
HE'S PLAYING IT UP...
...BUT HE WON'T SURVIVE LONG.
...
BUT I'LL ADMIT HE **WAS** WISE...
...TO WAIT FOR THE ENEMY TO SHOW HIMSELF!
STILL NO CONTACT WITH MARS?
NO, NOT YET.

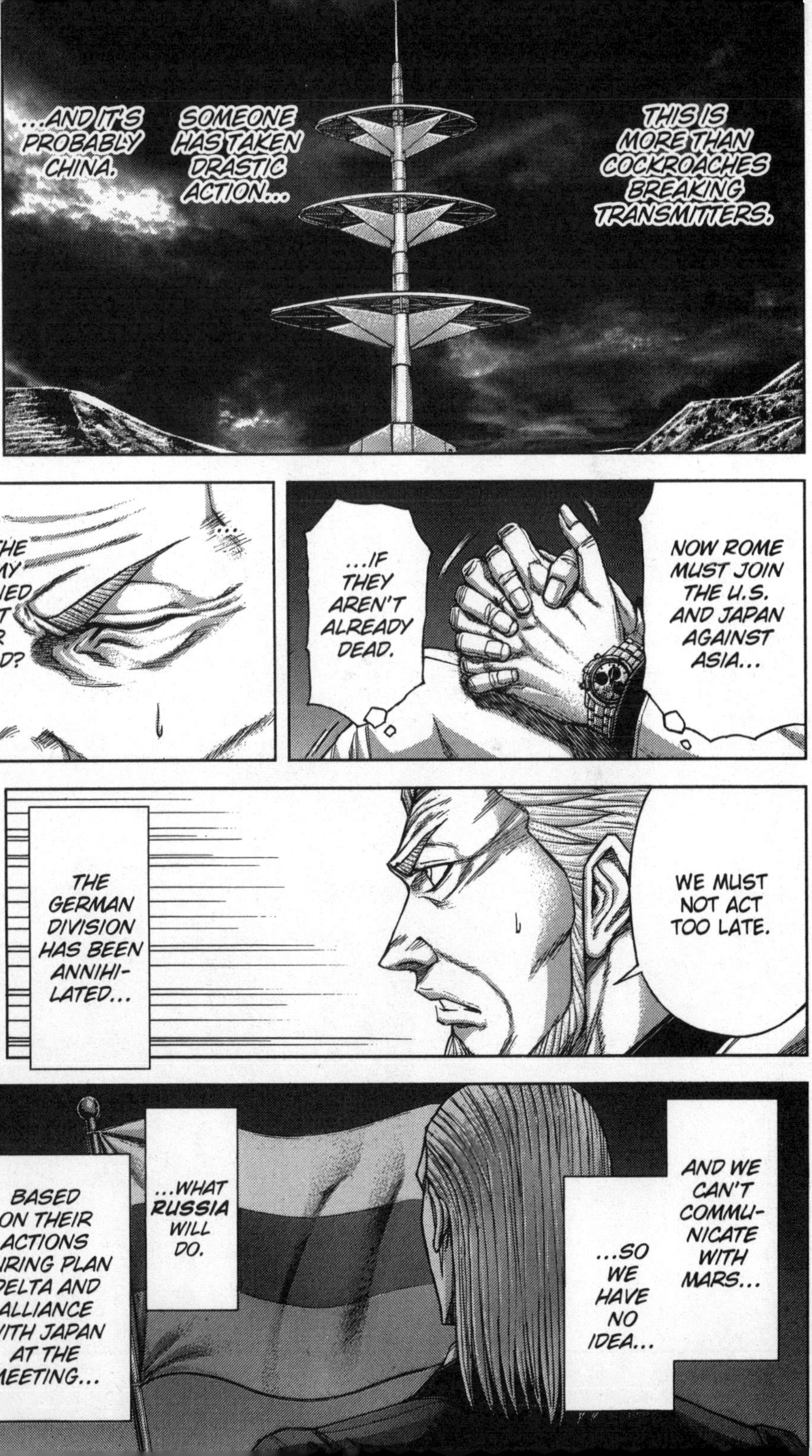
THIS IS MORE THAN COCKROACHES BREAKING TRANSMITTERS.
SOMEONE HAS TAKEN DRASTIC ACTION...
...AND IT'S PROBABLY CHINA.
NOW ROME MUST JOIN THE U.S. AND JAPAN AGAINST ASIA...
...IF THEY AREN'T ALREADY DEAD.
...
OR HAS THE ENEMY PLANNED THAT FAR AHEAD?
WE MUST NOT ACT TOO LATE.
THE GERMAN DIVISION HAS BEEN ANNIHILATED...
AND WE CAN'T COMMUNICATE WITH MARS...
...SO WE HAVE NO IDEA...
...WHAT RUSSIA WILL DO.
BASED ON THEIR ACTIONS DURING PLAN DELTA AND ALLIANCE WITH JAPAN AT THE MEETING...

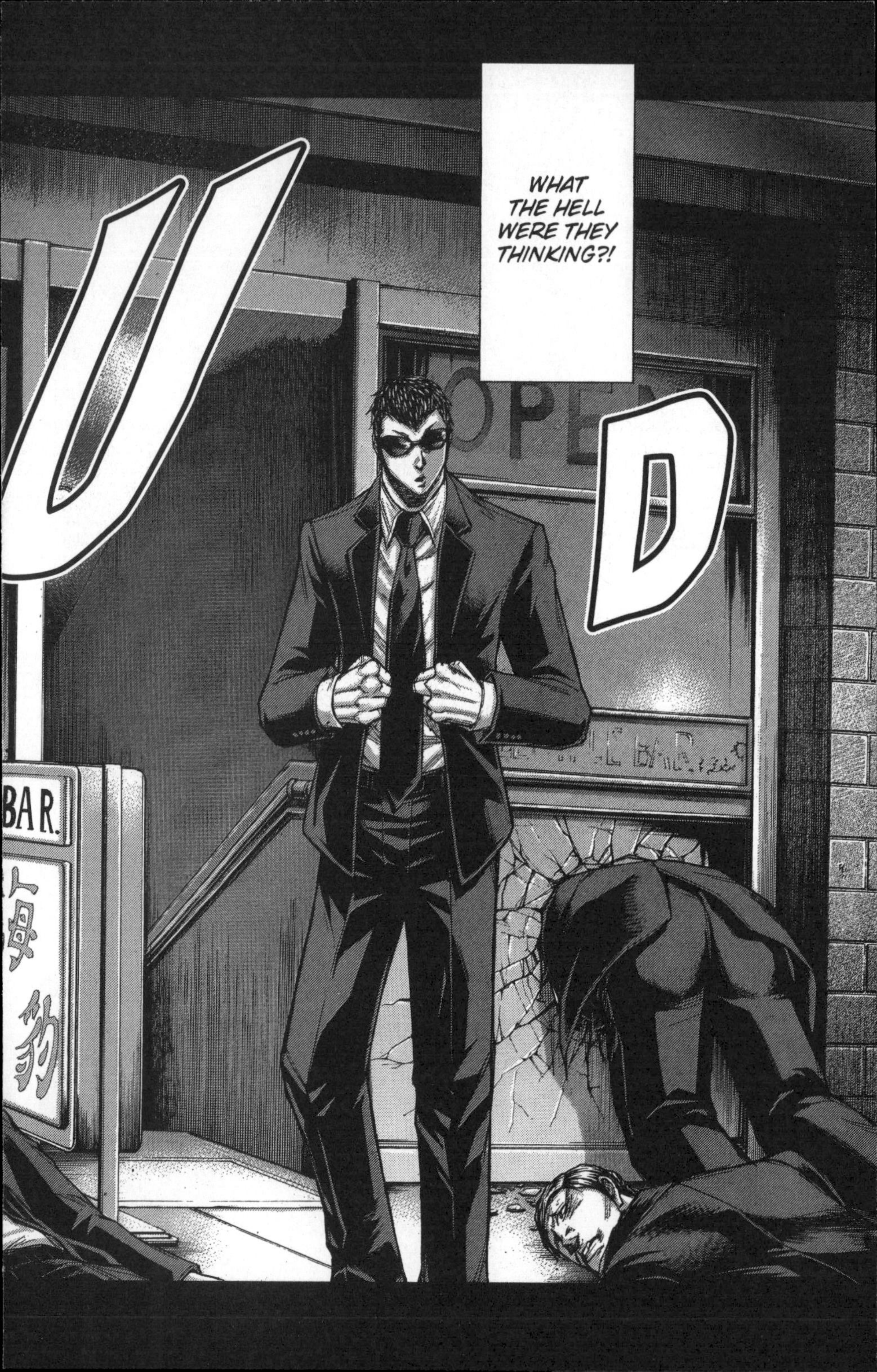
WHAT THE HELL WERE THEY THINKING?!
U
D
BAR.

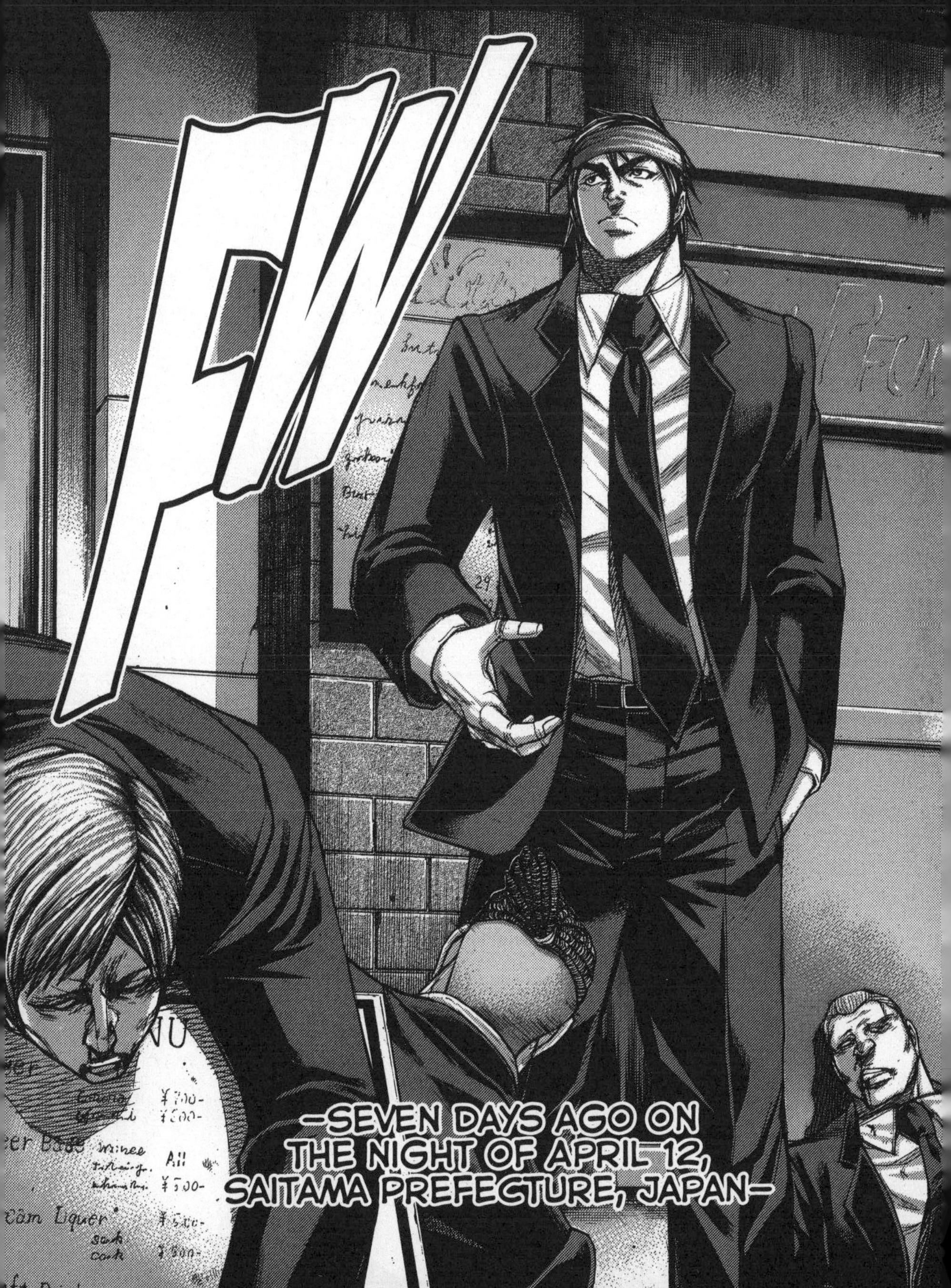
FW!
—SEVEN DAYS AGO ON THE NIGHT OF APRIL 12, SAITAMA PREFECTURE, JAPAN—

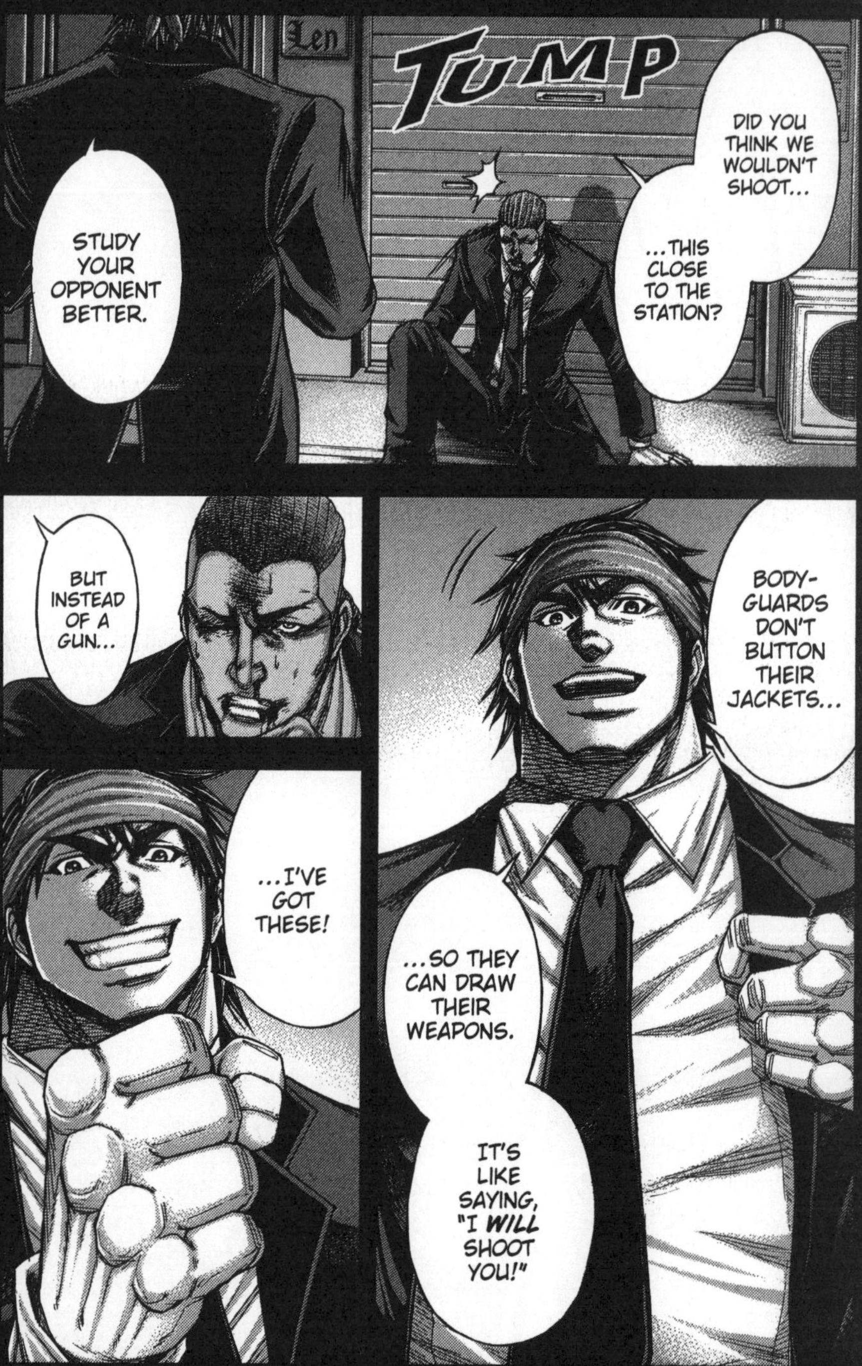
TUMP
DID YOU THINK WE WOULDN'T SHOOT...
...THIS CLOSE TO THE STATION?
Len
STUDY YOUR OPPONENT BETTER.
BODY-GUARDS DON'T BUTTON THEIR JACKETS...
...SO THEY CAN DRAW THEIR WEAPONS.
IT'S LIKE SAYING, "I *WILL* SHOOT YOU!"
BUT INSTEAD OF A GUN...
...I'VE GOT THESE!

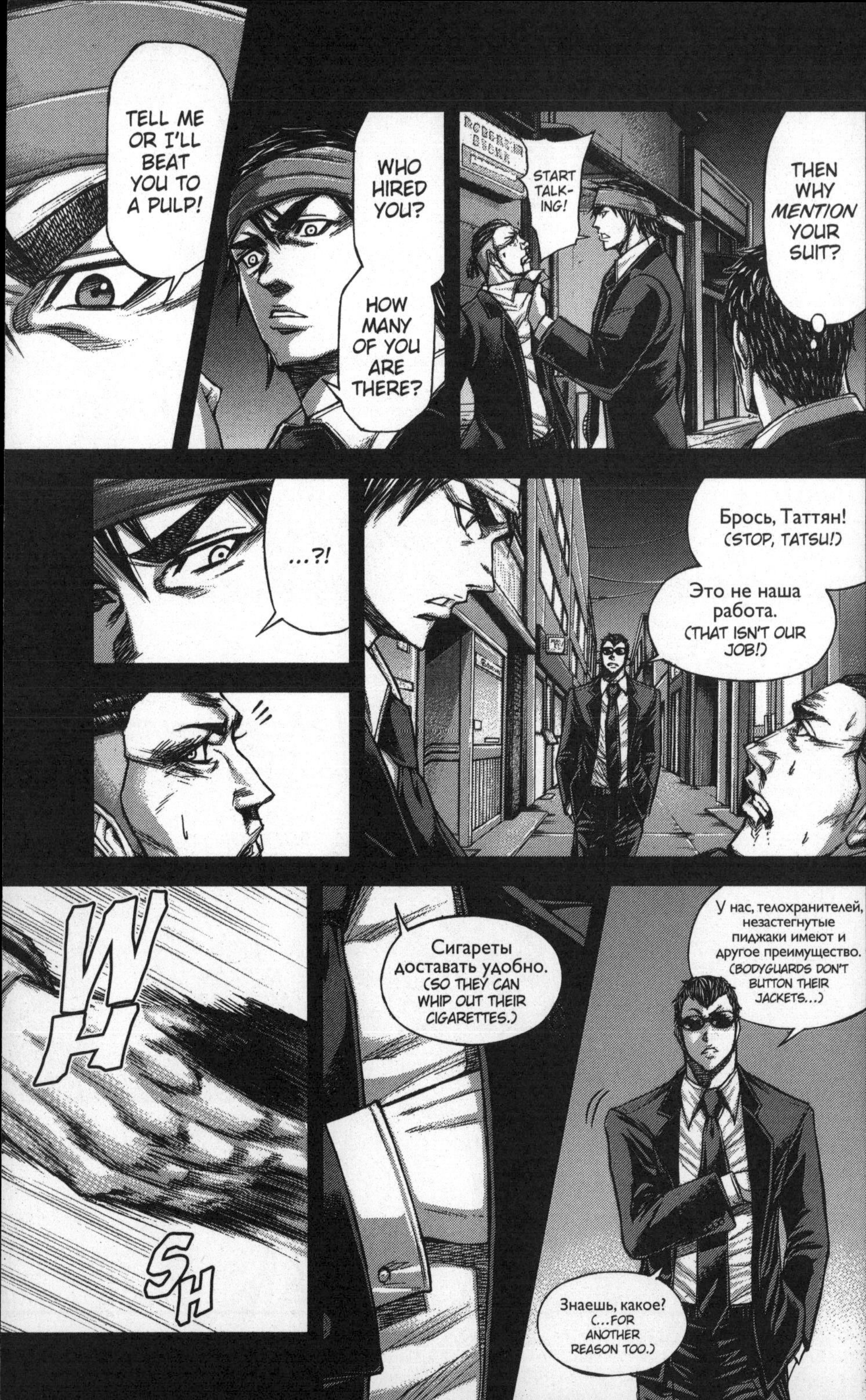
THEN WHY *MENTION* YOUR SUIT?
START TALKING!
WHO HIRED YOU?
HOW MANY OF YOU ARE THERE?
TELL ME OR I'LL BEAT YOU TO A PULP!
Брось, Таттян! (STOP, TATSU!)
Это не наша работа. (THAT ISN'T OUR JOB!)
...?!
У нас, телохранителей, незастегнутые пиджаки имеют и другое преимущество. (BODYGUARDS DON'T BUTTON THEIR JACKETS...)
Знаешь, какое? (...FOR ANOTHER REASON TOO.)
Сигареты доставать удобно. (SO THEY CAN WHIP OUT THEIR CIGARETTES.)
WH
SH

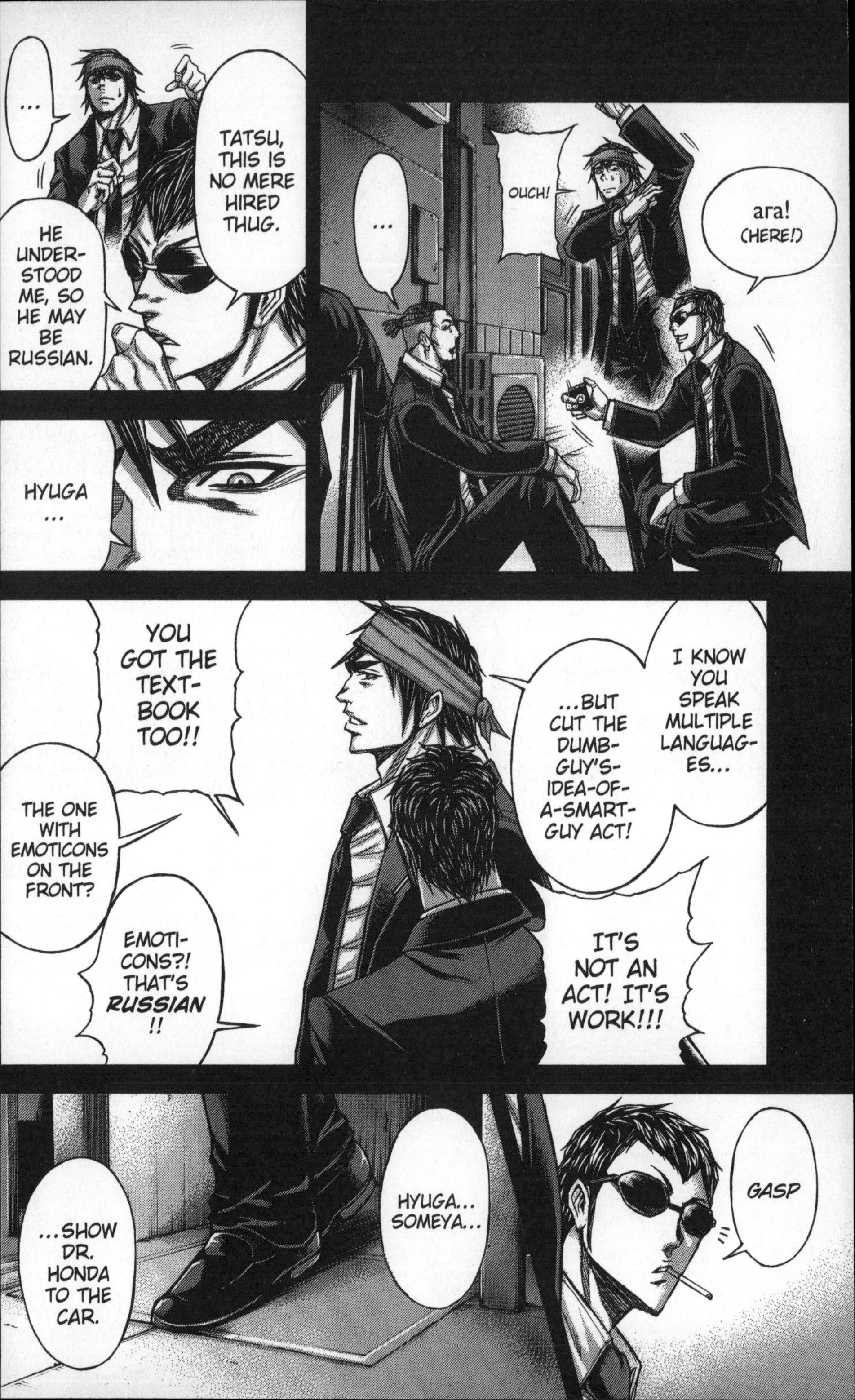
ara! (HERE!)
OUCH!
...
TATSU, THIS IS NO MERE HIRED THUG.
HE UNDER-STOOD ME, SO HE MAY BE RUSSIAN.
...
HYUGA ...
I KNOW YOU SPEAK MULTIPLE LANGUAG-ES...
...BUT CUT THE DUMB-GUY'S-IDEA-OF-A-SMART-GUY ACT!
YOU GOT THE TEXT-BOOK TOO!!
THE ONE WITH EMOTICONS ON THE FRONT?
IT'S NOT AN ACT! IT'S WORK!!!
EMOTI-CONS?! THAT'S *RUSSIAN* !!
GASP
HYUGA... SOMEYA...
...SHOW DR. HONDA TO THE CAR.

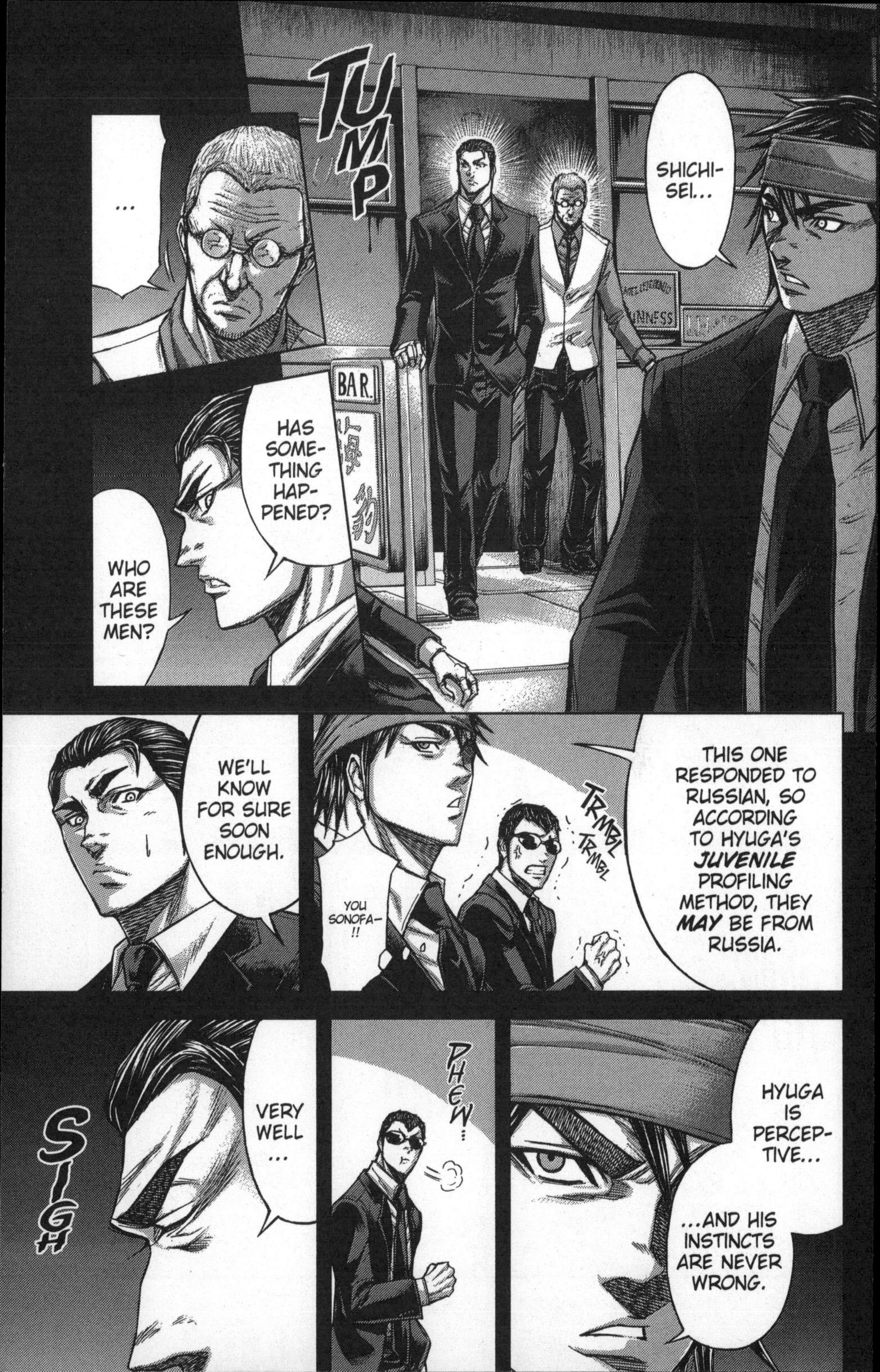
TUMP
SHICHI-SEI...
BAR.
...
HAS SOMETHING HAPPENED?
WHO ARE THESE MEN?
THIS ONE RESPONDED TO RUSSIAN, SO ACCORDING TO HYUGA'S JUVENILE PROFILING METHOD, THEY MAY BE FROM RUSSIA.
TRMBL TRMBL
YOU SONOFA-!!
WE'LL KNOW FOR SURE SOON ENOUGH.
HYUGA IS PERCEPTIVE...
...AND HIS INSTINCTS ARE NEVER WRONG.
PHEW...
VERY WELL...
SIGH

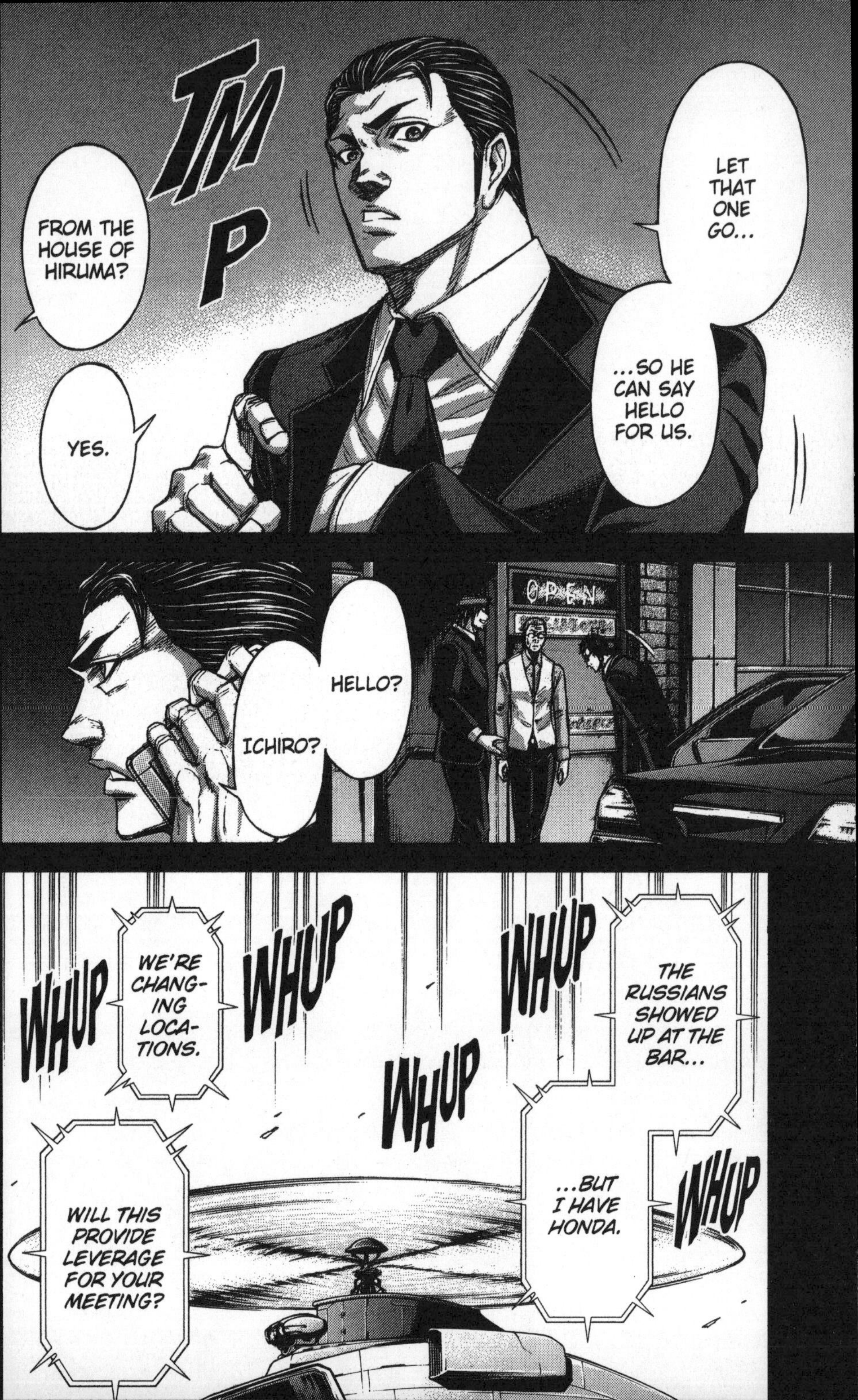
LET THAT ONE GO...
TMP
FROM THE HOUSE OF HIRUMA?
...SO HE CAN SAY HELLO FOR US.
YES.
HELLO?
ICHIRO?
WHUP
THE RUSSIANS SHOWED UP AT THE BAR...
WHUP
WHUP
WE'RE CHANGING LOCATIONS.
WHUP
WHUP
...BUT I HAVE HONDA.
WILL THIS PROVIDE LEVERAGE FOR YOUR MEETING?

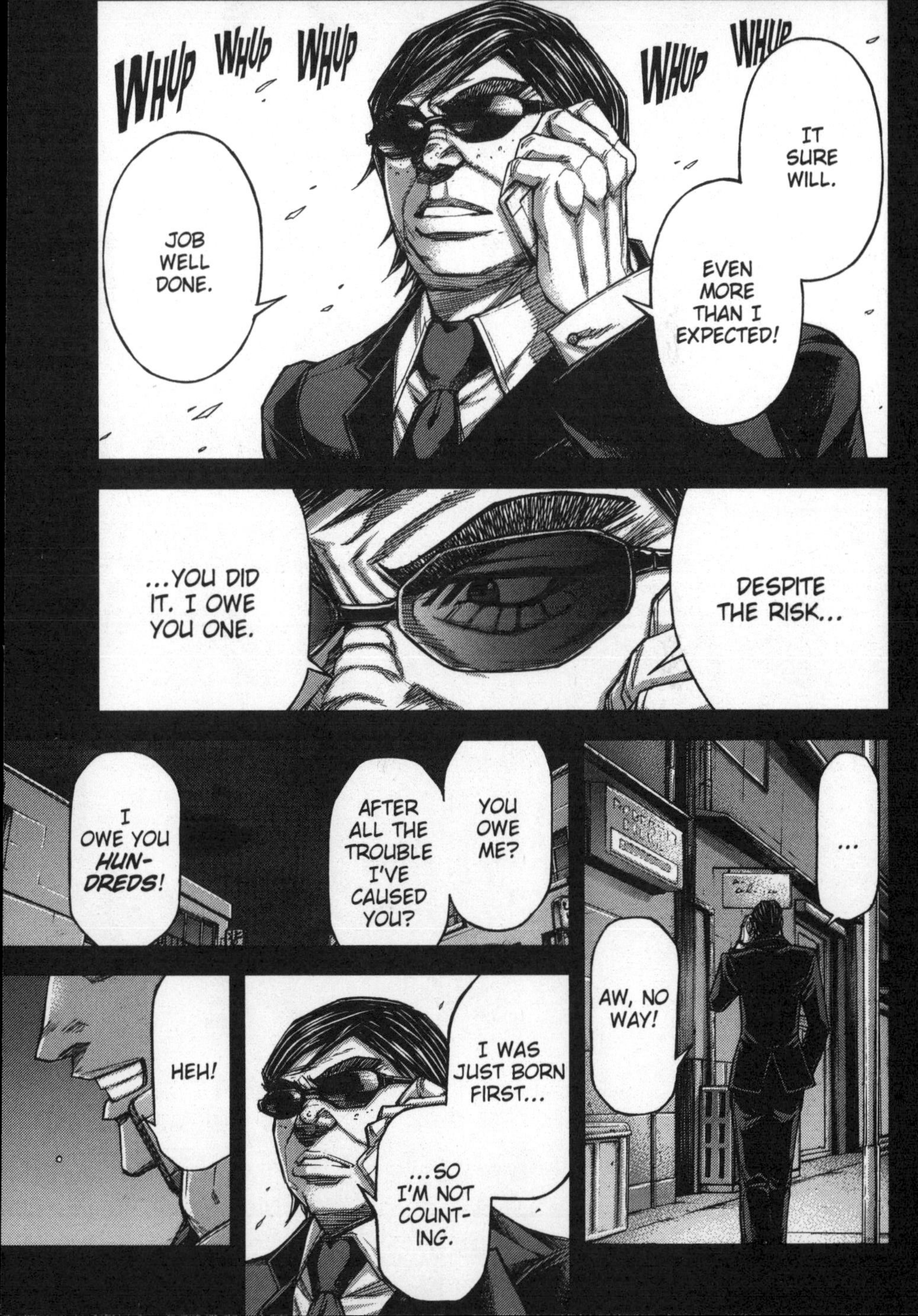

WHUP WHUP
WHUP WHUP WHUP
IT SURE WILL.
EVEN MORE THAN I EXPECTED!
JOB WELL DONE.
DESPITE THE RISK...
...YOU DID IT. I OWE YOU ONE.
...
AW, NO WAY!
YOU OWE ME?
AFTER ALL THE TROUBLE I'VE CAUSED YOU?
I OWE YOU *HUNDREDS!*
I WAS JUST BORN FIRST...
...SO I'M NOT COUNTING.
HEH!

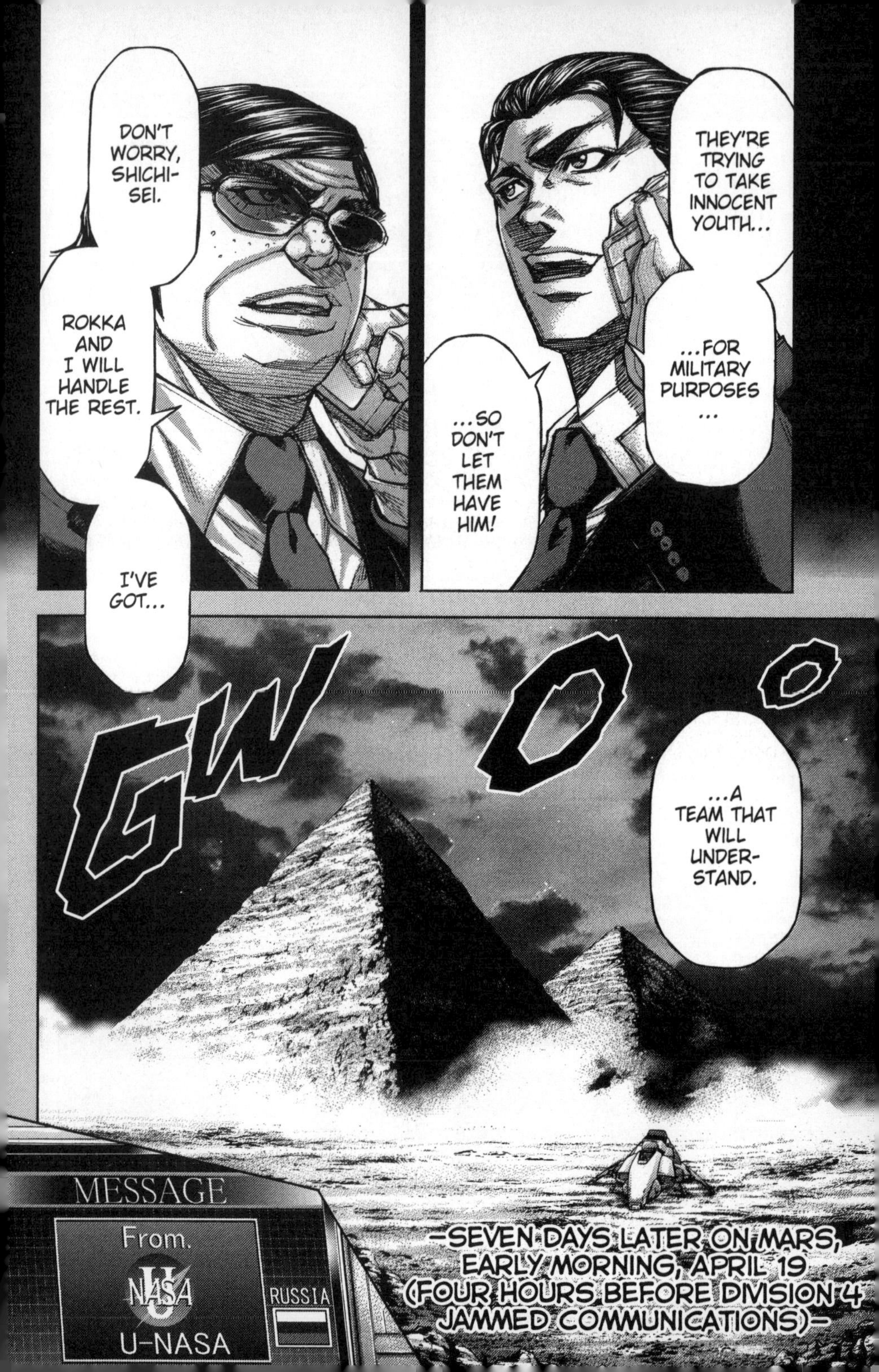
THEY'RE TRYING TO TAKE INNOCENT YOUTH...
...FOR MILITARY PURPOSES...
...SO DON'T LET THEM HAVE HIM!
DON'T WORRY, SHICHI-SEI.
ROKKA AND I WILL HANDLE THE REST.
I'VE GOT...
...A TEAM THAT WILL UNDER-STAND.
GWOO
MESSAGE
From.
U-NASA
RUSSIA
U-NASA
-SEVEN DAYS LATER ON MARS, EARLY MORNING, APRIL 19 (FOUR HOURS BEFORE DIVISION 4 JAMMED COMMUNICATIONS)-

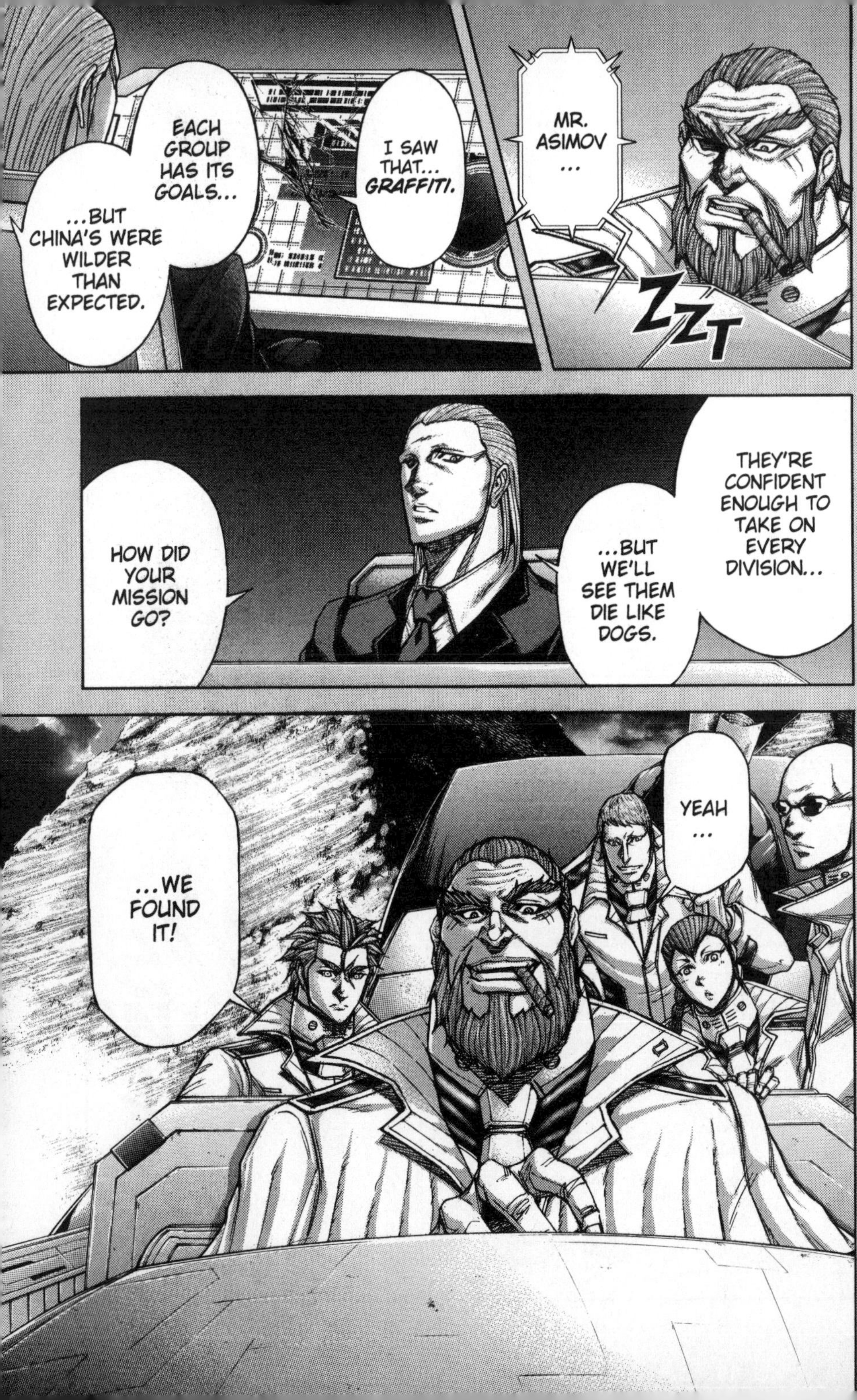
MR. ASIMOV...
ZZT
I SAW THAT... GRAFFITI.
EACH GROUP HAS ITS GOALS...
...BUT CHINA'S WERE WILDER THAN EXPECTED.
THEY'RE CONFIDENT ENOUGH TO TAKE ON EVERY DIVISION...
...BUT WE'LL SEE THEM DIE LIKE DOGS.
HOW DID YOUR MISSION GO?
YEAH...
...WE FOUND IT!

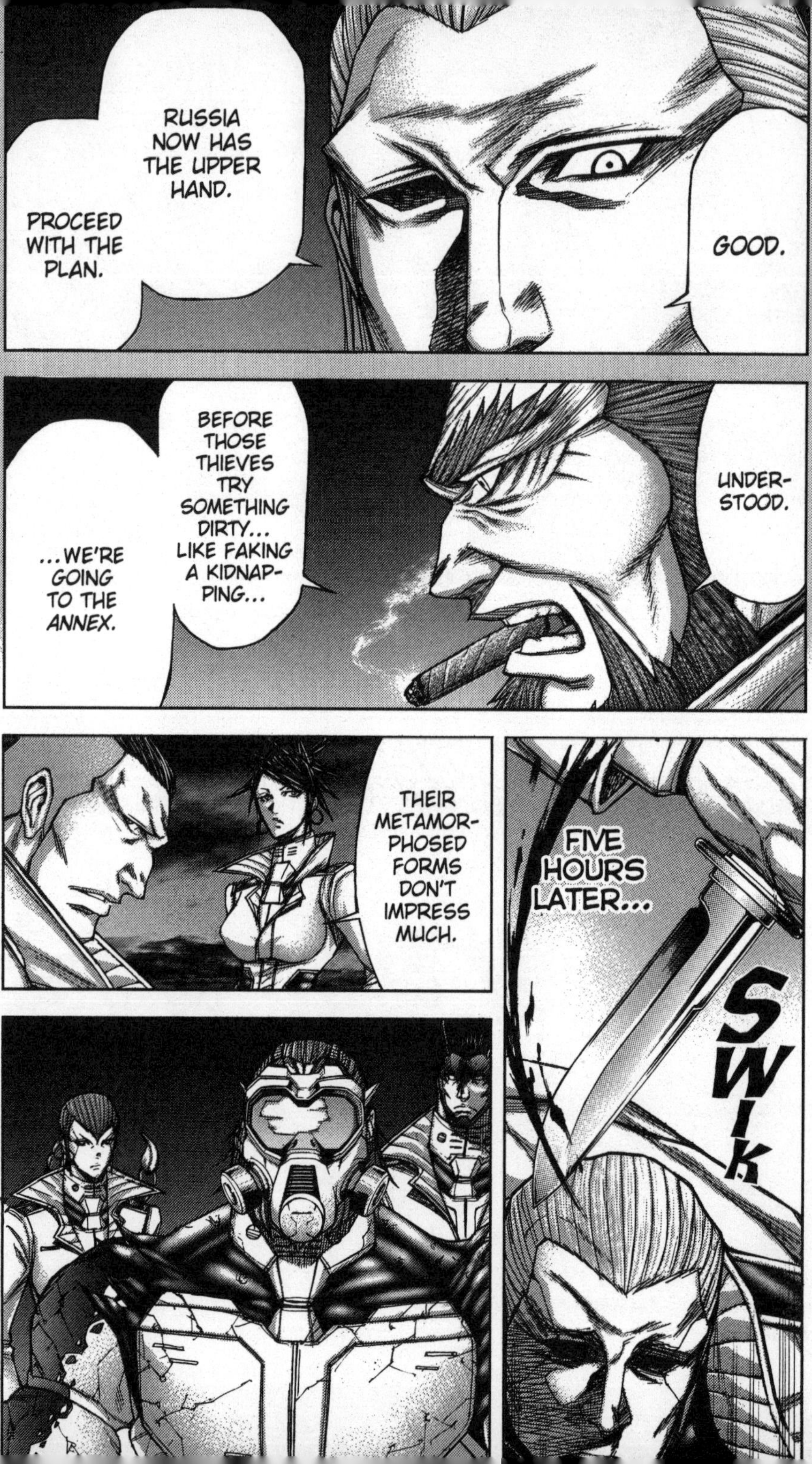
GOOD.
RUSSIA NOW HAS THE UPPER HAND.
PROCEED WITH THE PLAN.
UNDER-STOOD.
BEFORE THOSE THIEVES TRY SOMETHING DIRTY... LIKE FAKING A KIDNAP-PING...
...WE'RE GOING TO THE ANNEX.
FIVE HOURS LATER...
SWIK.
THEIR METAMOR-PHOSED FORMS DON'T IMPRESS MUCH.

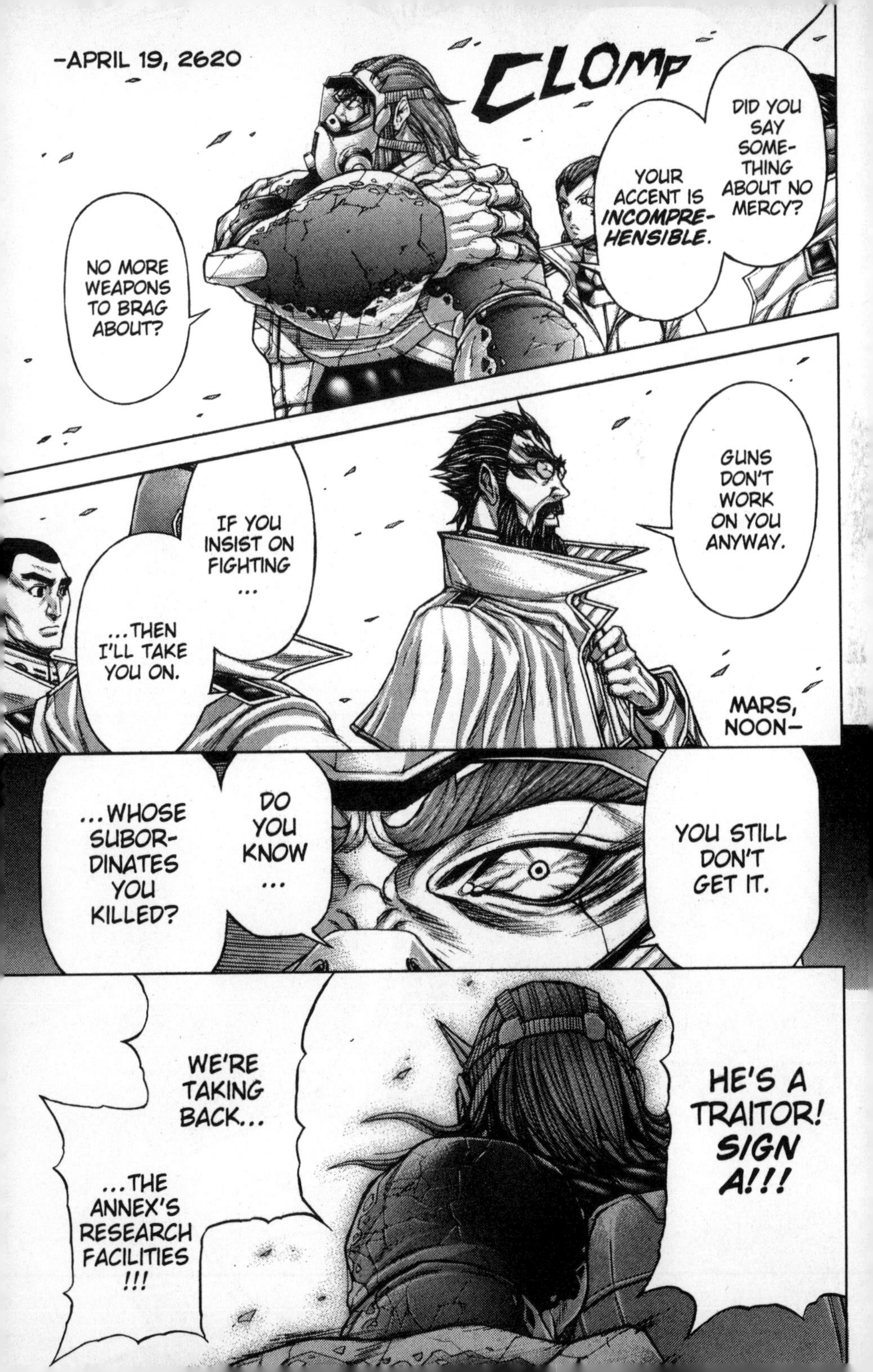
-APRIL 19, 2620
CLOMP
DID YOU SAY SOME-THING ABOUT NO MERCY?
YOUR ACCENT IS *INCOMPRE-HENSIBLE*.
NO MORE WEAPONS TO BRAG ABOUT?
GUNS DON'T WORK ON YOU ANYWAY.
MARS, NOON-
IF YOU INSIST ON FIGHTING...
...THEN I'LL TAKE YOU ON.
YOU STILL DON'T GET IT.
DO YOU KNOW...
...WHOSE SUBOR-DINATES YOU KILLED?
HE'S A TRAITOR! *SIGN A!!!*
WE'RE TAKING BACK...
...THE ANNEX'S RESEARCH FACILITIES!!!

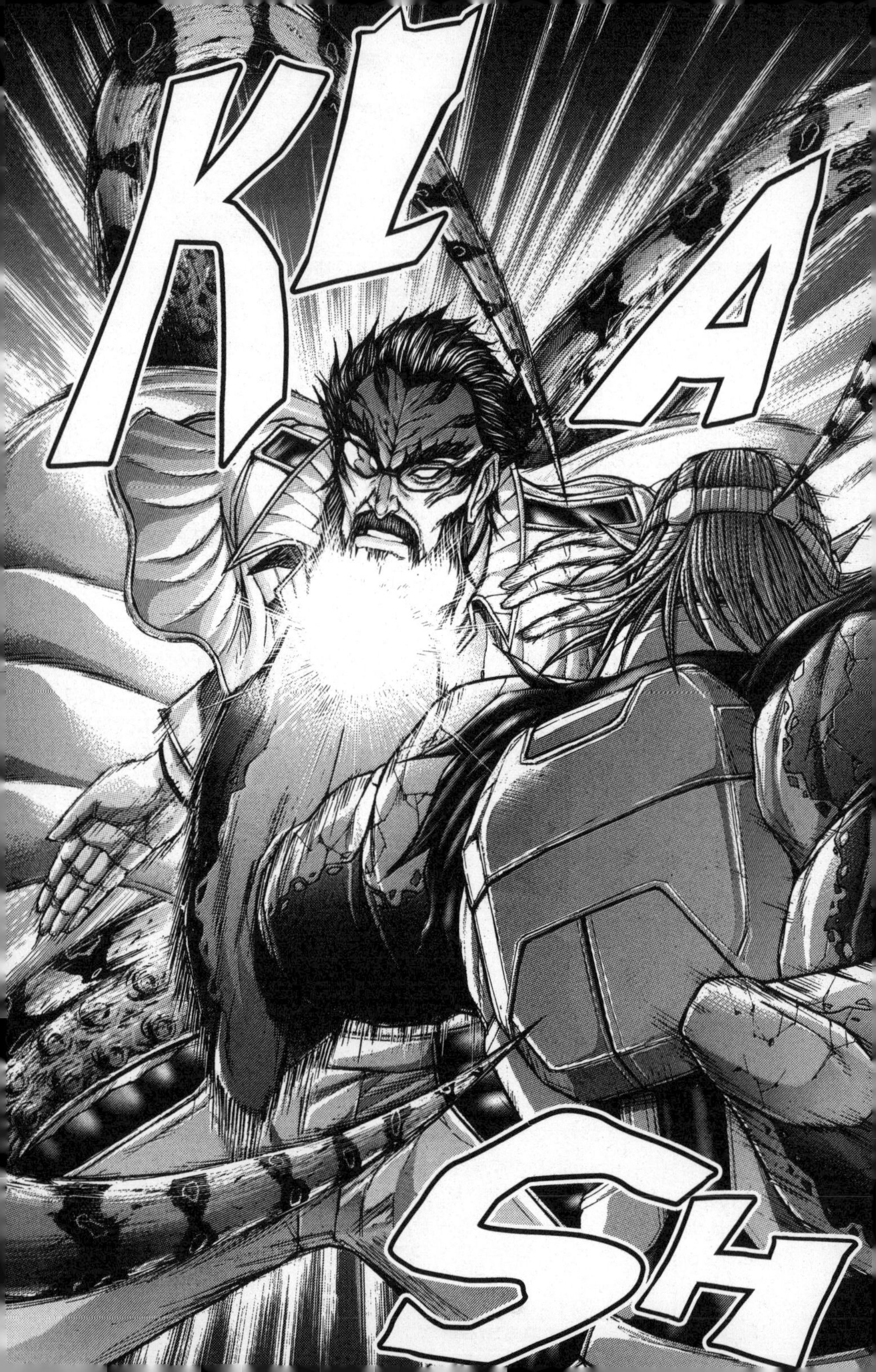
KLASH

TERRA FORMARS

Character

LIVE SAMPLES ARE BETTER, BUT...

Liu Yiwu ♂

China 42 yrs. 210 cm 99 kg

M.A.R.S. Ranking: 44

Operation Base: Blue-ringed octopus

Favorite Food: Super spicy food and anything with a strong taste
Dislikes: Keyboards with a small Enter key
Eye Color: Black Blood type: A
DOB: July 5 (Cancer)
Hobbies: Terrariums, breeding ancient fish

He's from a poor region, but thanks to an industrious personality and party connections, he was able to attend college and join the military after graduation.

At 24, he married the daughter of a high-ranking official and can't understand why the furniture she wants to buy is 100 times more expensive than the furniture he had.

His division and status as an officer were decided before his ranking. He became an officer because of his branch status and importance as an engineer, but ended up with a low rank.

Dina S. Asimov ♀

Russia 28 yrs. 176 cm 67 kg (before pregnancy)

Favorite Foods: Cheese, milkshakes, Siberia castella
Dislikes: Sexy actresses as the model for all girls
Eye Color: Light brown Blood type: B
DOB: December 19 (Sagittarius)
Hobbies: Skeet shooting

Her mother made her go to a co-ed school, but since her father was famous in the area, only other girls spoke to her. Even when she studied in Moscow, she attended a good school, so most of the boys knew about her father.

Contracting the A.E. Virus while pregnant has damaged her pancreas and lungs. The latest medical technology saved her life, but her condition, as well as that of her child, is precarious.

She has two cell phones. She claims she can eat as much as she wants and never get fat.

CHAPTER 65: FABLE COMBAT

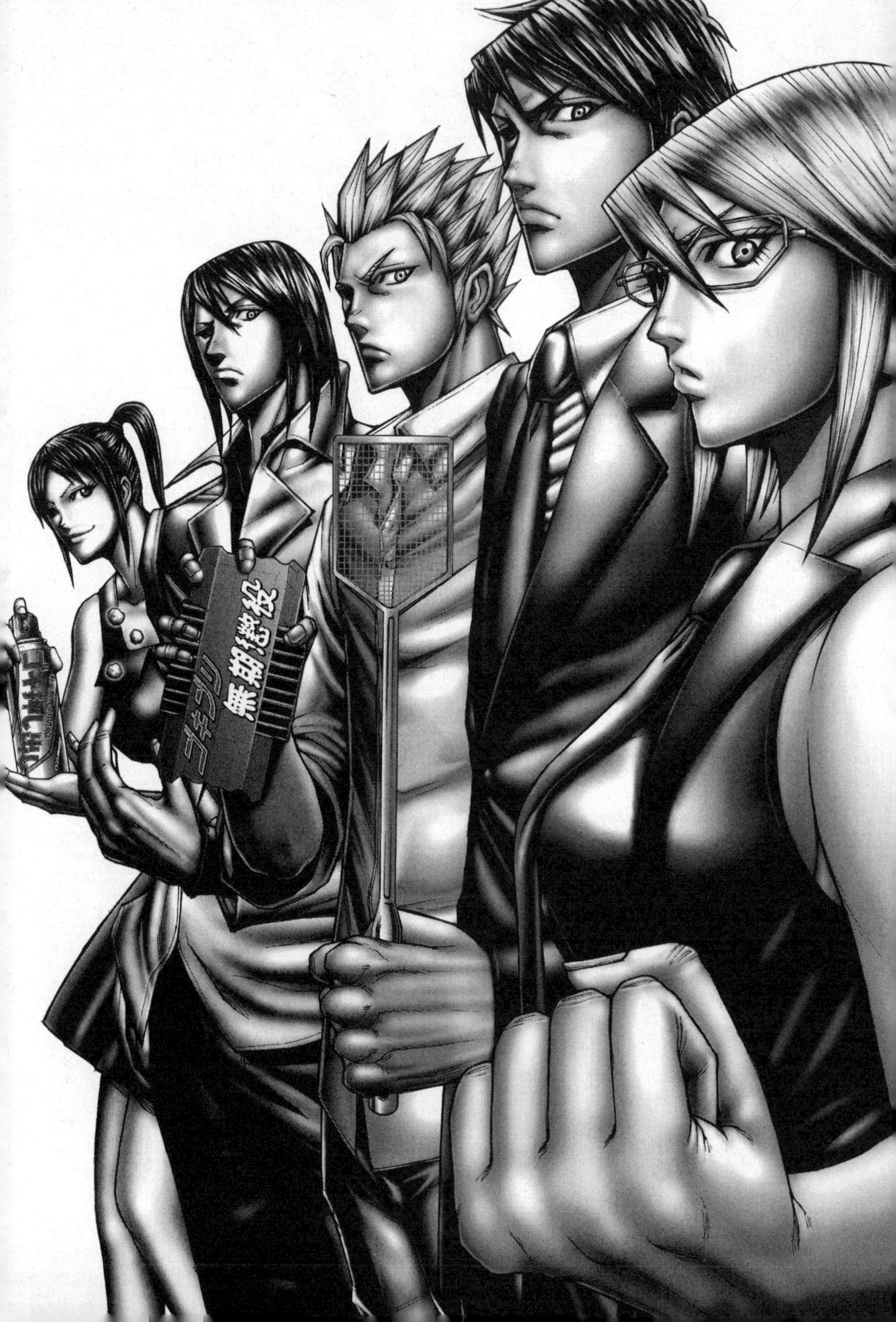

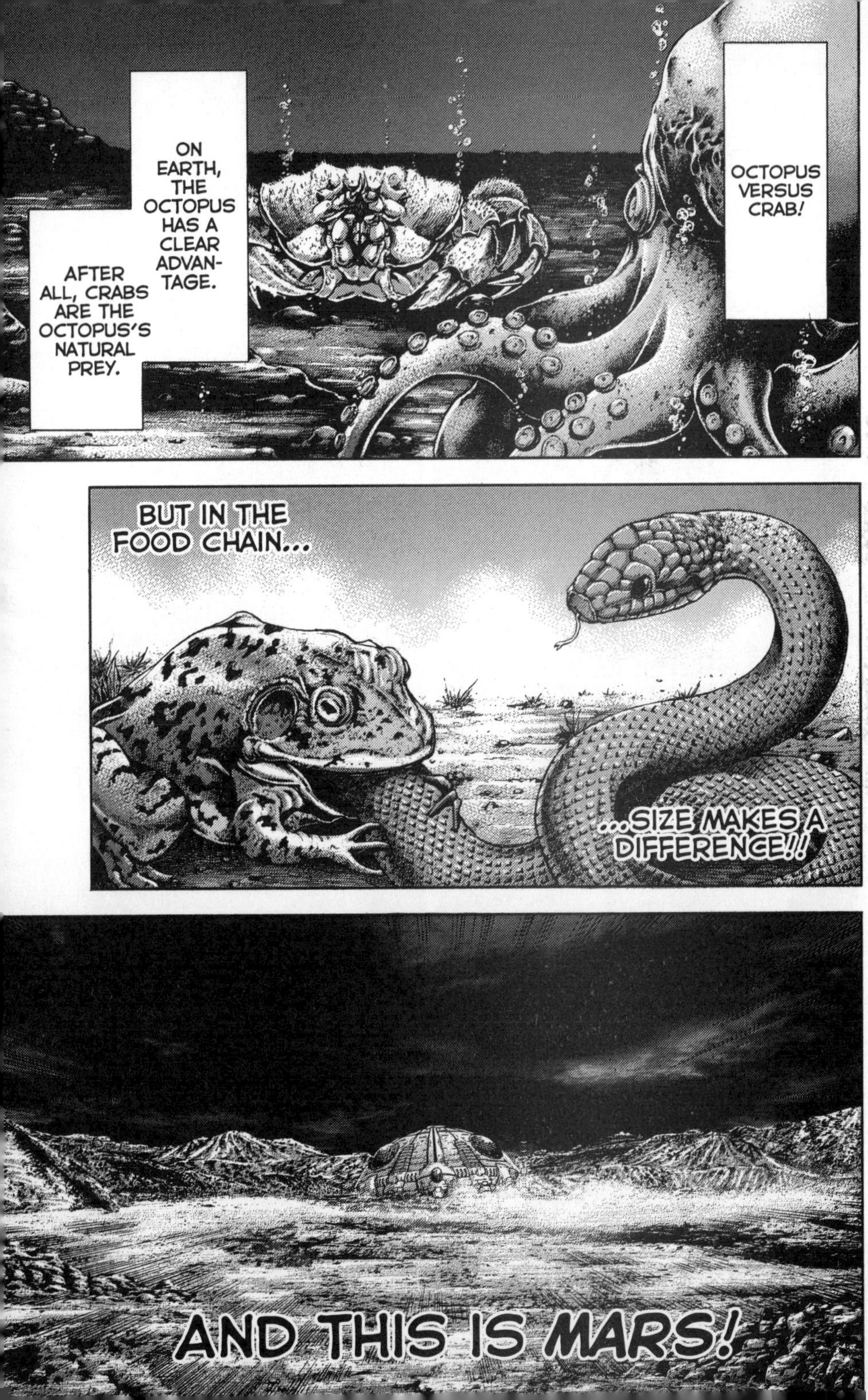
OCTOPUS VERSUS CRAB!
ON EARTH, THE OCTOPUS HAS A CLEAR ADVAN-TAGE.
AFTER ALL, CRABS ARE THE OCTOPUS'S NATURAL PREY.
BUT IN THE FOOD CHAIN...
...SIZE MAKES A DIFFERENCE!!
AND THIS IS MARS!

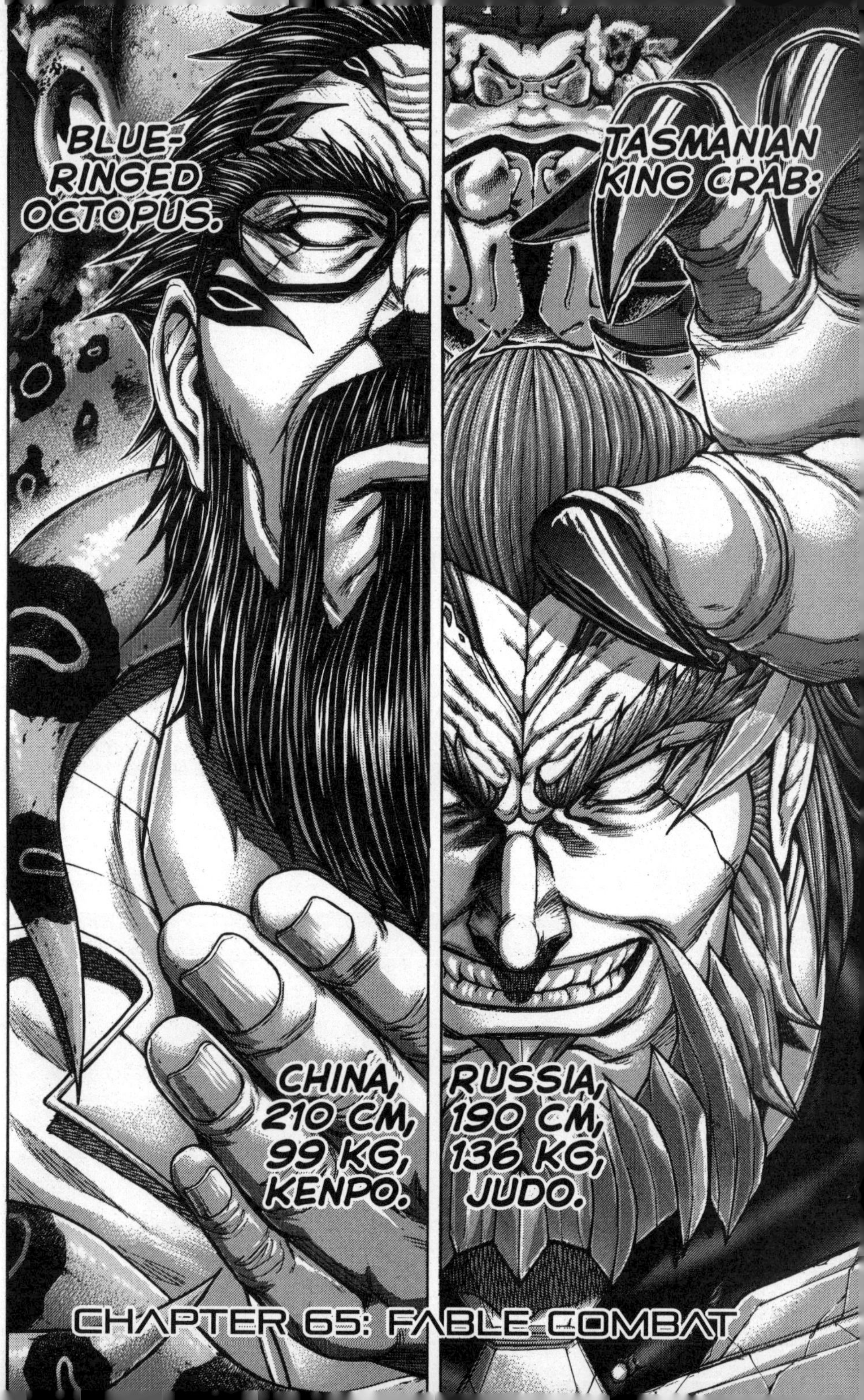
TASMANIAN KING CRAB:
RUSSIA, 190 CM, 136 KG, JUDO.
BLUE-RINGED OCTOPUS.
CHINA, 210 CM, 99 KG, KENPO.
CHAPTER 65: FABLE COMBAT

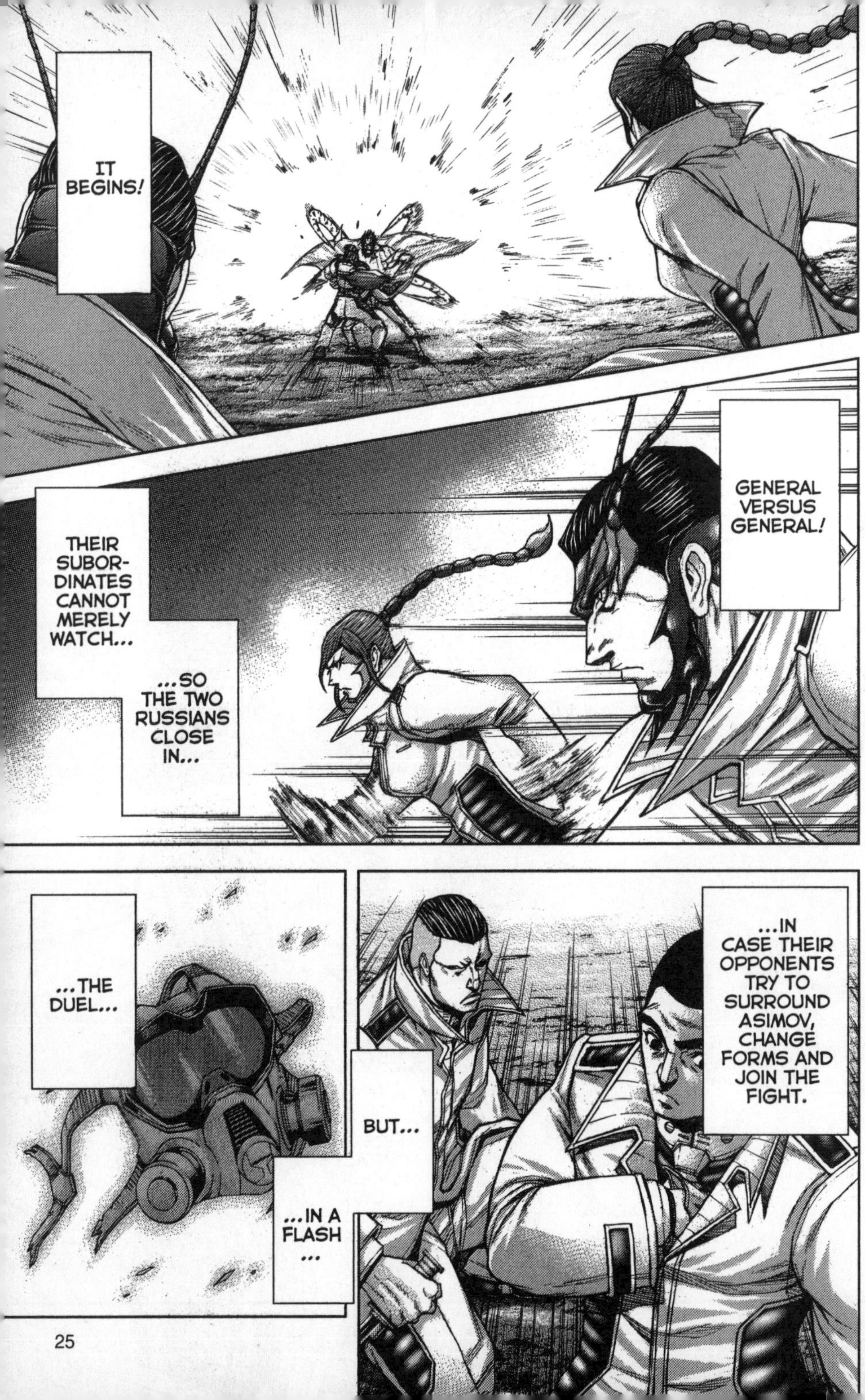
IT BEGINS!
GENERAL VERSUS GENERAL!
THEIR SUBOR-DINATES CANNOT MERELY WATCH...
...SO THE TWO RUSSIANS CLOSE IN...
...IN CASE THEIR OPPONENTS TRY TO SURROUND ASIMOV, CHANGE FORMS AND JOIN THE FIGHT.
BUT...
...IN A FLASH...
...THE DUEL...

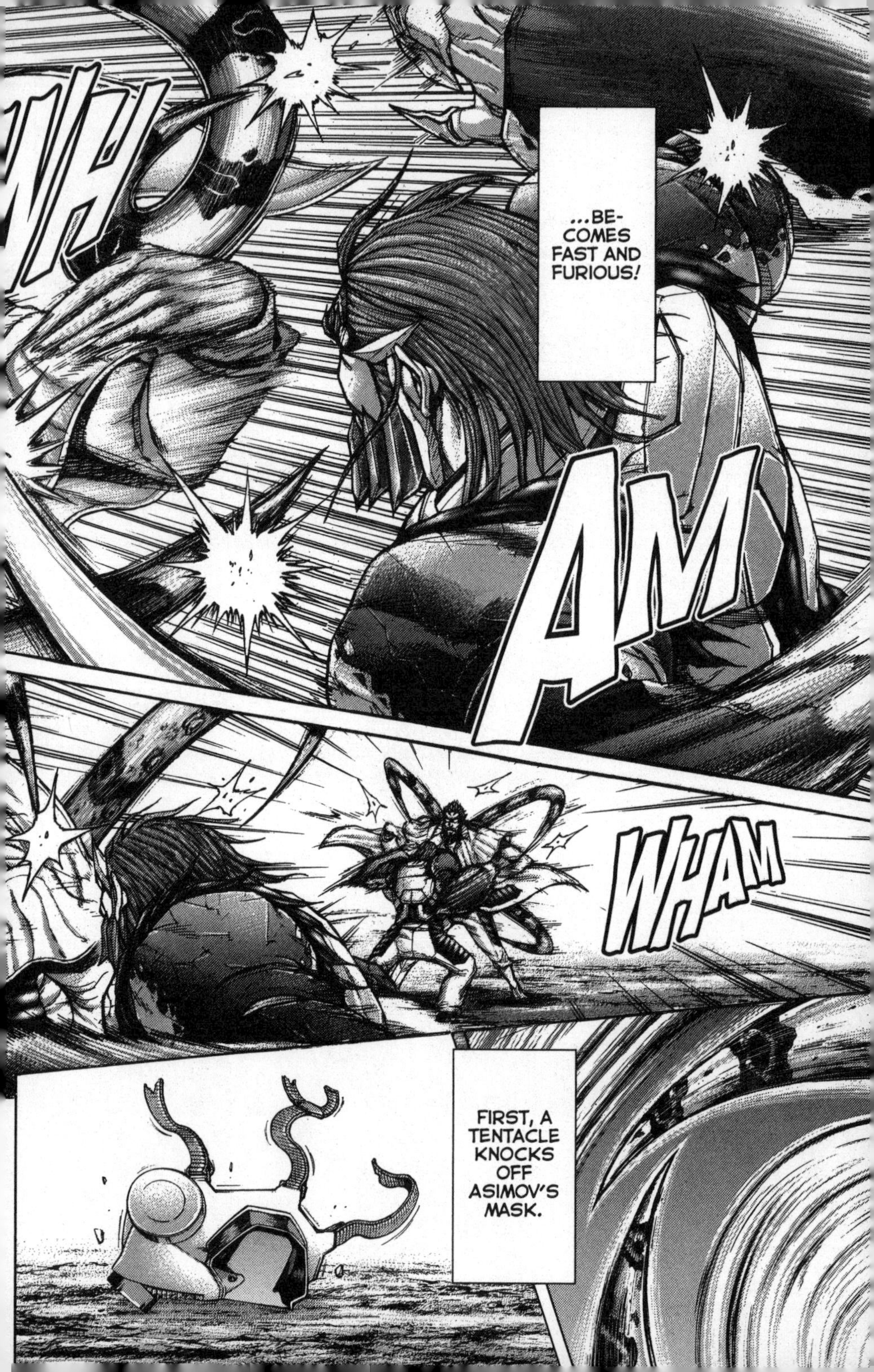
...BE-
COMES
FAST AND
FURIOUS!
WH
AM
WHAM
FIRST, A
TENTACLE
KNOCKS
OFF
ASIMOV'S
MASK.

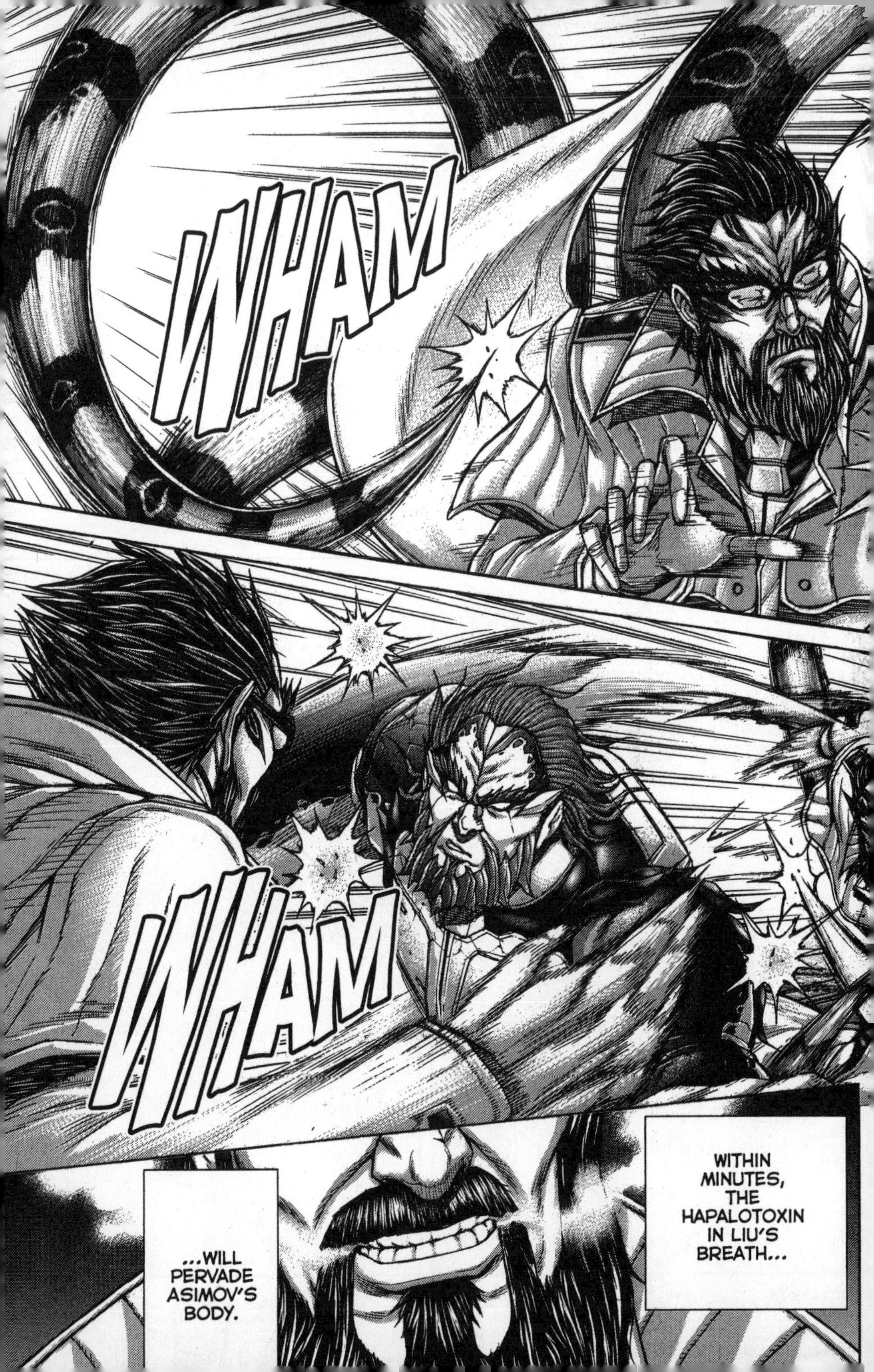
WHAM
WHAM
WITHIN MINUTES, THE HAPALOTOXIN IN LIU'S BREATH...
...WILL PERVADE ASIMOV'S BODY.

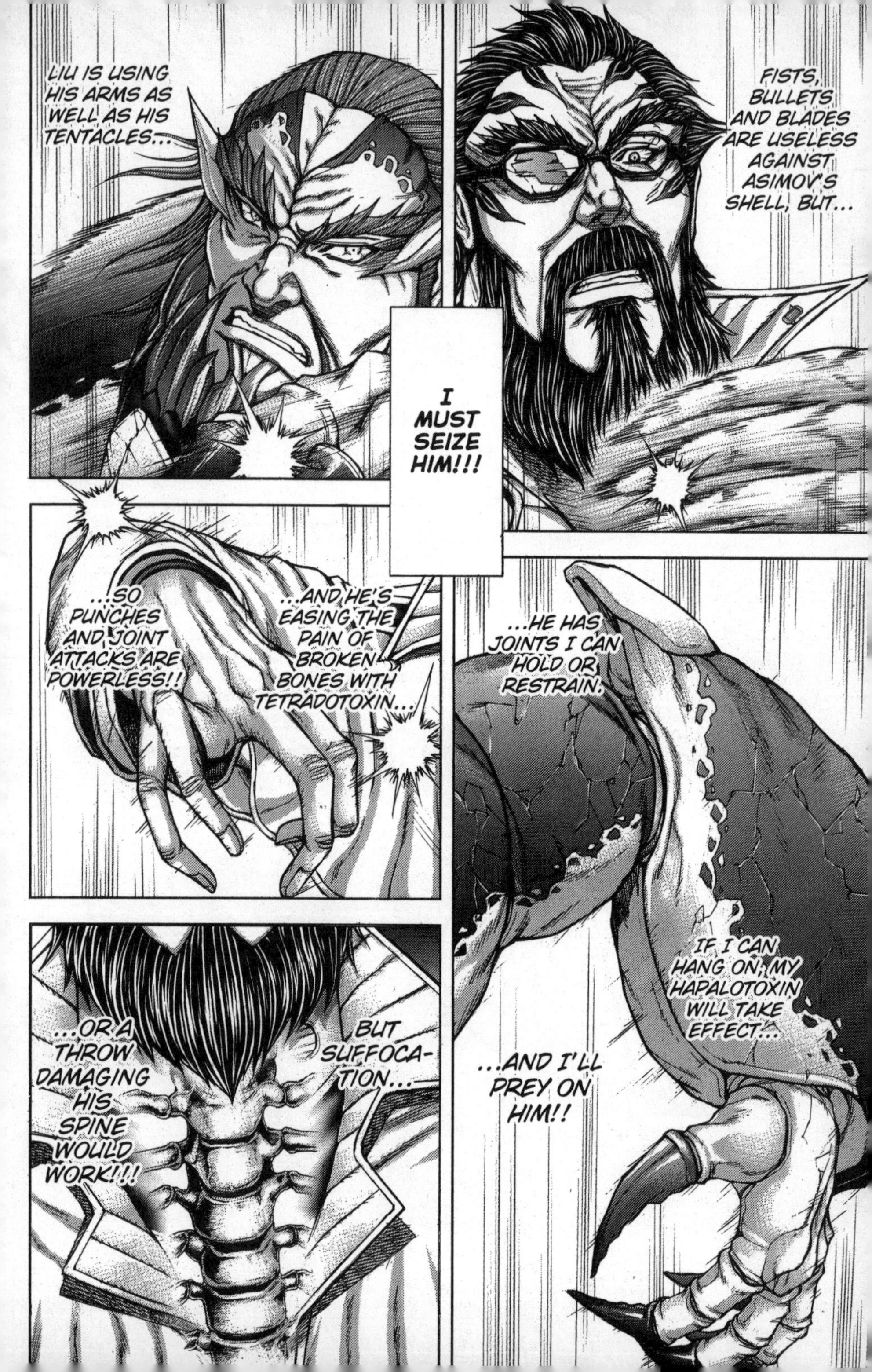
FISTS, BULLETS AND BLADES ARE USELESS AGAINST ASIMOV'S SHELL, BUT...
LIU IS USING HIS ARMS AS WELL AS HIS TENTACLES...
I MUST SEIZE HIM!!!
...HE HAS JOINTS I CAN HOLD OR RESTRAIN.
IF I CAN HANG ON, MY HAPALOTOXIN WILL TAKE EFFECT...
...AND I'LL PREY ON HIM!!
...AND HE'S EASING THE PAIN OF BROKEN BONES WITH TETRADOTOXIN...
...SO PUNCHES AND JOINT ATTACKS ARE POWERLESS!!
BUT SUFFOCATION...
...OR A THROW DAMAGING HIS SPINE WOULD WORK!!!

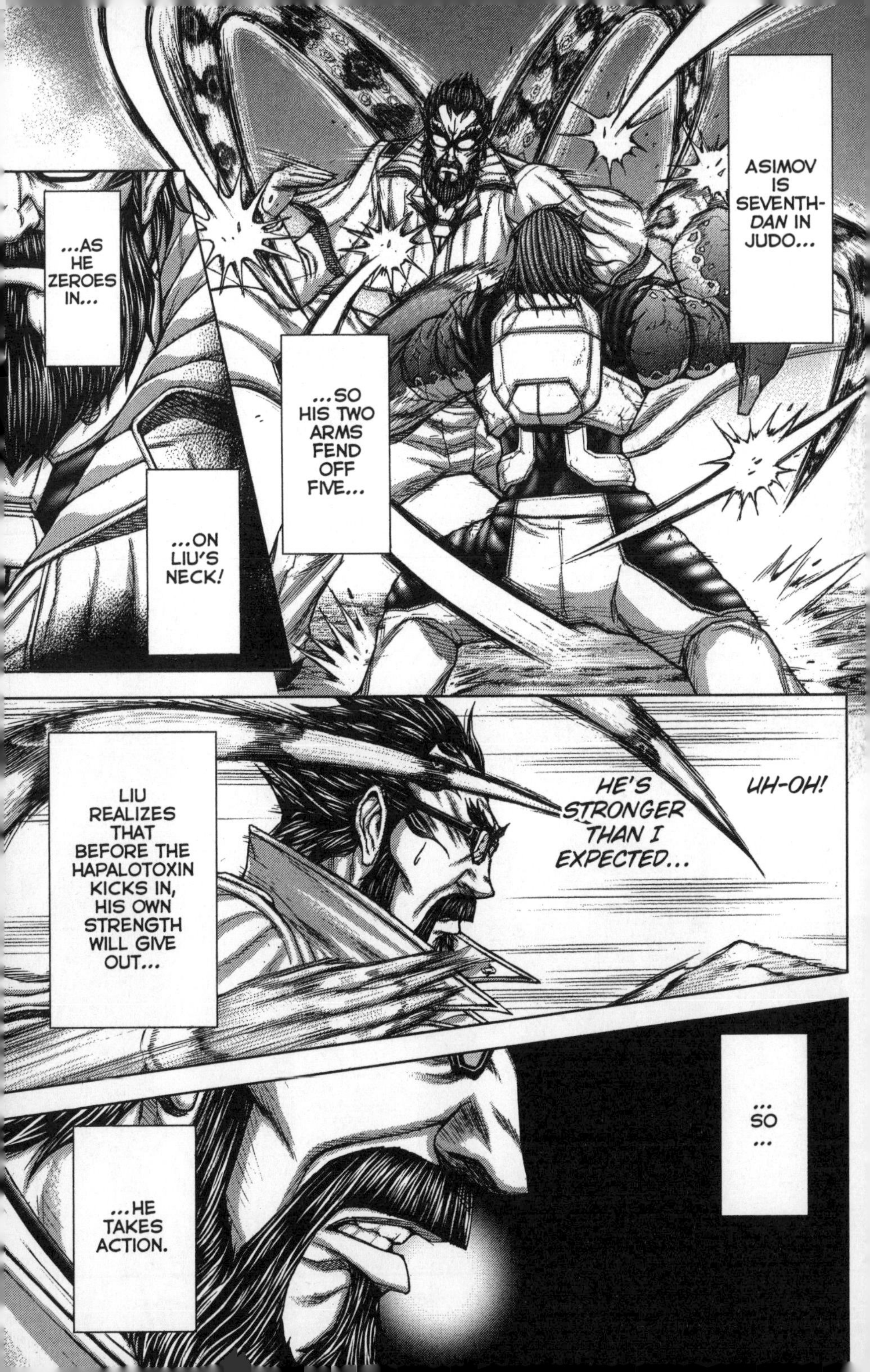
ASIMOV IS SEVENTH-*DAN* IN JUDO...
...SO HIS TWO ARMS FEND OFF FIVE...
...AS HE ZEROES IN...
...ON LIU'S NECK!
UH-OH!
HE'S STRONGER THAN I EXPECTED...
LIU REALIZES THAT BEFORE THE HAPALOTOXIN KICKS IN, HIS OWN STRENGTH WILL GIVE OUT...
...SO...
...HE TAKES ACTION.

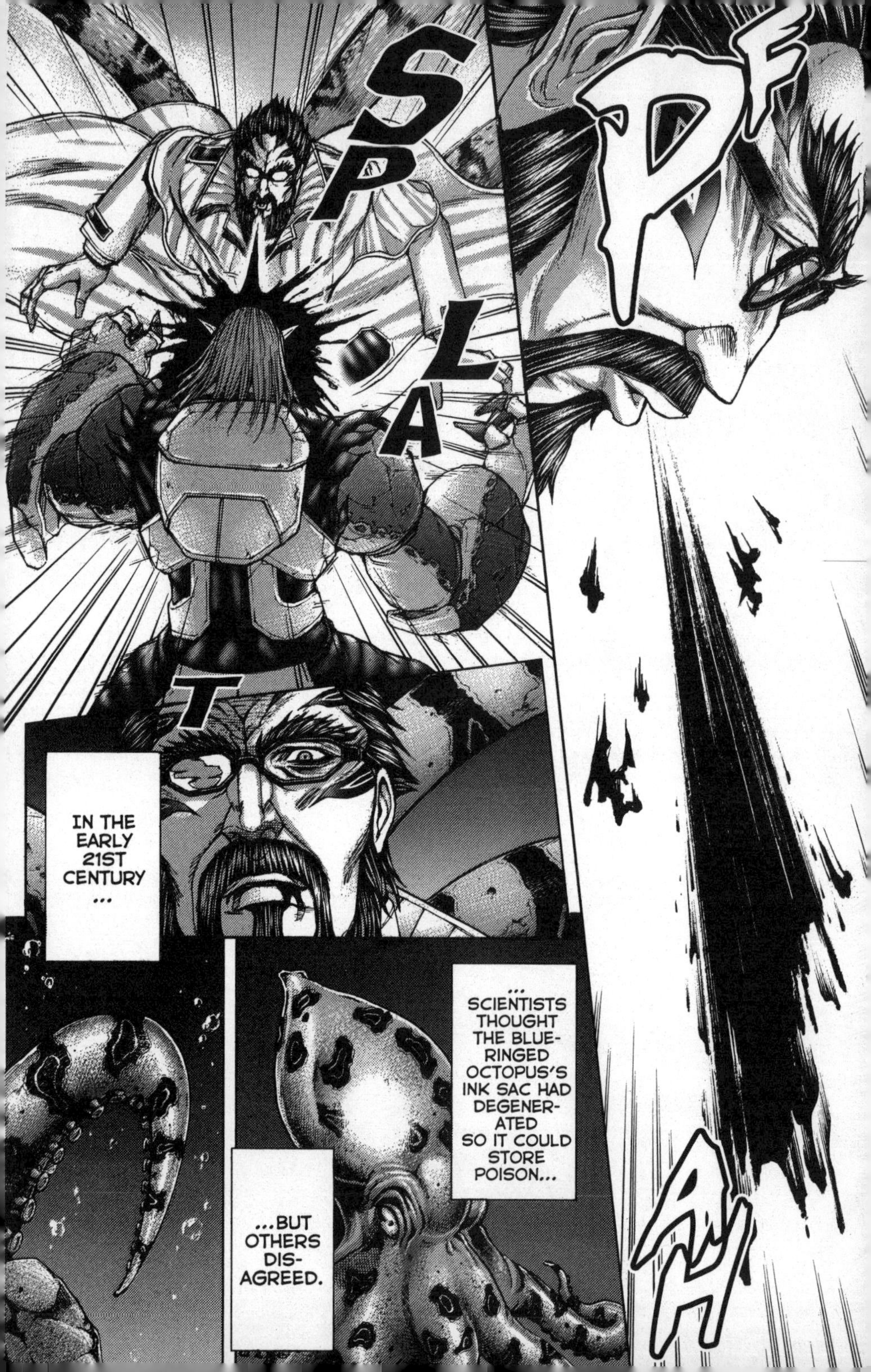
SPLAT
IN THE EARLY 21ST CENTURY...
...SCIENTISTS THOUGHT THE BLUE-RINGED OCTOPUS'S INK SAC HAD DEGENER-ATED SO IT COULD STORE POISON...
...BUT OTHERS DIS-AGREED.

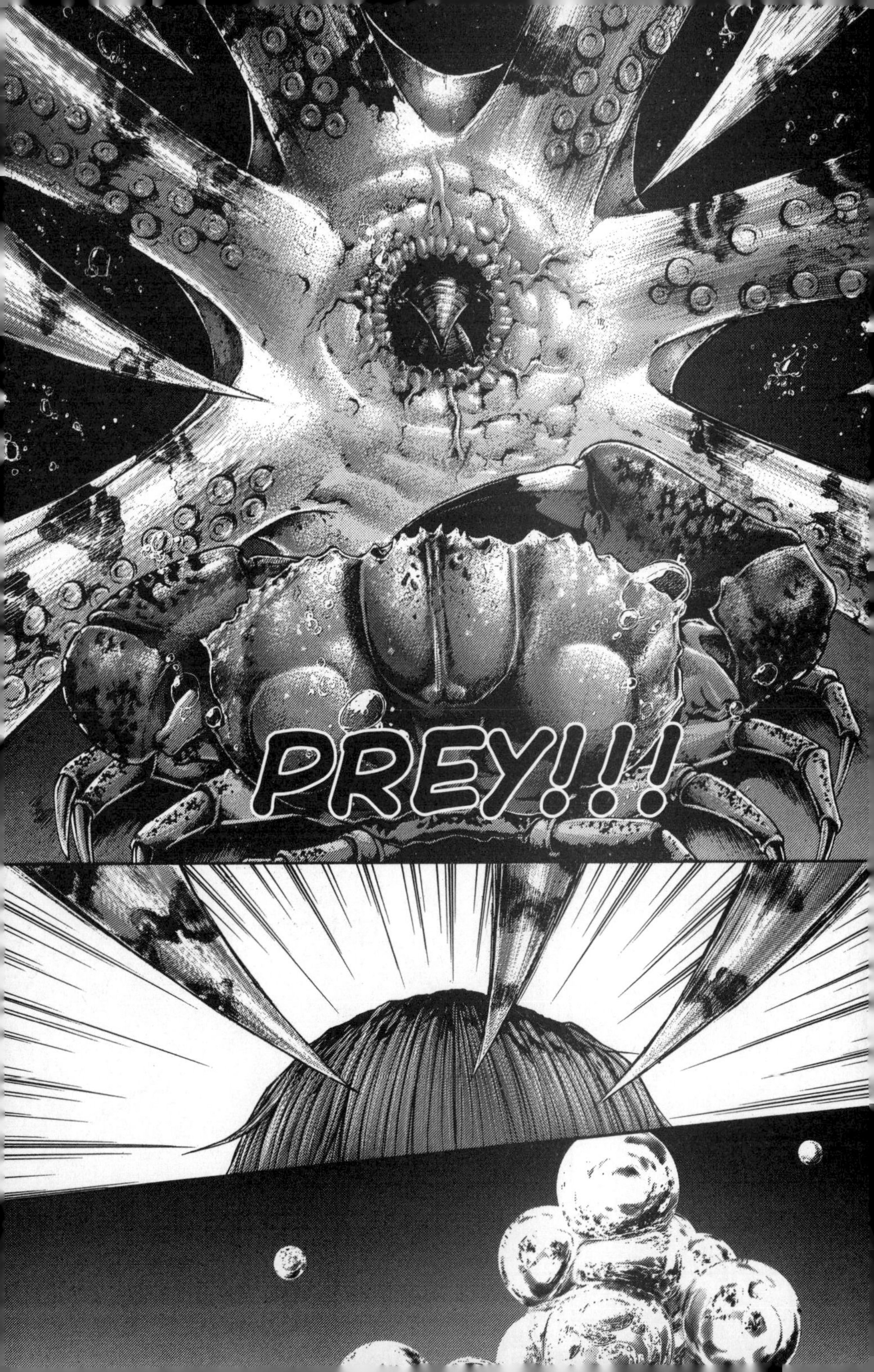
PREY!!!

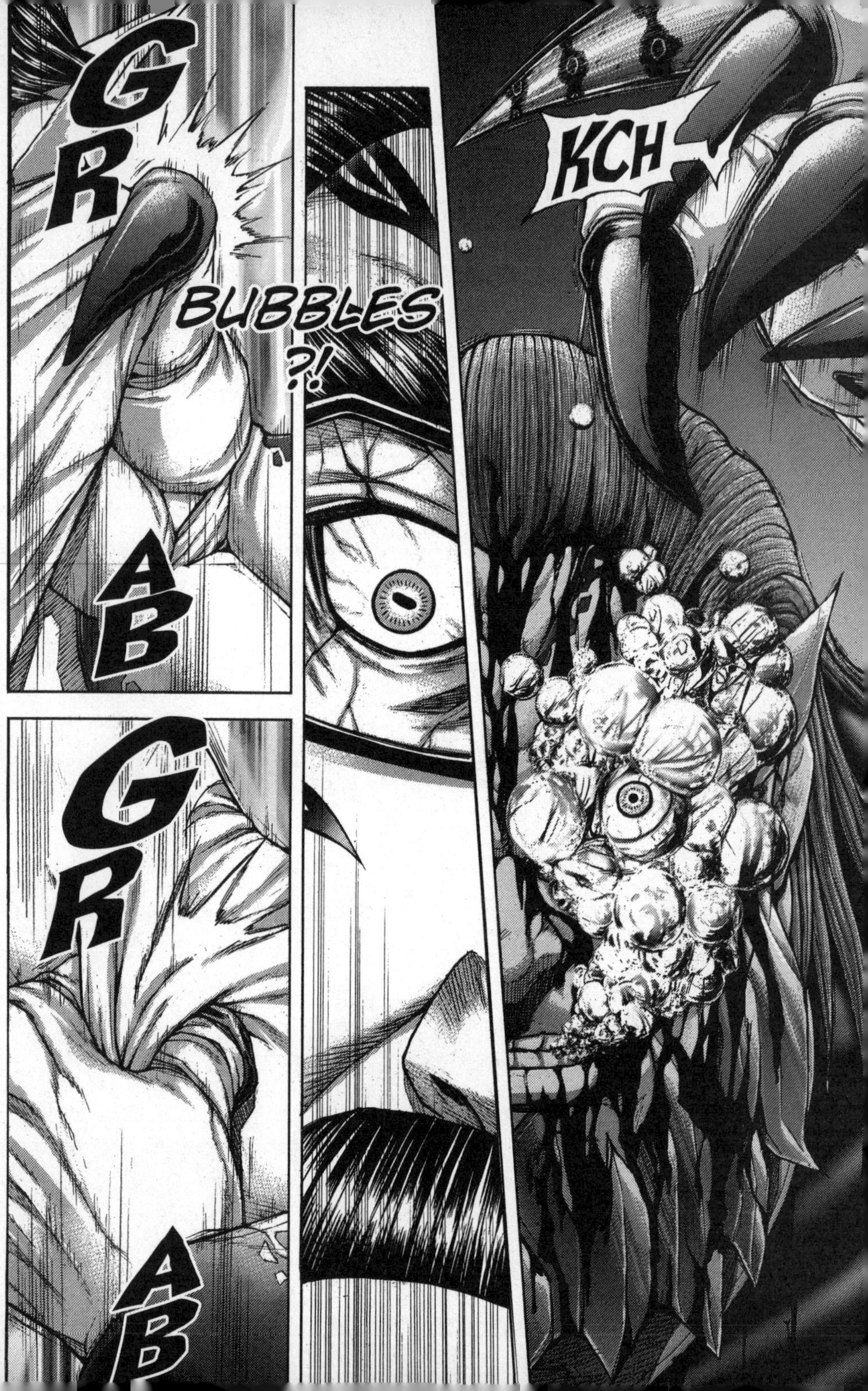
KCH
BUBBLES ?!
GRAB
GRAB

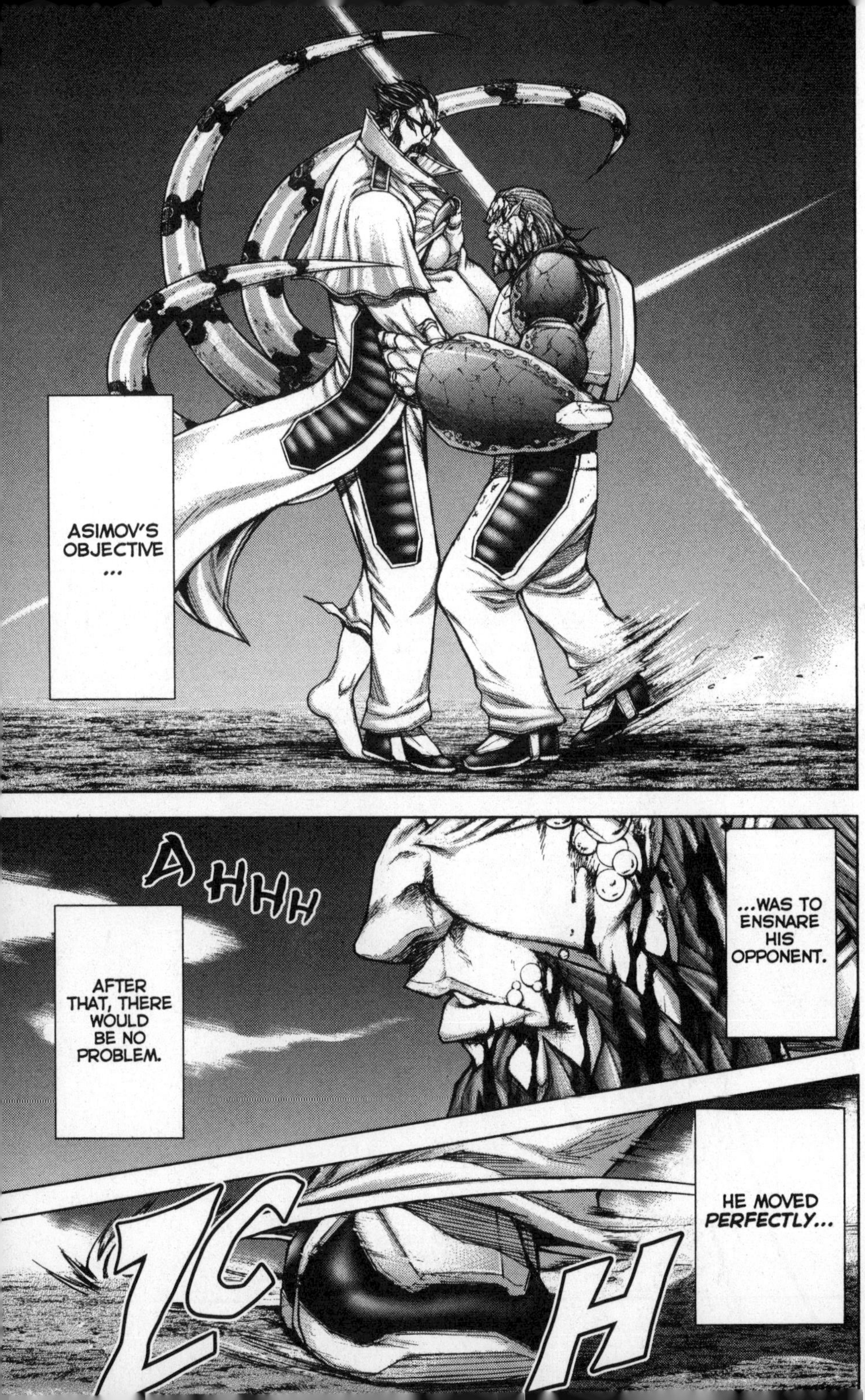
ASIMOV'S OBJECTIVE ...
...WAS TO ENSNARE HIS OPPONENT.
AHHH
AFTER THAT, THERE WOULD BE NO PROBLEM.
HE MOVED *PERFECTLY*...
ZCH

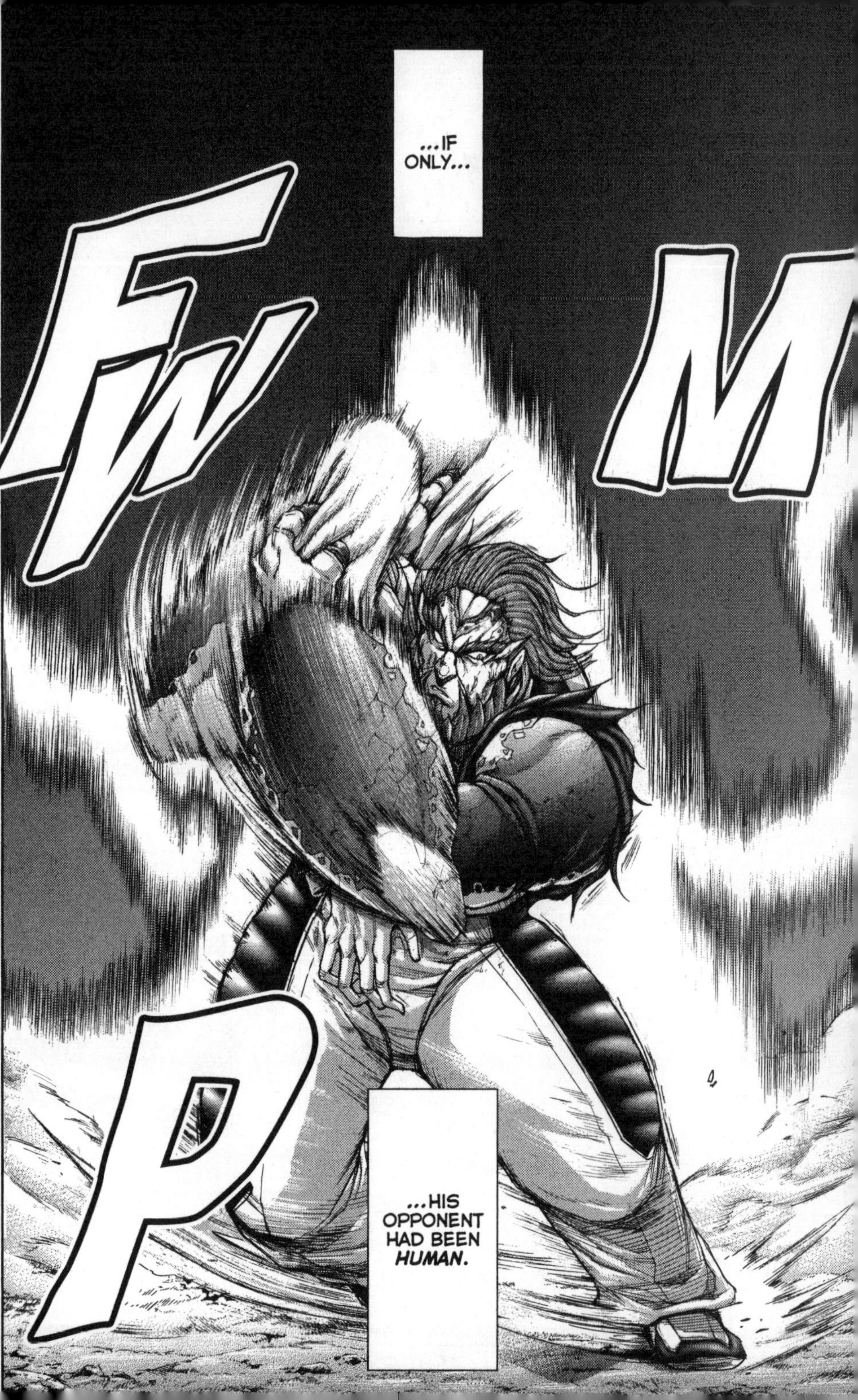
...IF ONLY...
FWMP
...HIS OPPONENT HAD BEEN *HUMAN*.

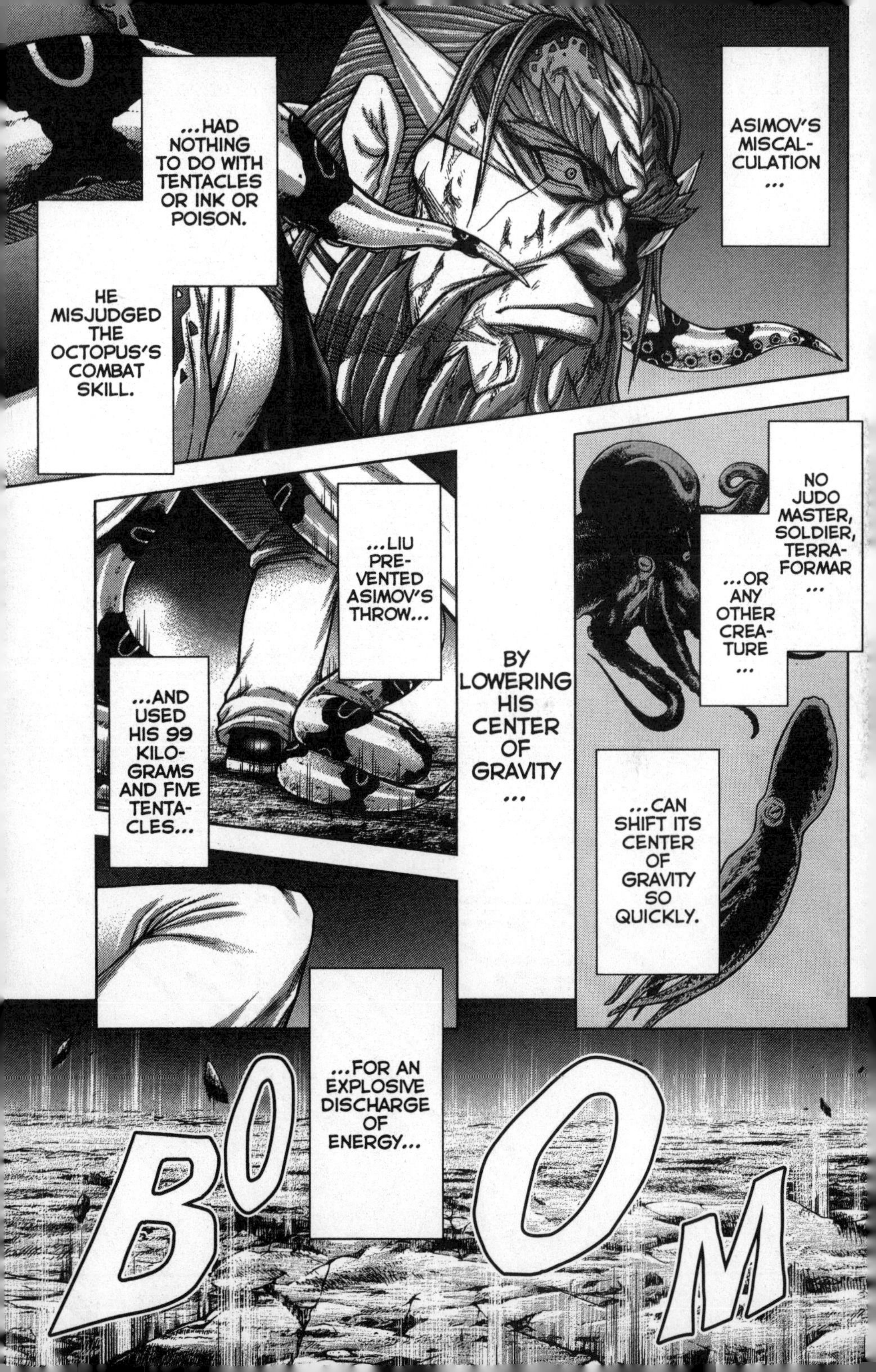
ASIMOV'S MISCAL- CULATION ...
...HAD NOTHING TO DO WITH TENTACLES OR INK OR POISON.
HE MISJUDGED THE OCTOPUS'S COMBAT SKILL.
NO JUDO MASTER, SOLDIER, TERRA- FORMAR ...
...OR ANY OTHER CREA- TURE ...
...CAN SHIFT ITS CENTER OF GRAVITY SO QUICKLY.
BY LOWERING HIS CENTER OF GRAVITY ...
...LIU PRE- VENTED ASIMOV'S THROW...
...AND USED HIS 99 KILO- GRAMS AND FIVE TENTA- CLES...
...FOR AN EXPLOSIVE DISCHARGE OF ENERGY...
BOOOM

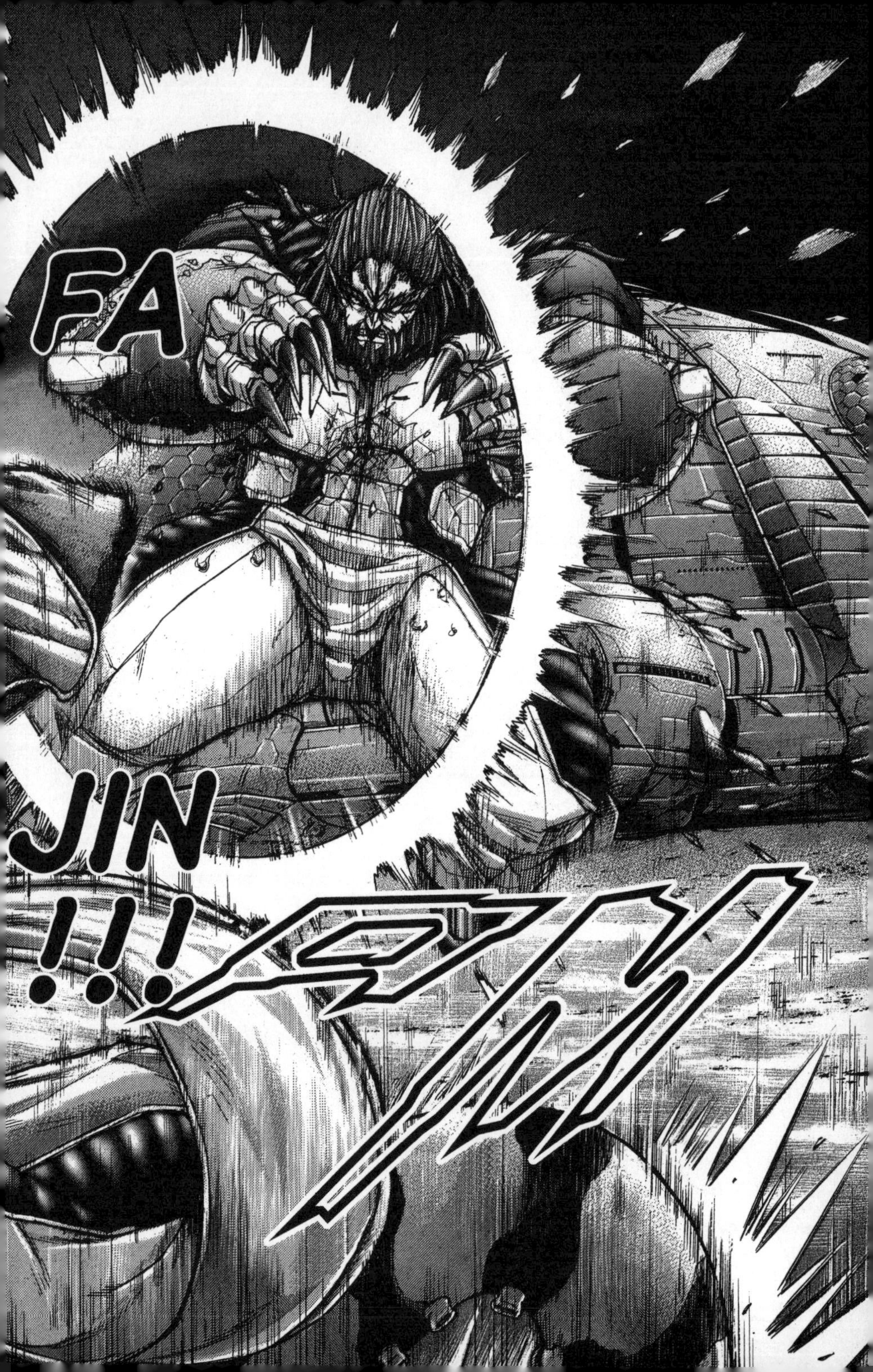
FA
JIN
!!!

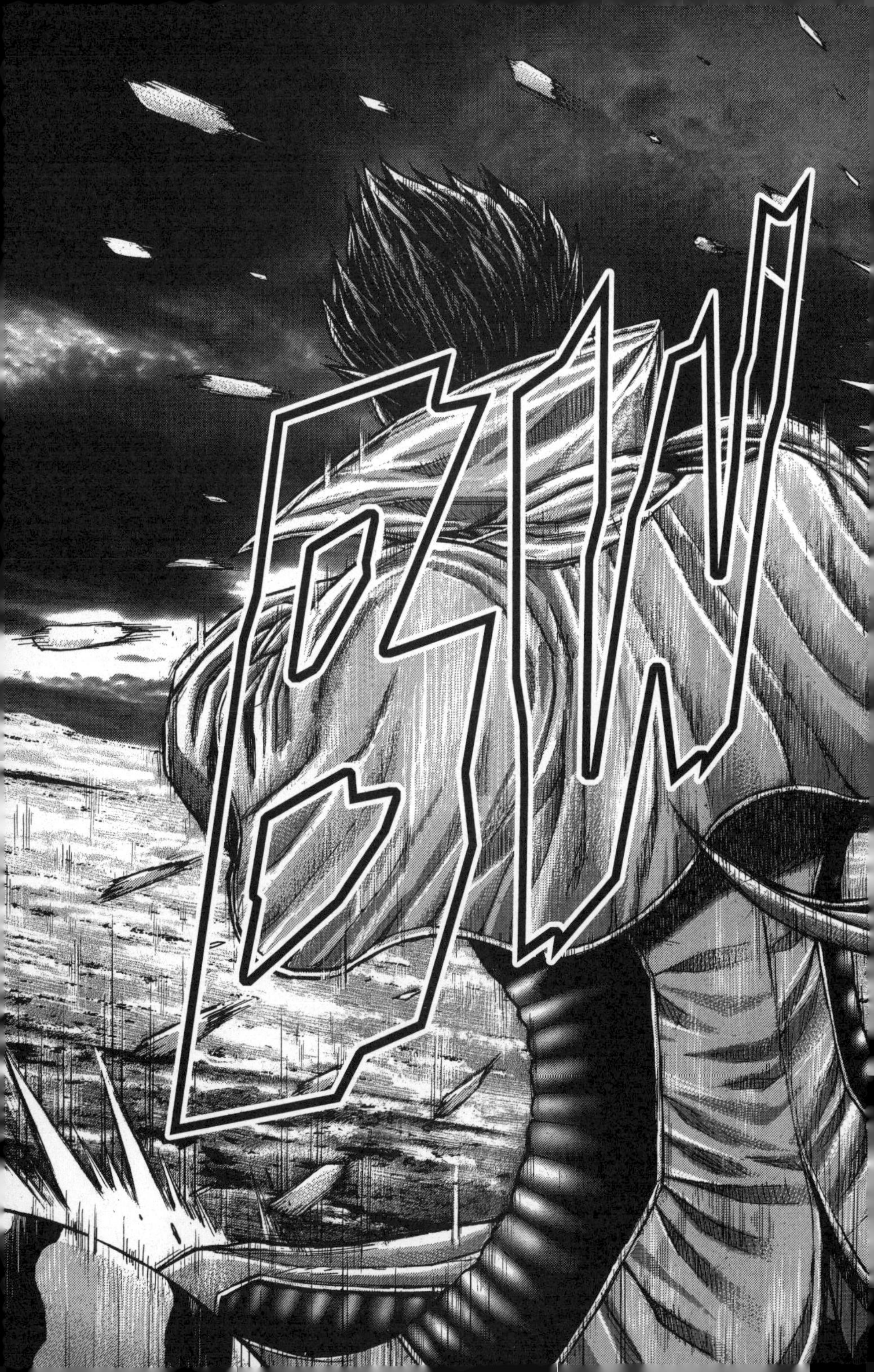

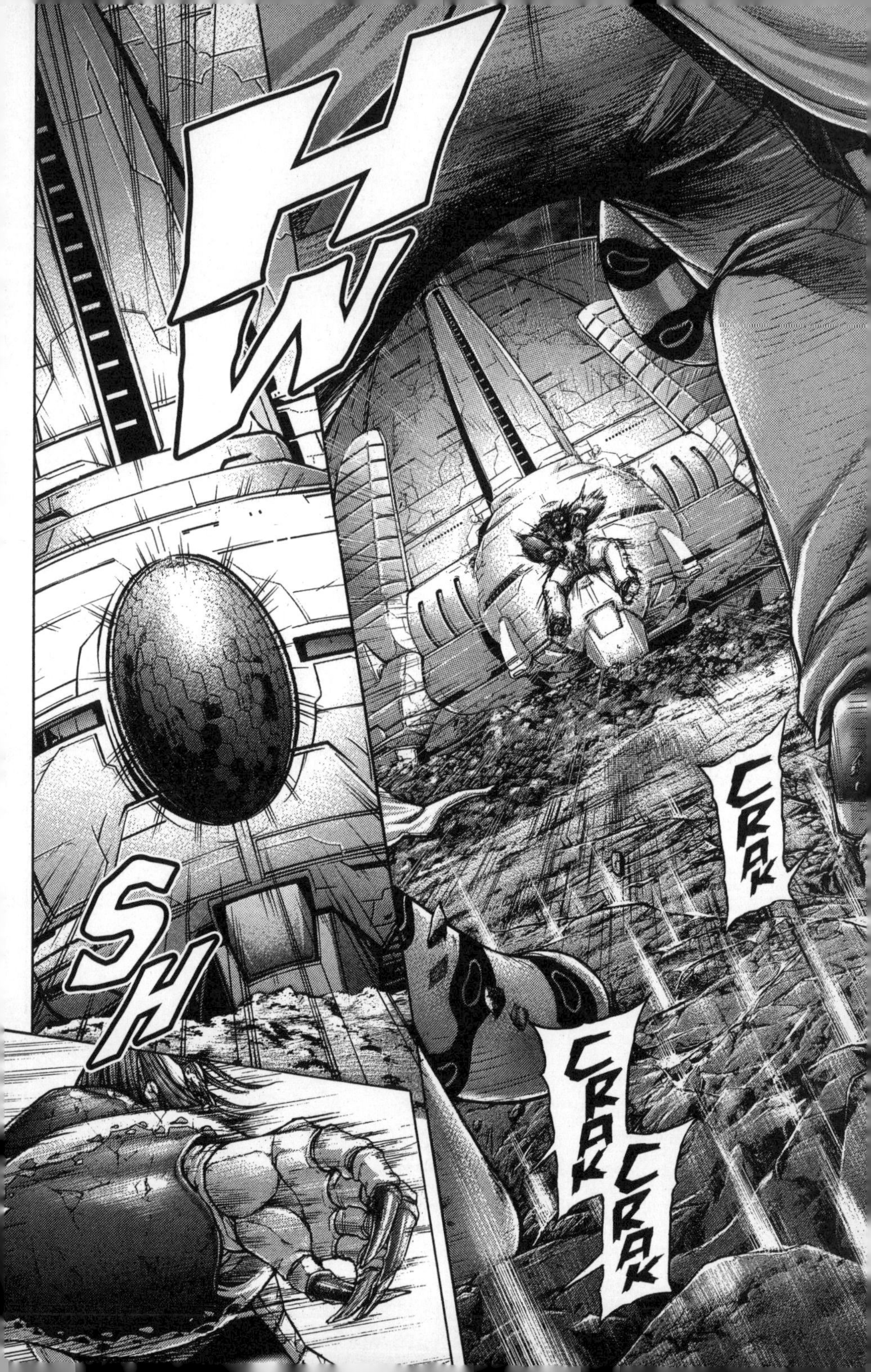
CRAK
CRAK
CRAK
SH

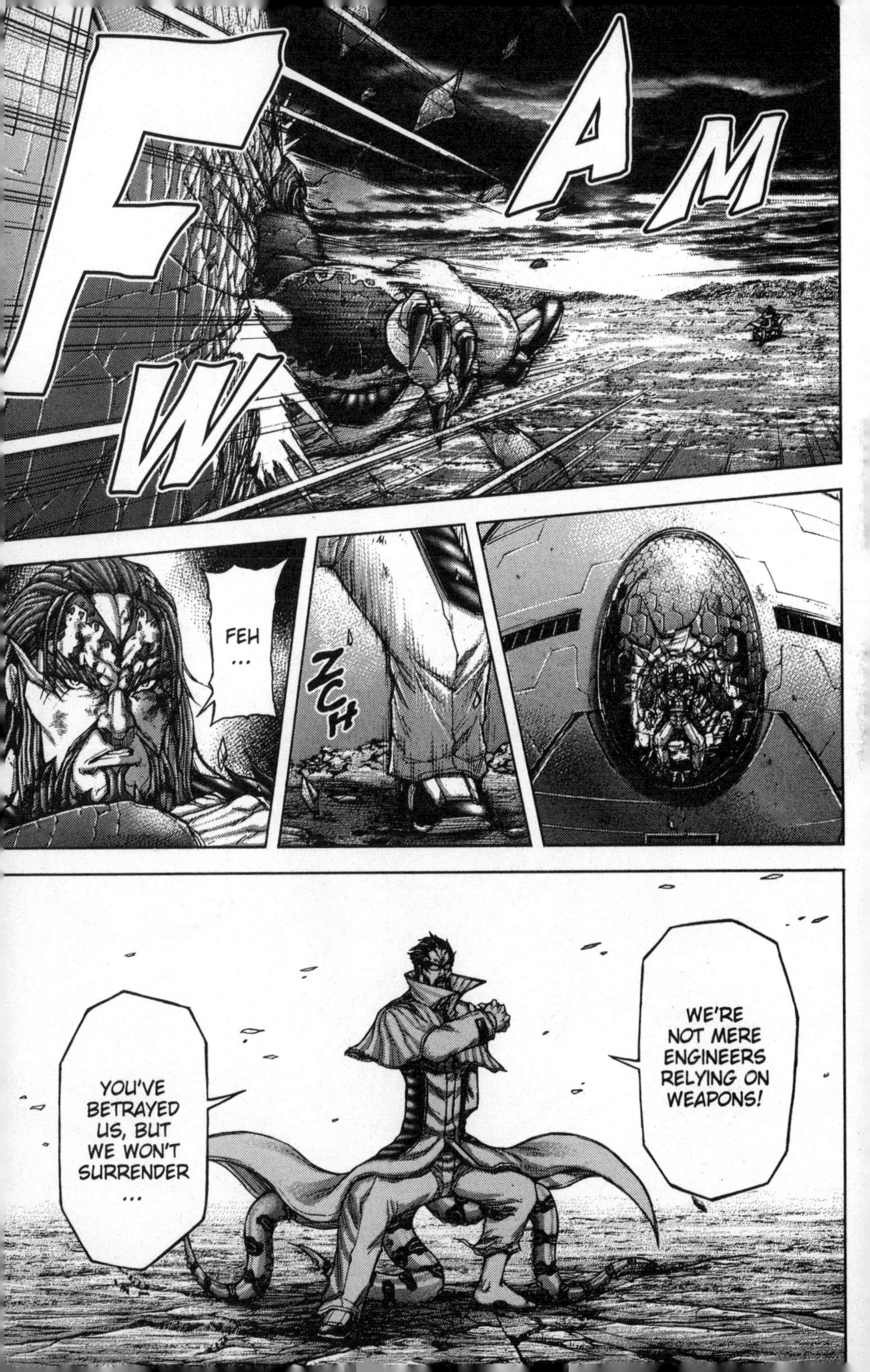
FWAM
ZCH
FEH ...
WE'RE NOT MERE ENGINEERS RELYING ON WEAPONS!
YOU'VE BETRAYED US, BUT WE WON'T SURRENDER ...

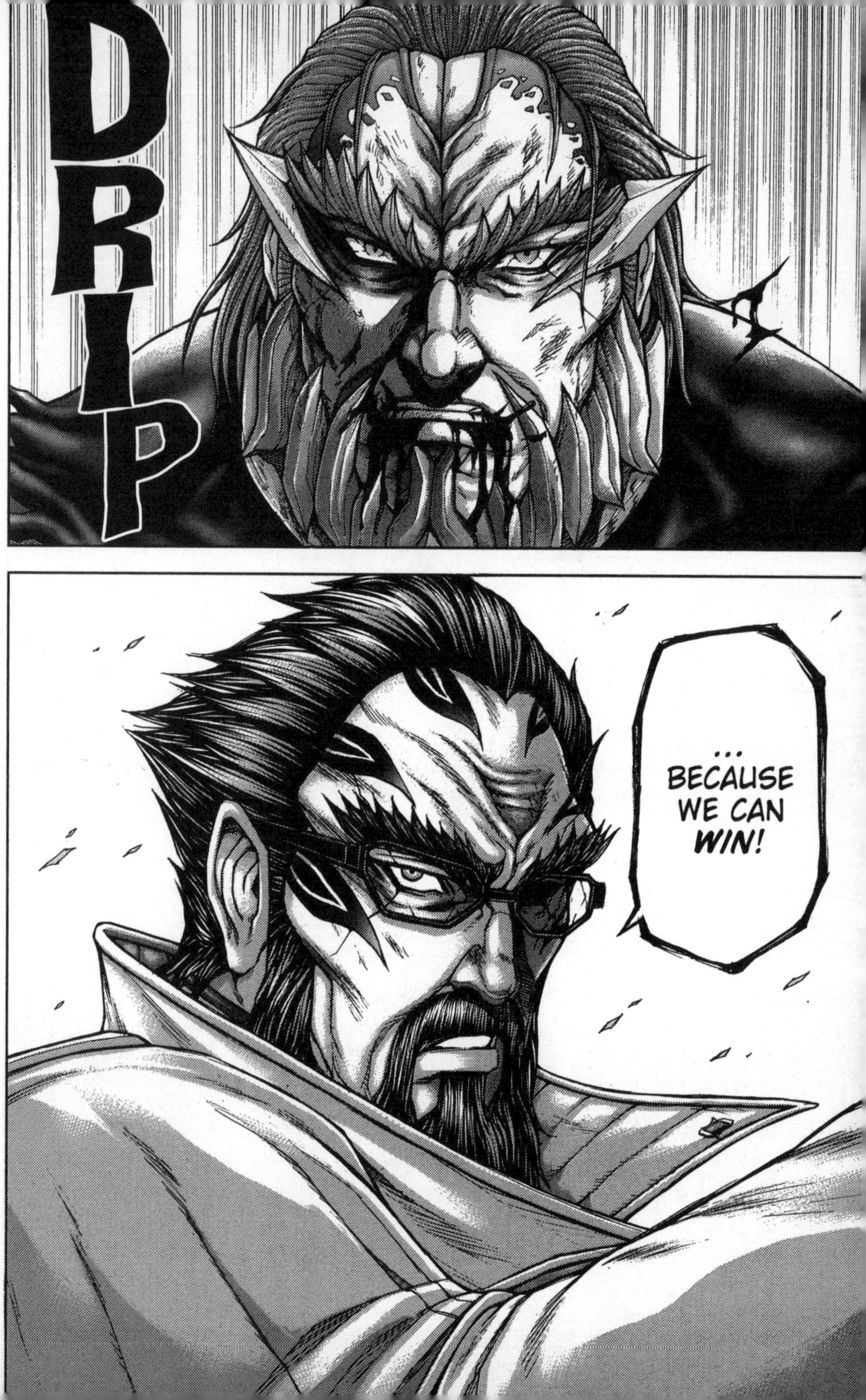
DRIP
... BECAUSE WE CAN WIN!

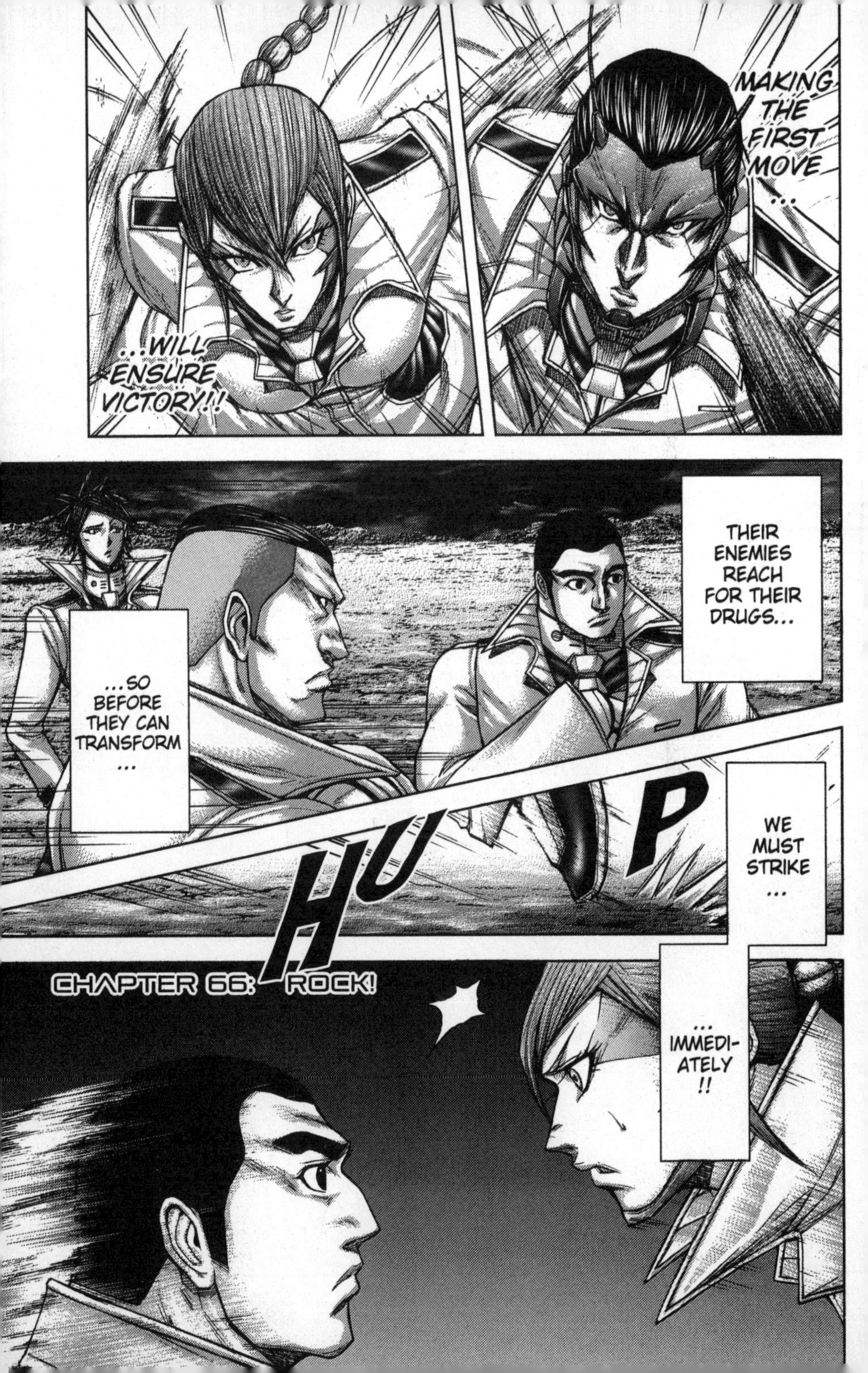
MAKING THE FIRST MOVE...
...WILL ENSURE VICTORY!!
THEIR ENEMIES REACH FOR THEIR DRUGS...
...SO BEFORE THEY CAN TRANSFORM...
WE MUST STRIKE...
HUP
...IMMEDIATELY!!
CHAPTER 66: ROCK!

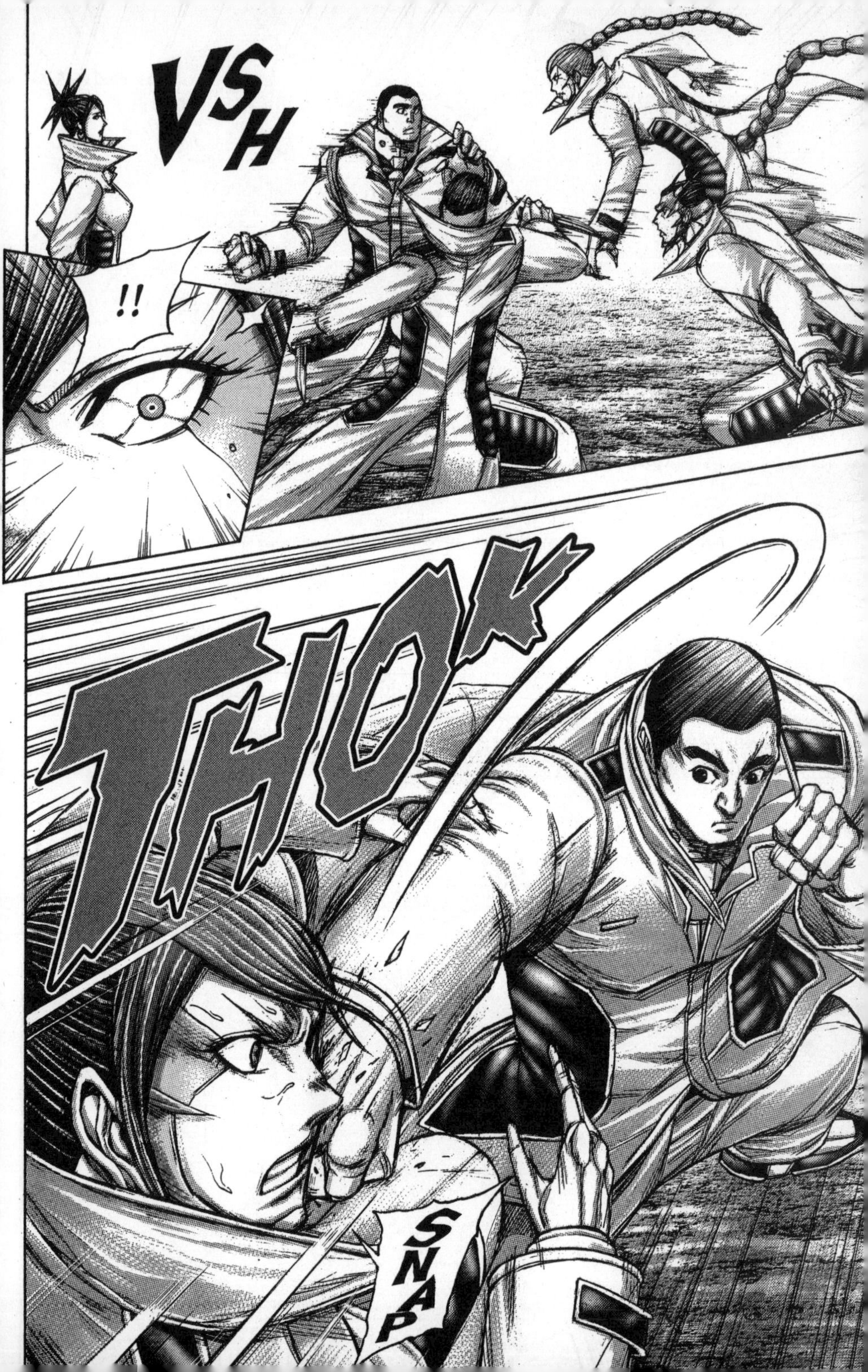
VSH
!!
THOK
SNAP

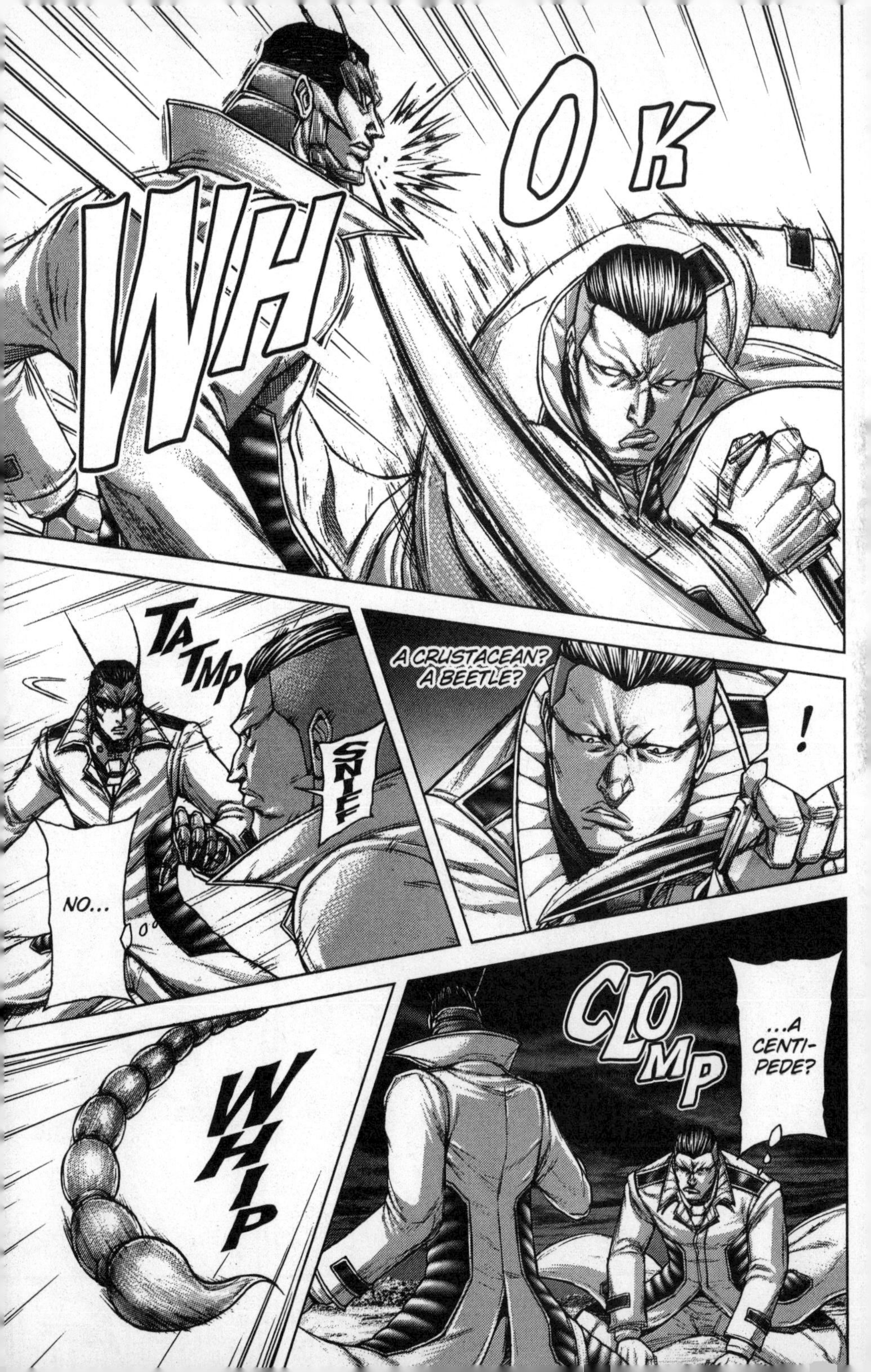
WHOK
A CRUSTACEAN? A BEETLE?
!
TATMP
SNIFF
NO...
CLOMP
...A CENTI-PEDE?
WHIP

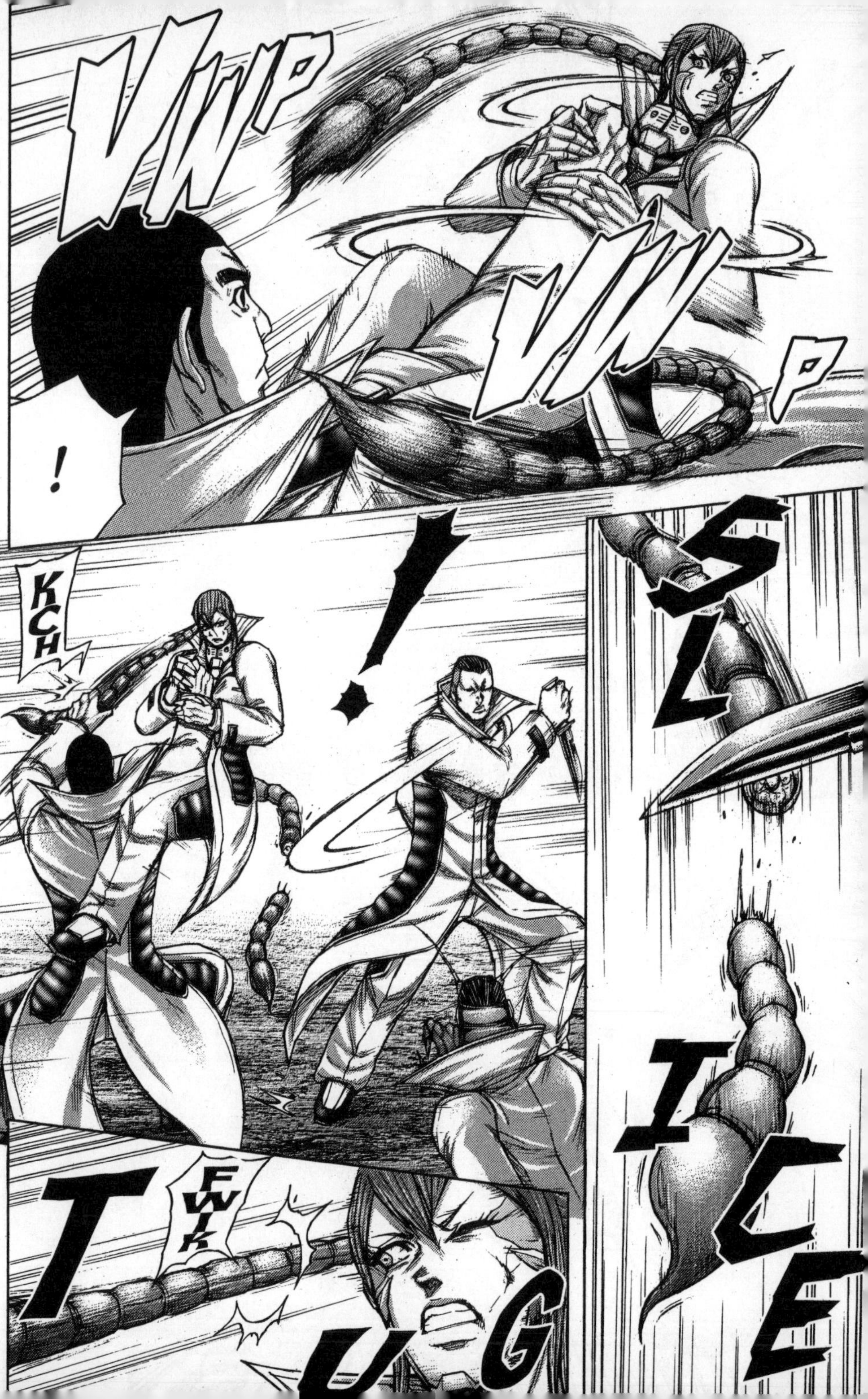
VWP
VWIP
!
SLICE
!
KCH
FWIK
TUG

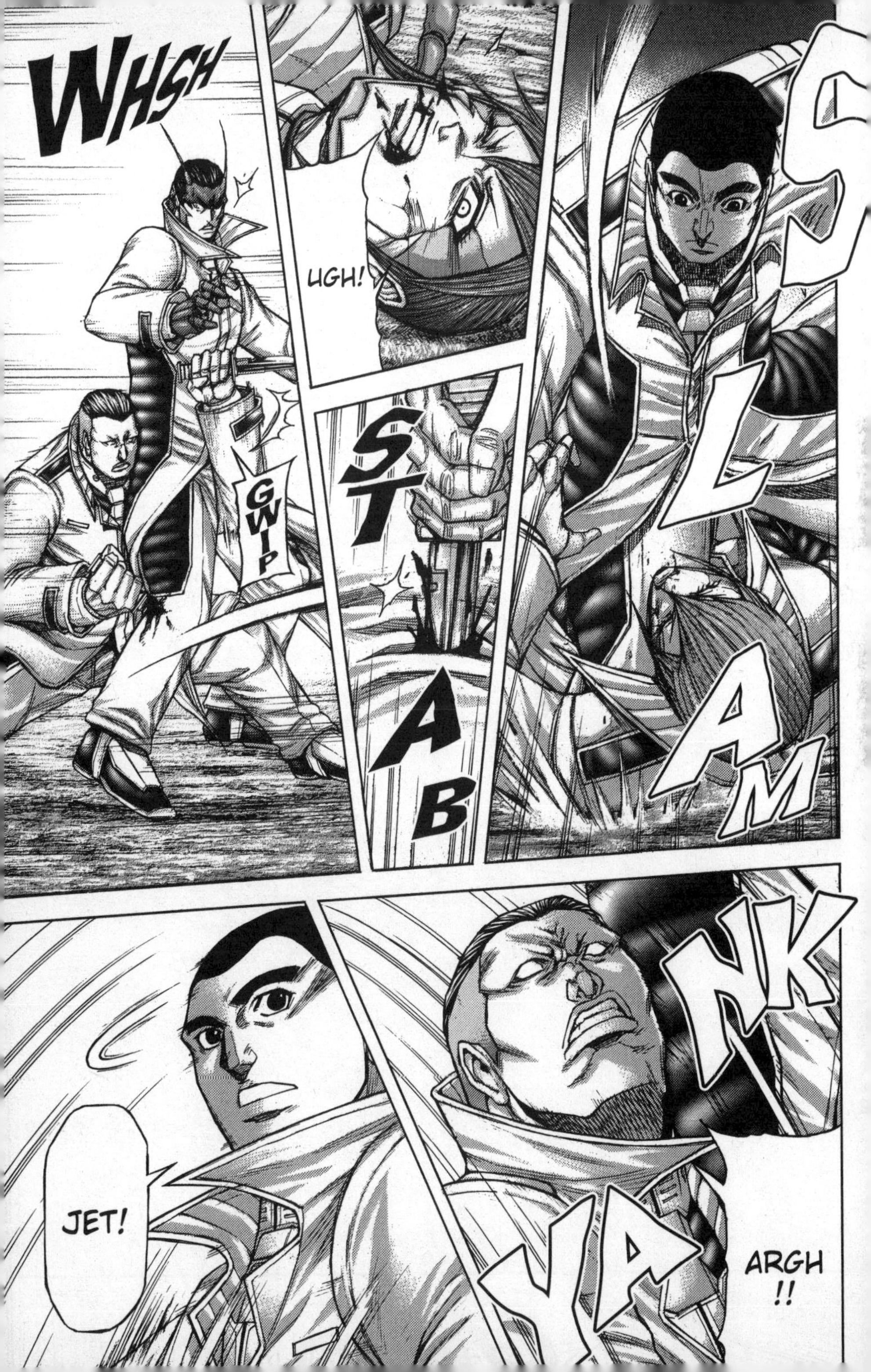
SLAM
UGH!
STAB
WHSH
GWIP
YANK
ARGH!!
JET!

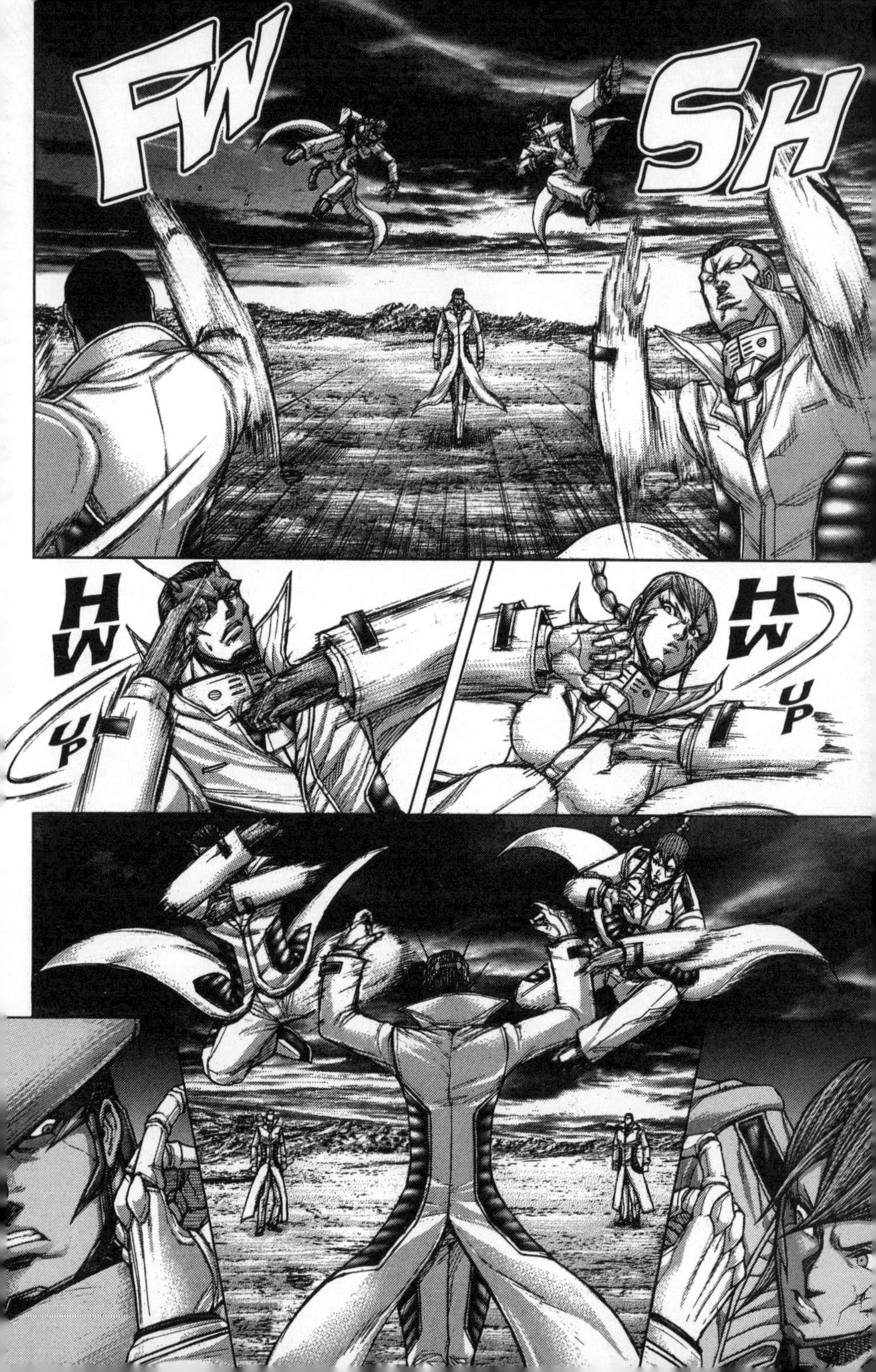
FWSH
HWUP
HWUP

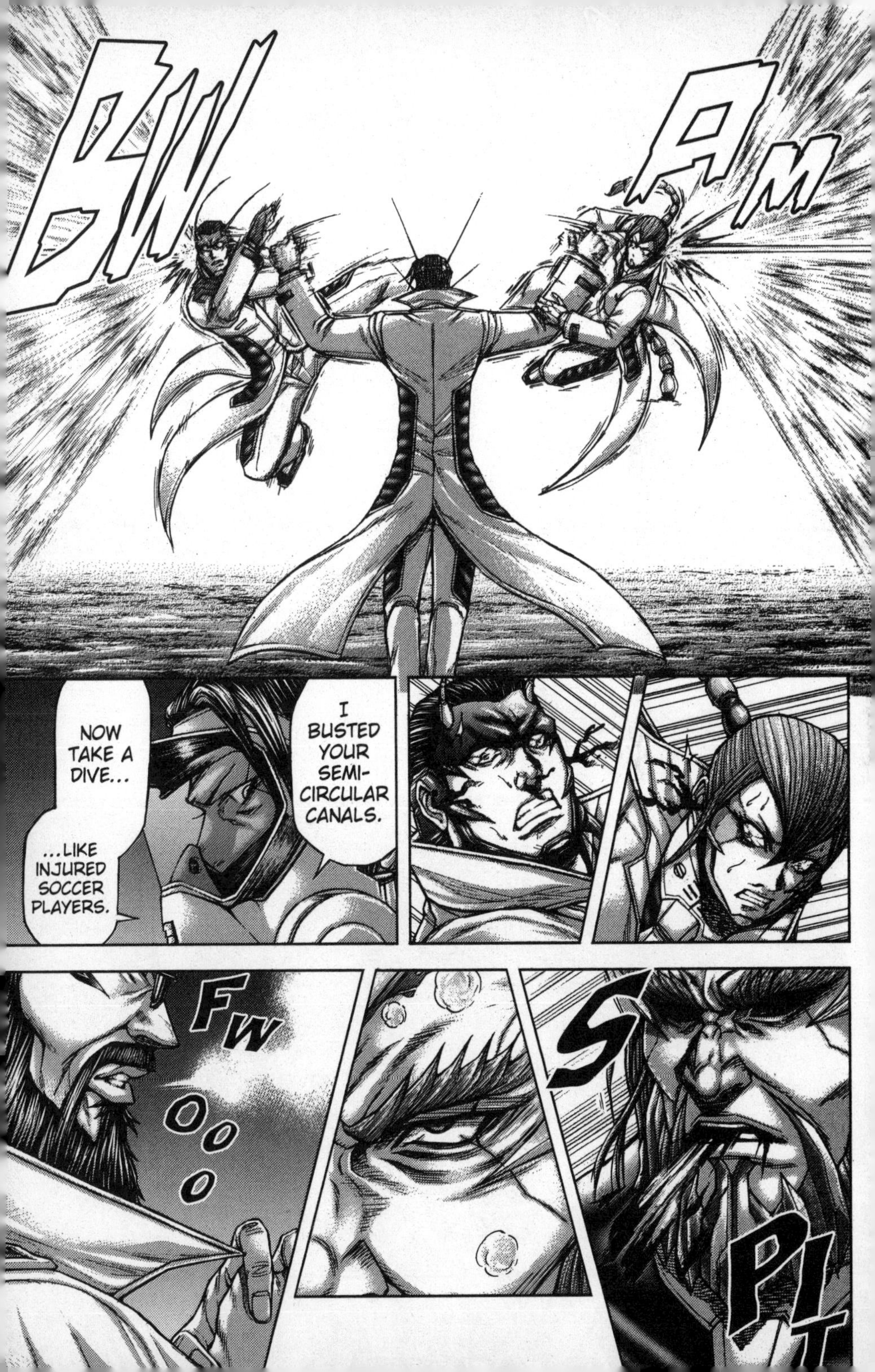
BAM
I BUSTED YOUR SEMI-CIRCULAR CANALS.
NOW TAKE A DIVE...
...LIKE INJURED SOCCER PLAYERS.
S
PIT
FW
OOO

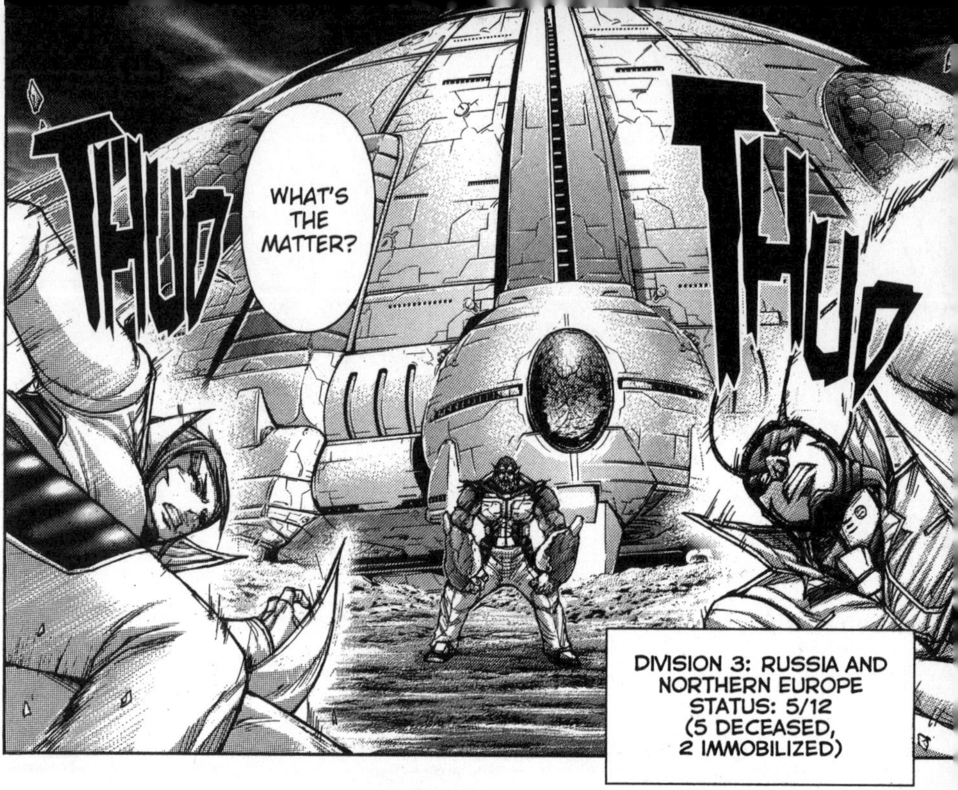
THUD
WHAT'S THE MATTER?
THUD
DIVISION 3: RUSSIA AND NORTHERN EUROPE STATUS: 5/12 (5 DECEASED, 2 IMMOBILIZED)

CHAPTER 66: ROCK!

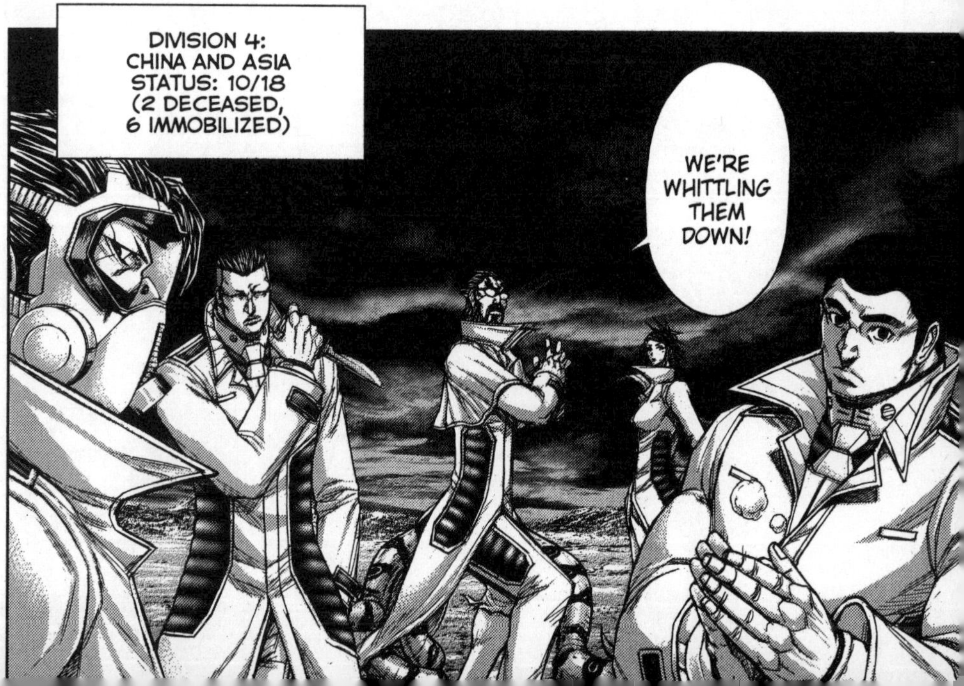
DIVISION 4: CHINA AND ASIA STATUS: 10/18 (2 DECEASED, 6 IMMOBILIZED)
WE'RE WHITTLING THEM DOWN!

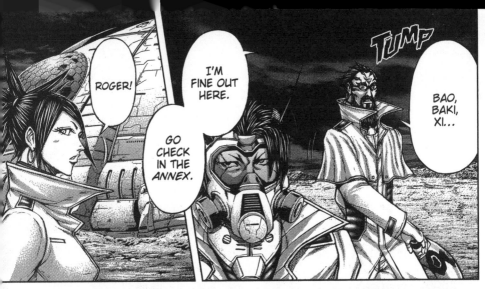

TUMP
BAO, BAKI, XI...
I'M FINE OUT HERE.
GO CHECK IN THE ANNEX.
ROGER!
KRUMBL
IMPULSE...
...IS A PRODUCT OF FORCE APPLIED OVER TIME...*
...SUCH AS WHEN ONE OBJECT STRIKES ANOTHER.
Force
Impulse
Time
Impact
FA JIN IS NOT SUPER-NATURAL.
LIKE ANY BLOW, IT DRAWS UPON LIMITED MUSCLE STRENGTH AND BODY WEIGHT.
THE STRENGTH APPLIED IS NOT MUCH DIFFER-ENT...
... BUT ...

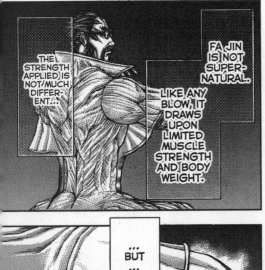

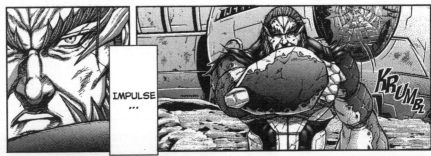

*WHEN FORCE ISN'T CONSTANT, IT BECOMES A FORCE-TIME INTEGRAL.

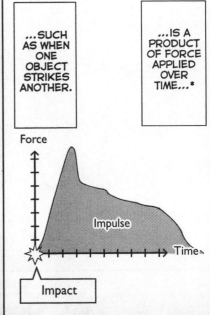

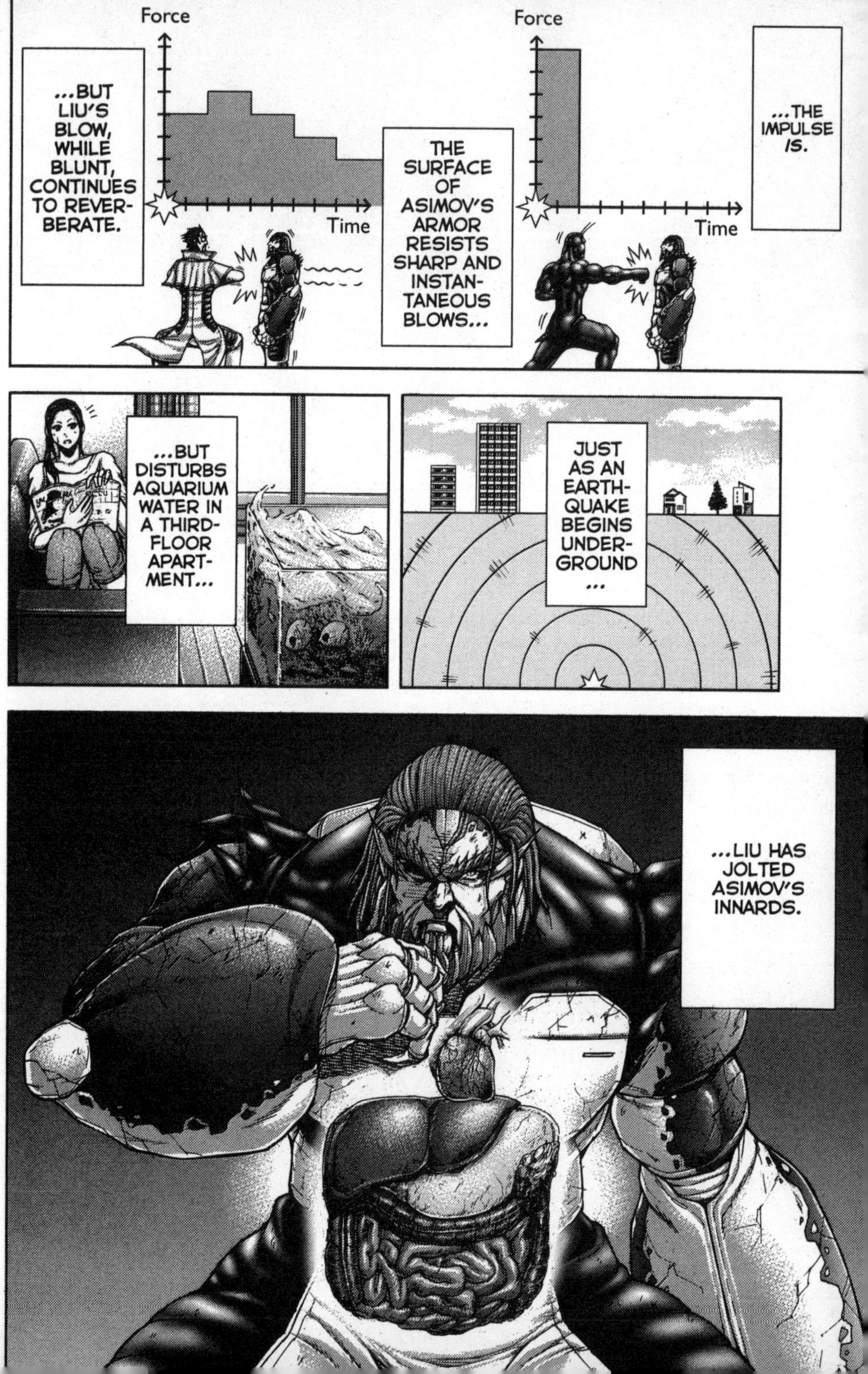
...THE IMPULSE IS.
Force
Time
THE SURFACE OF ASIMOV'S ARMOR RESISTS SHARP AND INSTANTANEOUS BLOWS...
Force
Time
...BUT LIU'S BLOW, WHILE BLUNT, CONTINUES TO REVERBERATE.
JUST AS AN EARTHQUAKE BEGINS UNDERGROUND...
...BUT DISTURBS AQUARIUM WATER IN A THIRD-FLOOR APARTMENT...
...LIU HAS JOLTED ASIMOV'S INNARDS.

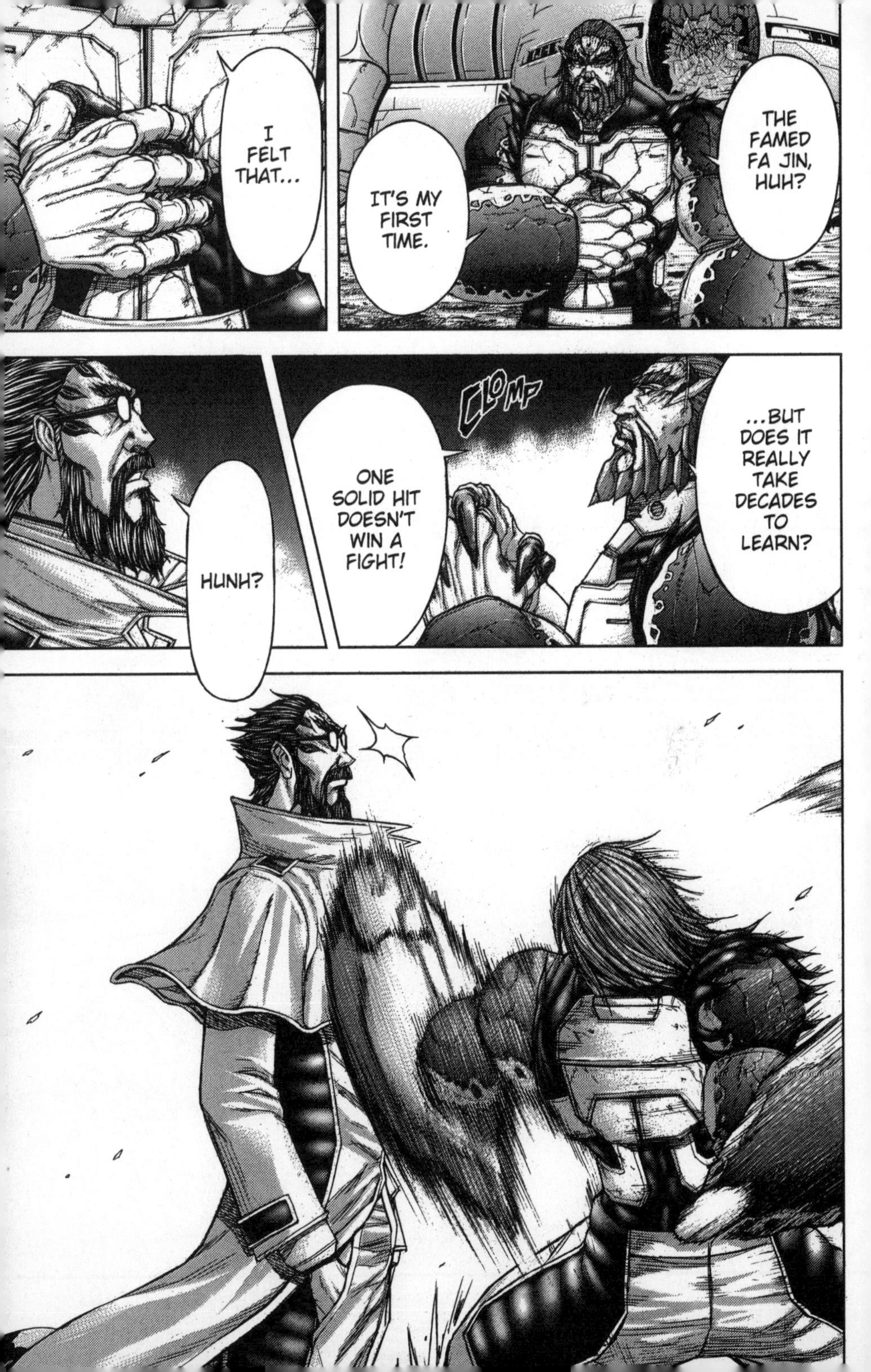
THE FAMED FA JIN, HUH?
IT'S MY FIRST TIME.
I FELT THAT...
...BUT DOES IT REALLY TAKE DECADES TO LEARN?
CLOMP
ONE SOLID HIT DOESN'T WIN A FIGHT!
HUNH?

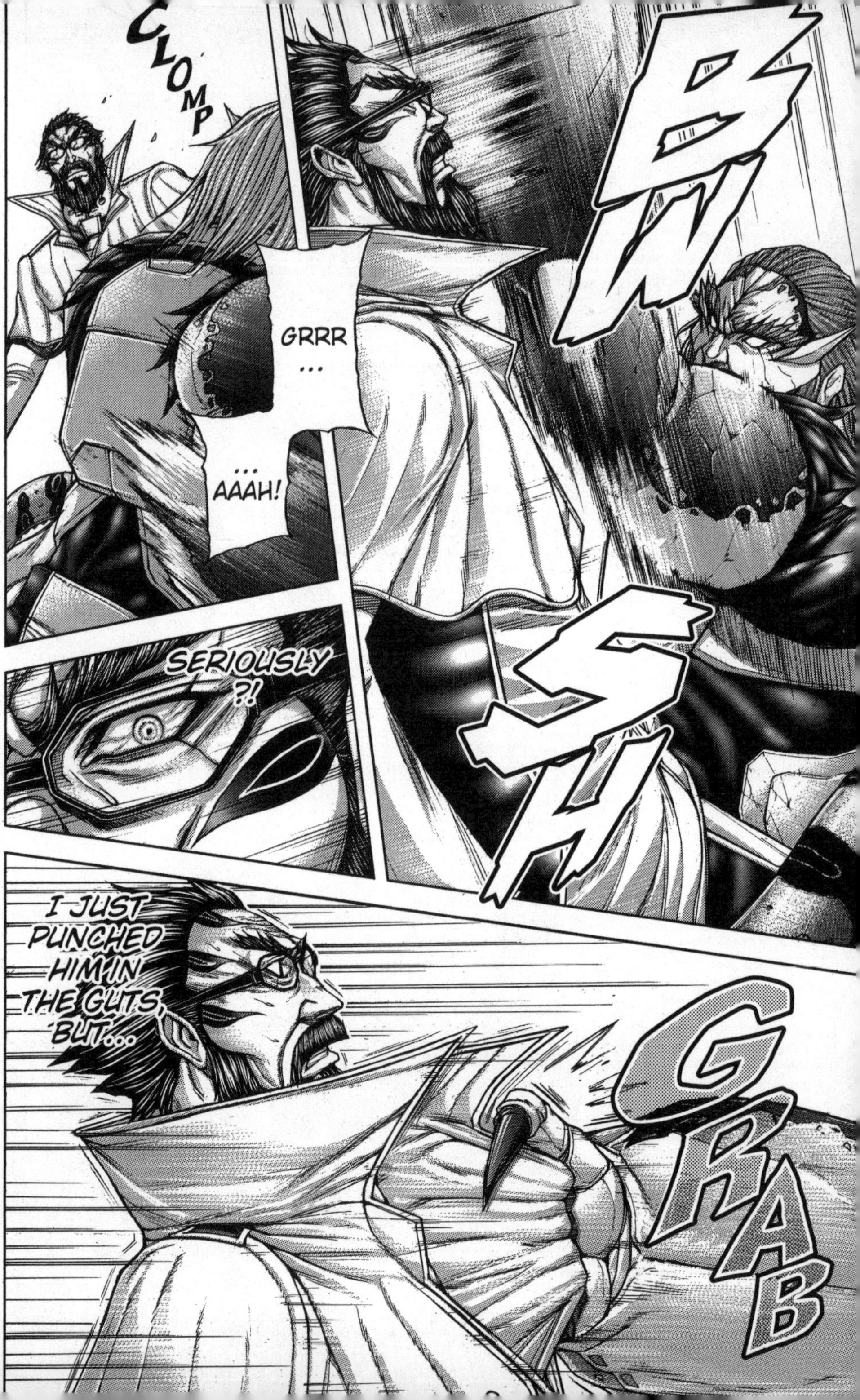
BW
SH
CLOMP
GRRR ...
... AAAH!
SERIOUSLY ?!
I JUST PUNCHED HIM IN THE GUTS, BUT...
GRAB

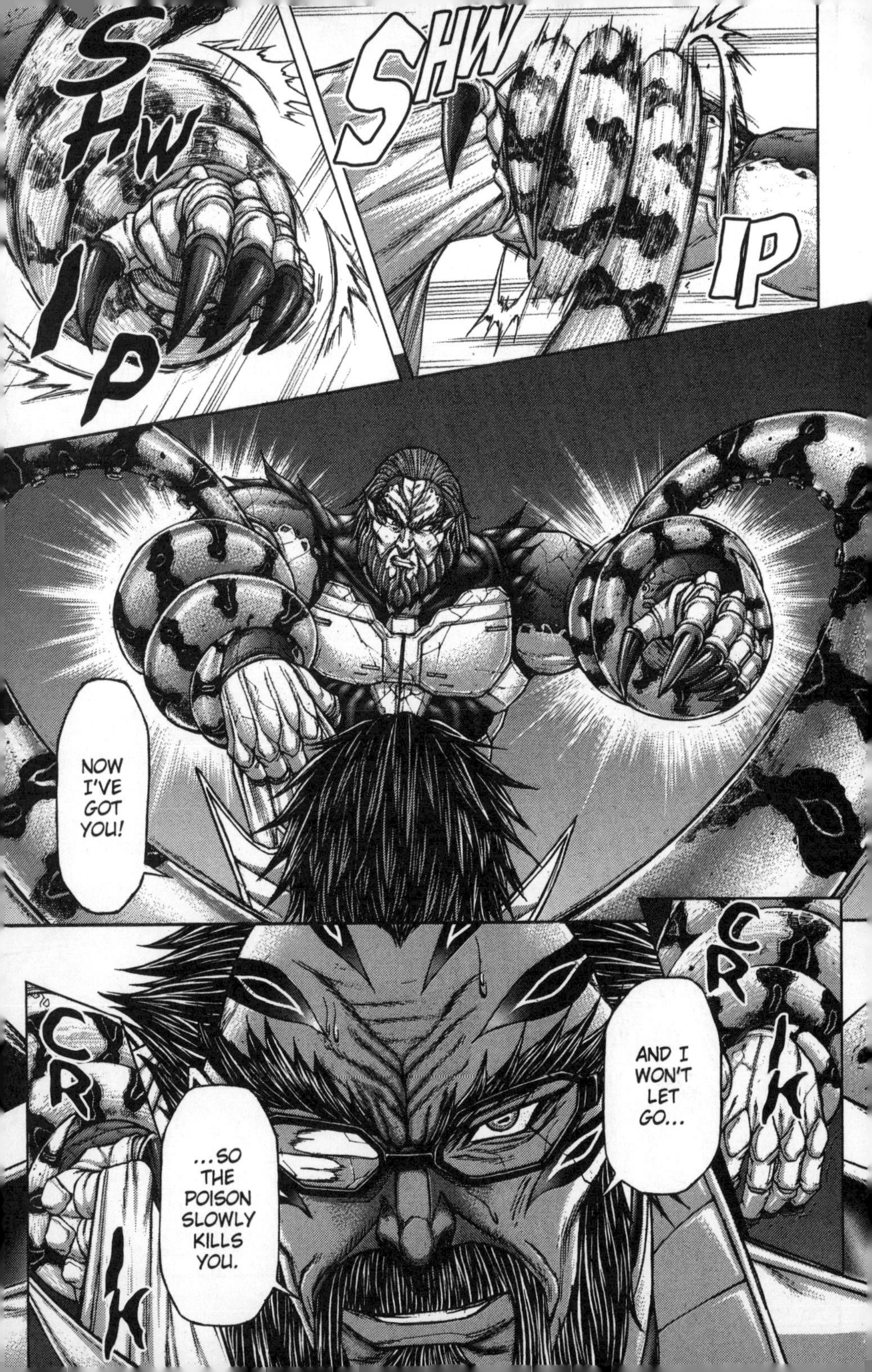
SHWIP
SHWIP
NOW I'VE GOT YOU!
CRIK
AND I WON'T LET GO...
...SO THE POISON SLOWLY KILLS YOU.
CRIK

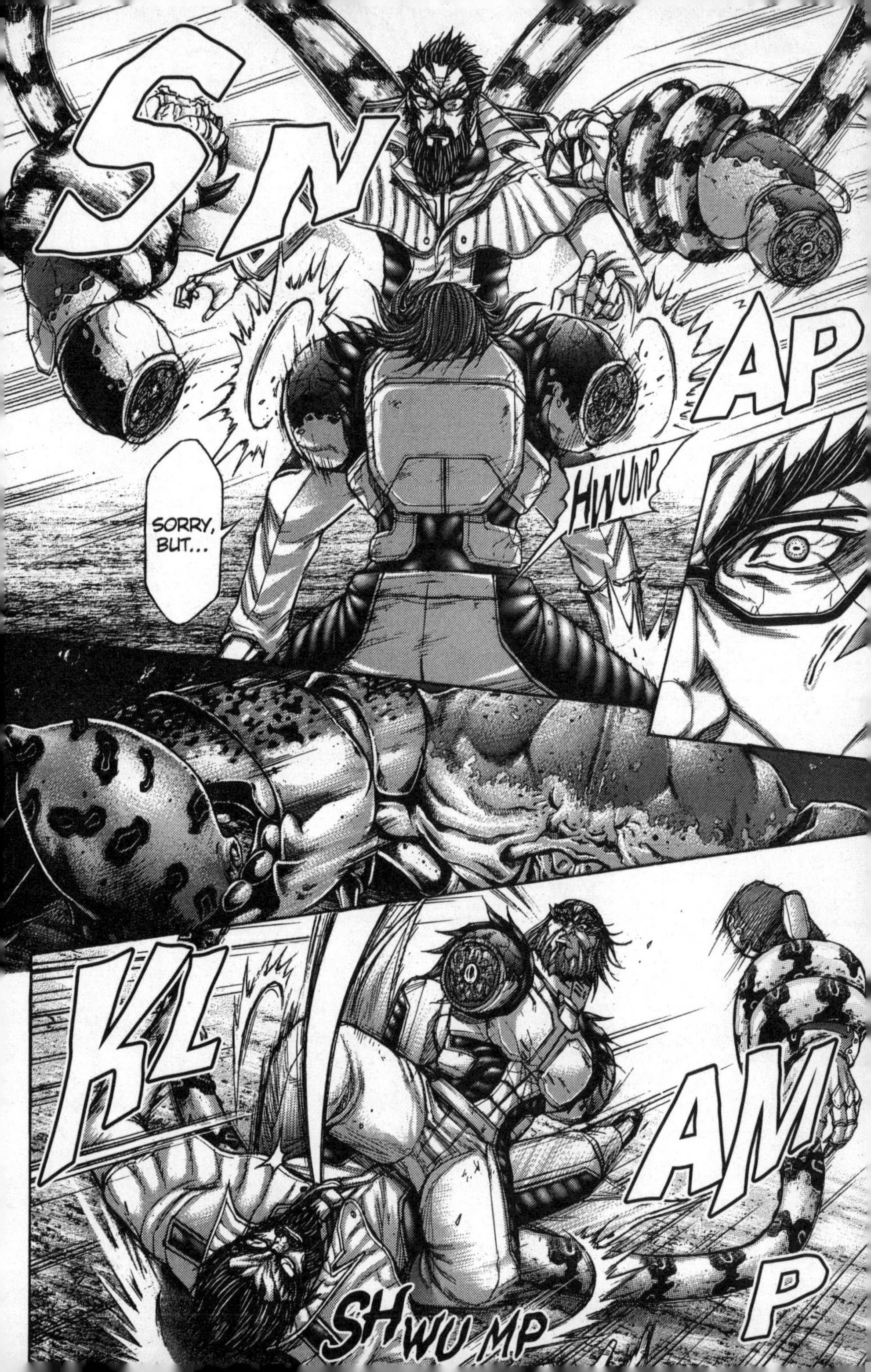
SNAP
HWUMP
SORRY, BUT...
KLAMP
SHWUMP

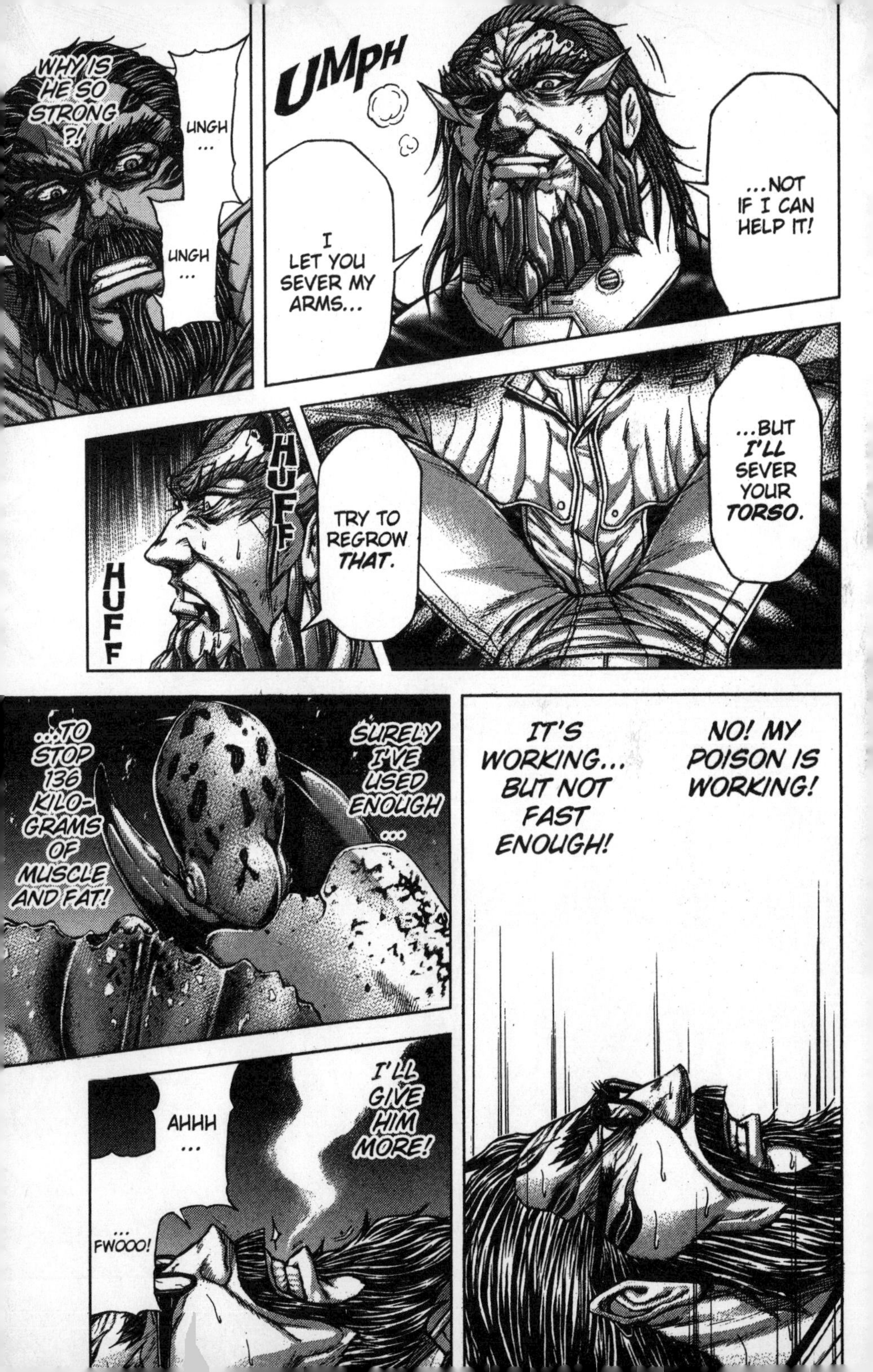
UMPH
...NOT IF I CAN HELP IT!
I LET YOU SEVER MY ARMS...
WHY IS HE SO STRONG?!
UNGH...
UNGH...
...BUT I'LL SEVER YOUR TORSO.
TRY TO REGROW THAT.
HUFF
HUFF
NO! MY POISON IS WORKING!
IT'S WORKING... BUT NOT FAST ENOUGH!
SURELY I'VE USED ENOUGH...
...TO STOP 136 KILOGRAMS OF MUSCLE AND FAT!
I'LL GIVE HIM MORE!
AHHH...
...FWOOO!

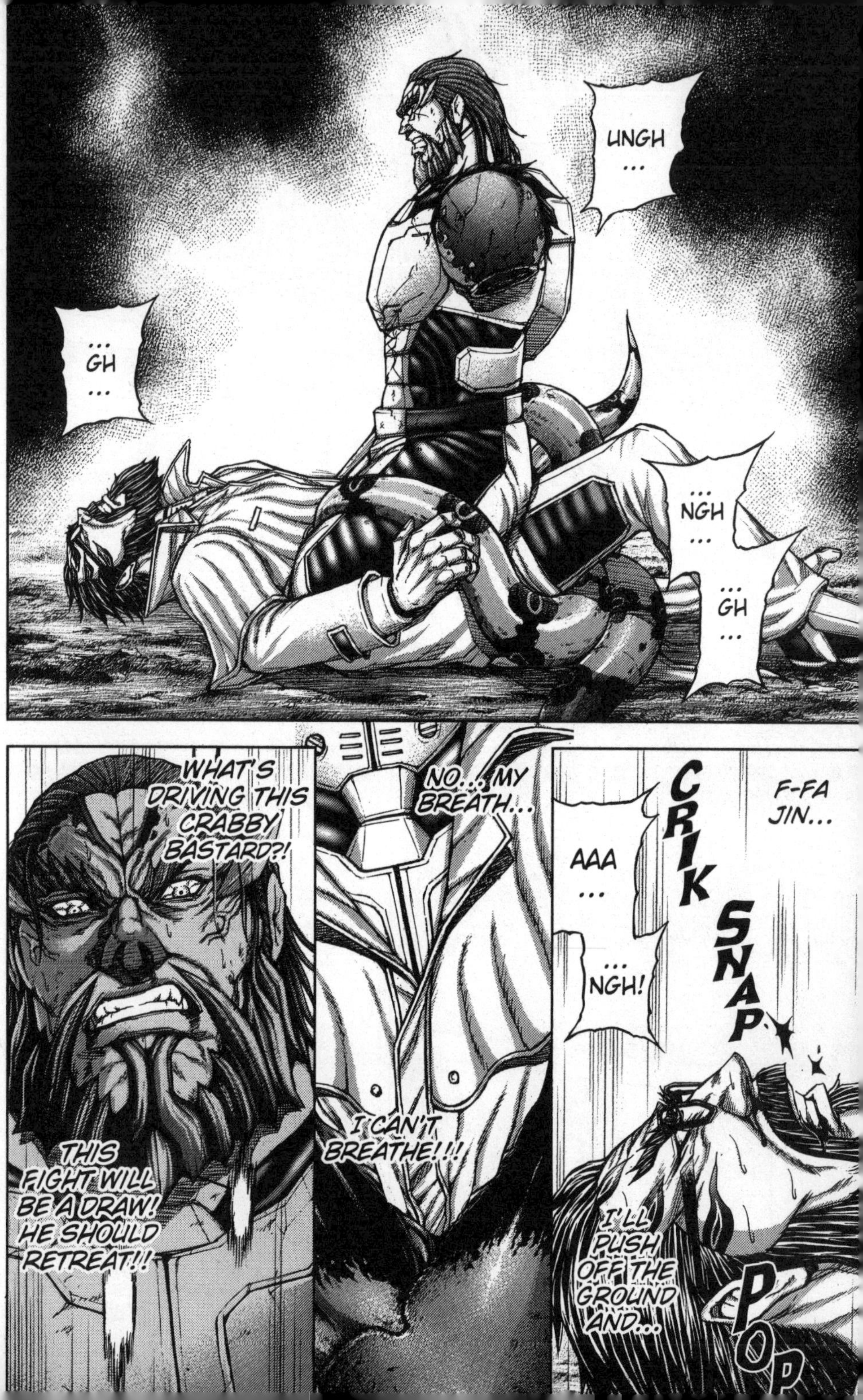
UNGH ...
... NGH ...
... GH ...
... GH ...
F-FA JIN...
AAA ...
... NGH!
CRIK
SNAP
I'LL PUSH OFF THE GROUND AND...
POP
NO... MY BREATH...
I CAN'T BREATHE!!!
WHAT'S DRIVING THIS CRABBY BASTARD?!
THIS FIGHT WILL BE A DRAW! HE SHOULD RETREAT!!

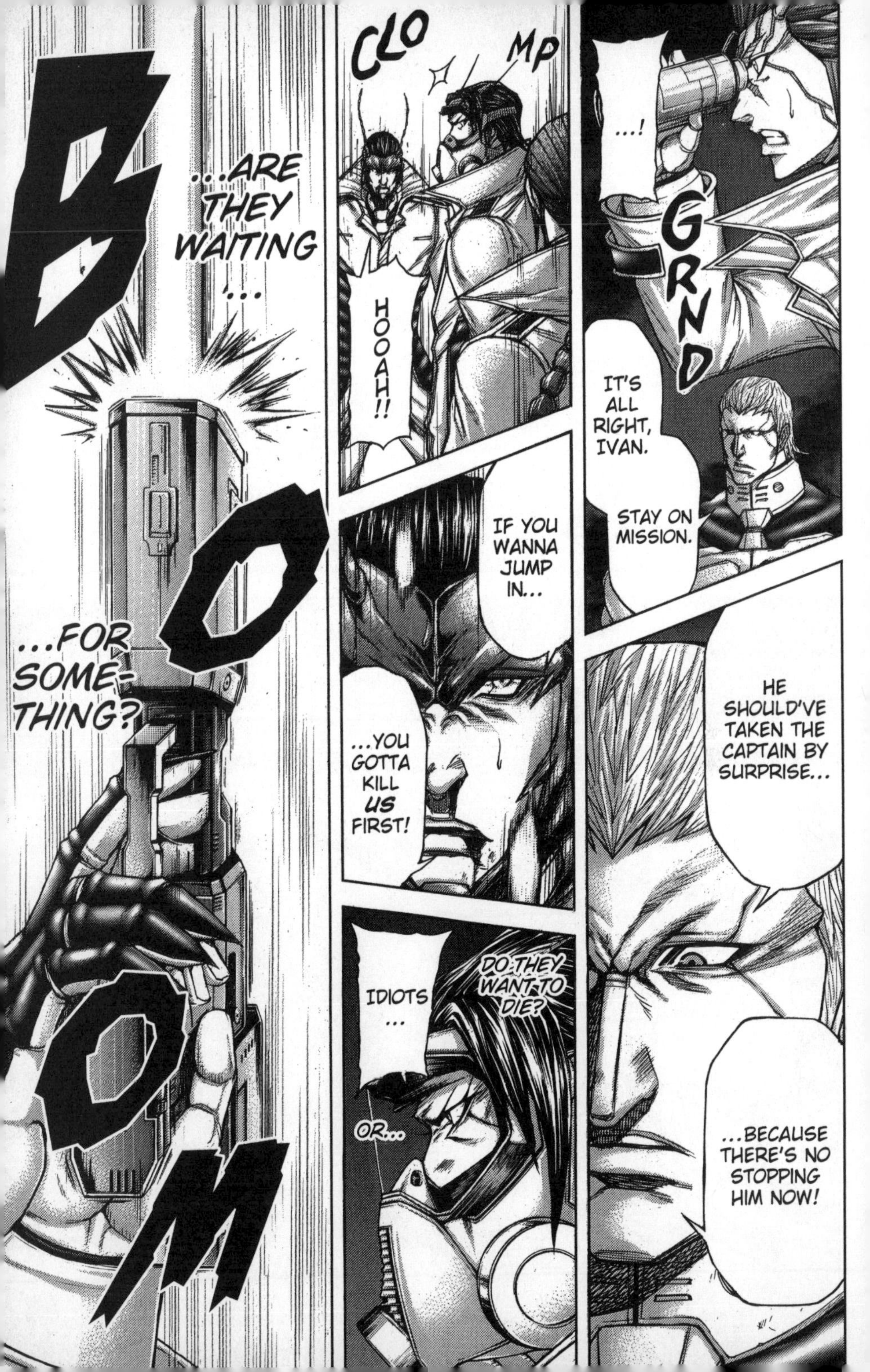

...!
GRND
IT'S ALL RIGHT, IVAN.
STAY ON MISSION.
HE SHOULD'VE TAKEN THE CAPTAIN BY SURPRISE...
...BECAUSE THERE'S NO STOPPING HIM NOW!
CLOMP
HOOAH!!
IF YOU WANNA JUMP IN...
...YOU GOTTA KILL US FIRST!
IDIOTS...
DO THEY WANT TO DIE?
OR...
BOOM
...ARE THEY WAITING...
...FOR SOME-THING?

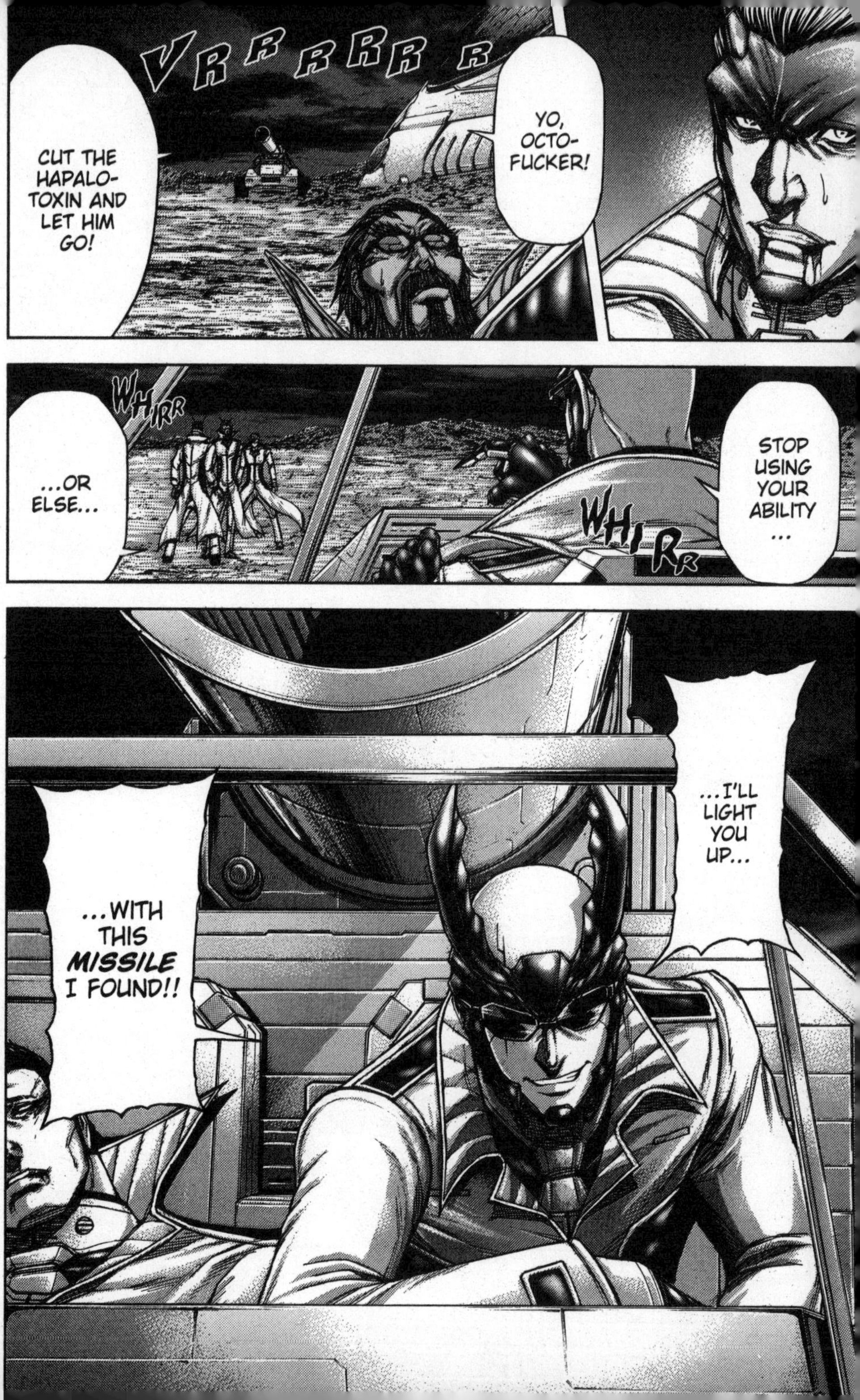
VRRRRRR
YO, OCTO-FUCKER!
CUT THE HAPALO-TOXIN AND LET HIM GO!
WHIRR
STOP USING YOUR ABILITY...
WHIRR
...OR ELSE...
...I'LL LIGHT YOU UP...
...WITH THIS *MISSILE* I FOUND!!

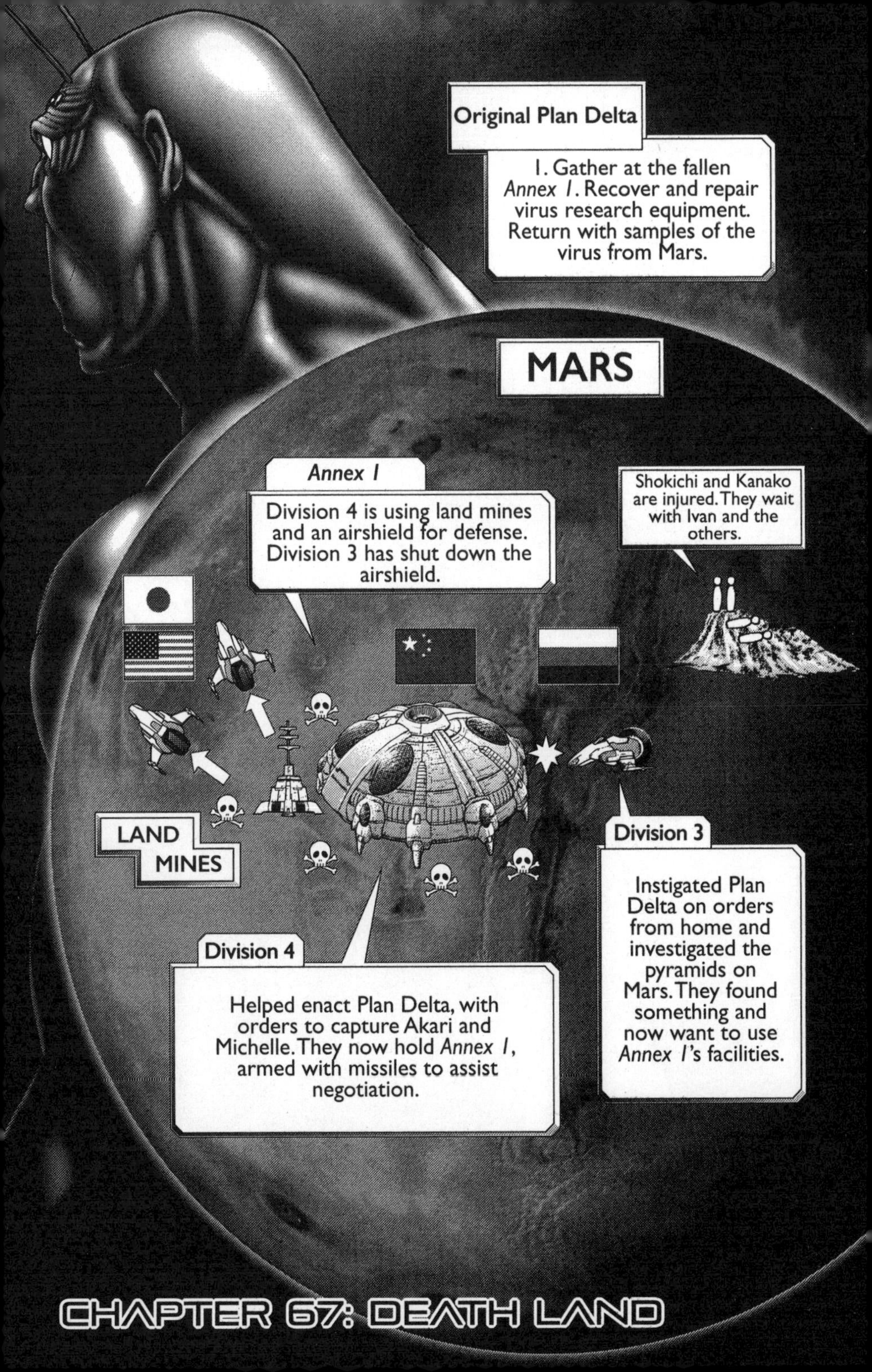

Original Plan Delta
1. Gather at the fallen *Annex 1*. Recover and repair virus research equipment. Return with samples of the virus from Mars.
MARS
Shokichi and Kanako are injured. They wait with Ivan and the others.
Annex 1
Division 4 is using land mines and an airshield for defense. Division 3 has shut down the airshield.
Division 3
Instigated Plan Delta on orders from home and investigated the pyramids on Mars. They found something and now want to use *Annex 1*'s facilities.
LAND MINES
Division 4
Helped enact Plan Delta, with orders to capture Akari and Michelle. They now hold *Annex 1*, armed with missiles to assist negotiation.
CHAPTER 67: DEATH LAND

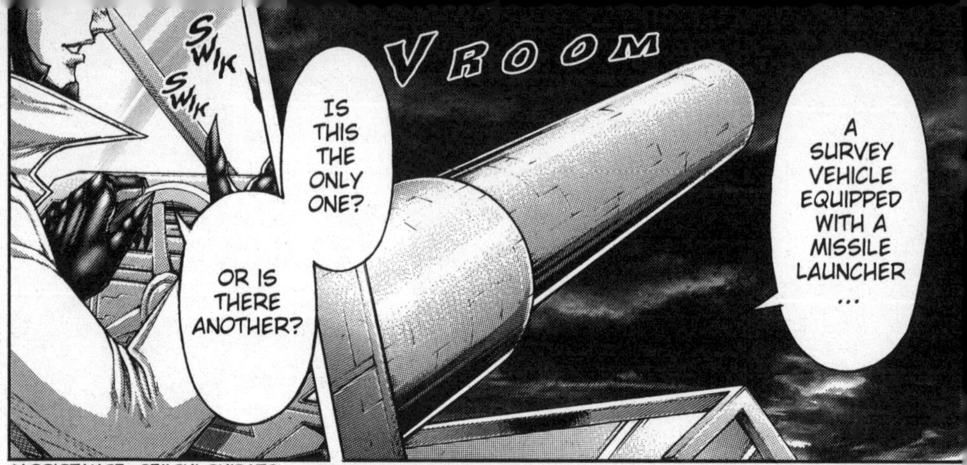
VROOM
A SURVEY VEHICLE EQUIPPED WITH A MISSILE LAUNCHER ...
IS THIS THE ONLY ONE?
OR IS THERE ANOTHER?
SWIK SWIK

*ASSISTANCE: SEIICHI SHIRATO

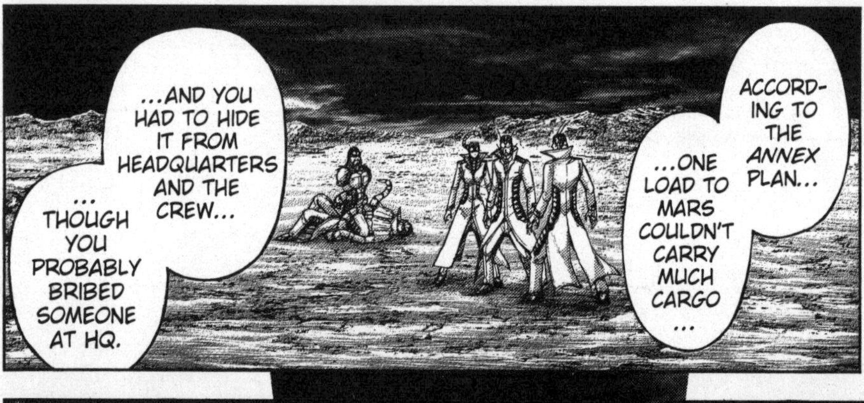
ACCORD-ING TO THE *ANNEX* PLAN...
...ONE LOAD TO MARS COULDN'T CARRY MUCH CARGO ...
...AND YOU HAD TO HIDE IT FROM HEADQUARTERS AND THE CREW...
... THOUGH YOU PROBABLY BRIBED SOMEONE AT HQ.

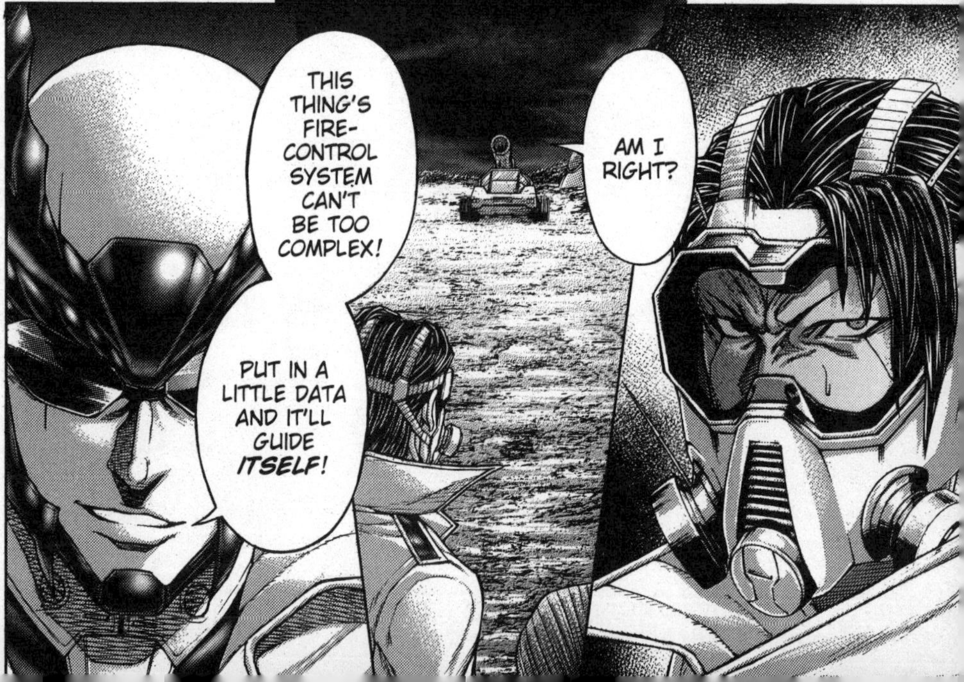
AM I RIGHT?
THIS THING'S FIRE-CONTROL SYSTEM CAN'T BE TOO COMPLEX!
PUT IN A LITTLE DATA AND IT'LL GUIDE *ITSELF*!

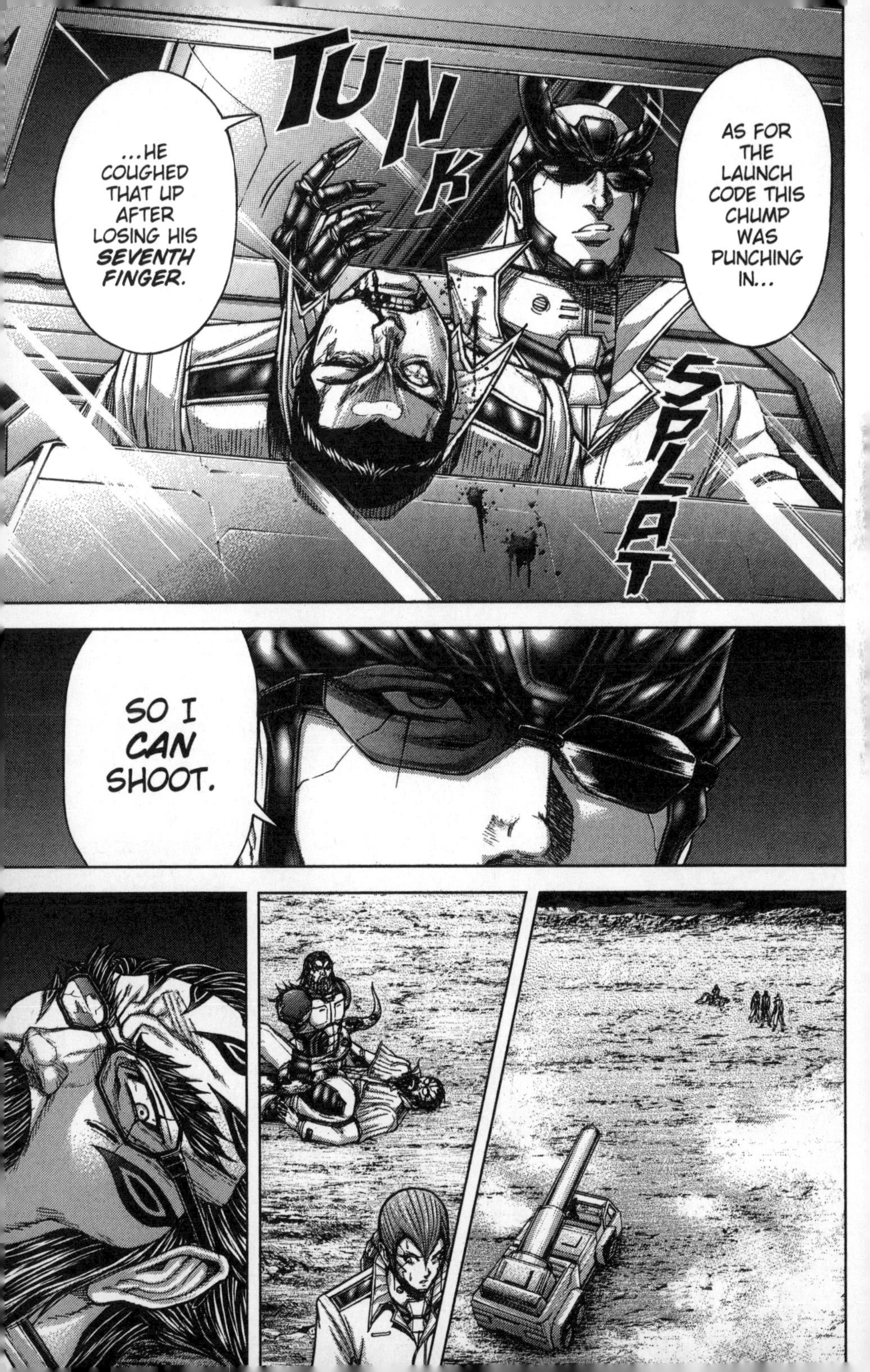
AS FOR THE LAUNCH CODE THIS CHUMP WAS PUNCHING IN...
TUNK
...HE COUGHED THAT UP AFTER LOSING HIS SEVENTH FINGER.
SPLAT
SO I CAN SHOOT.

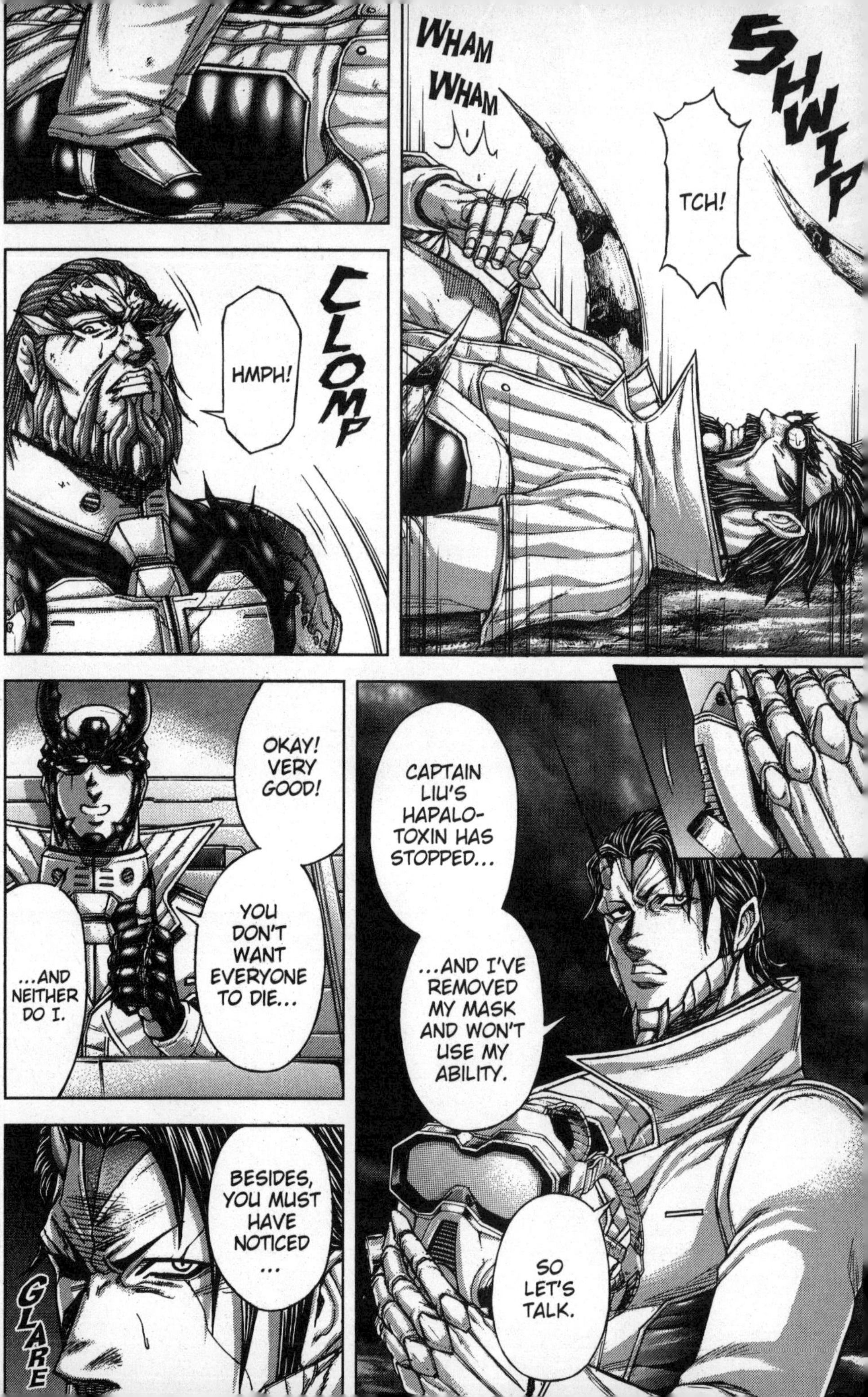
SHWIP
TCH!
WHAM
WHAM
HMPH!
CLOMP
CAPTAIN LIU'S HAPALO-TOXIN HAS STOPPED...
...AND I'VE REMOVED MY MASK AND WON'T USE MY ABILITY.
SO LET'S TALK.
OKAY! VERY GOOD!
YOU DON'T WANT EVERYONE TO DIE...
...AND NEITHER DO I.
BESIDES, YOU MUST HAVE NOTICED ...
GLARE

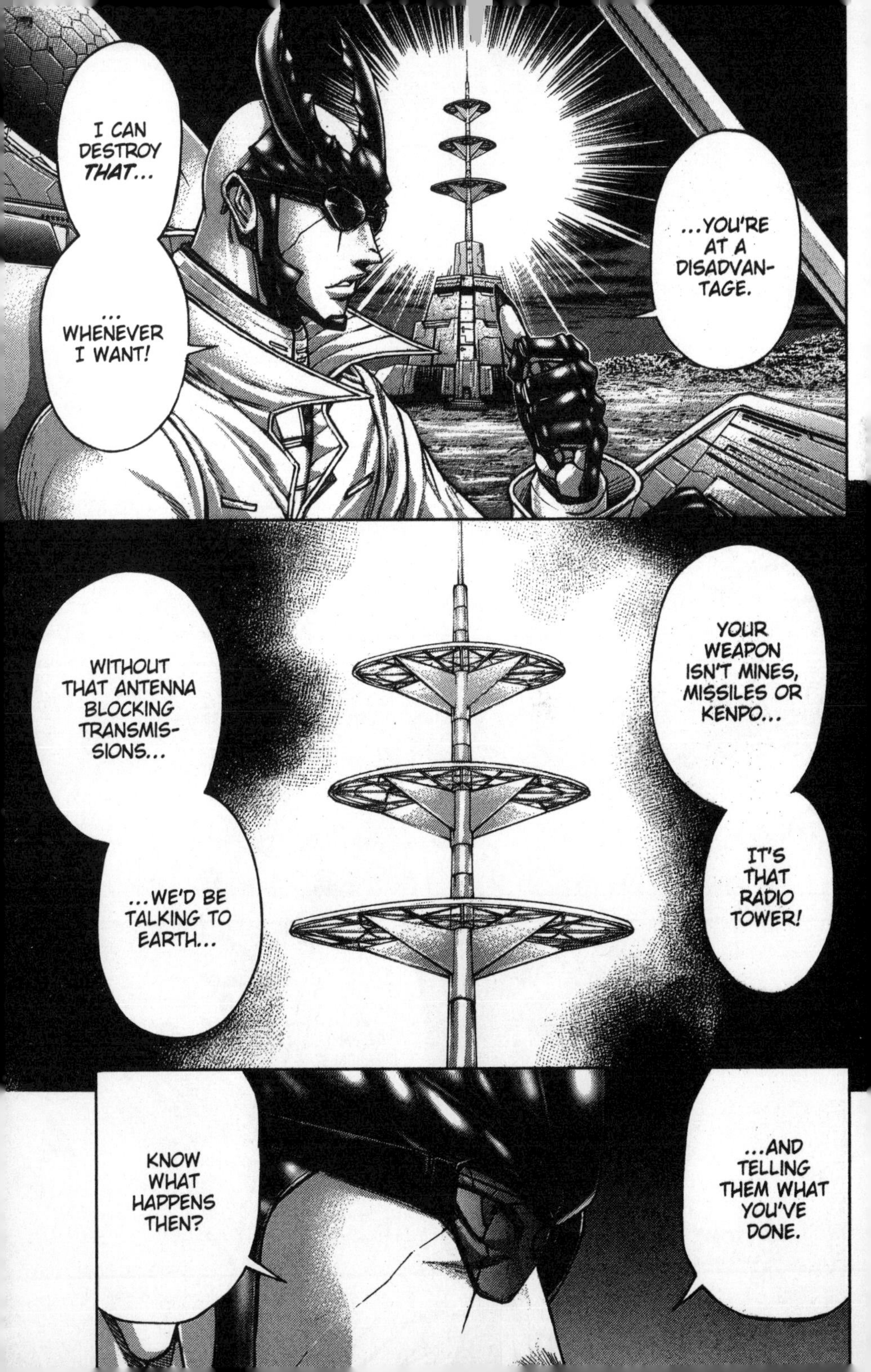
...YOU'RE AT A DISADVANTAGE.
I CAN DESTROY *THAT*...
...WHENEVER I WANT!
YOUR WEAPON ISN'T MINES, MISSILES OR KENPO...
IT'S THAT RADIO TOWER!
WITHOUT THAT ANTENNA BLOCKING TRANSMISSIONS...
...WE'D BE TALKING TO EARTH...
...AND TELLING THEM WHAT YOU'VE DONE.
KNOW WHAT HAPPENS THEN?

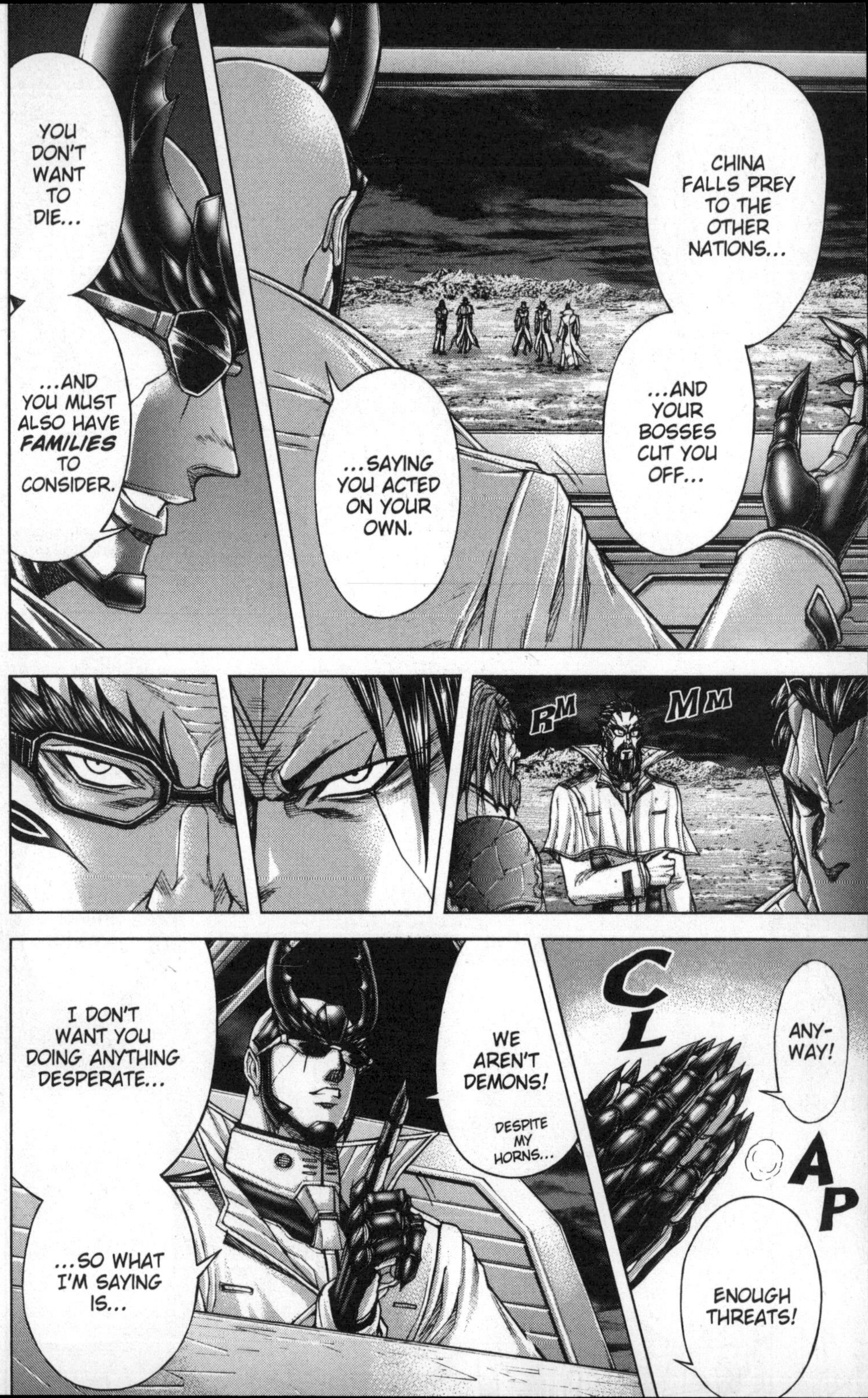
CHINA FALLS PREY TO THE OTHER NATIONS...
...AND YOUR BOSSES CUT YOU OFF...
...SAYING YOU ACTED ON YOUR OWN.
YOU DON'T WANT TO DIE...
...AND YOU MUST ALSO HAVE FAMILIES TO CONSIDER.
RMMM
ANY-WAY!
CLAP
ENOUGH THREATS!
WE AREN'T DEMONS!
DESPITE MY HORNS...
I DON'T WANT YOU DOING ANYTHING DESPERATE...
...SO WHAT I'M SAYING IS...

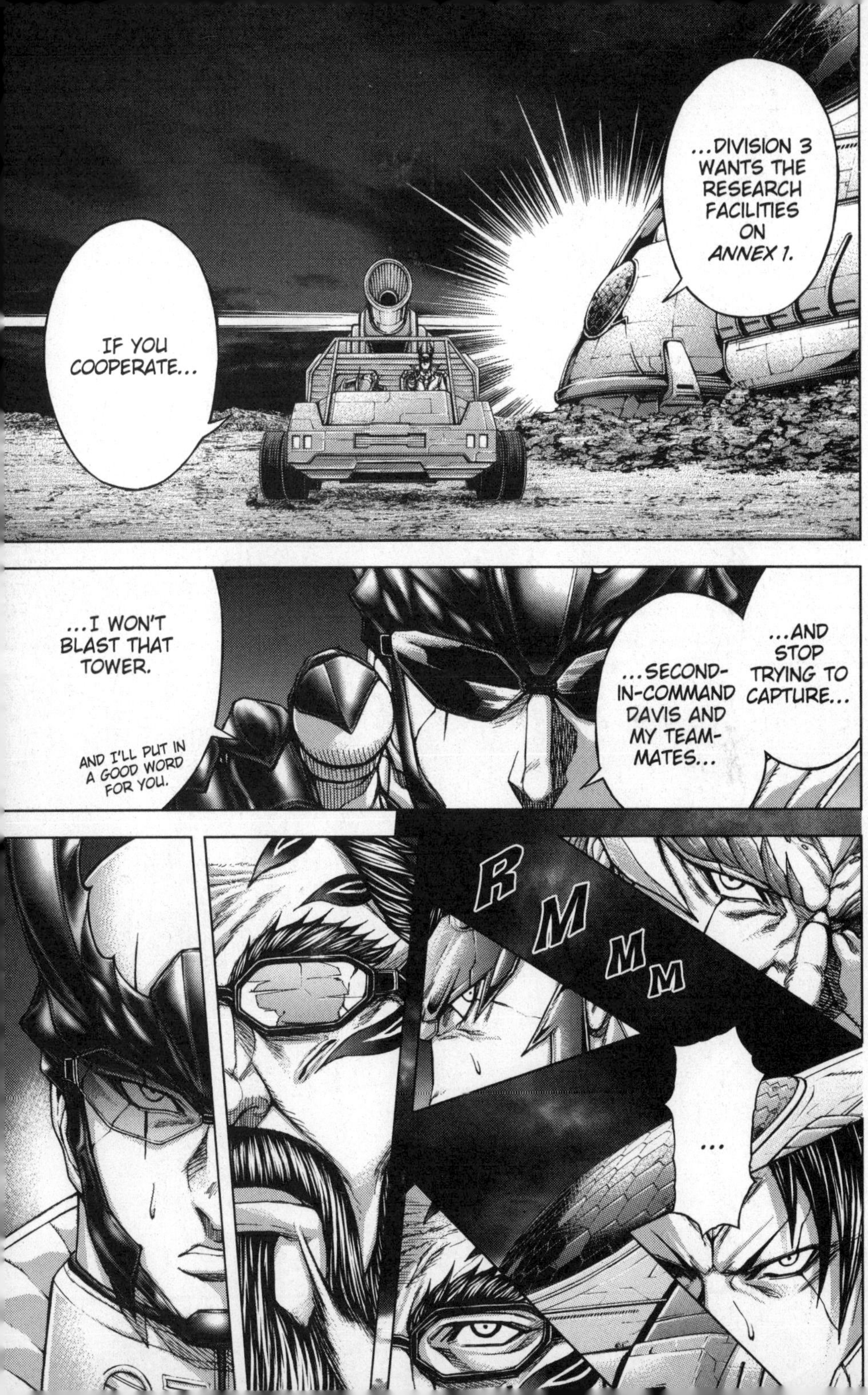
...DIVISION 3 WANTS THE RESEARCH FACILITIES ON ANNEX 1.
IF YOU COOPERATE...
...AND STOP TRYING TO CAPTURE...
...SECOND-IN-COMMAND DAVIS AND MY TEAM-MATES...
...I WON'T BLAST THAT TOWER.
AND I'LL PUT IN A GOOD WORD FOR YOU.
RMMM
...

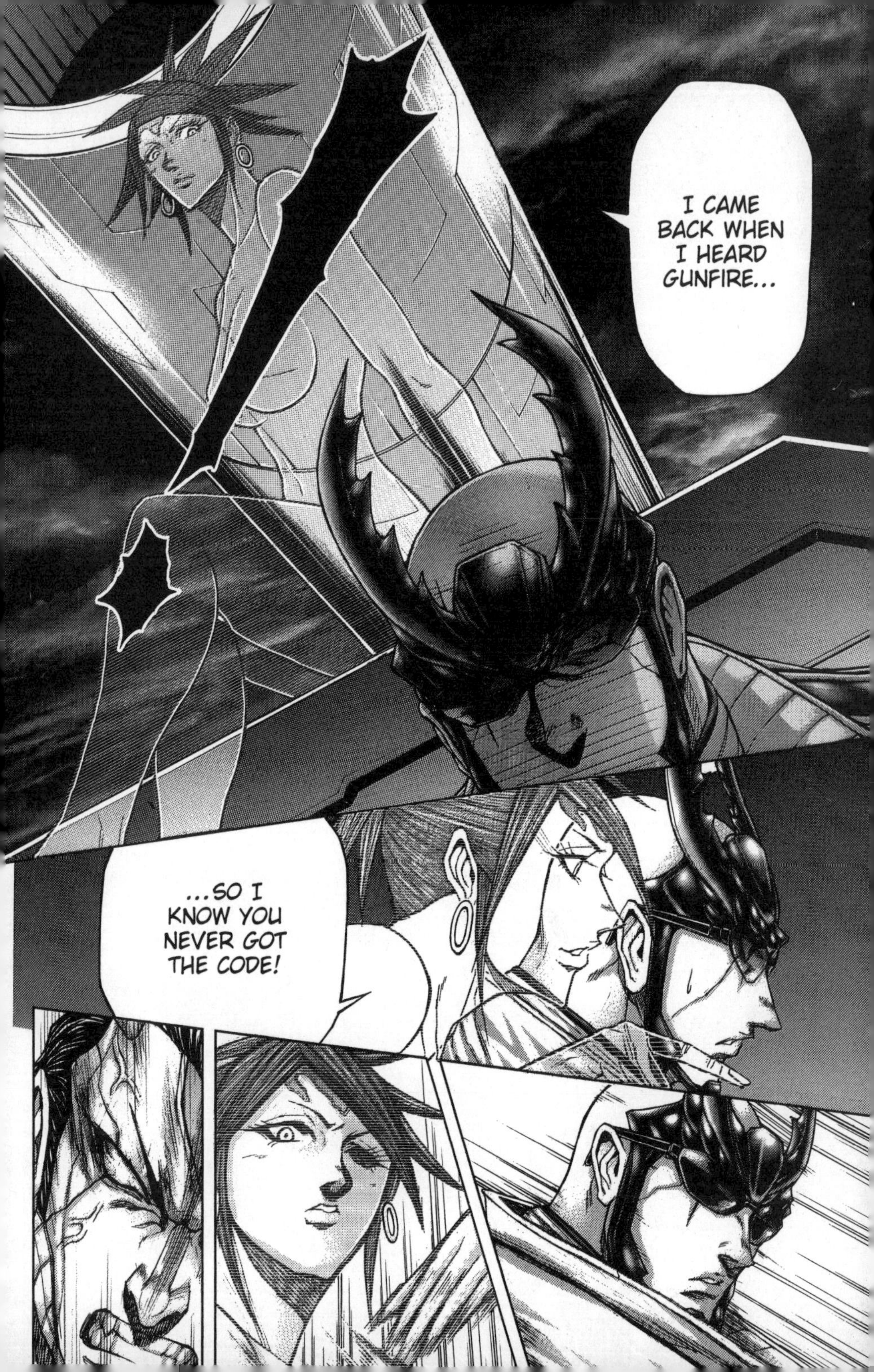
I CAME BACK WHEN I HEARD GUNFIRE...
...SO I KNOW YOU NEVER GOT THE CODE!

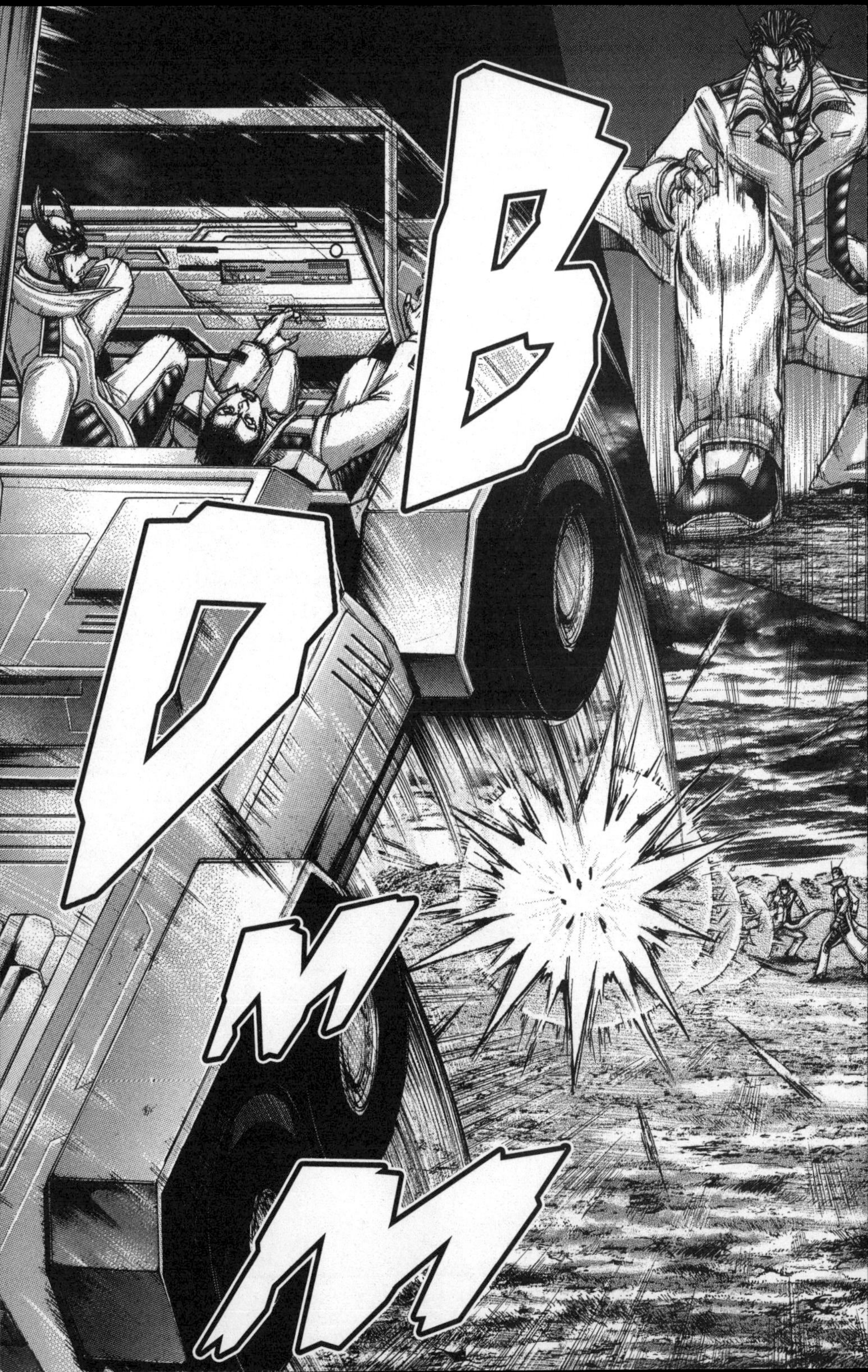
BDMM

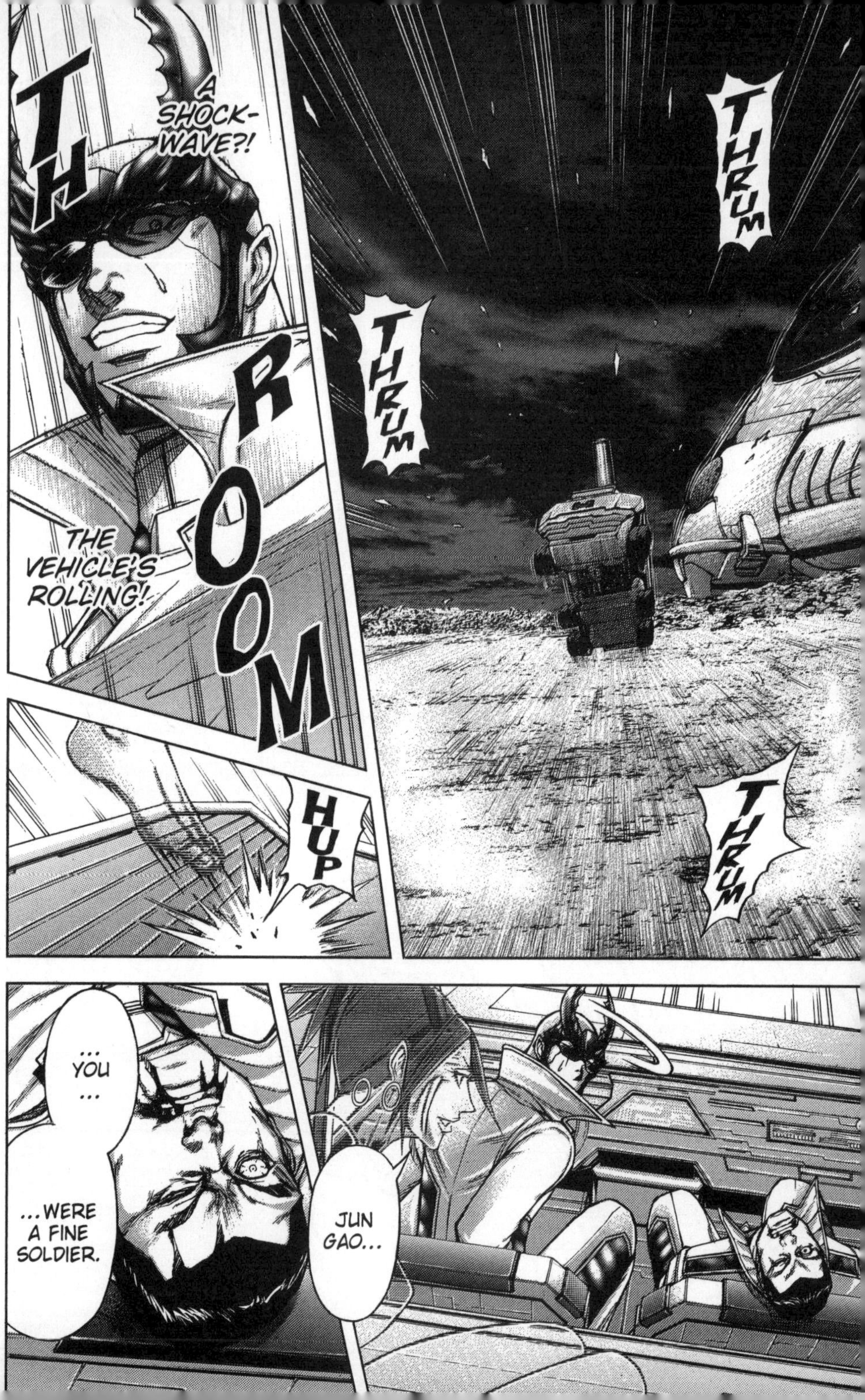
THRUM
THRUM
THRUM
A SHOCK-WAVE?!
THROOM
THE VEHICLE'S ROLLING!
HUP
JUN GAO...
... YOU ...
...WERE A FINE SOLDIER.

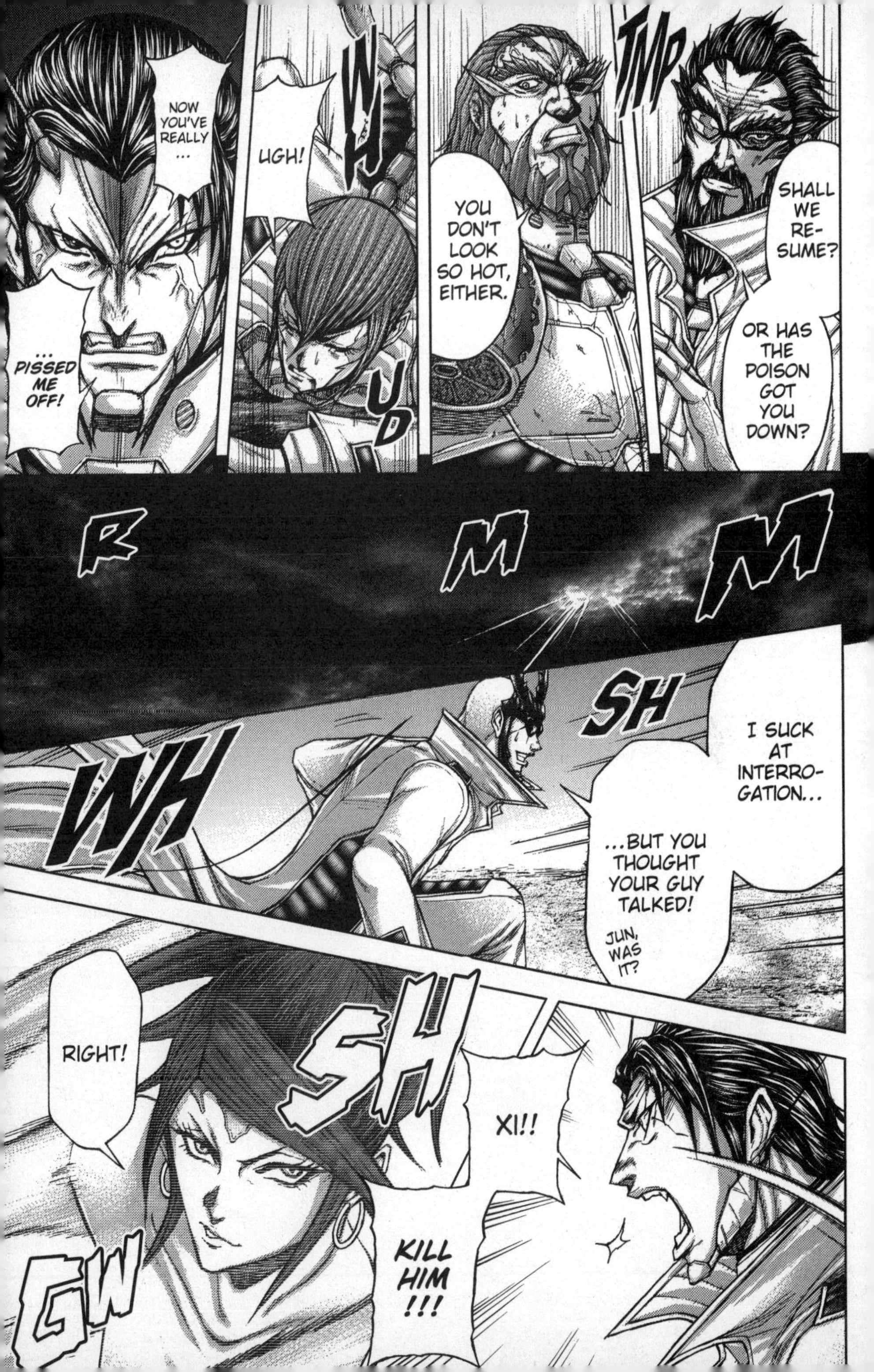
TMP
SHALL WE RE-SUME?
OR HAS THE POISON GOT YOU DOWN?
YOU DON'T LOOK SO HOT, EITHER.
WH
UGH!
UD
NOW YOU'VE REALLY ...
... PISSED ME OFF!
R
M
M
SH
I SUCK AT INTERROGATION...
...BUT YOU THOUGHT YOUR GUY TALKED!
JUN, WAS IT?
WH
XI!!
SH
RIGHT!
KILL HIM!!!
GW

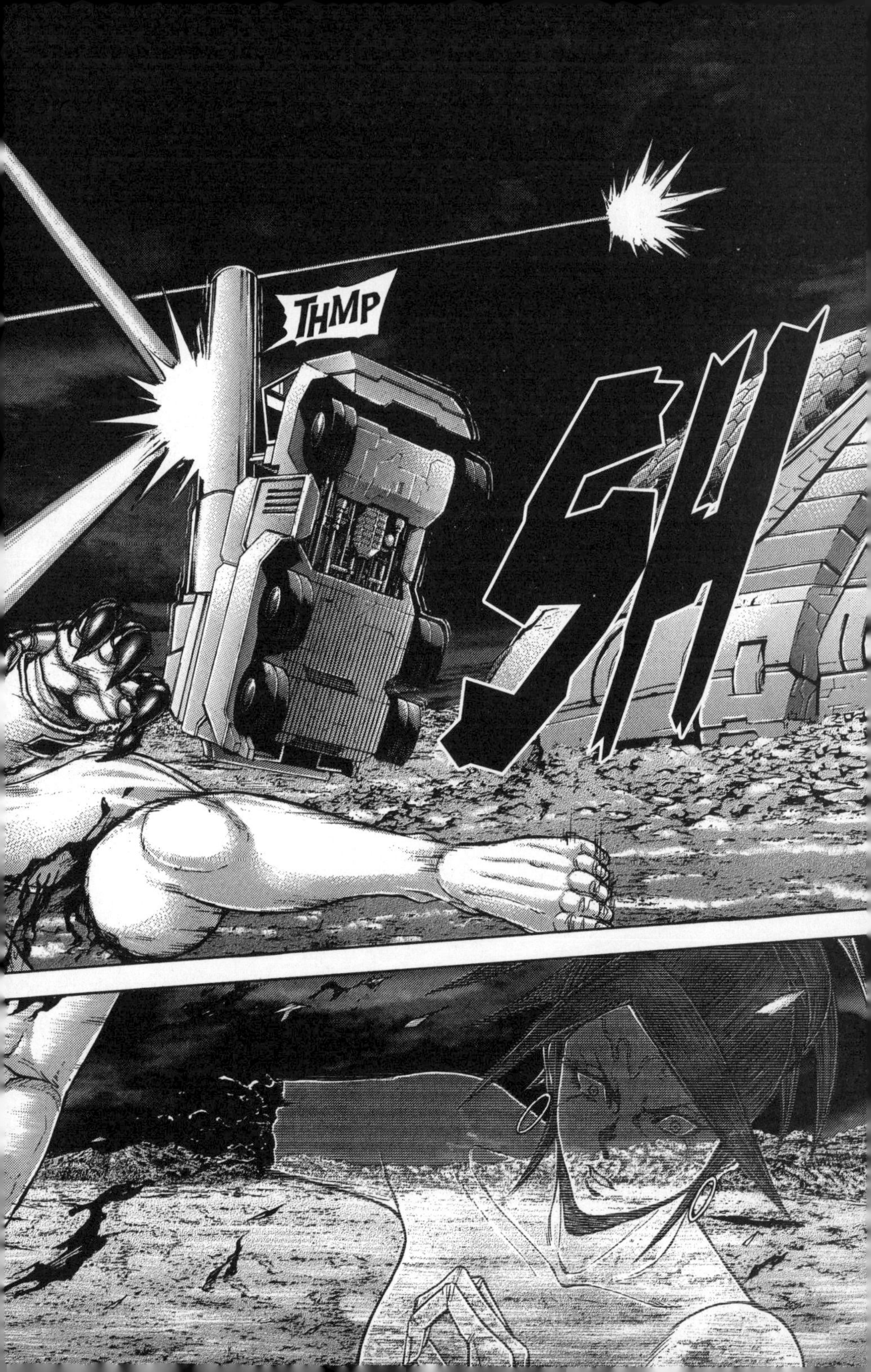
THMP

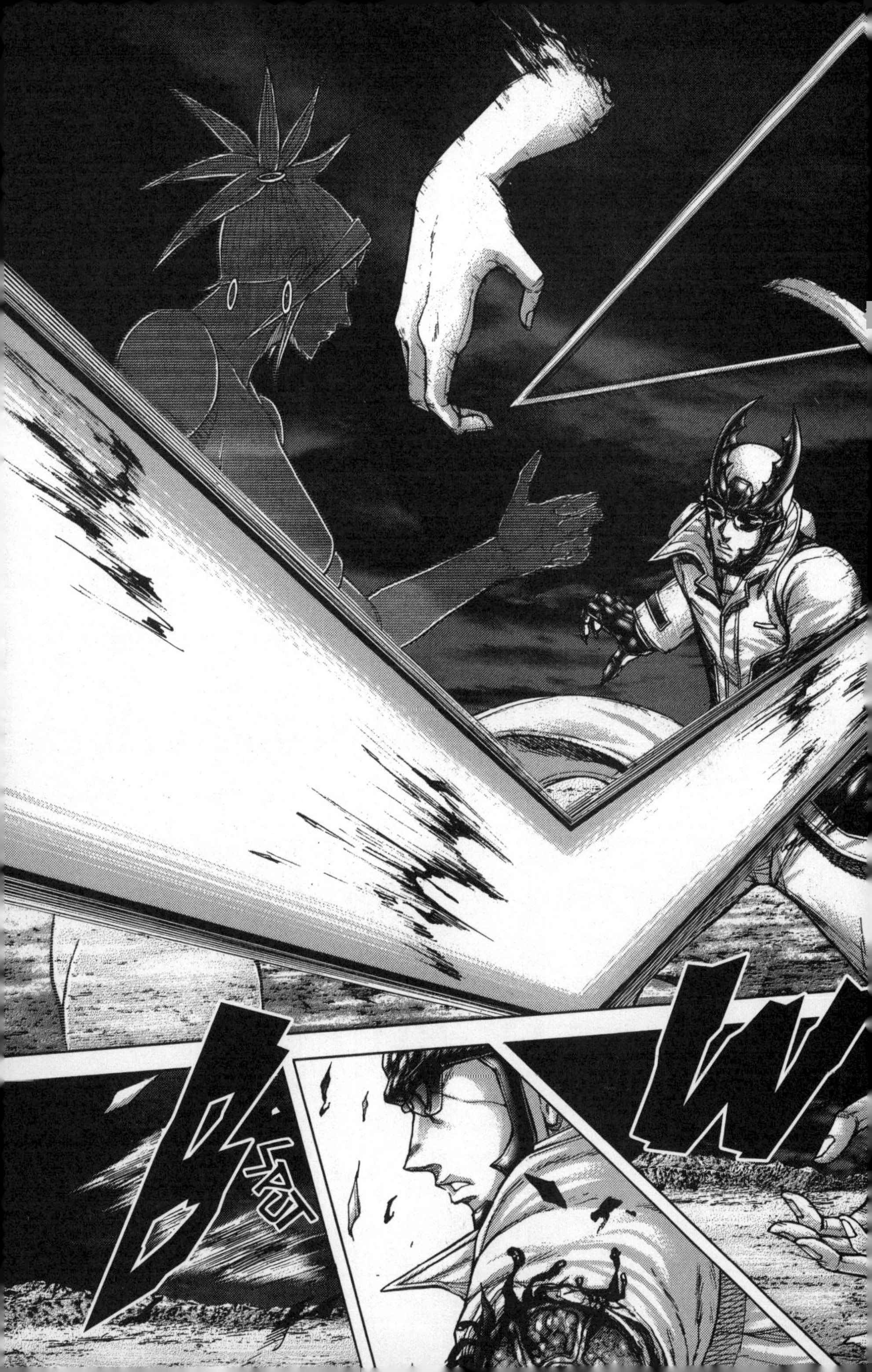
SPUT

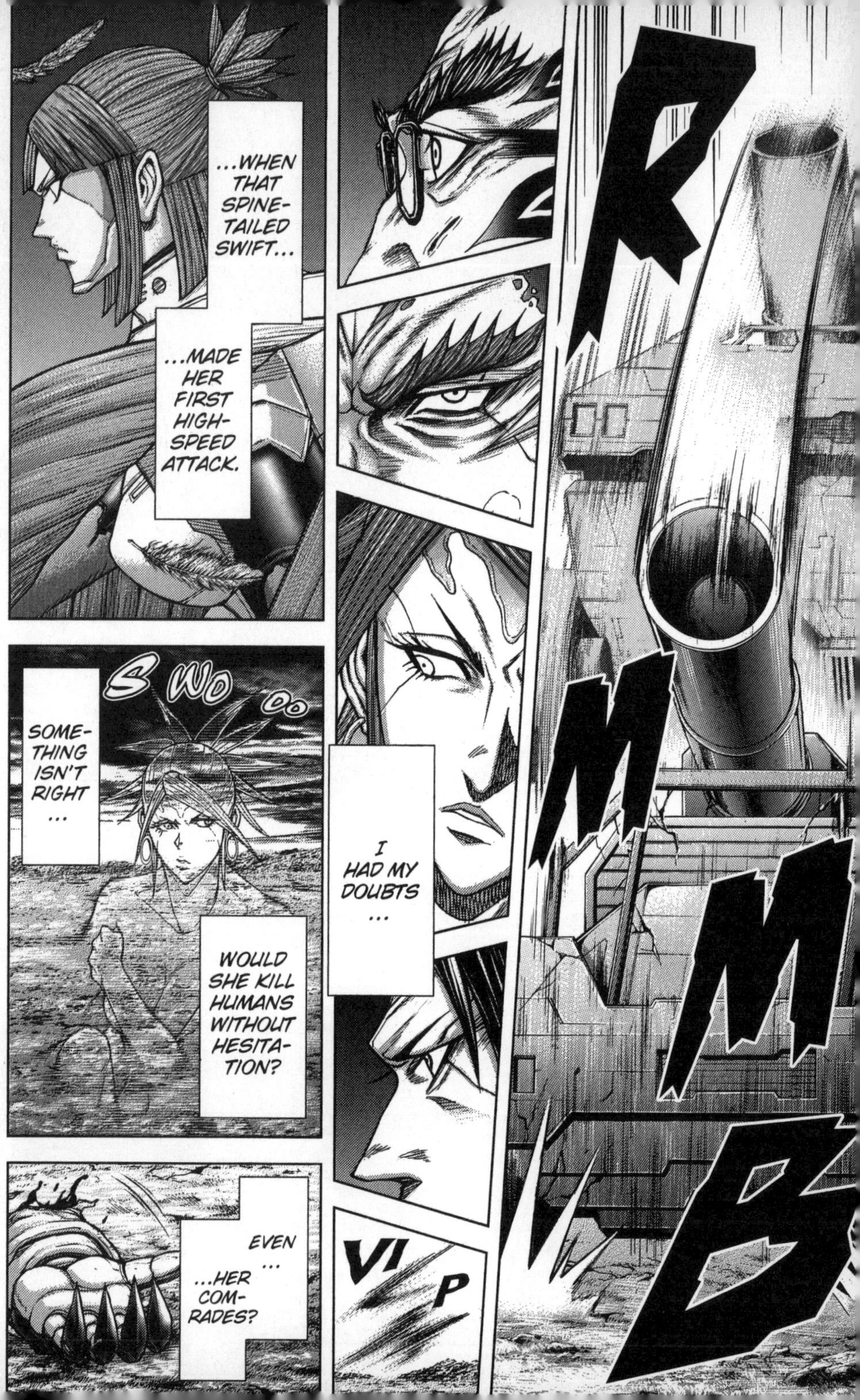
RMMB
I HAD MY DOUBTS ...
VIP
...WHEN THAT SPINE-TAILED SWIFT...
...MADE HER FIRST HIGH-SPEED ATTACK.
SWOOO
SOMETHING ISN'T RIGHT ...
WOULD SHE KILL HUMANS WITHOUT HESITATION?
EVEN ...
...HER COMRADES?

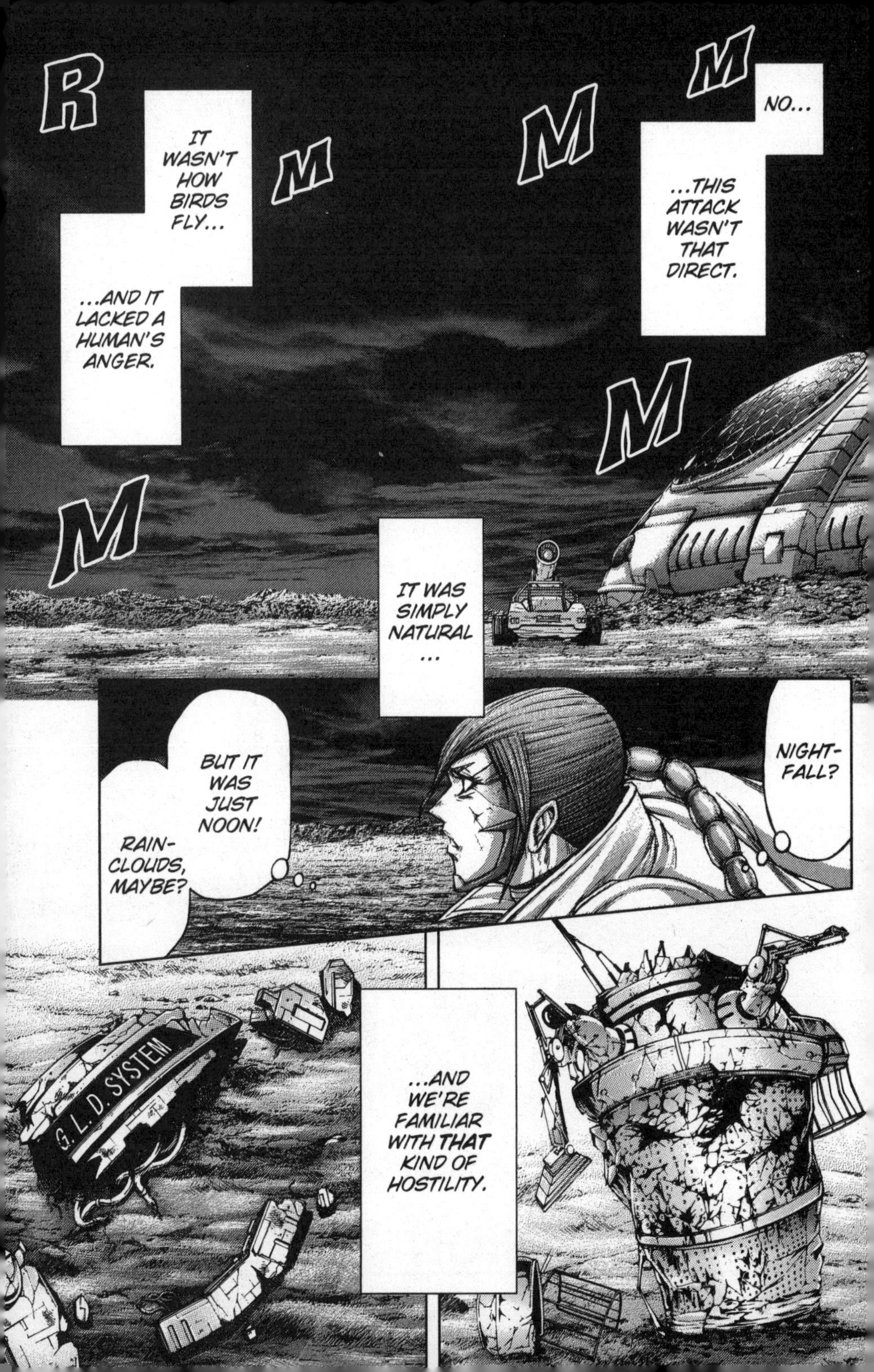
RMMMMM
NO...
...THIS ATTACK WASN'T THAT DIRECT.
IT WASN'T HOW BIRDS FLY...
...AND IT LACKED A HUMAN'S ANGER.
IT WAS SIMPLY NATURAL...
NIGHT-FALL?
BUT IT WAS JUST NOON!
RAIN-CLOUDS, MAYBE?
...AND WE'RE FAMILIAR WITH THAT KIND OF HOSTILITY.
G.L.D. SYSTEM

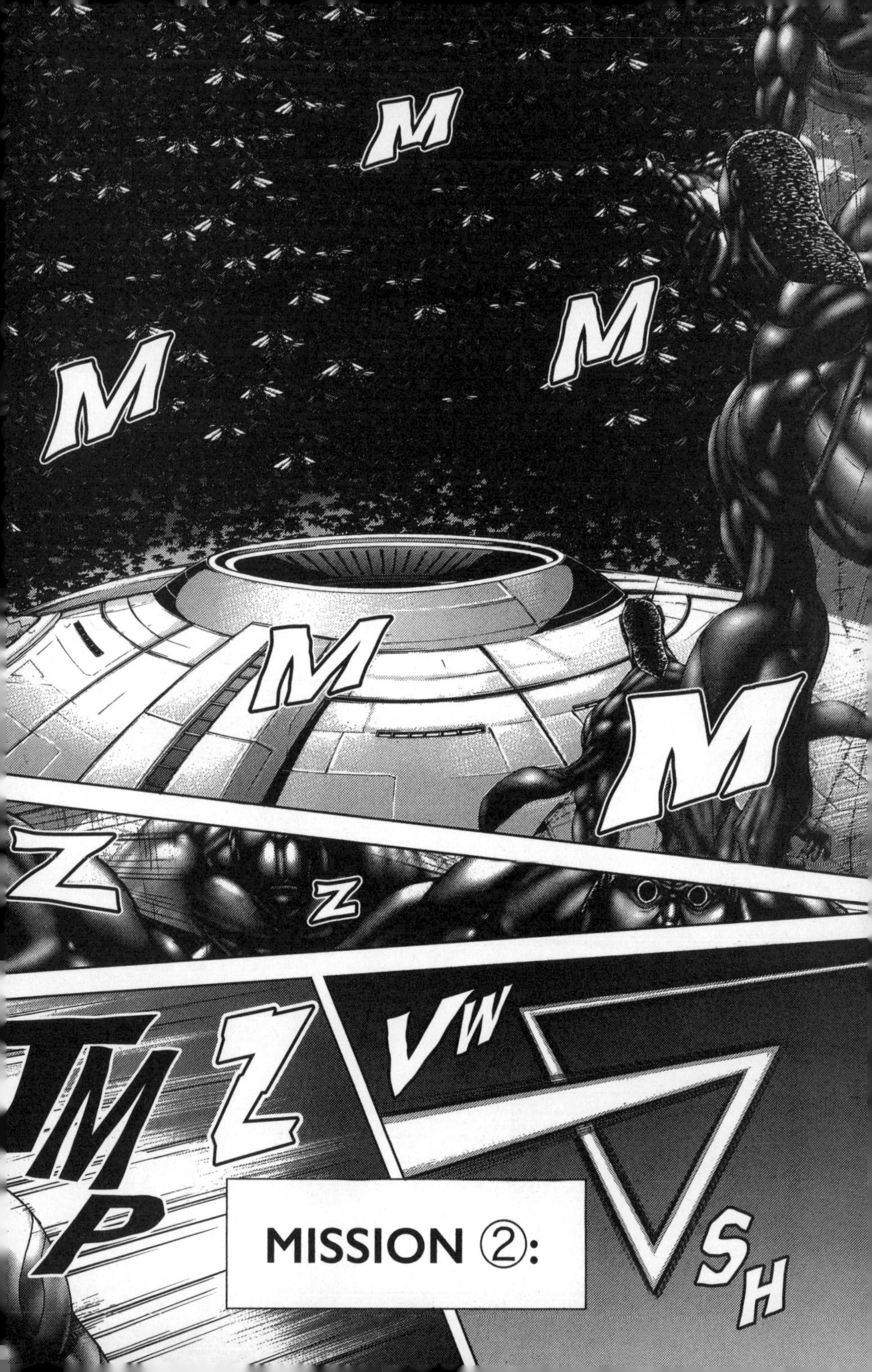
M
M
M
M
M
Z
Z
VW
SH
Z
M
P
MISSION ②:

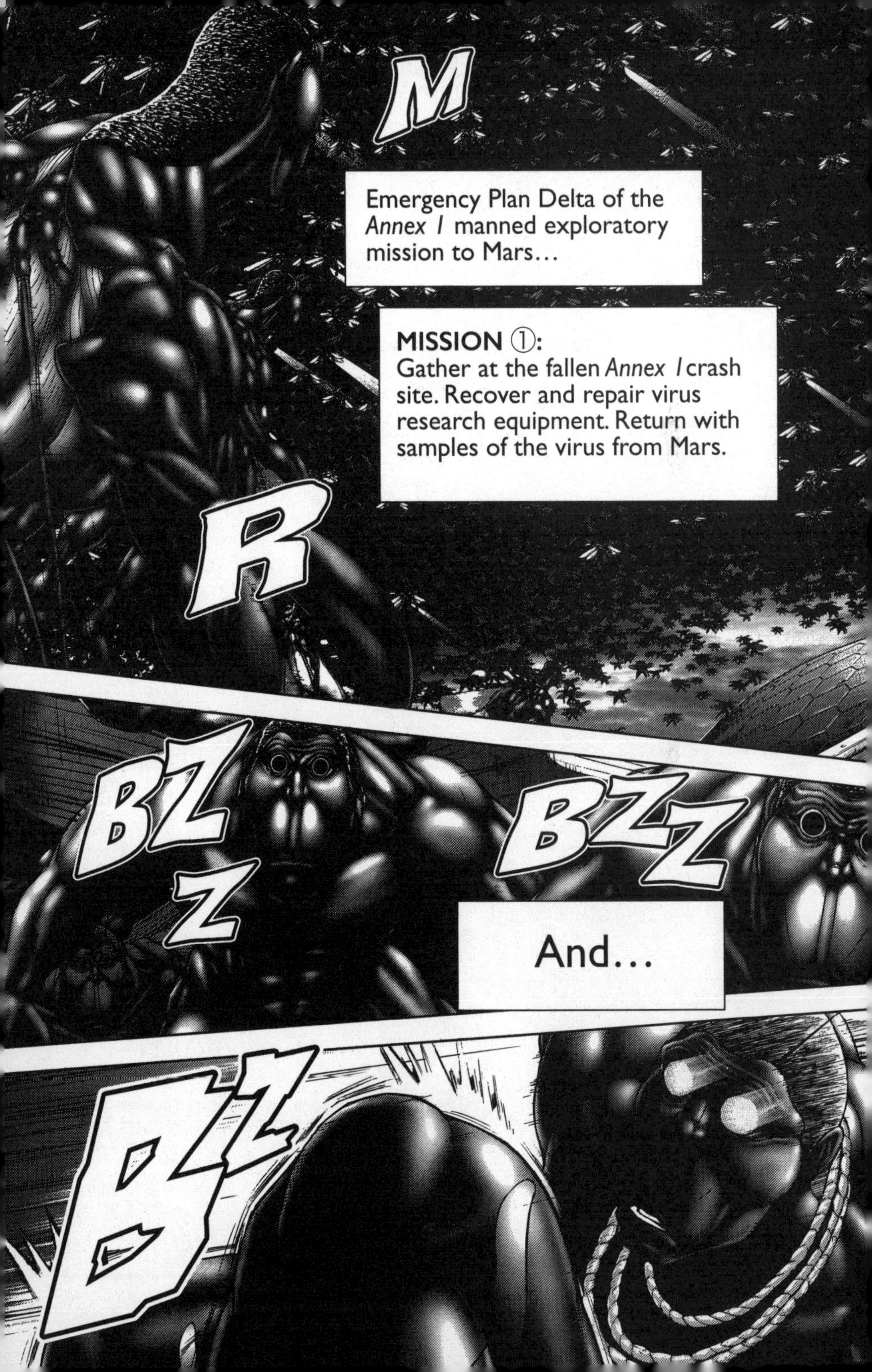
M
Emergency Plan Delta of the *Annex I* manned exploratory mission to Mars…
MISSION ①:
Gather at the fallen *Annex I* crash site. Recover and repair virus research equipment. Return with samples of the virus from Mars.
R
BZZ
And…
BZ
Z
BZ

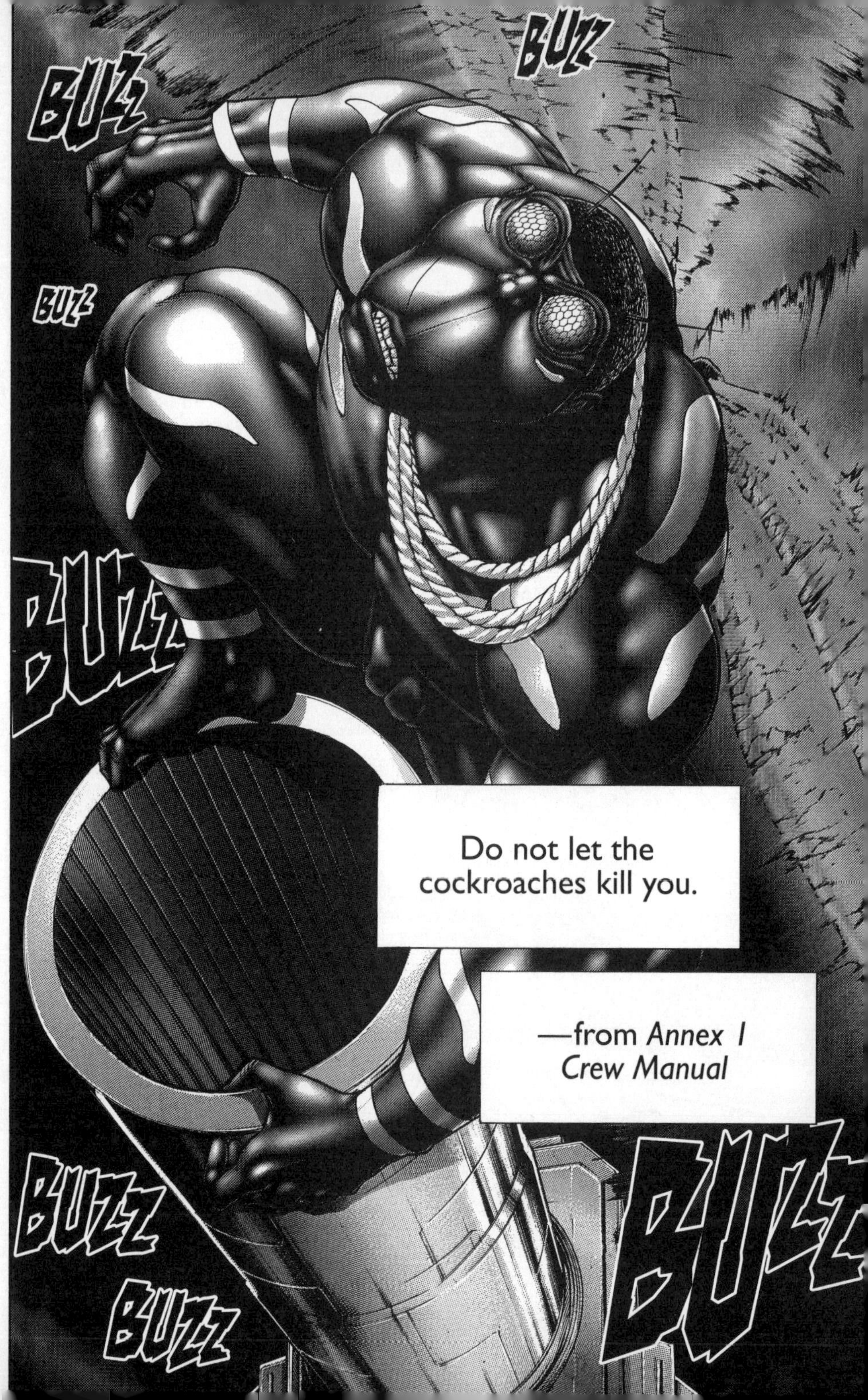
BUZZ
BUZZ
BUZZ
BUZZ
Do not let the cockroaches kill you.
—from *Annex I Crew Manual*
BUZZ
BUZZ
BUZZ

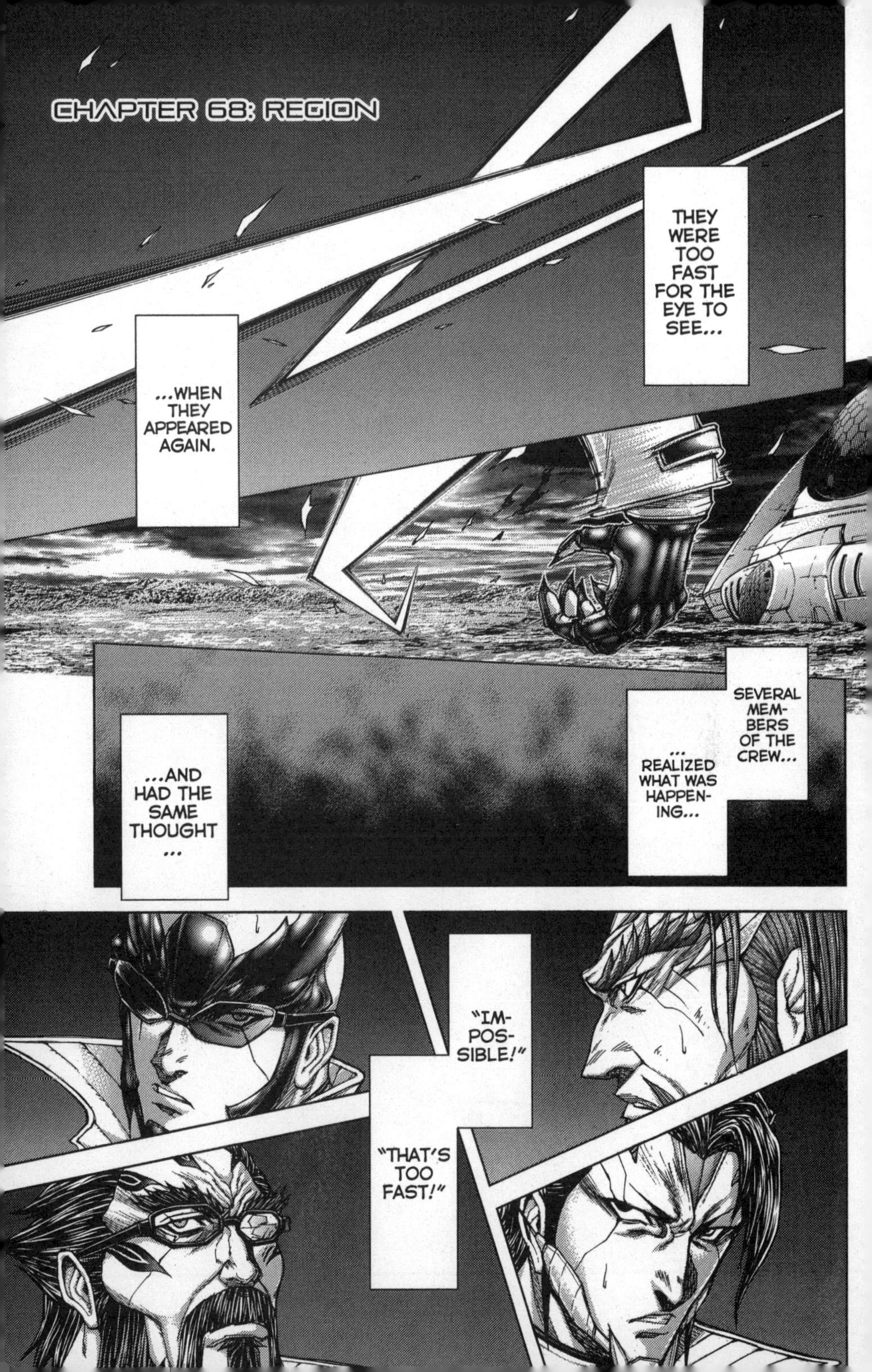
CHAPTER 68: REGION
THEY WERE TOO FAST FOR THE EYE TO SEE...
...WHEN THEY APPEARED AGAIN.
SEVERAL MEMBERS OF THE CREW...
...REALIZED WHAT WAS HAPPENING...
...AND HAD THE SAME THOUGHT...
"IMPOSSIBLE!"
"THAT'S TOO FAST!"

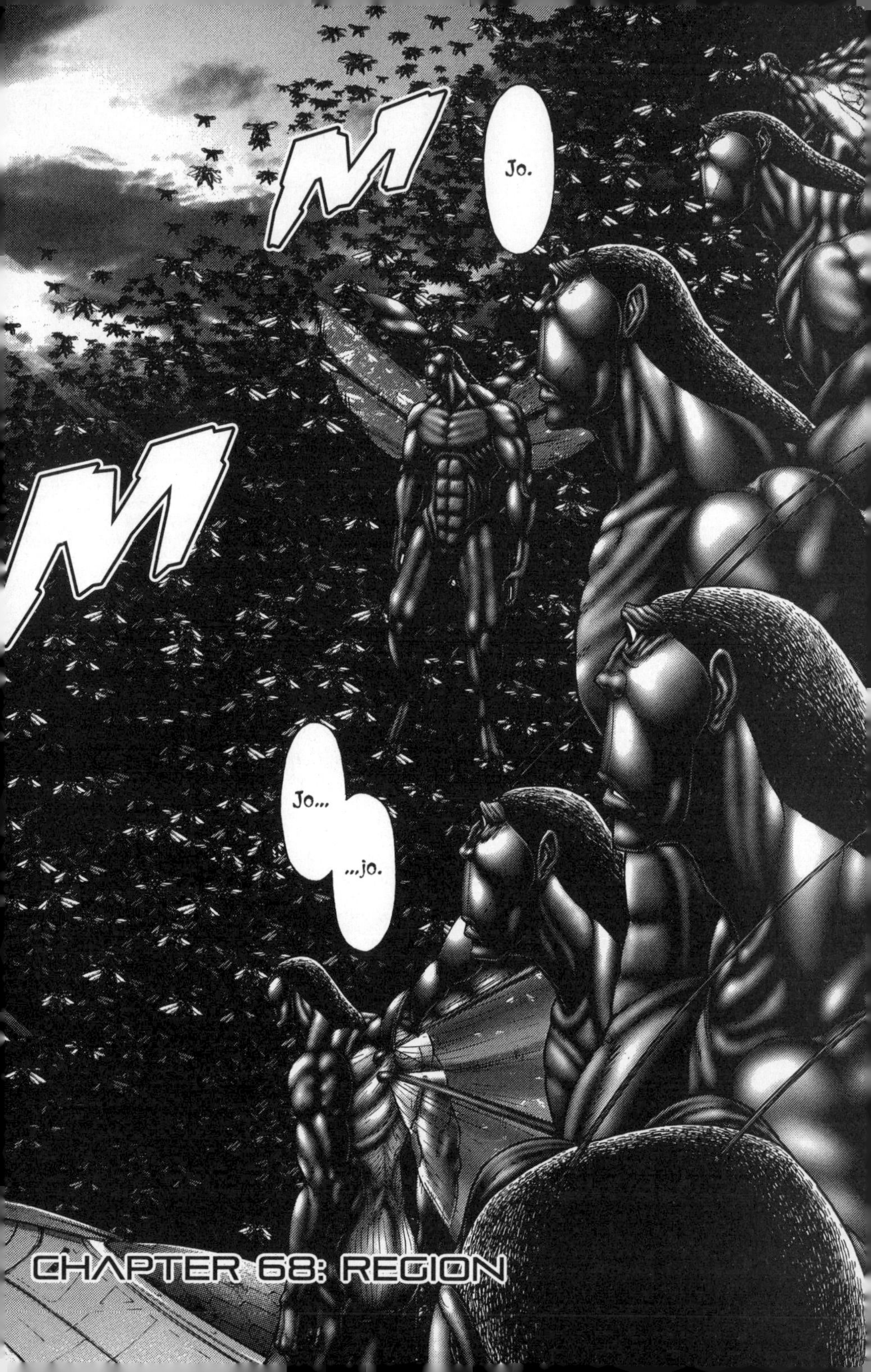
Jo.
M
M
Jo... ...jo.
CHAPTER 68: REGION

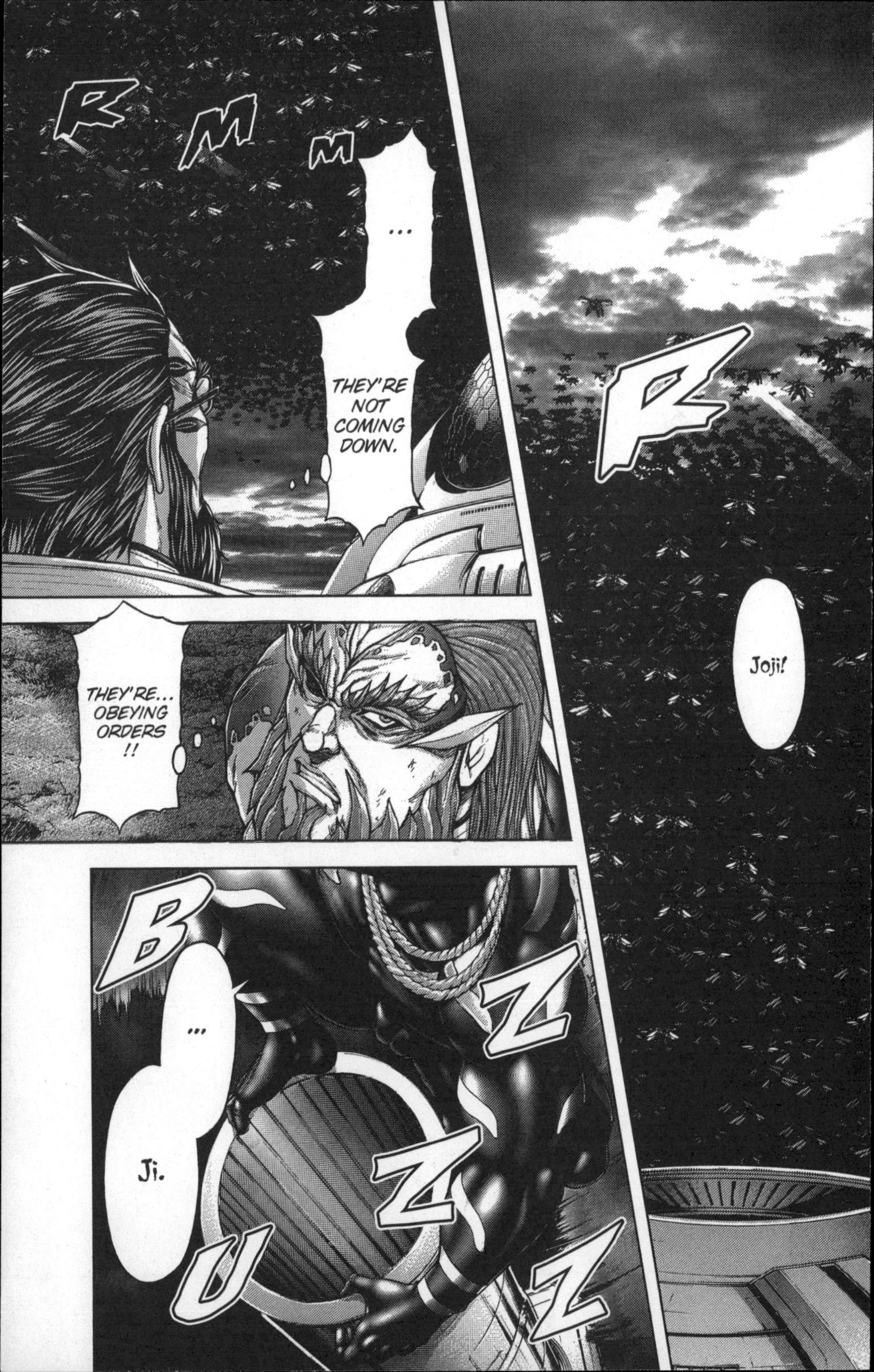
R
Joji!
RMM
...
THEY'RE NOT COMING DOWN.
THEY'RE... OBEYING ORDERS !!
BUZZZ
...
Ji.

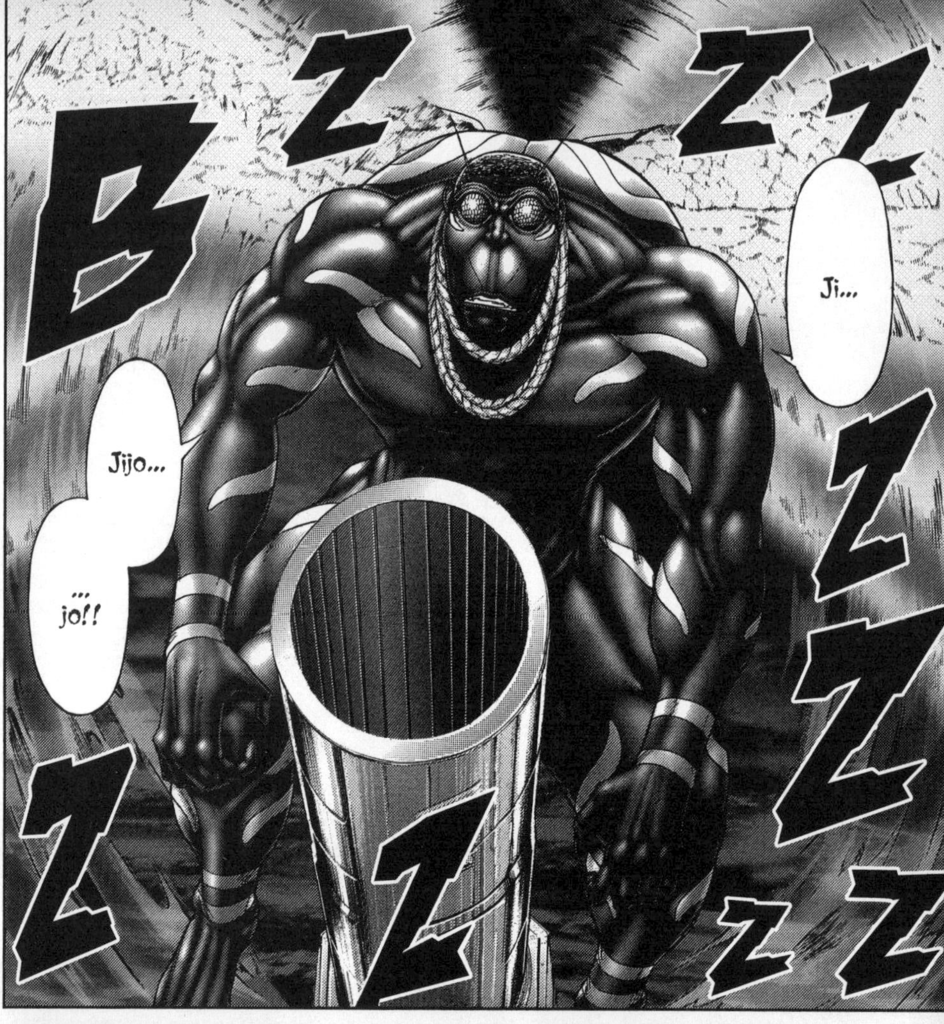
BZZZZZZZZZZ
Ji...
Jijo...
... jo!!
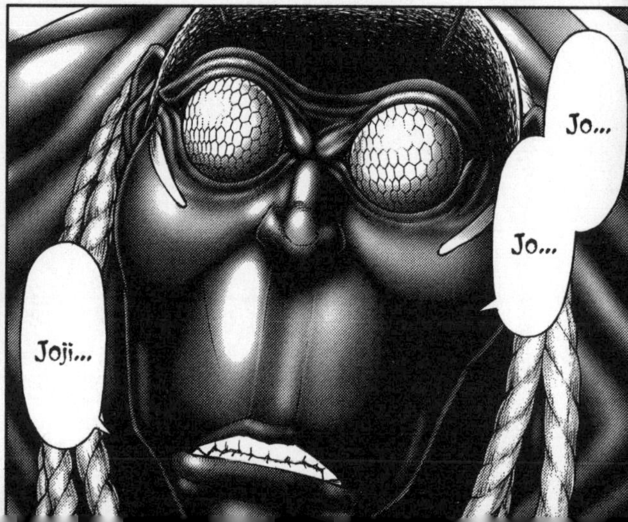
Jo...
Jo...
Joji...
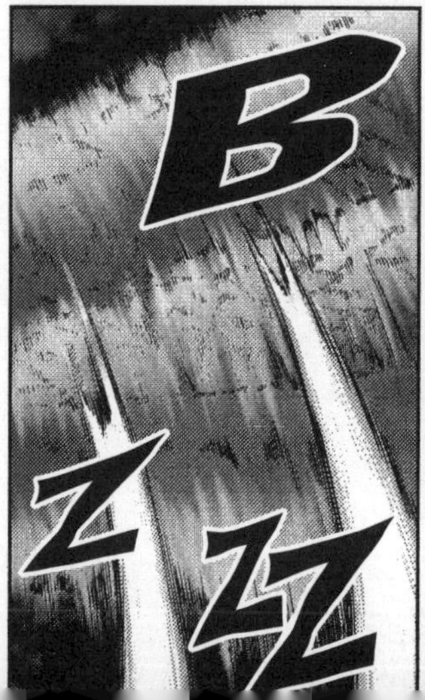
BZZZ

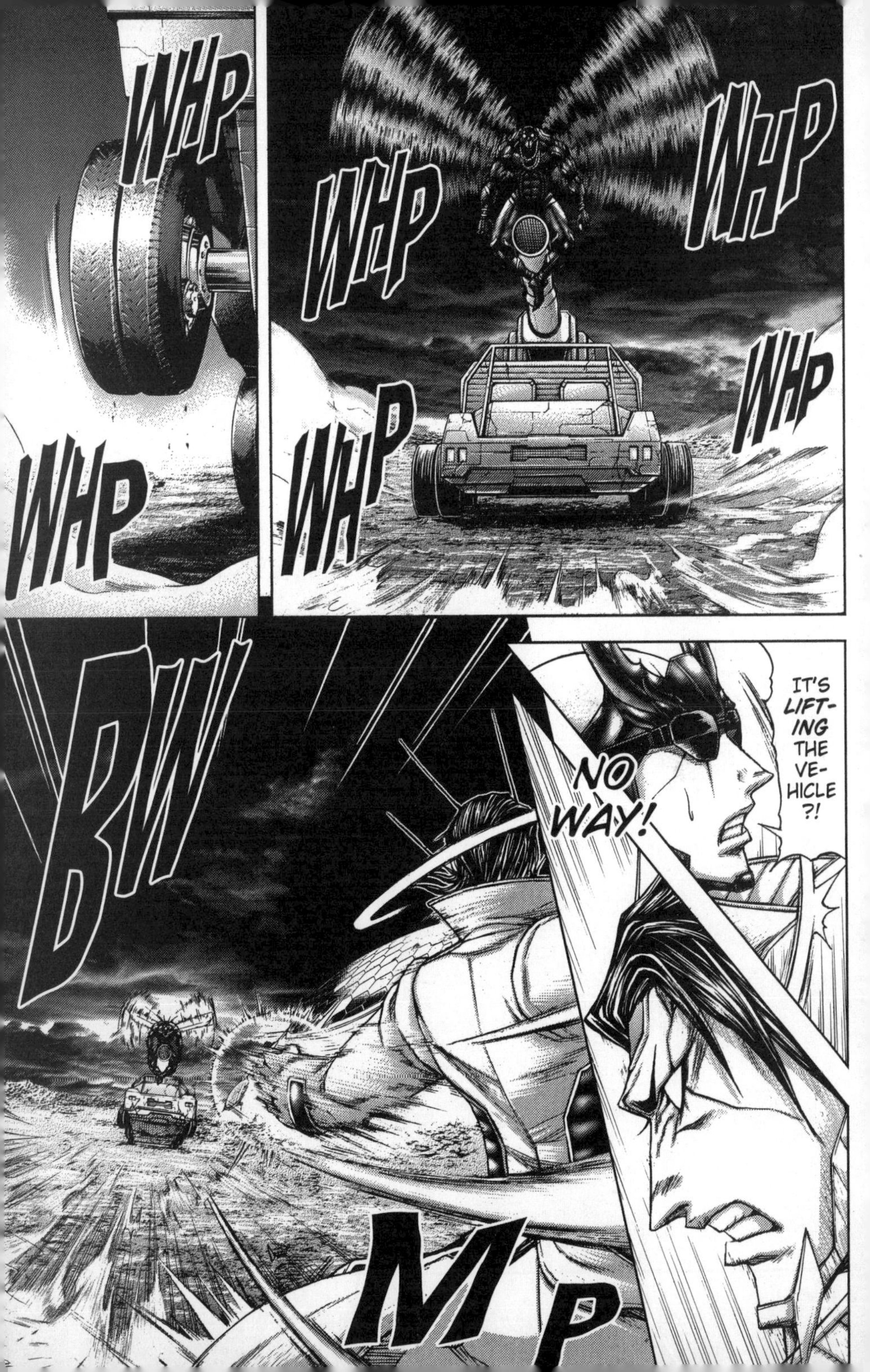
WHP
WHP
WHP
WHP
WHP
WHP
IT'S LIFTING THE VEHICLE?!
NO WAY!
BW
MP

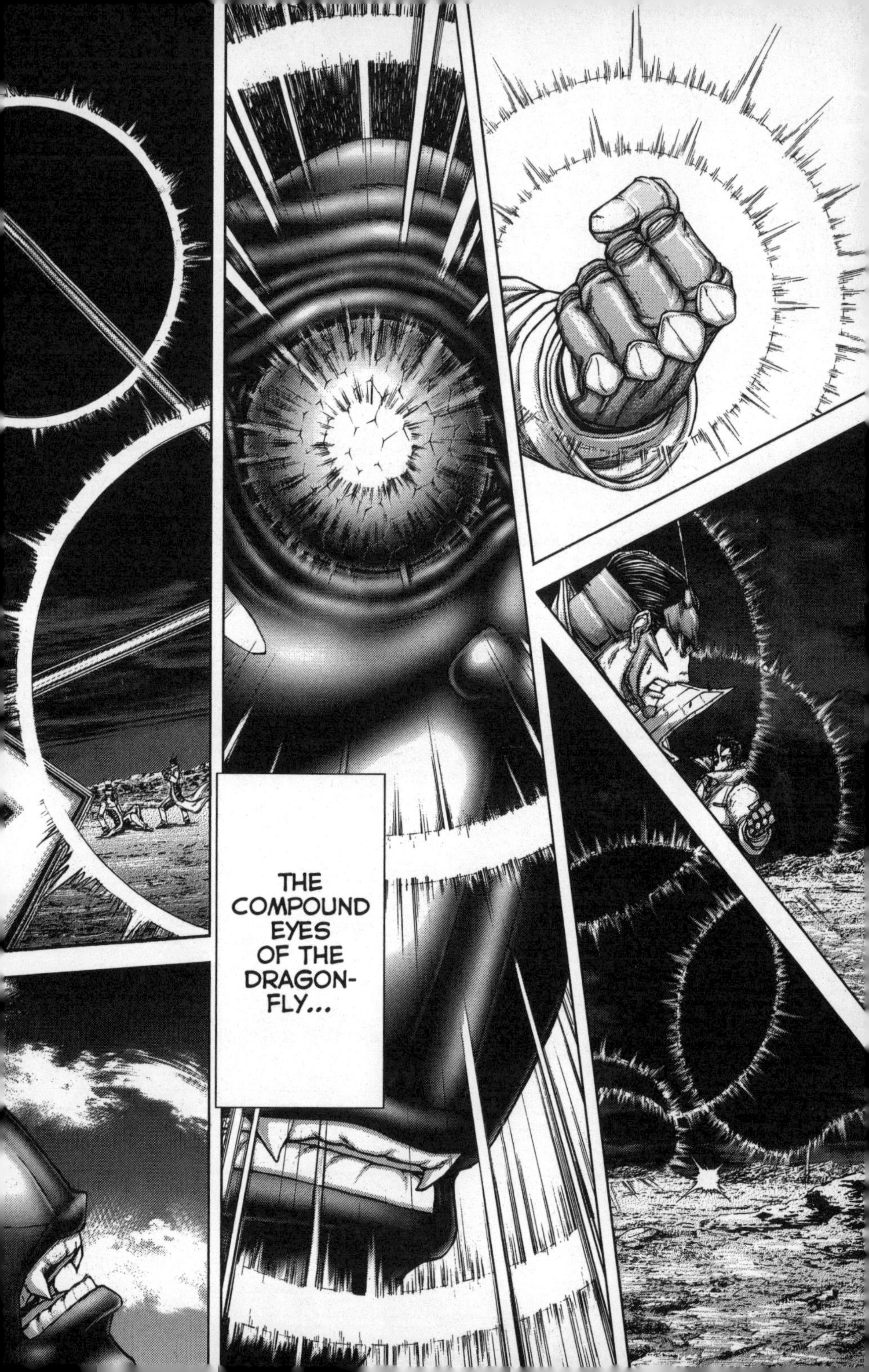
THE COMPOUND EYES OF THE DRAGON-FLY...

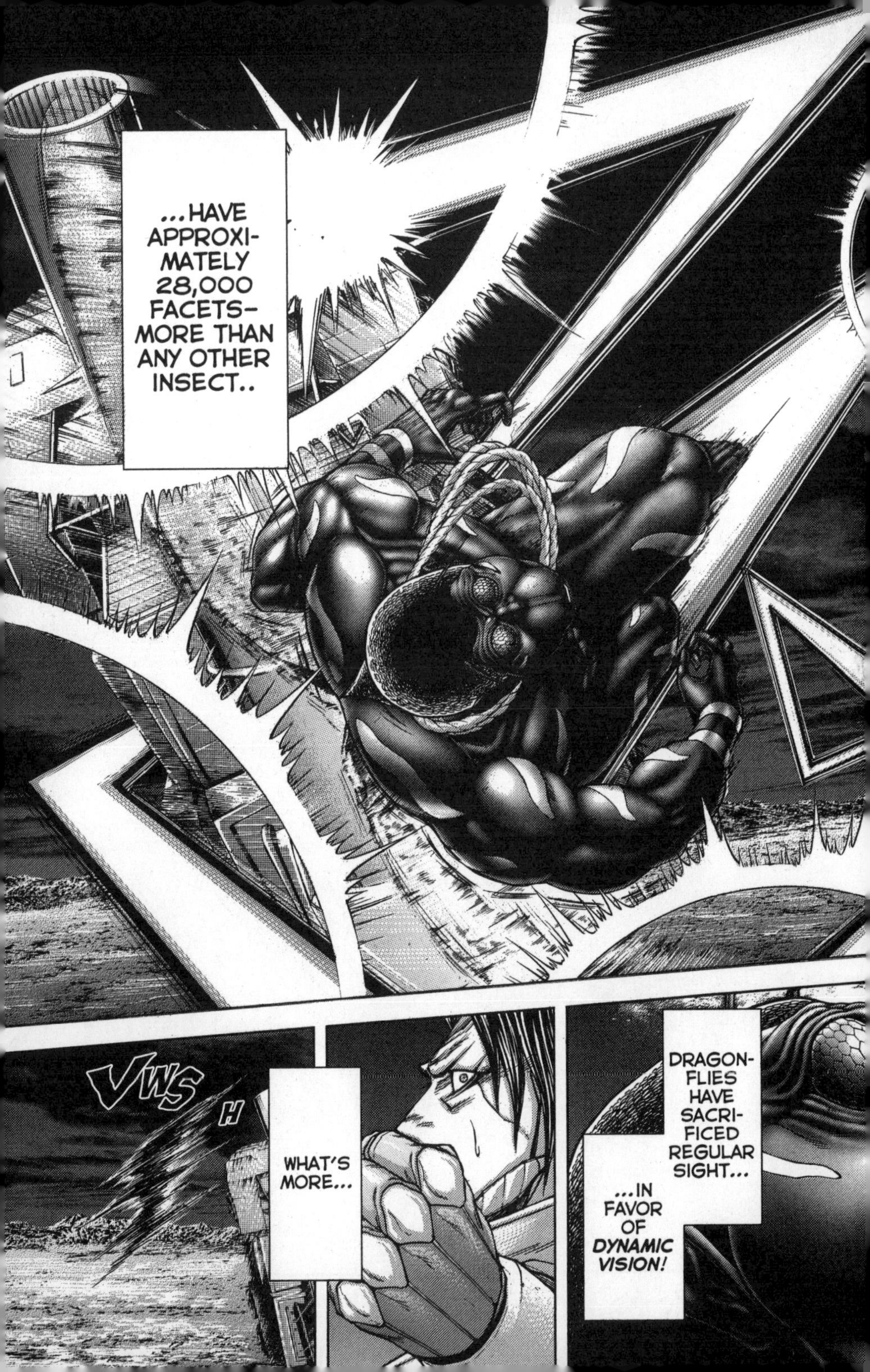
...HAVE APPROXIMATELY 28,000 FACETS—MORE THAN ANY OTHER INSECT..
DRAGONFLIES HAVE SACRIFICED REGULAR SIGHT...
...IN FAVOR OF *DYNAMIC VISION!*
WHAT'S MORE...
VWSH

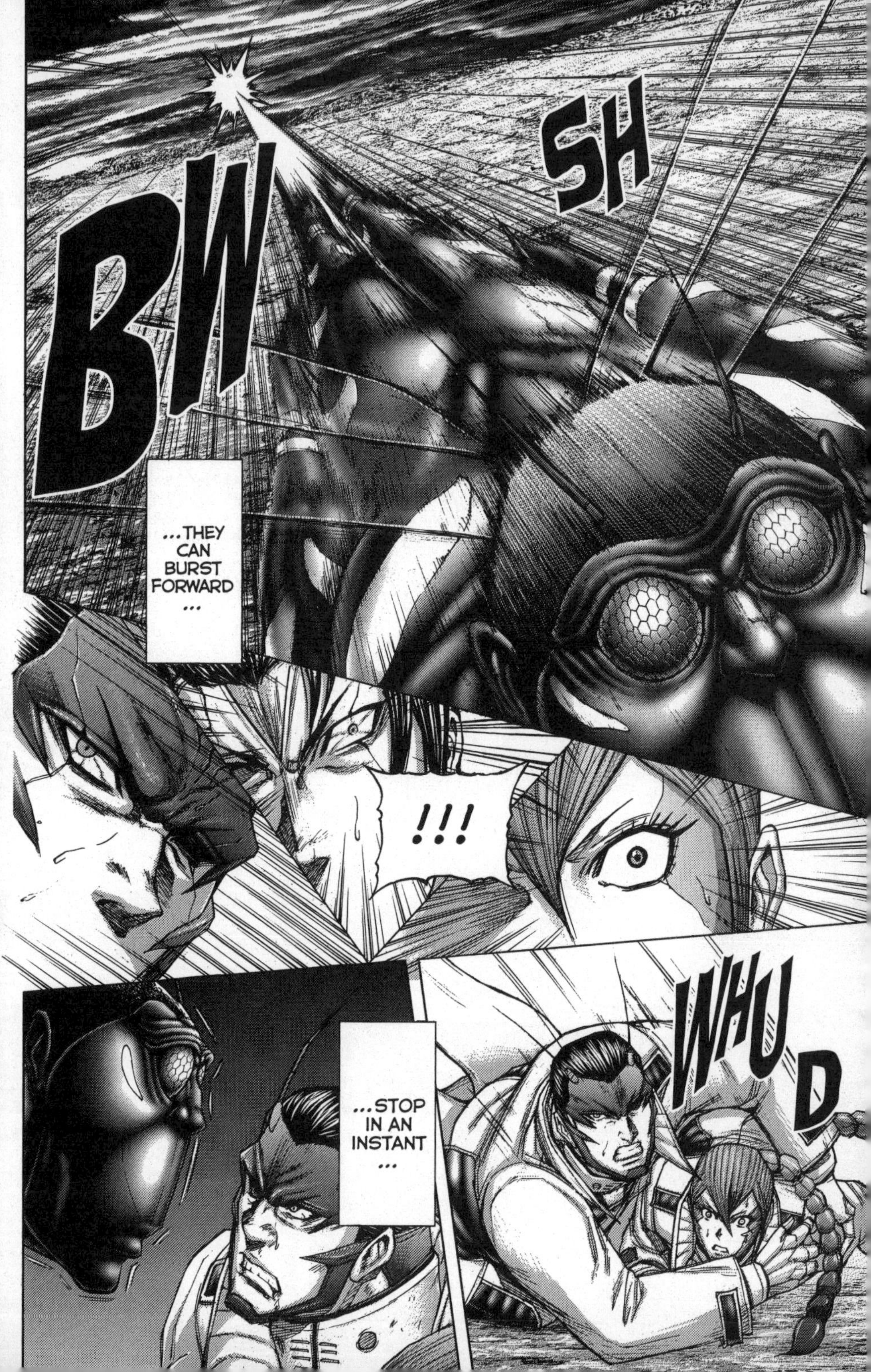
BWSH
...THEY CAN BURST FORWARD ...
!!!
WHUD
...STOP IN AN INSTANT ...

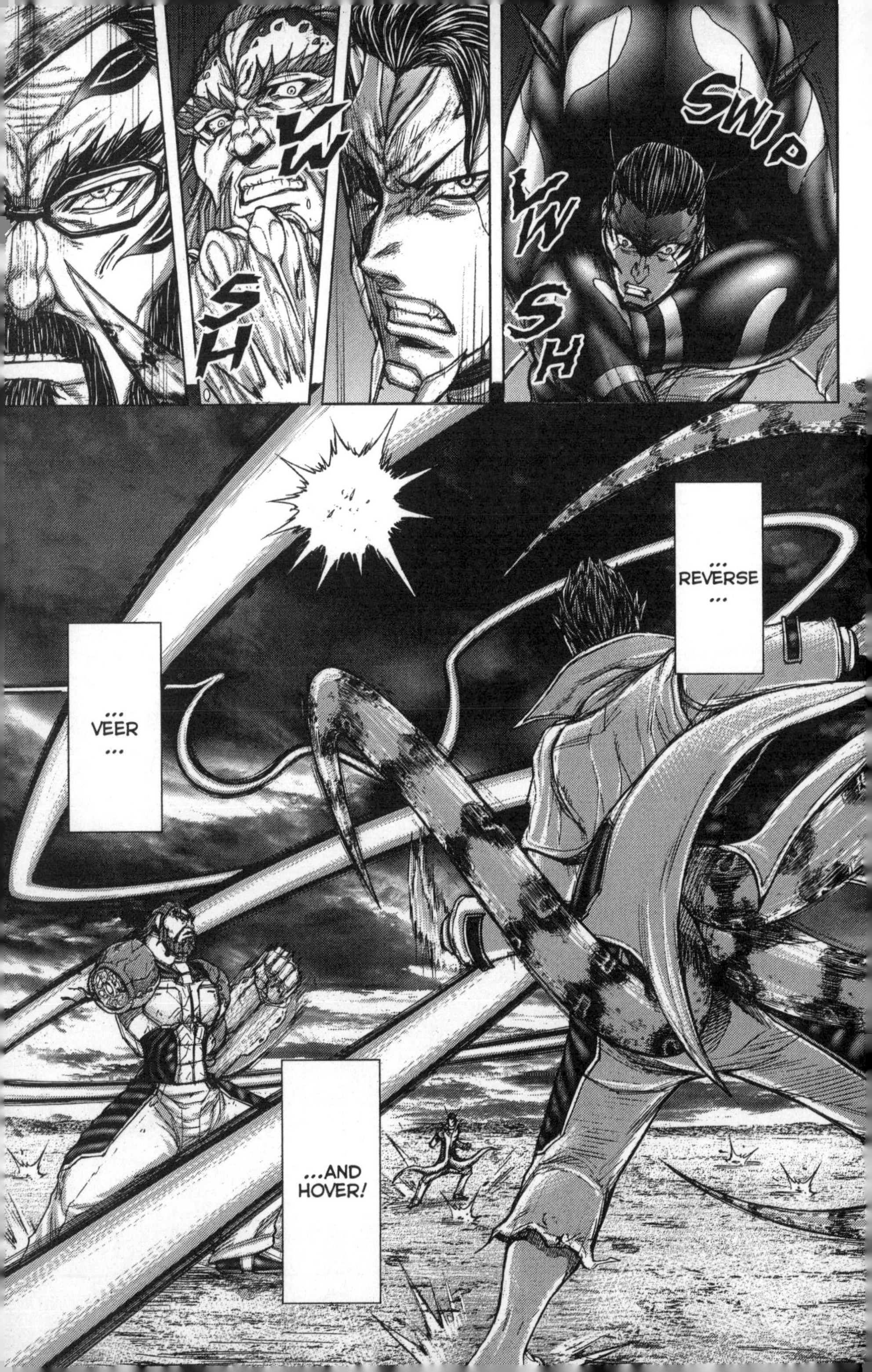
SWIP
VWSH
VWSH
...REVERSE...
...VEER...
...AND HOVER!

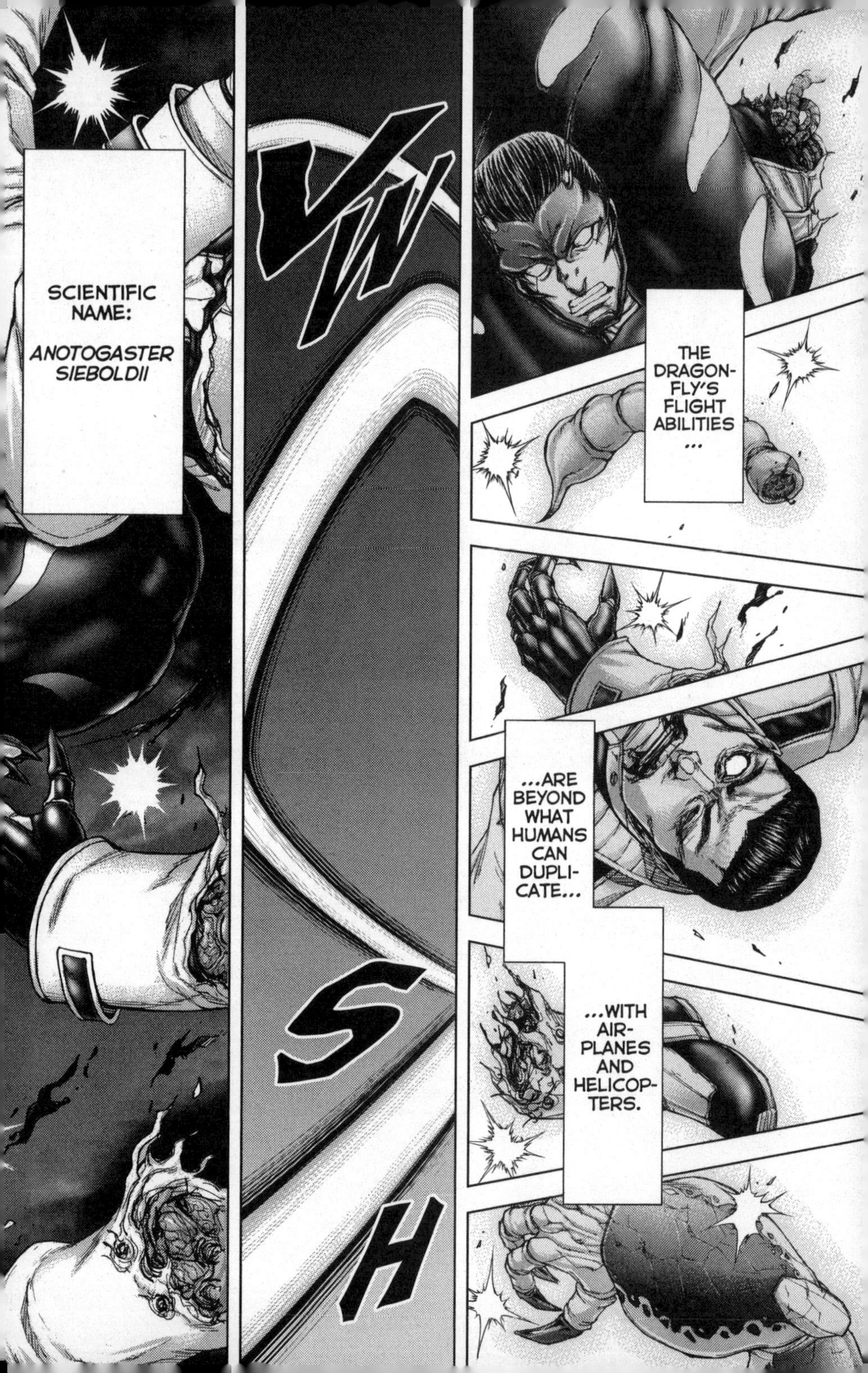
THE DRAGON-FLY'S FLIGHT ABILITIES ...
...ARE BEYOND WHAT HUMANS CAN DUPLI-CATE...
...WITH AIR-PLANES AND HELICOP-TERS.
SH
SCIENTIFIC NAME:
ANOTOGASTER SIEBOLDII

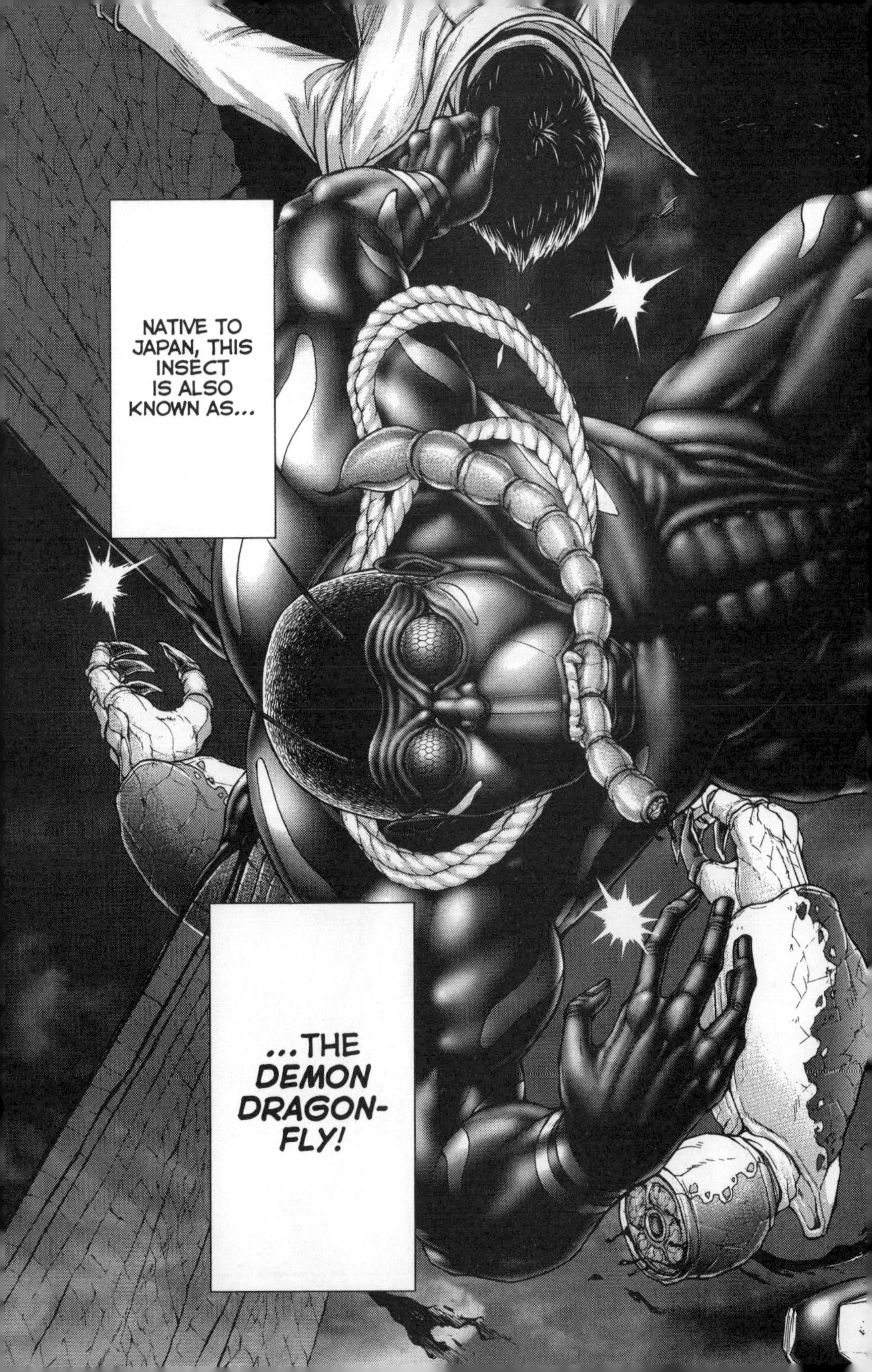
NATIVE TO JAPAN, THIS INSECT IS ALSO KNOWN AS...
...THE DEMON DRAGON-FLY!

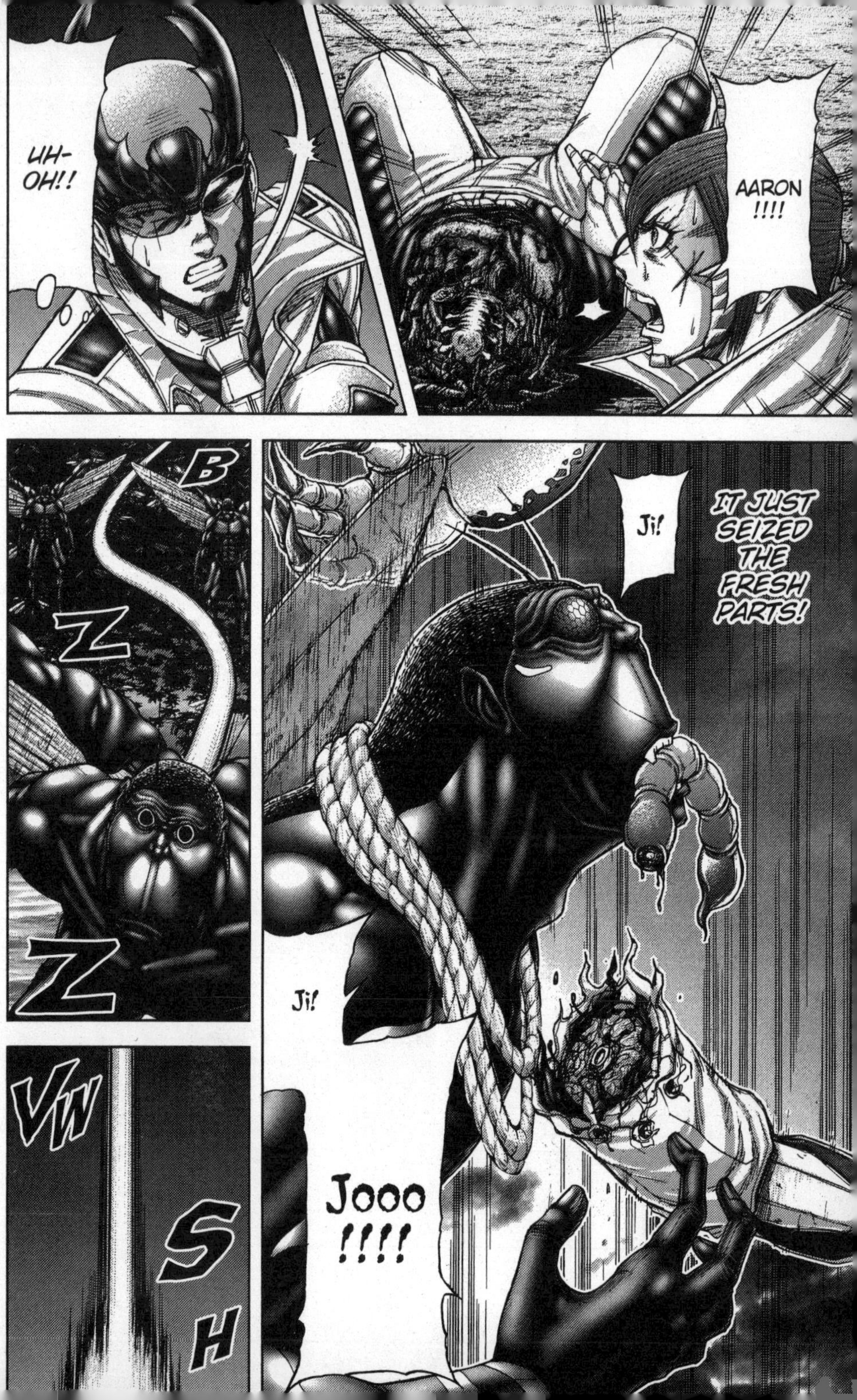
AARON !!!!
UH-OH!!
IT JUST SEIZED THE FRESH PARTS!
Ji!
Ji!
Jooo !!!!
BZZ
VWSH

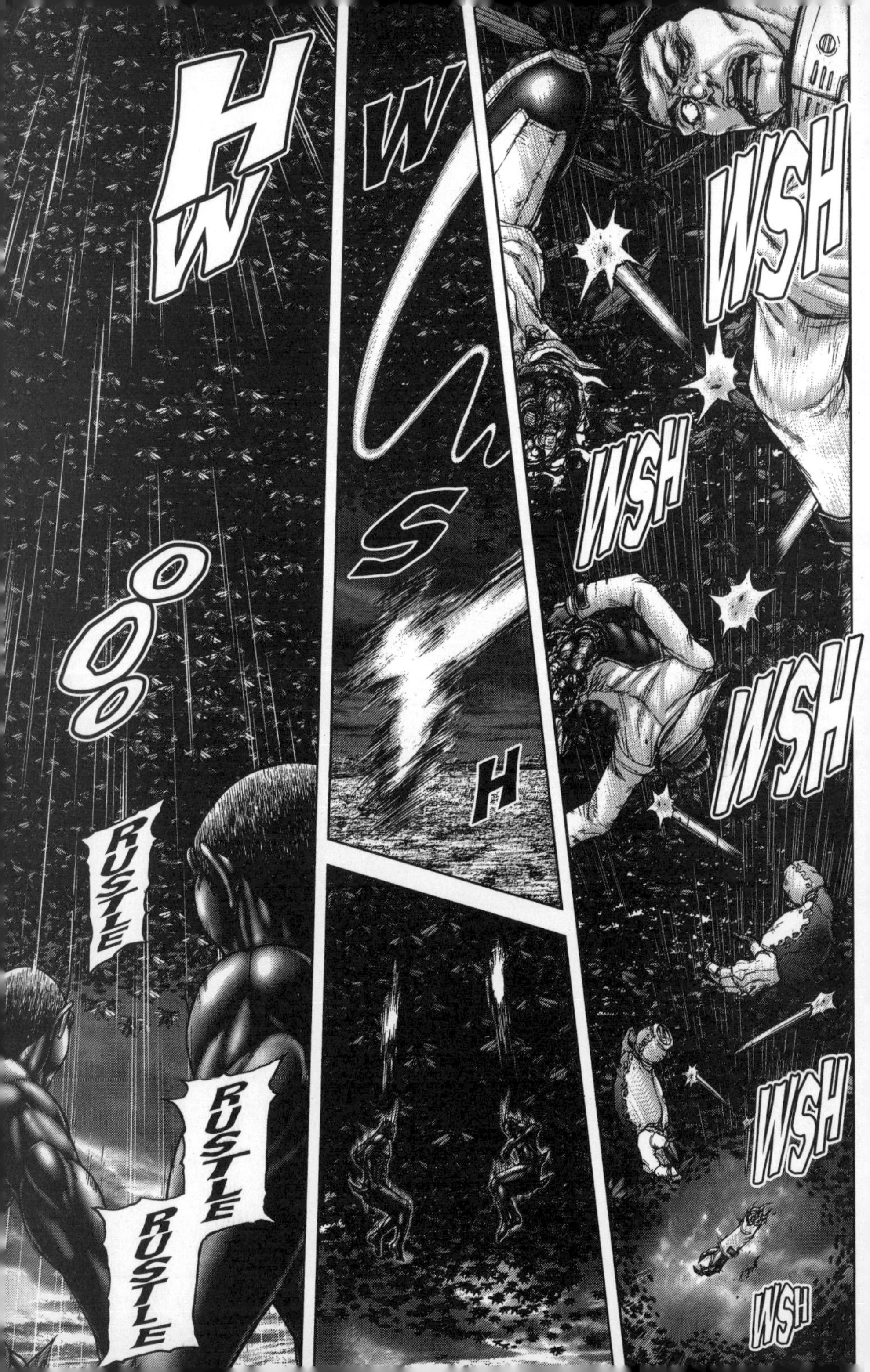
WSH
WSH
WSH
WSH
WSH
WWSH
HWW
OOOO
RUSTLE
RUSTLE
RUSTLE

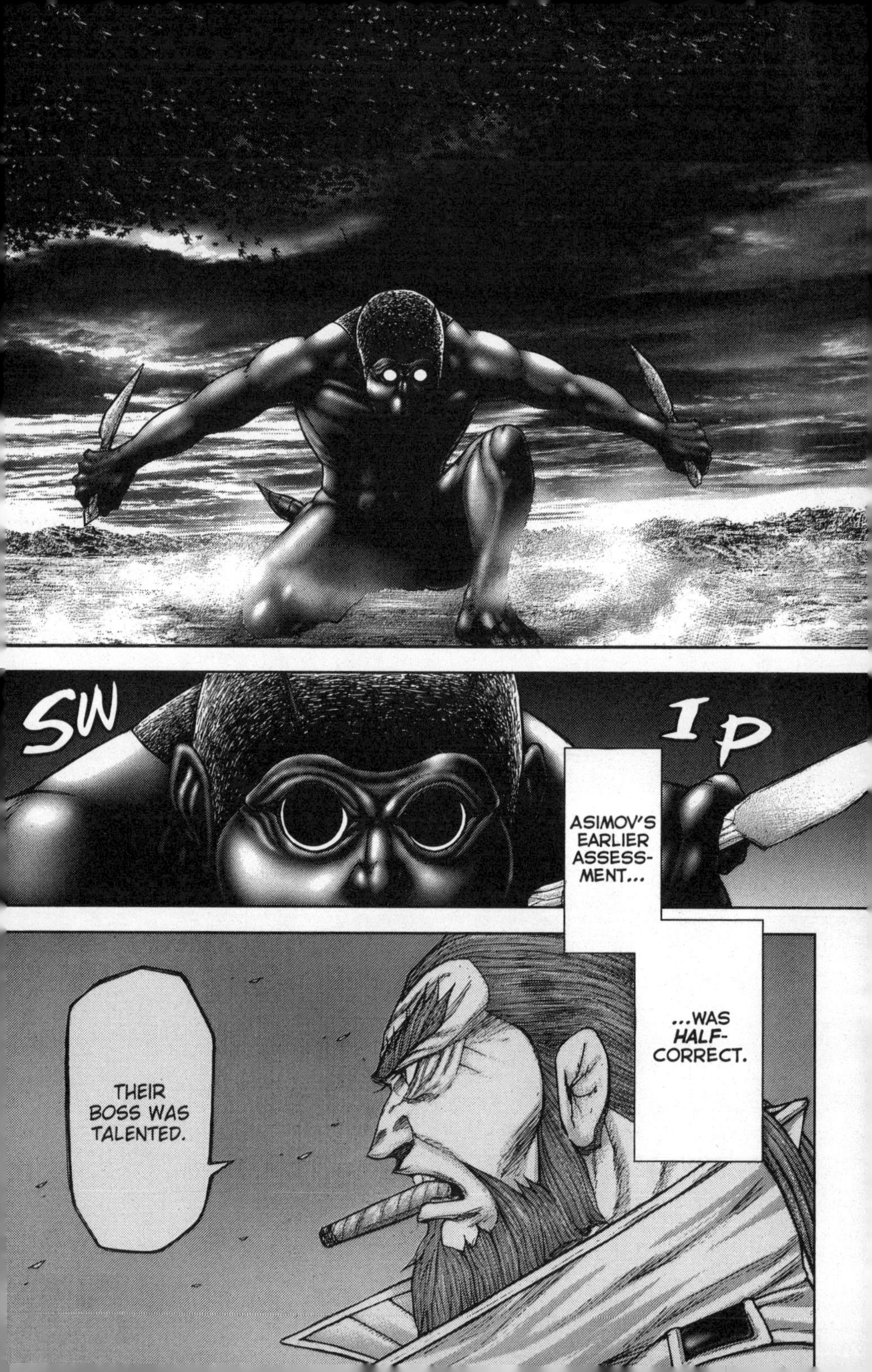
SWIP
ASIMOV'S EARLIER ASSESSMENT...
...WAS *HALF*-CORRECT.
THEIR BOSS WAS TALENTED.

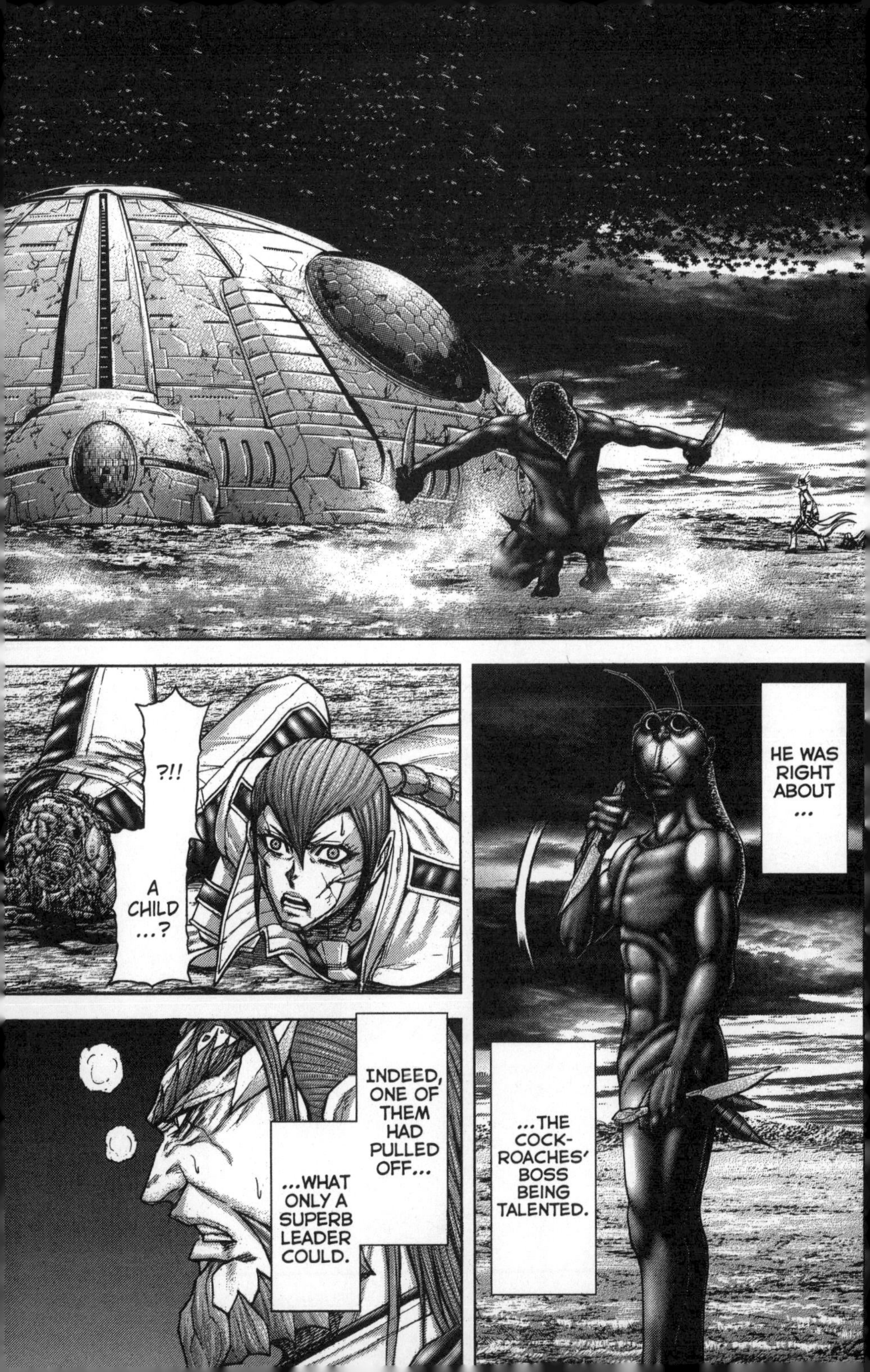
HE WAS RIGHT ABOUT ...
...THE COCK-ROACHES' BOSS BEING TALENTED.
?!!
A CHILD ...?
INDEED, ONE OF THEM HAD PULLED OFF...
...WHAT ONLY A SUPERB LEADER COULD.

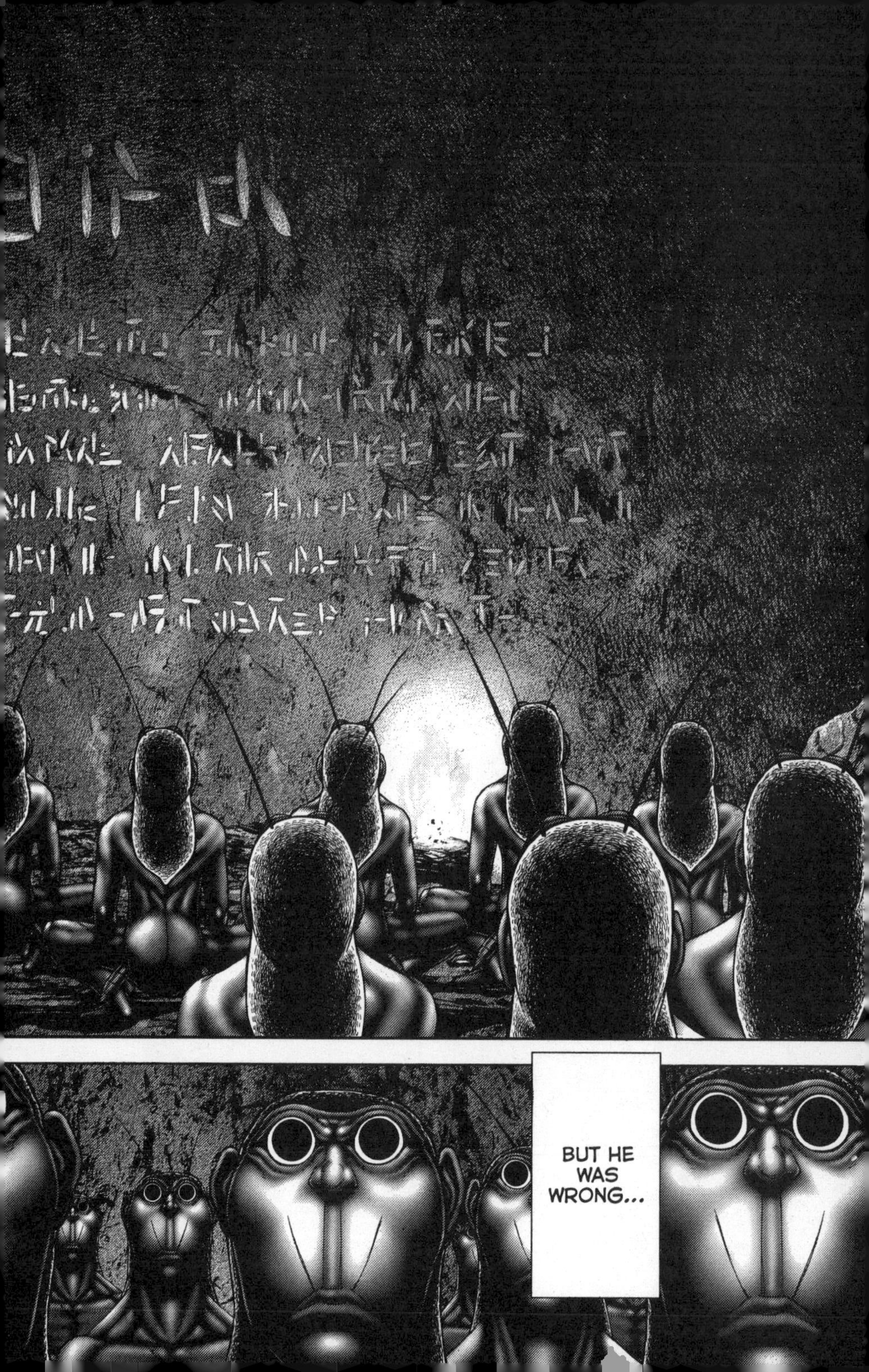
BUT HE WAS WRONG...

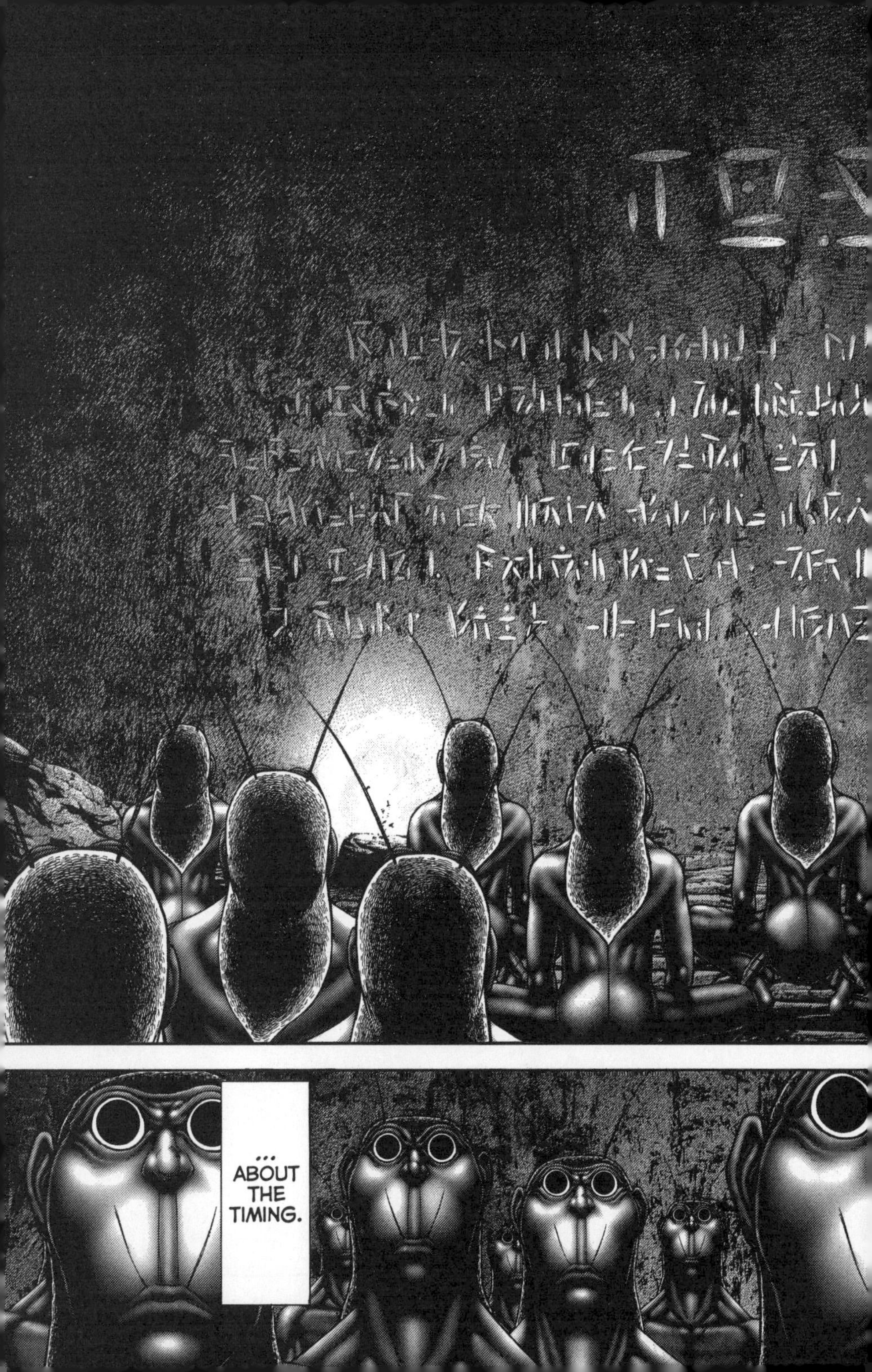
...ABOUT THE TIMING.

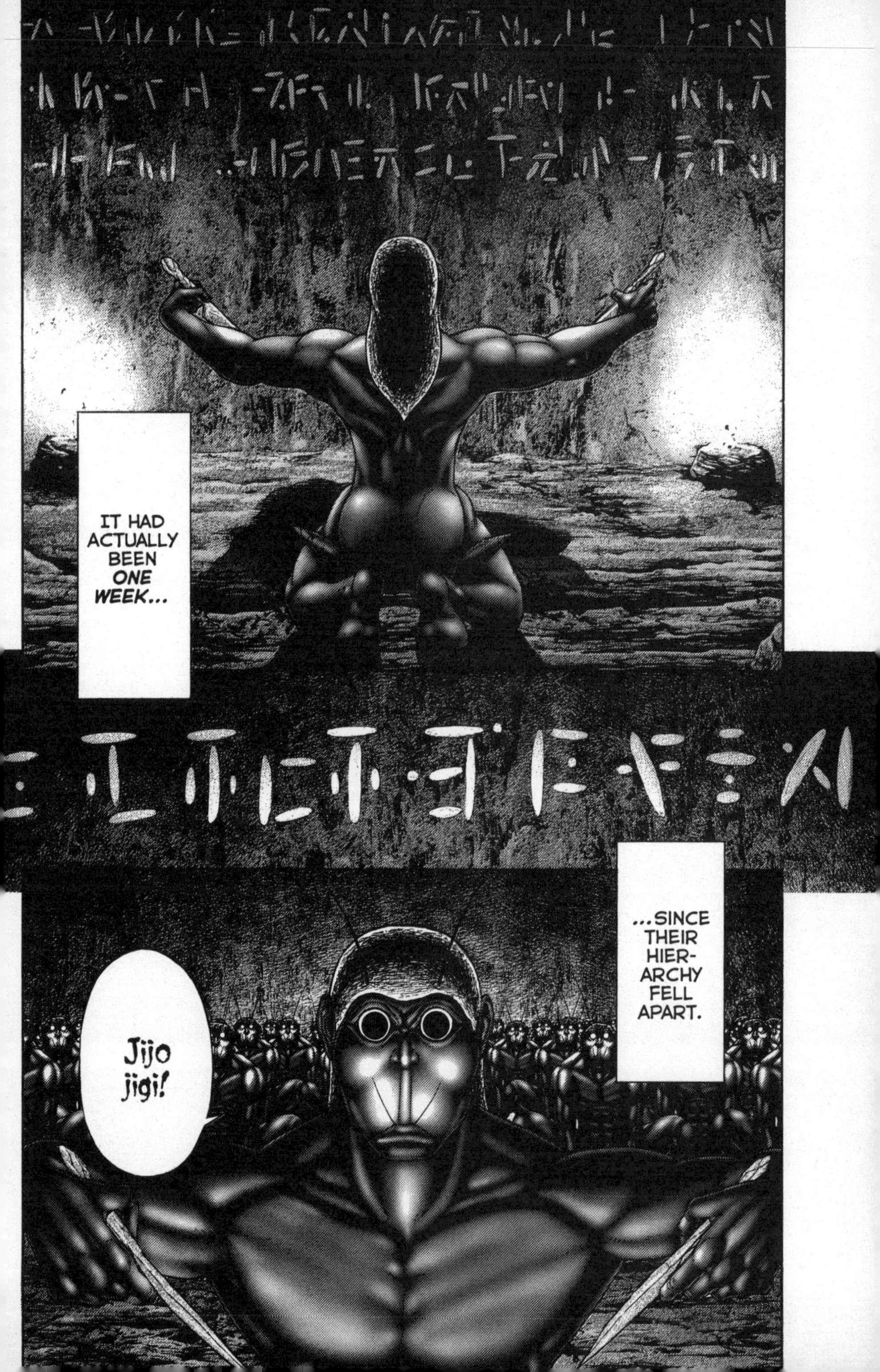
IT HAD ACTUALLY BEEN ONE WEEK...
...SINCE THEIR HIERARCHY FELL APART.
Jijo jigi!

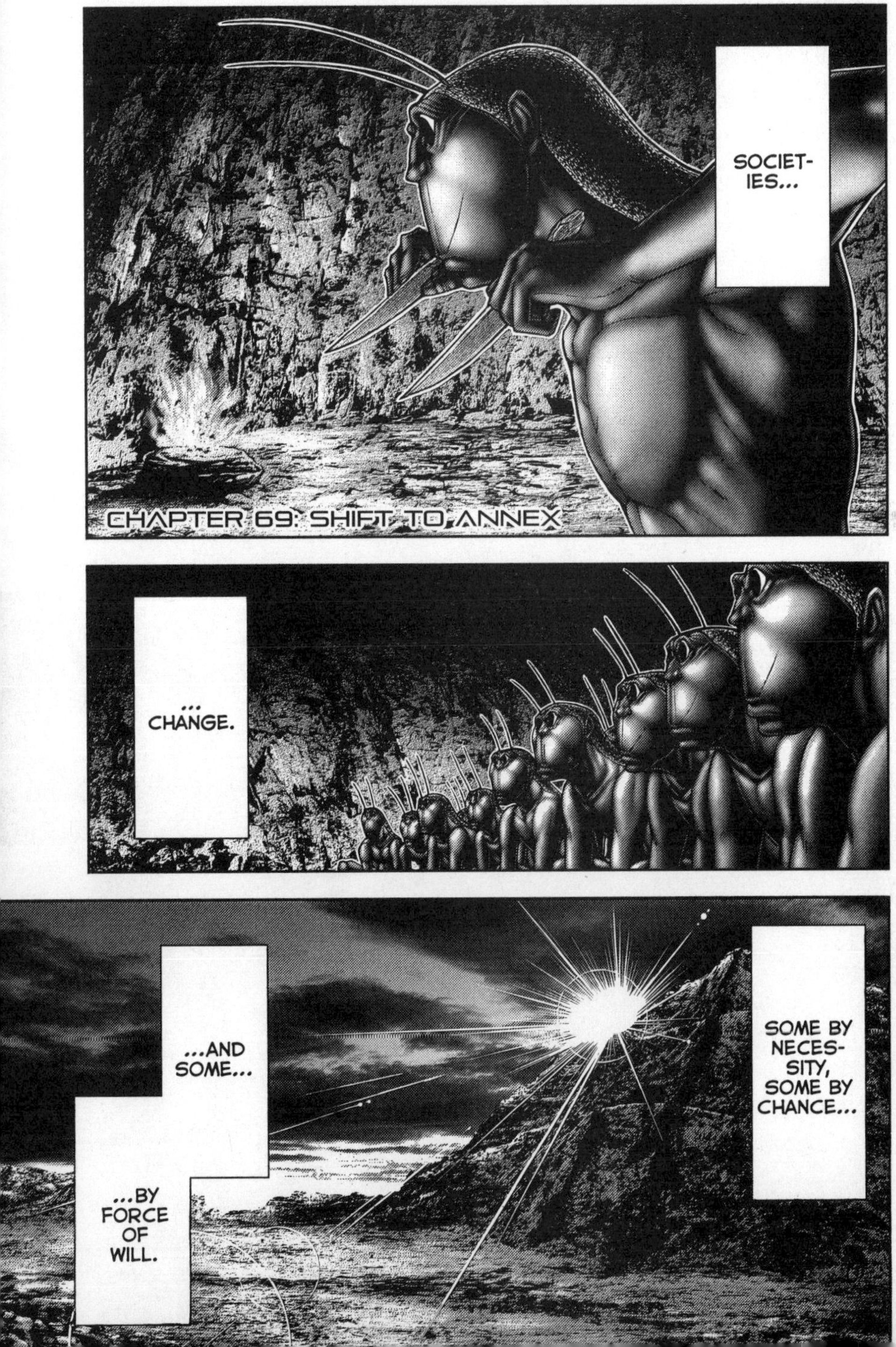
SOCIET-IES...
CHAPTER 69: SHIFT TO ANNEX
... CHANGE.
SOME BY NECES-SITY, SOME BY CHANCE...
...AND SOME...
...BY FORCE OF WILL.

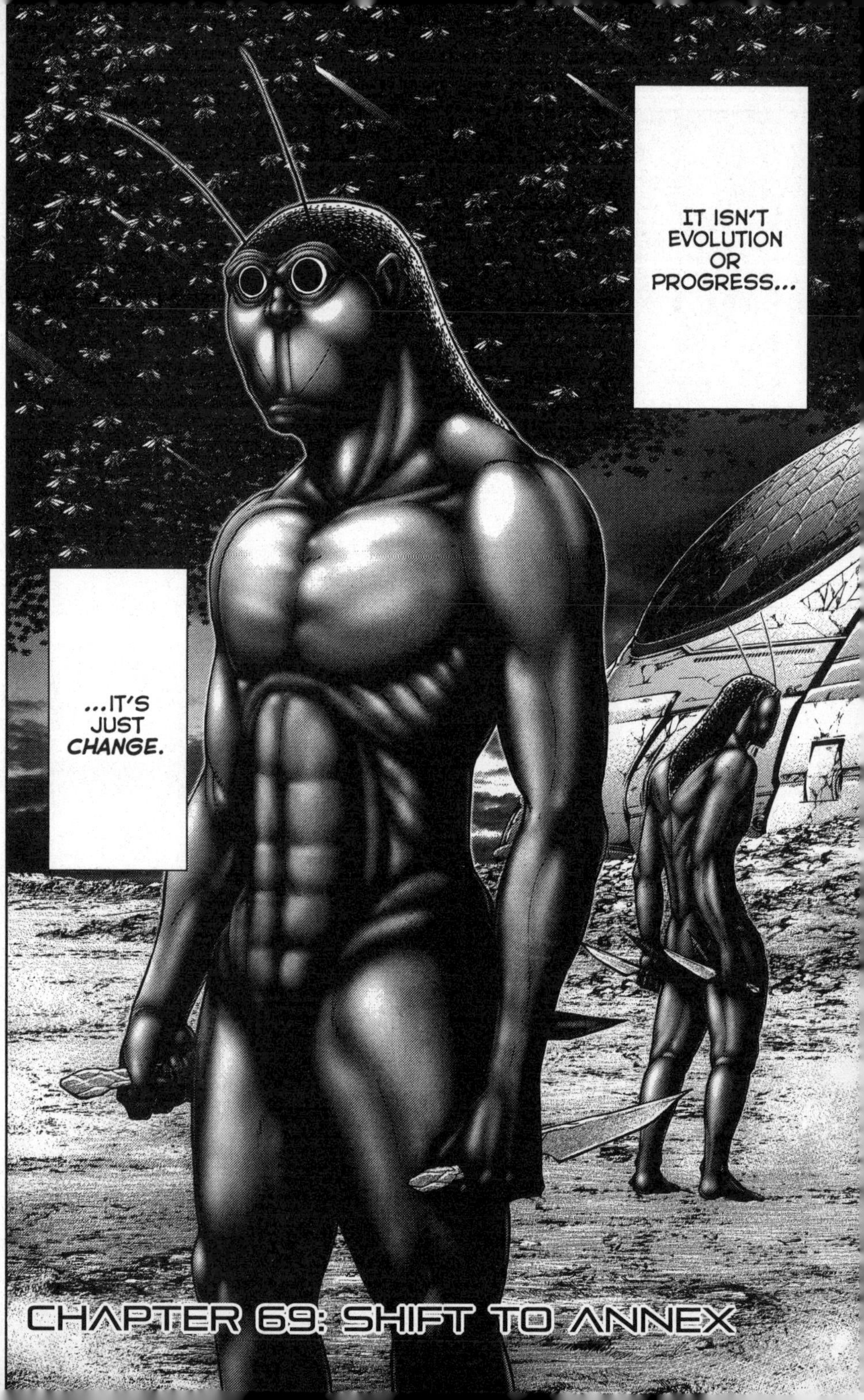
IT ISN'T EVOLUTION OR PROGRESS...
...IT'S JUST CHANGE.
CHAPTER 69: SHIFT TO ANNEX

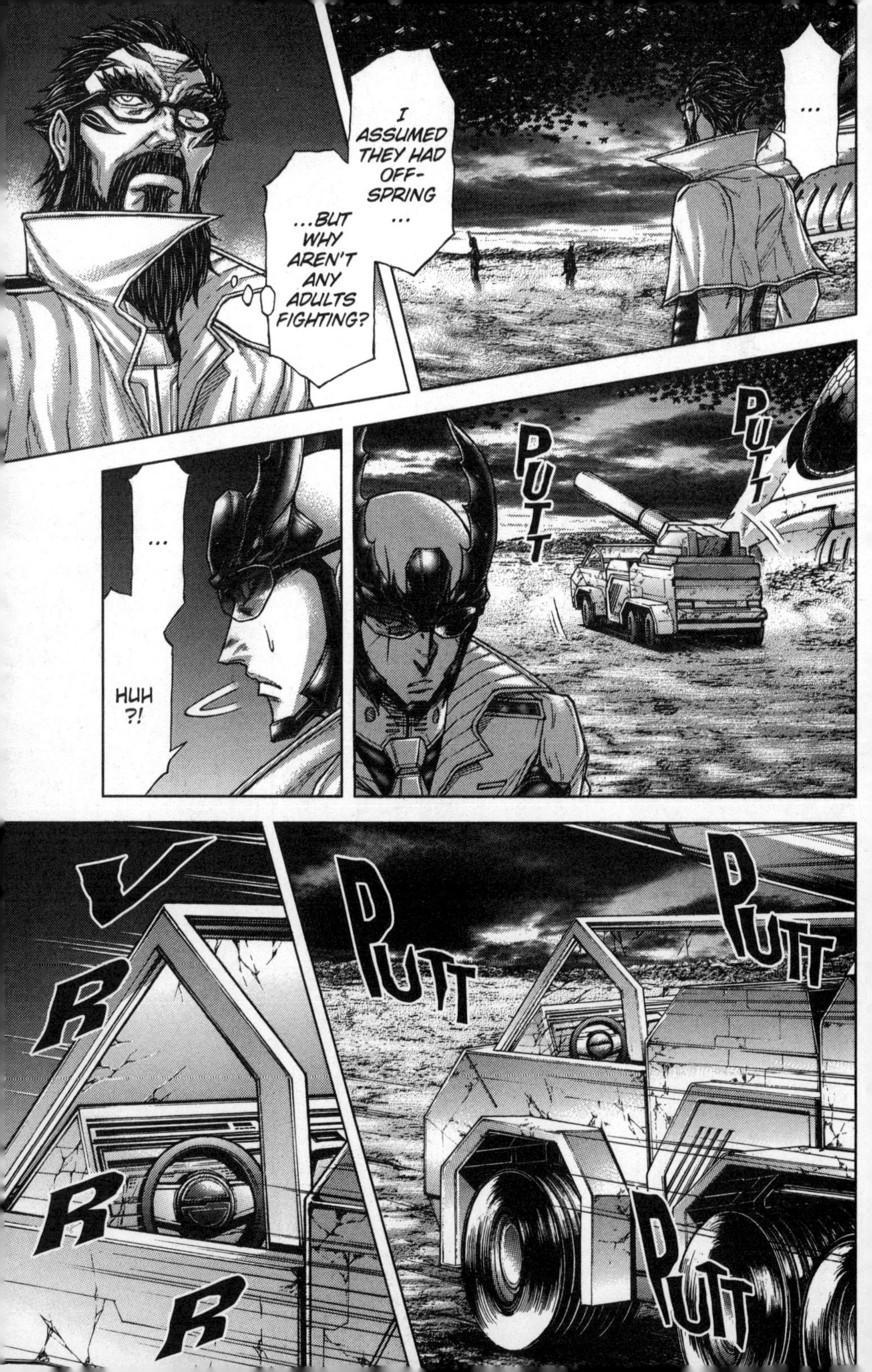
...
I ASSUMED THEY HAD OFF-SPRING ...
...BUT WHY AREN'T ANY ADULTS FIGHTING?
PUTT
PUTT
...
HUH ?!
PUTT
PUTT
PUTT
VRRR

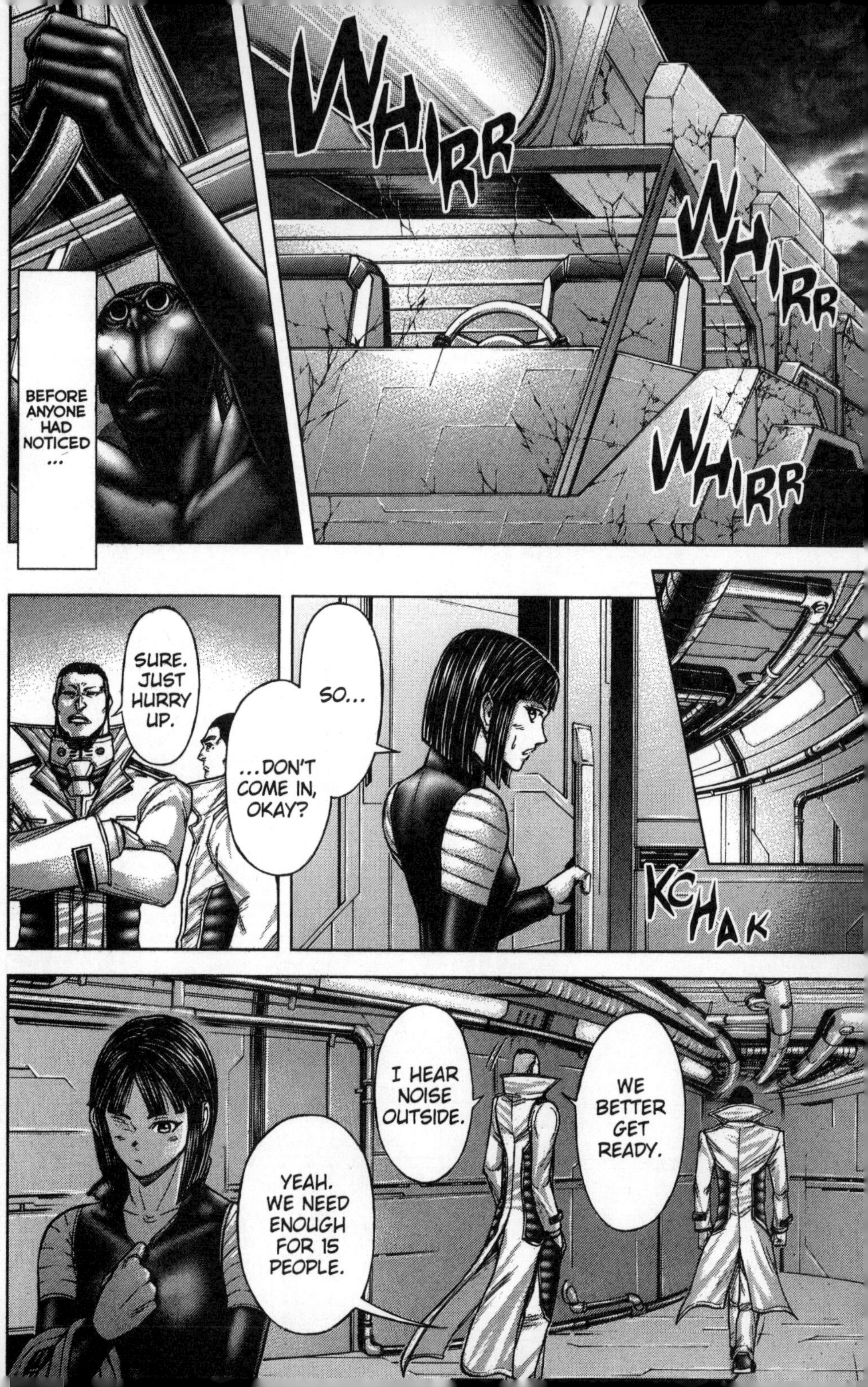
WHIRR
WHIRR
WHIRR
BEFORE ANYONE HAD NOTICED...
KCHAK
SO...
...DON'T COME IN, OKAY?
SURE. JUST HURRY UP.
WE BETTER GET READY.
I HEAR NOISE OUTSIDE.
YEAH. WE NEED ENOUGH FOR 15 PEOPLE.

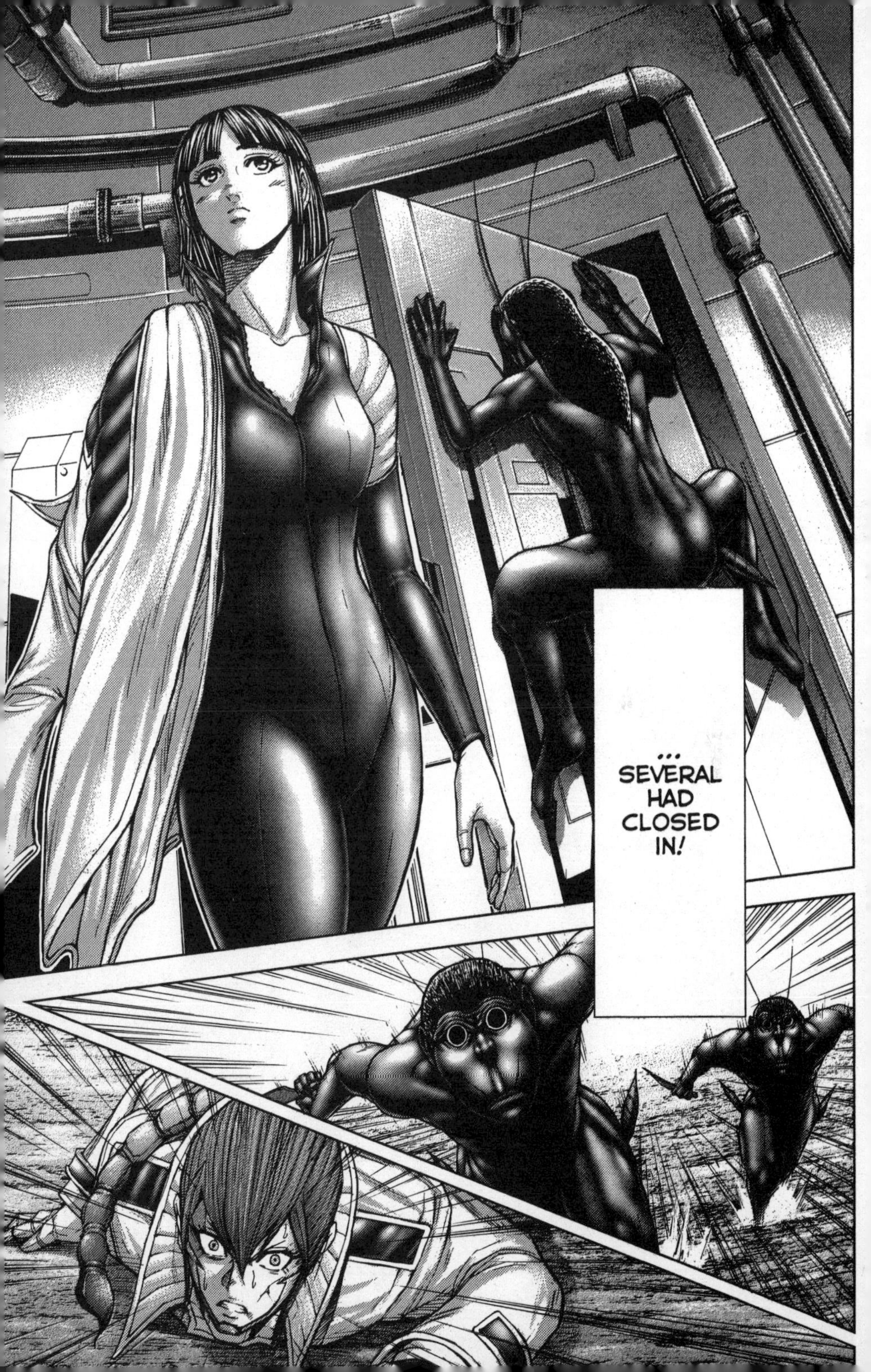
...SEVERAL HAD CLOSED IN!

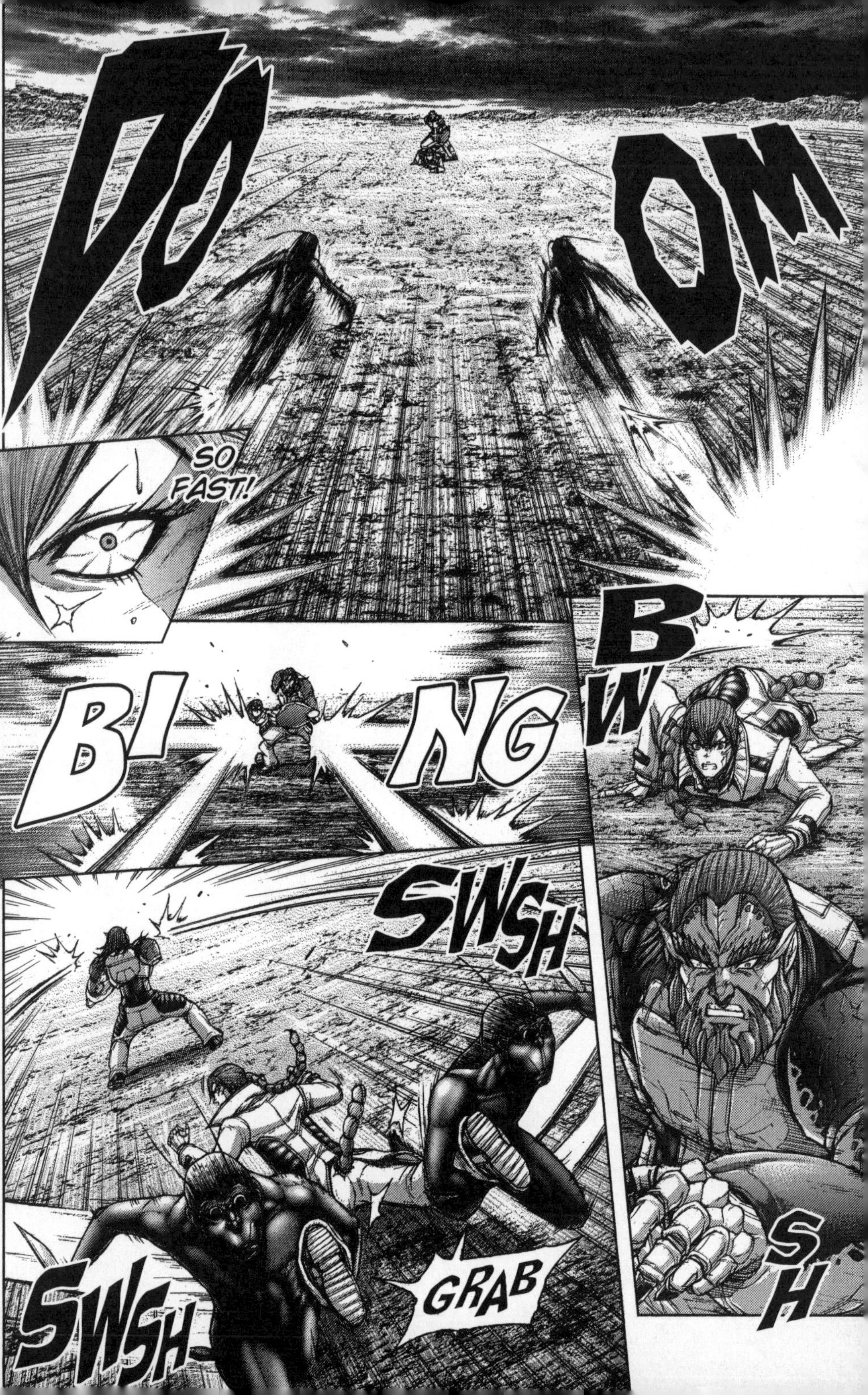
DO
OM
SO FAST!
BW
SH
BI
NG
SWSH
GRAB
SWSH

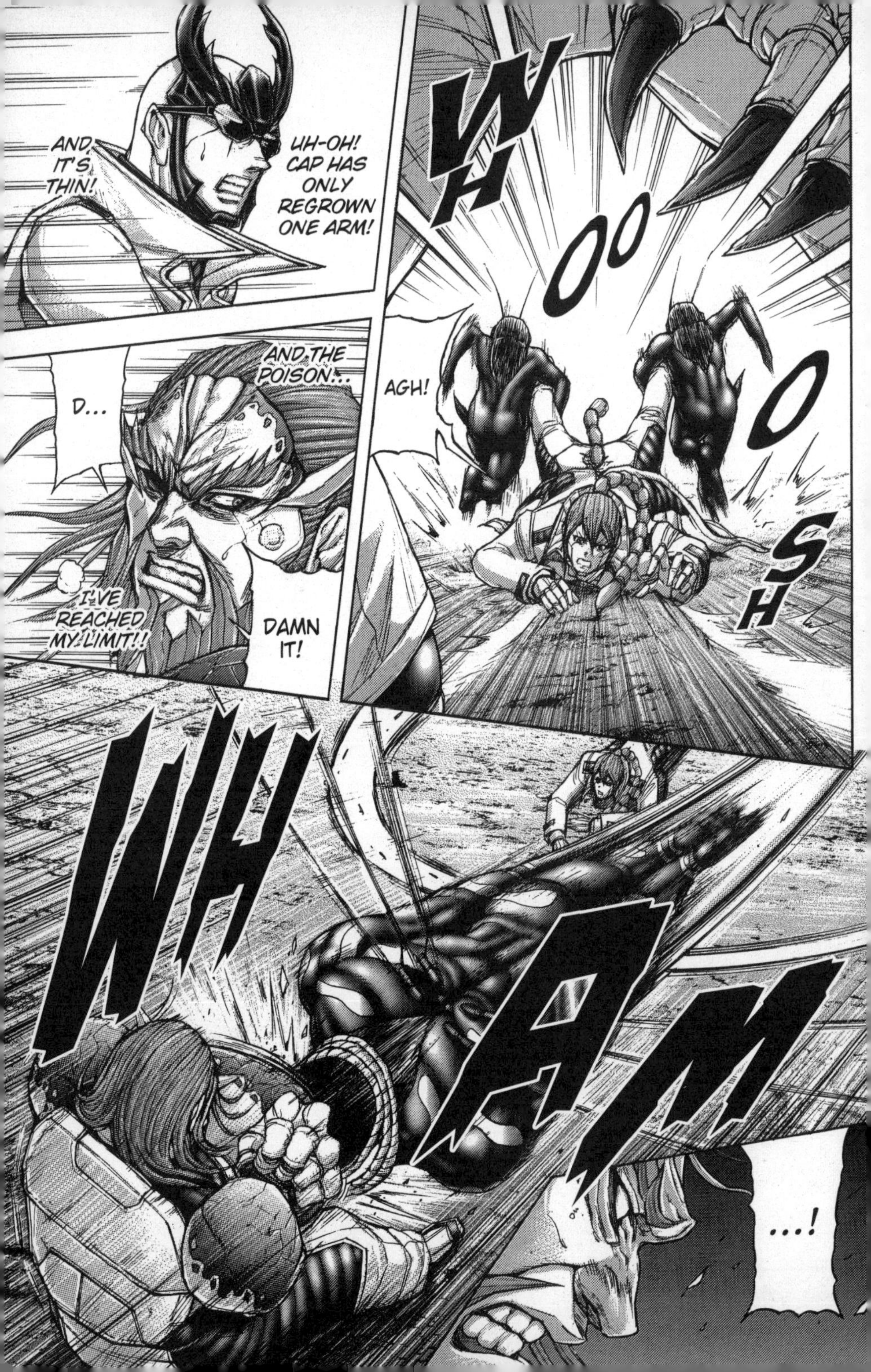
WHOOOOSH
AGH!
UH-OH! CAP HAS ONLY REGROWN ONE ARM!
AND IT'S THIN!
AND THE POISON...
D...
I'VE REACHED MY LIMIT!!
DAMN IT!
WHAM
...!

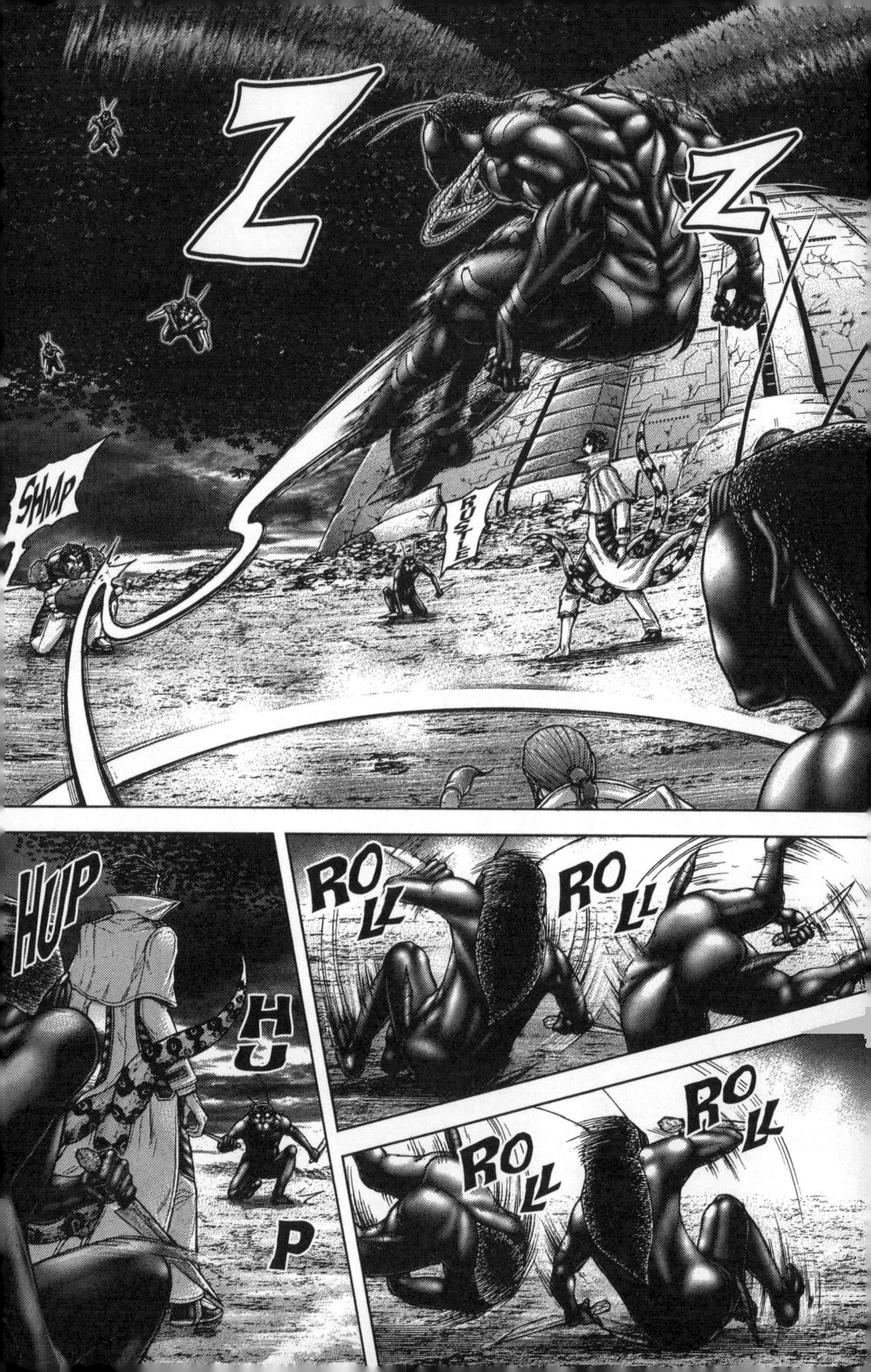
Z
Z
RUSTLE
SHMP
ROLL
ROLL
ROLL
ROLL
HUP
HUP

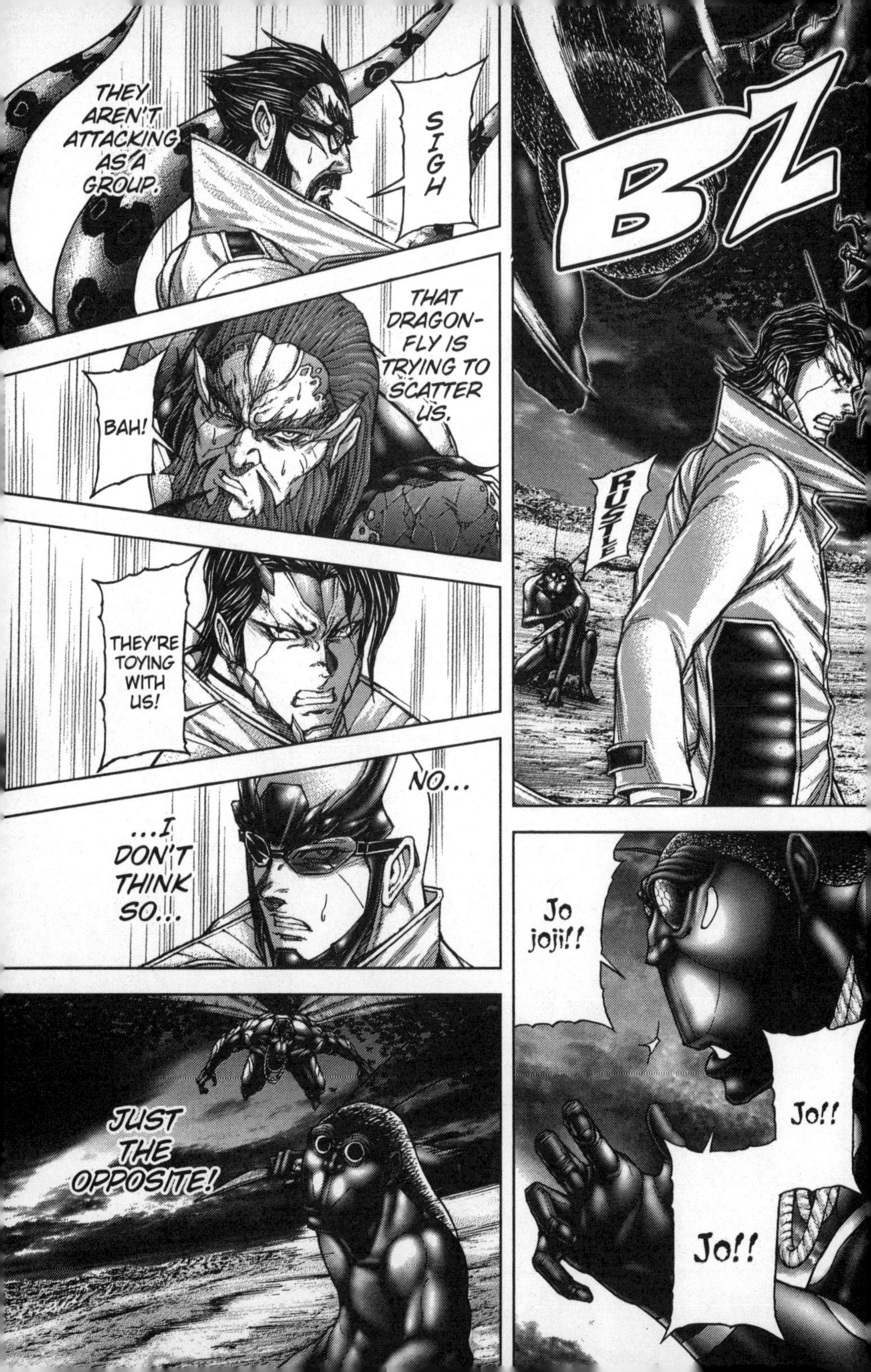

BZ
RUSTLE
SIGH
THEY AREN'T ATTACKING AS A GROUP.
THAT DRAGON-FLY IS TRYING TO SCATTER US.
BAH!
THEY'RE TOYING WITH US!
NO...
...I DON'T THINK SO...
JUST THE OPPOSITE!
Jo joji!!
Jo!!
Jo!!

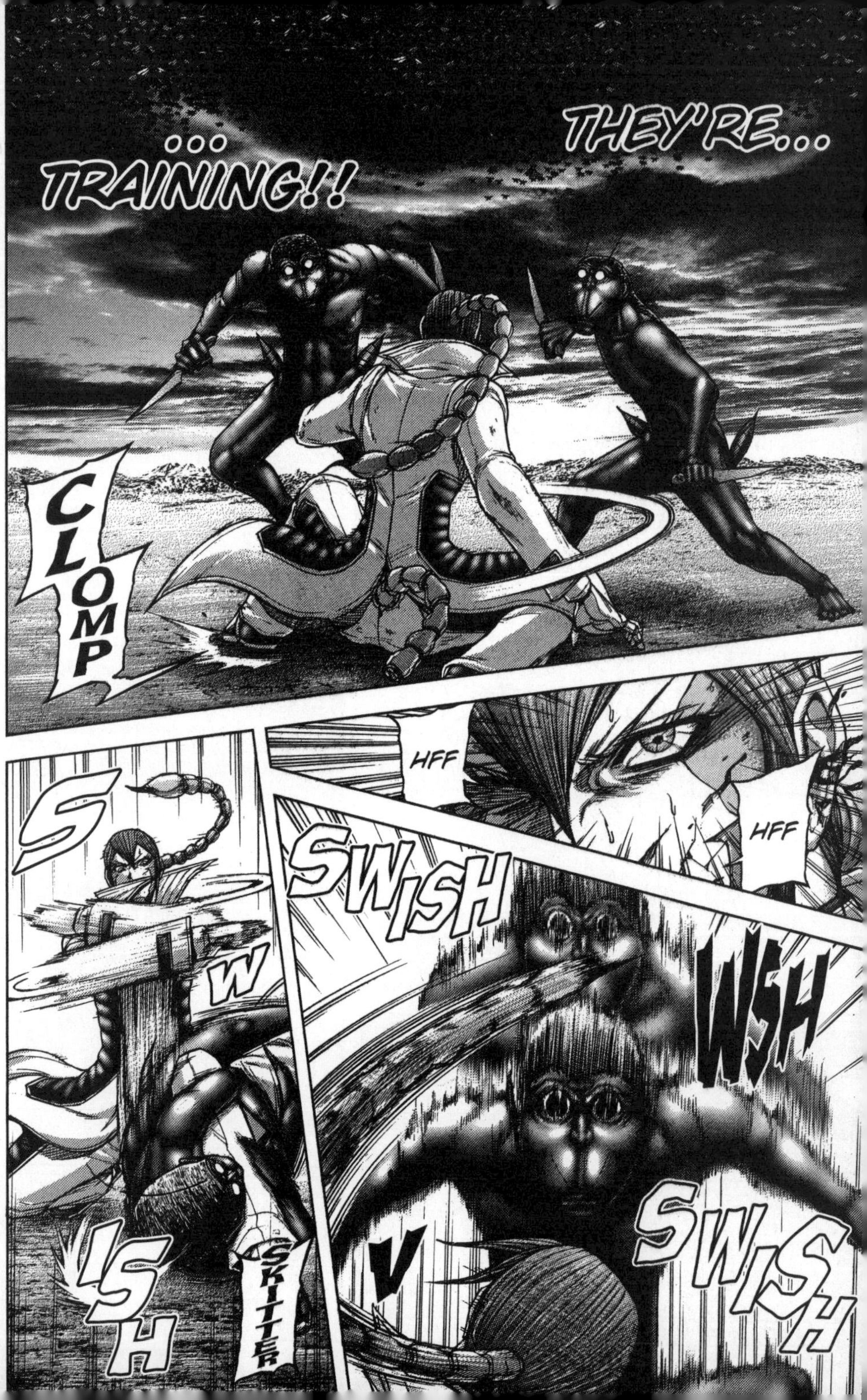
THEY'RE...
...TRAINING!!
CLOMP
HFF
HFF
SWISH
WSH
SWISH
V
S
W
ISH
SKITTER

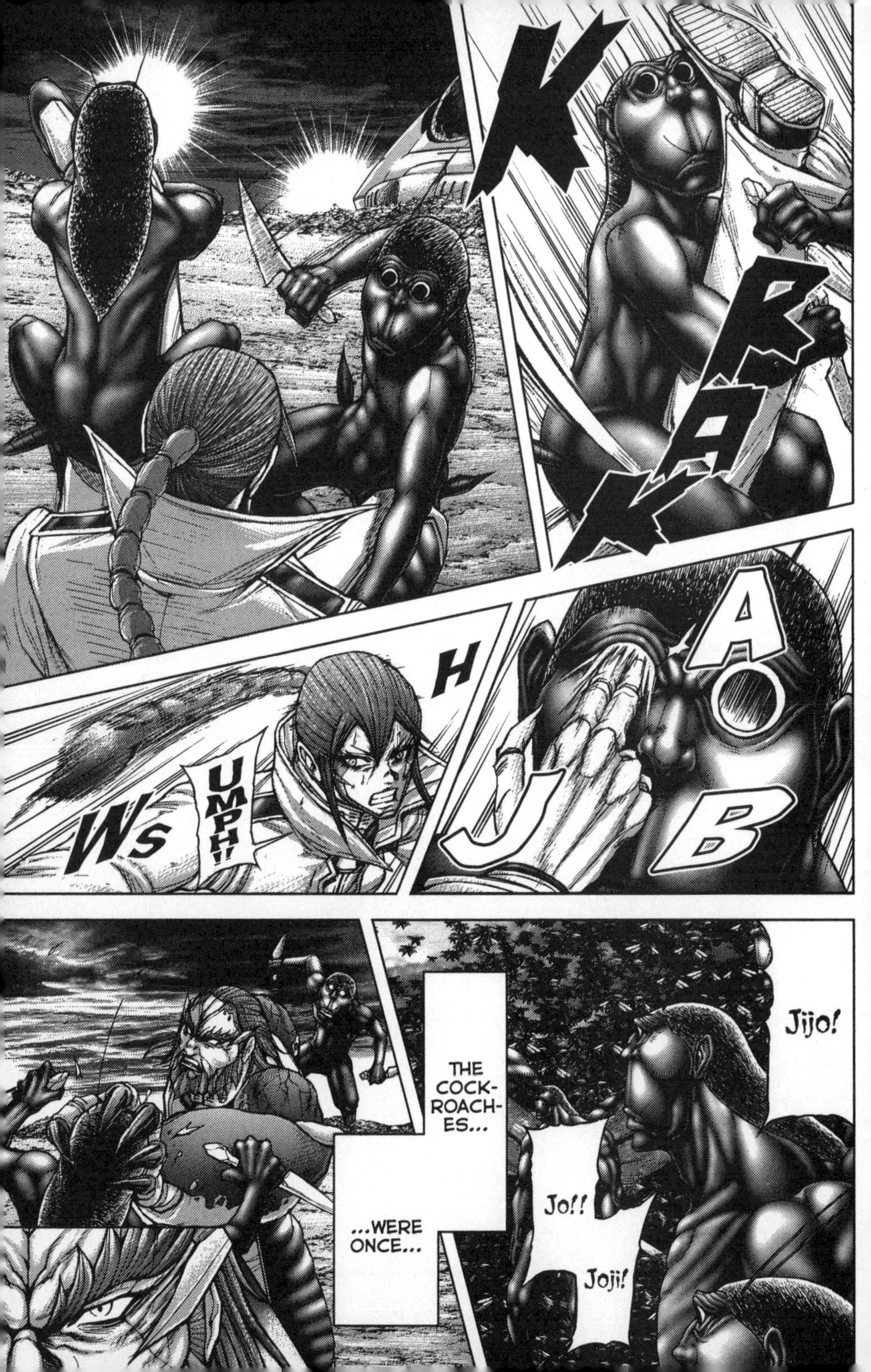
KRAK
JAB
WSH
UMPH!!
Jijo!
THE COCKROACHES...
Jo!!
...WERE ONCE...
Joji!

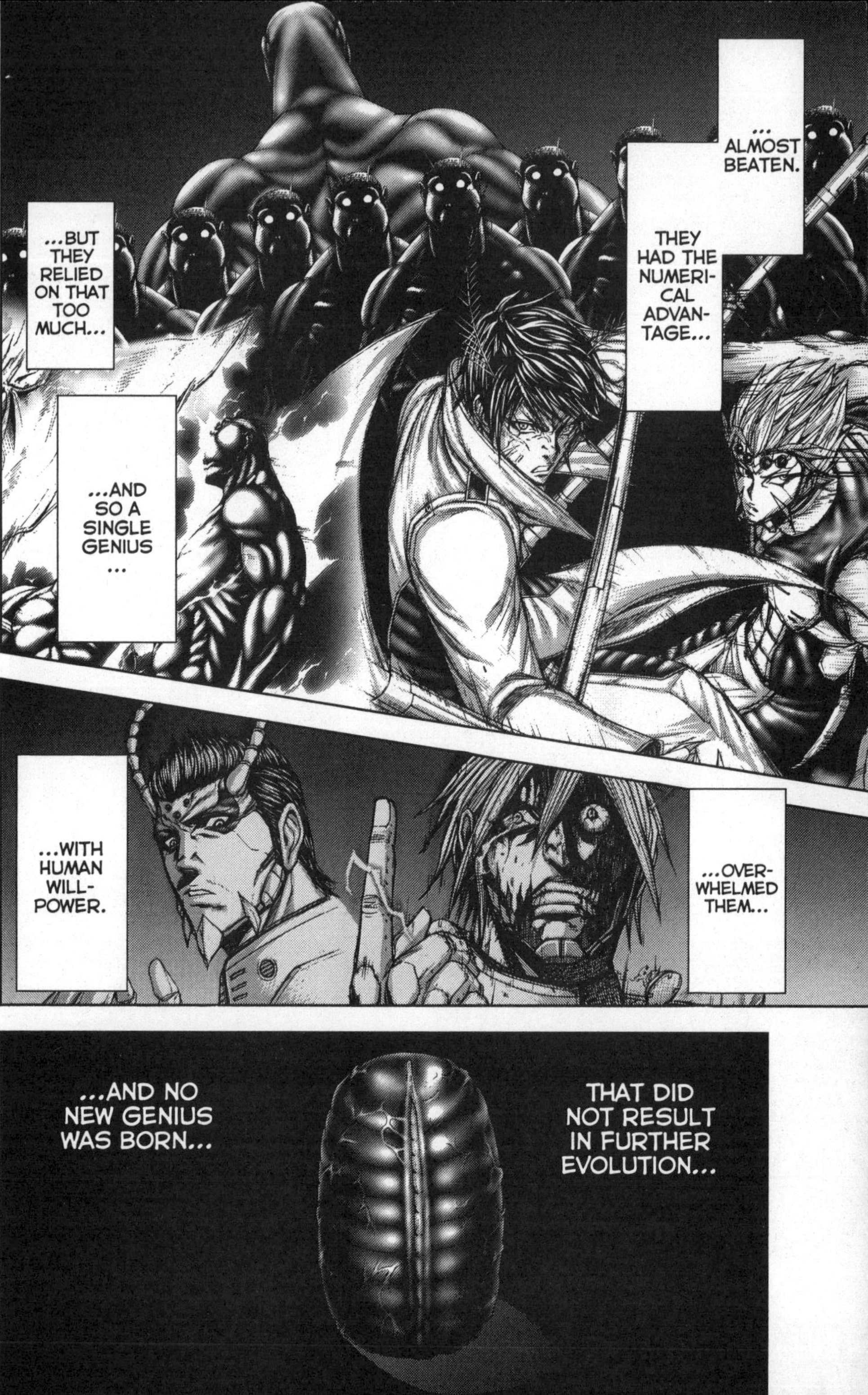
...ALMOST BEATEN.
THEY HAD THE NUMERI-CAL ADVAN-TAGE...
...BUT THEY RELIED ON THAT TOO MUCH...
...AND SO A SINGLE GENIUS...
...OVER-WHELMED THEM...
...WITH HUMAN WILL-POWER.
THAT DID NOT RESULT IN FURTHER EVOLUTION...
...AND NO NEW GENIUS WAS BORN...

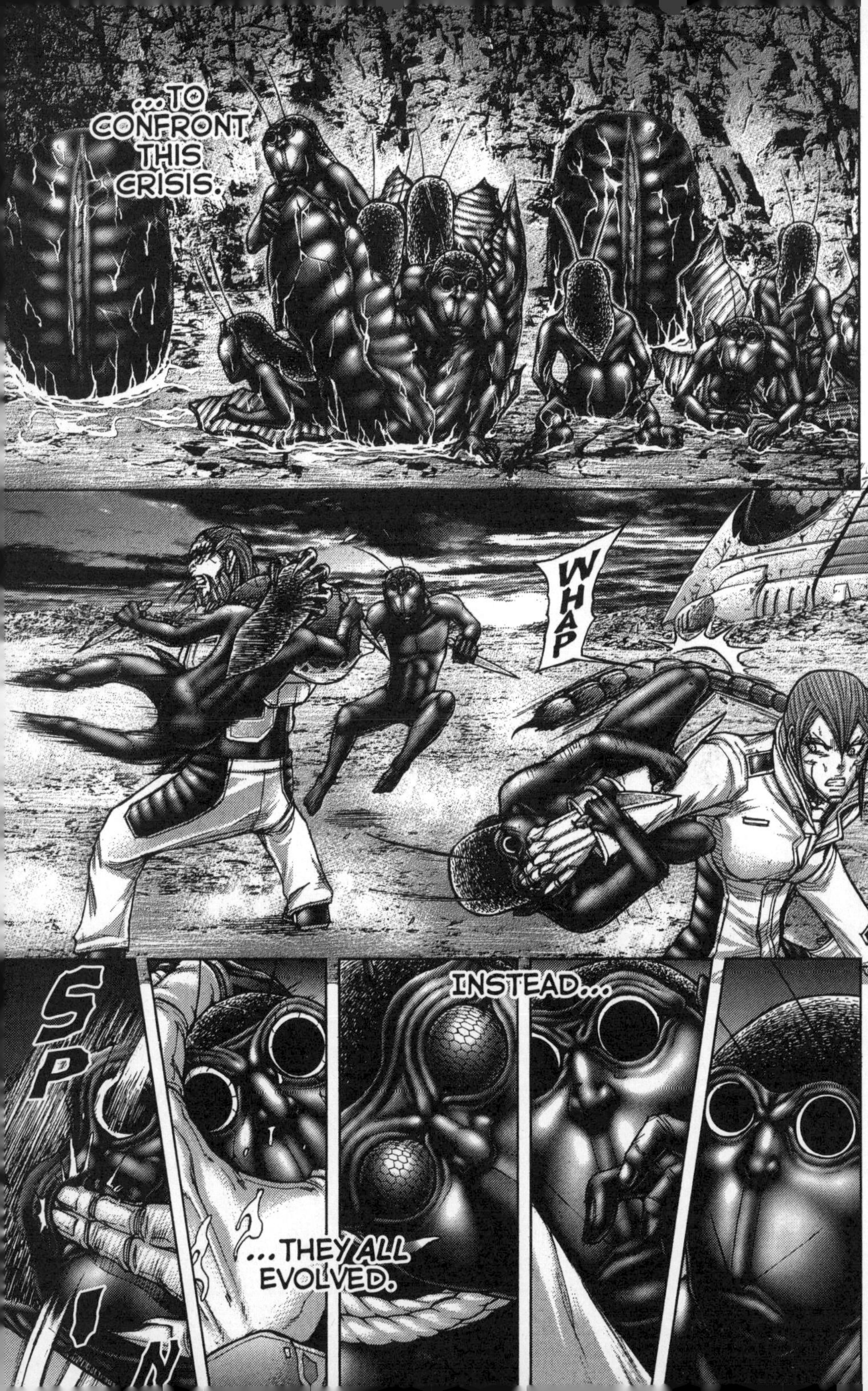
...TO CONFRONT THIS CRISIS.
WHAP
INSTEAD...
...THEY ALL EVOLVED.
SPIN

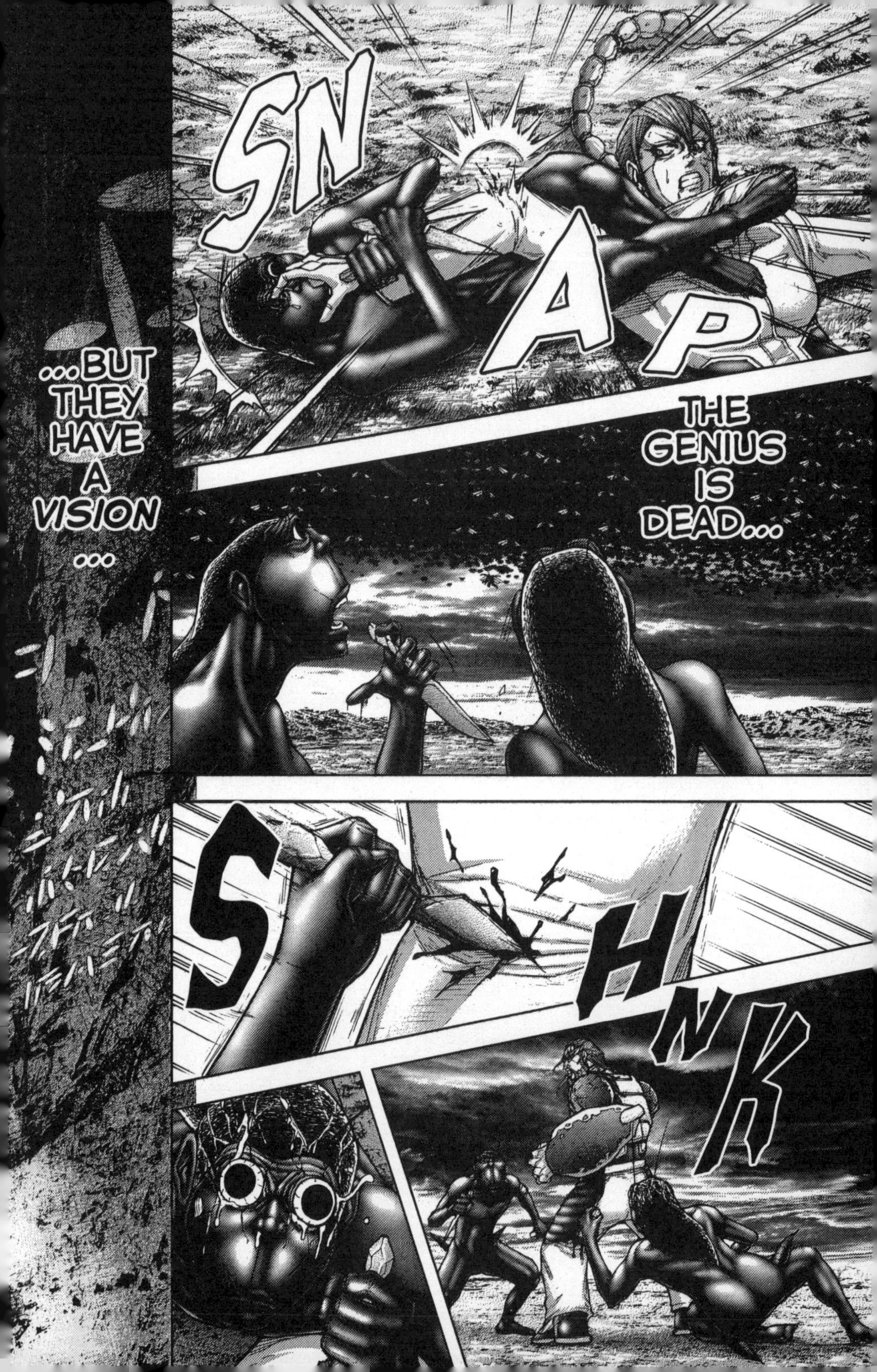
SNAP
THE GENIUS IS DEAD...
SHNK
...BUT THEY HAVE A VISION...

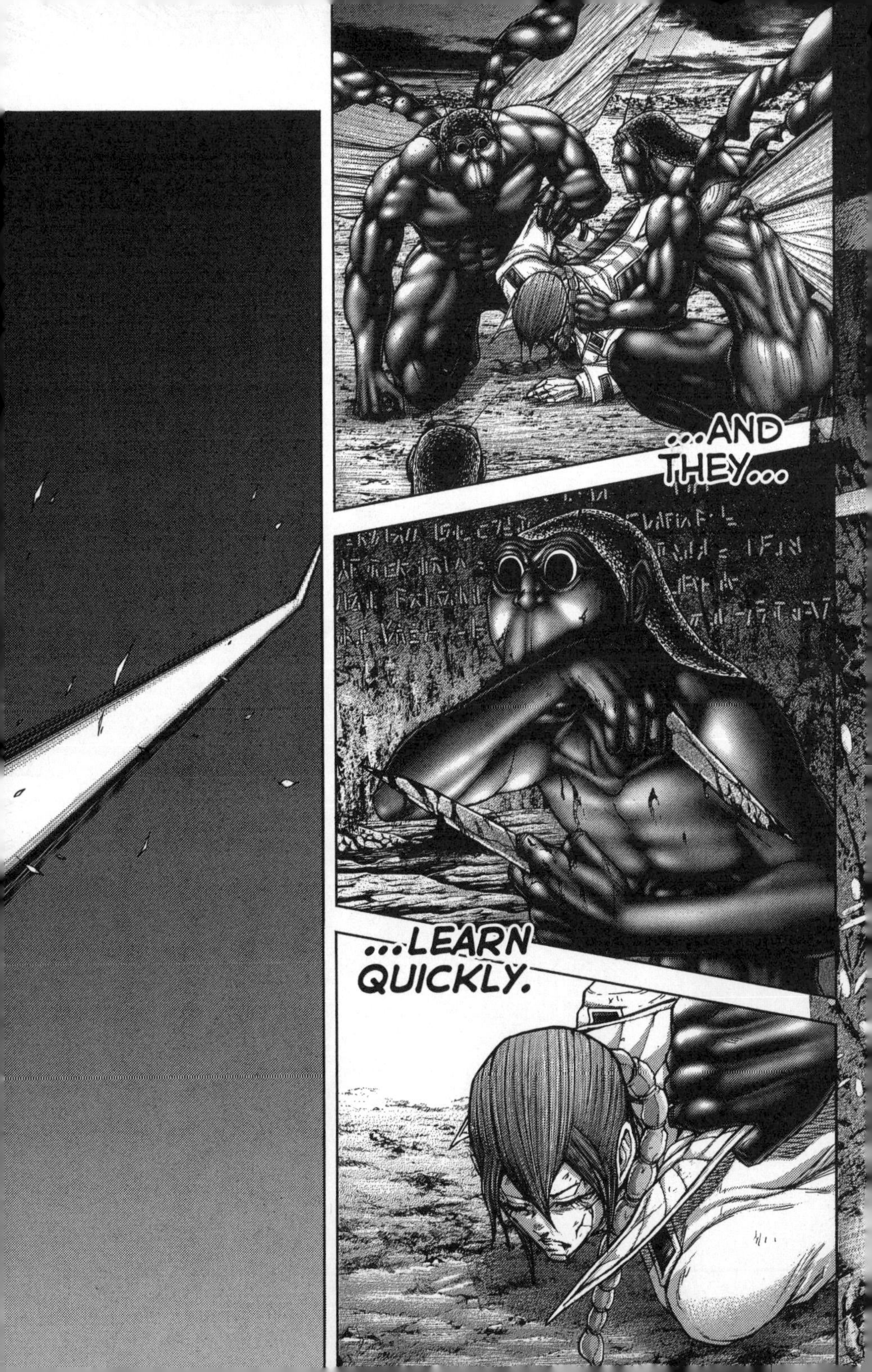
...AND THEY...
...LEARN QUICKLY.

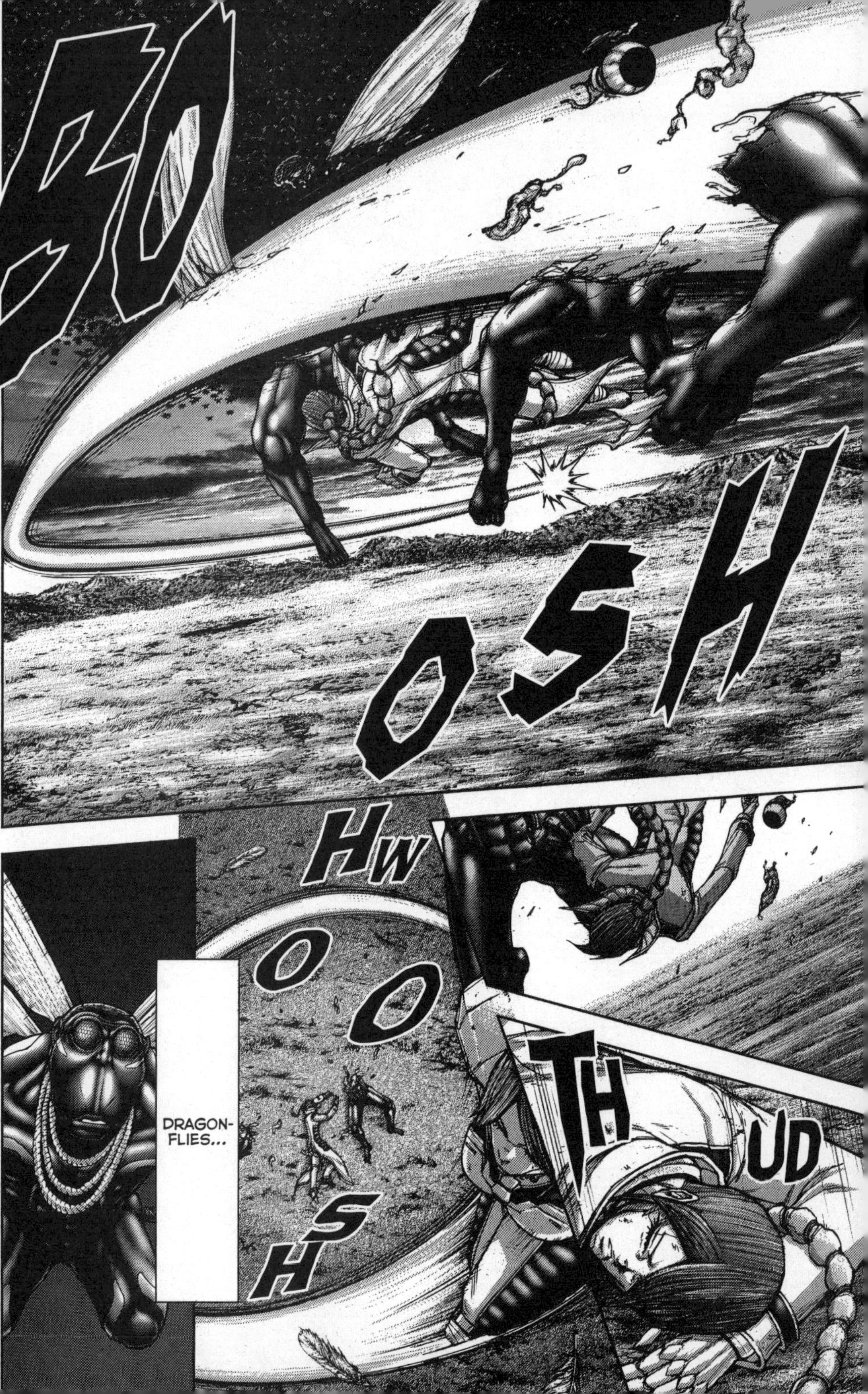
OSH
THUD
HWOOSH
DRAGON-FLIES...

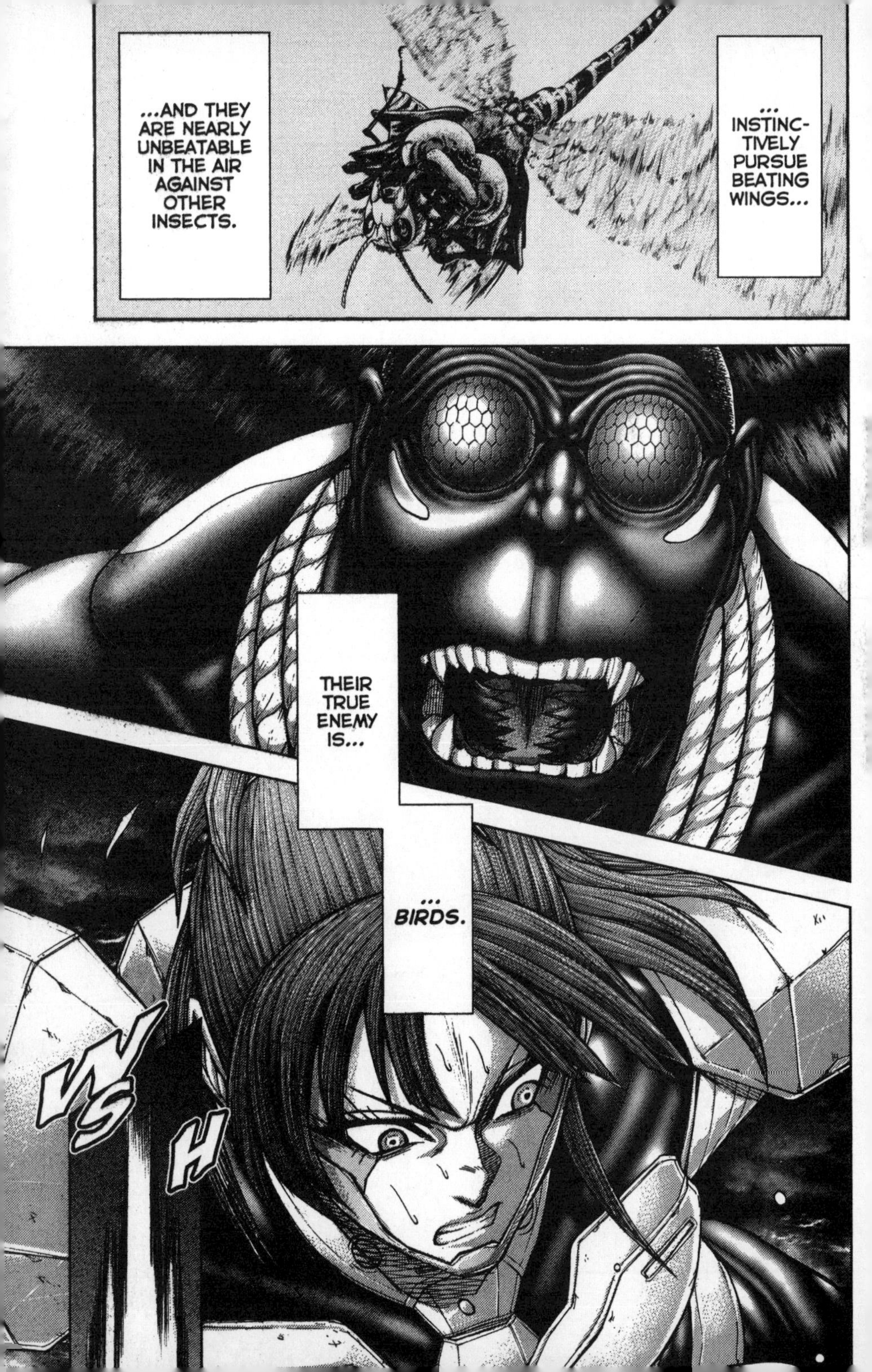
...INSTINCTIVELY PURSUE BEATING WINGS...
...AND THEY ARE NEARLY UNBEATABLE IN THE AIR AGAINST OTHER INSECTS.
THEIR TRUE ENEMY IS...
...BIRDS.
WSH

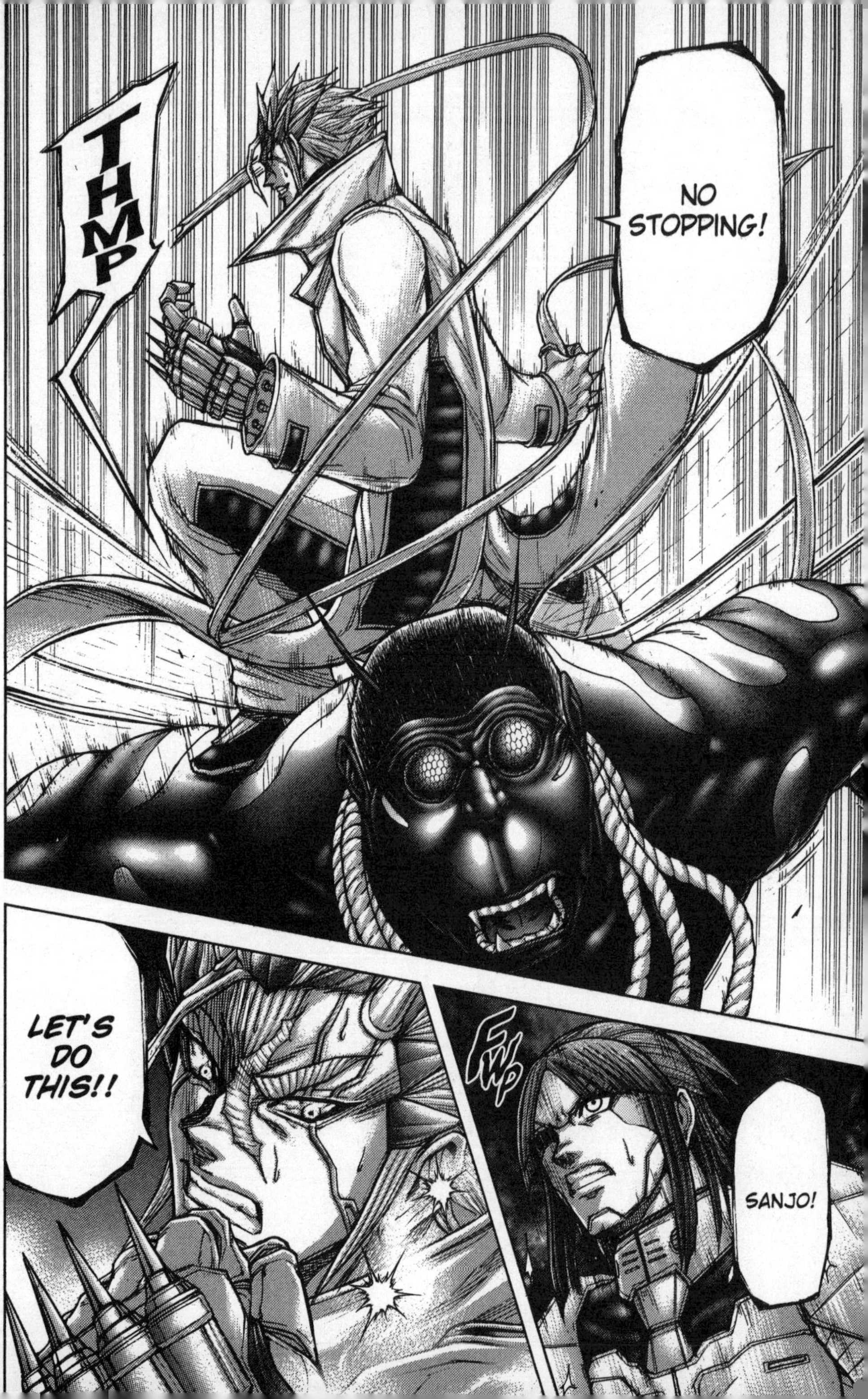
NO STOPPING!
THMP
FWP
SANJO!
LET'S DO THIS!!

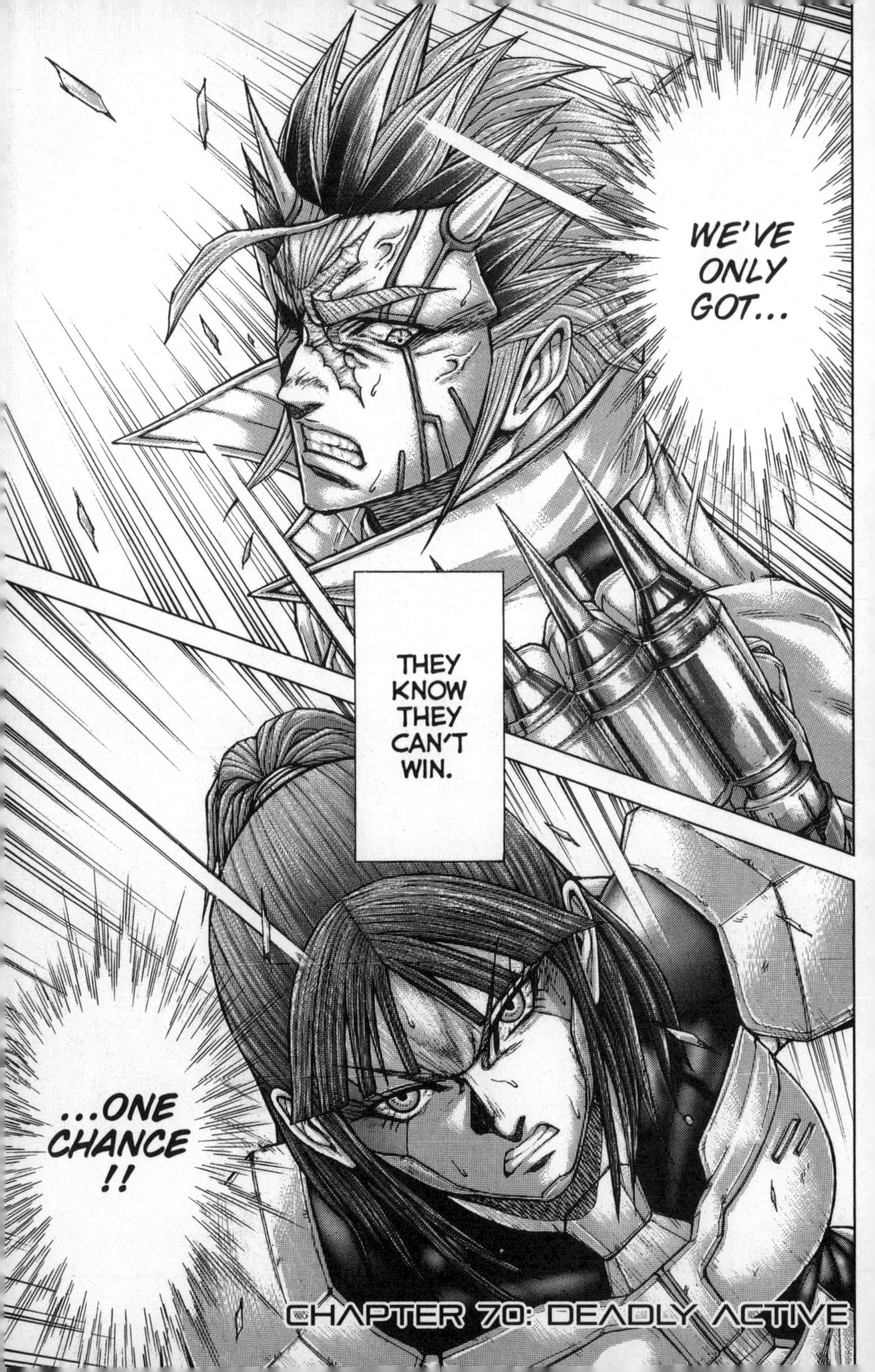
WE'VE ONLY GOT...
THEY KNOW THEY CAN'T WIN.
...ONE CHANCE!!
CHAPTER 70: DEADLY ACTIVE

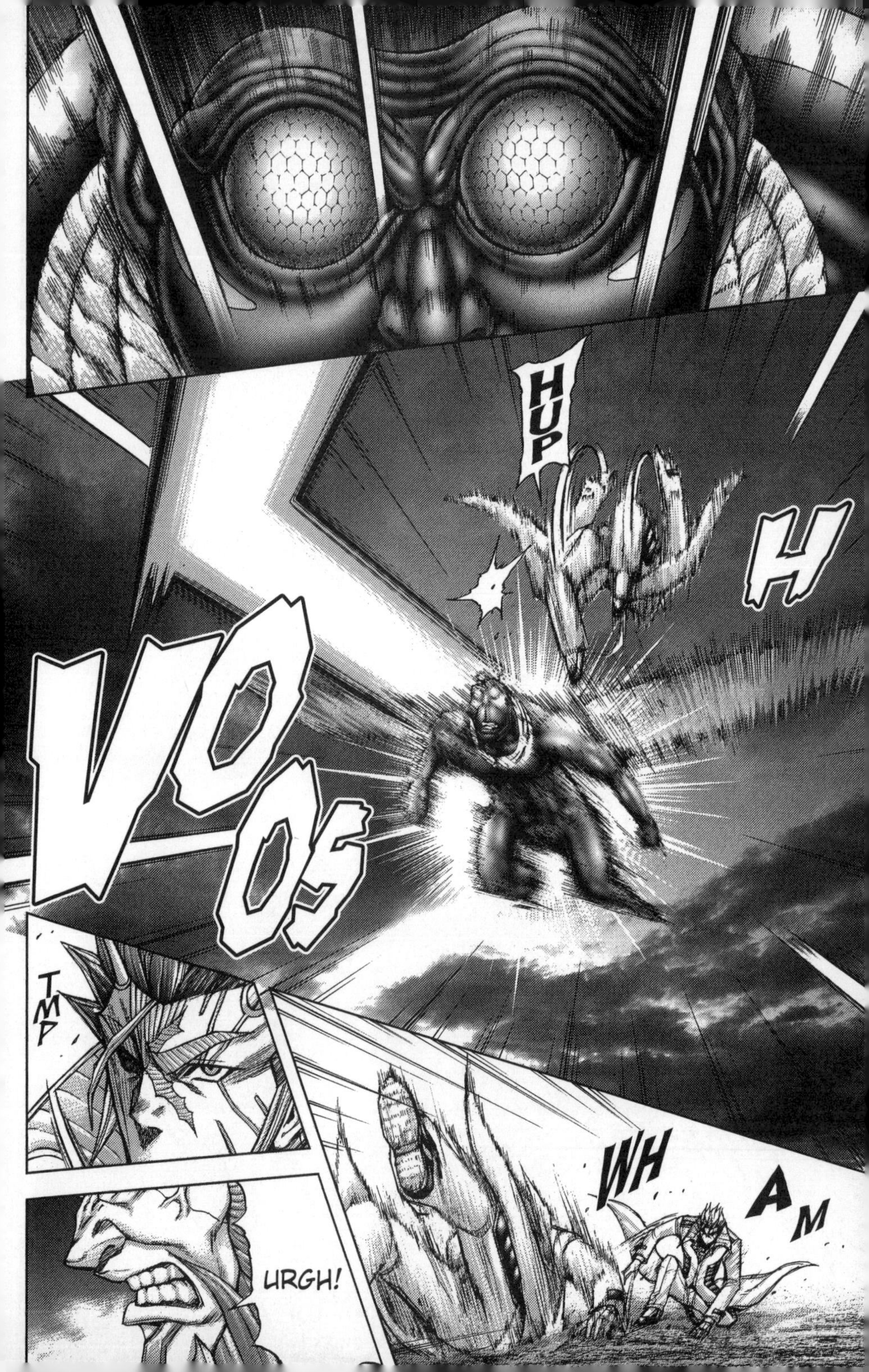
H
HUP
VO
OS
WH
AM
TMP
URGH!

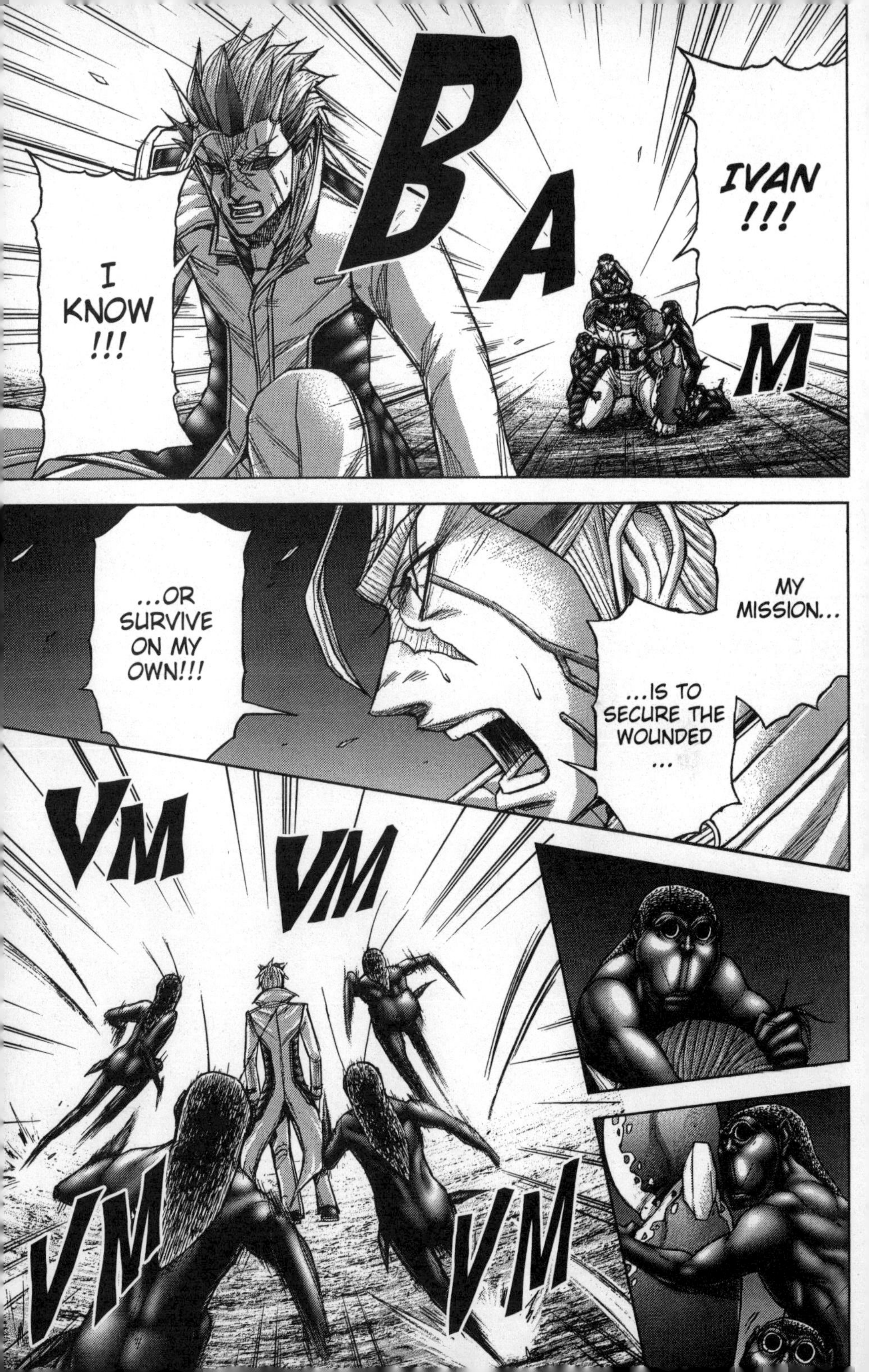
IVAN !!!
BAM
I KNOW !!!
MY MISSION...
...IS TO SECURE THE WOUNDED ...
...OR SURVIVE ON MY OWN!!!
VM
VM
VM
VM

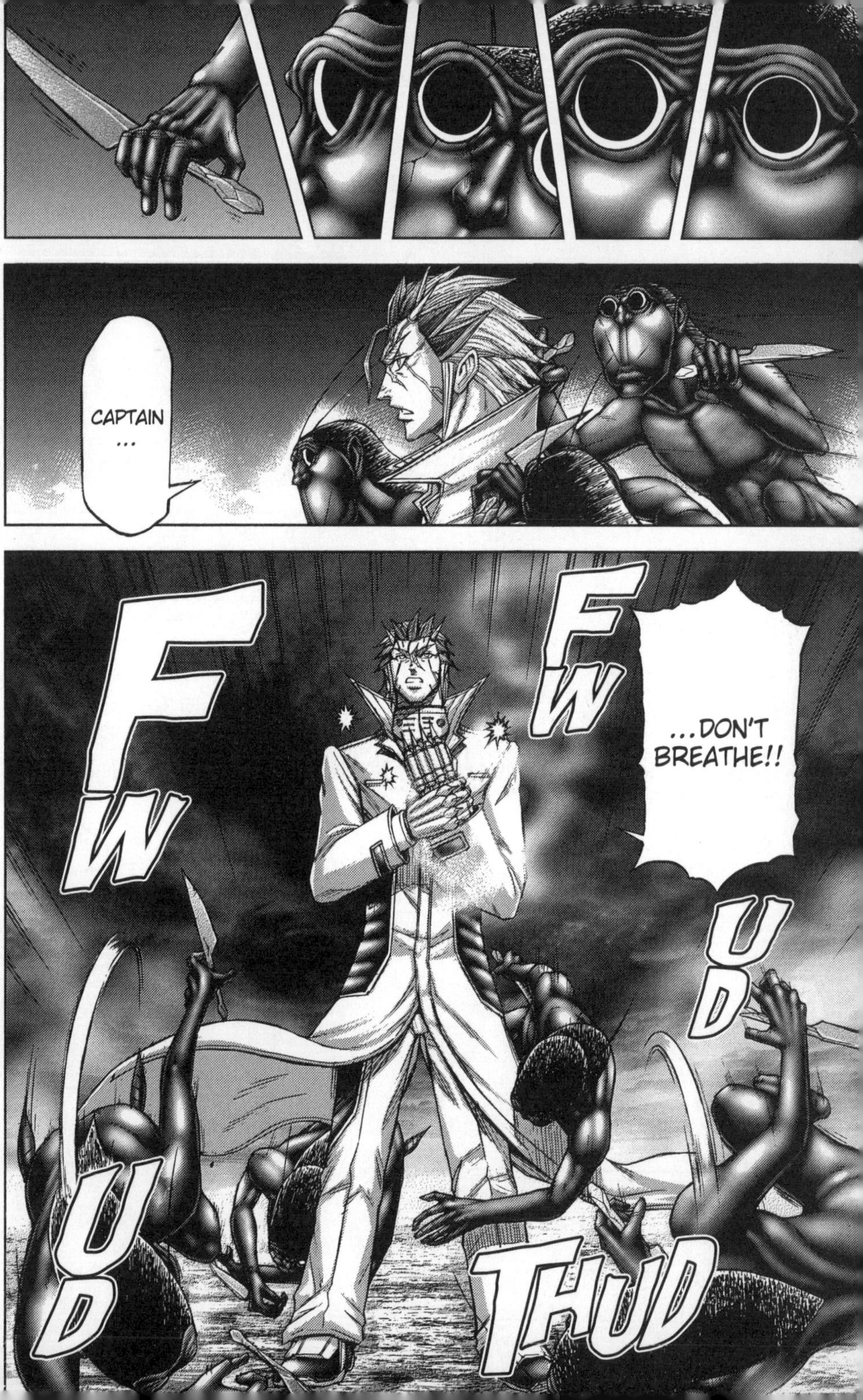
CAPTAIN
...
...DON'T BREATHE!!
FWUD
FWUD
THUD

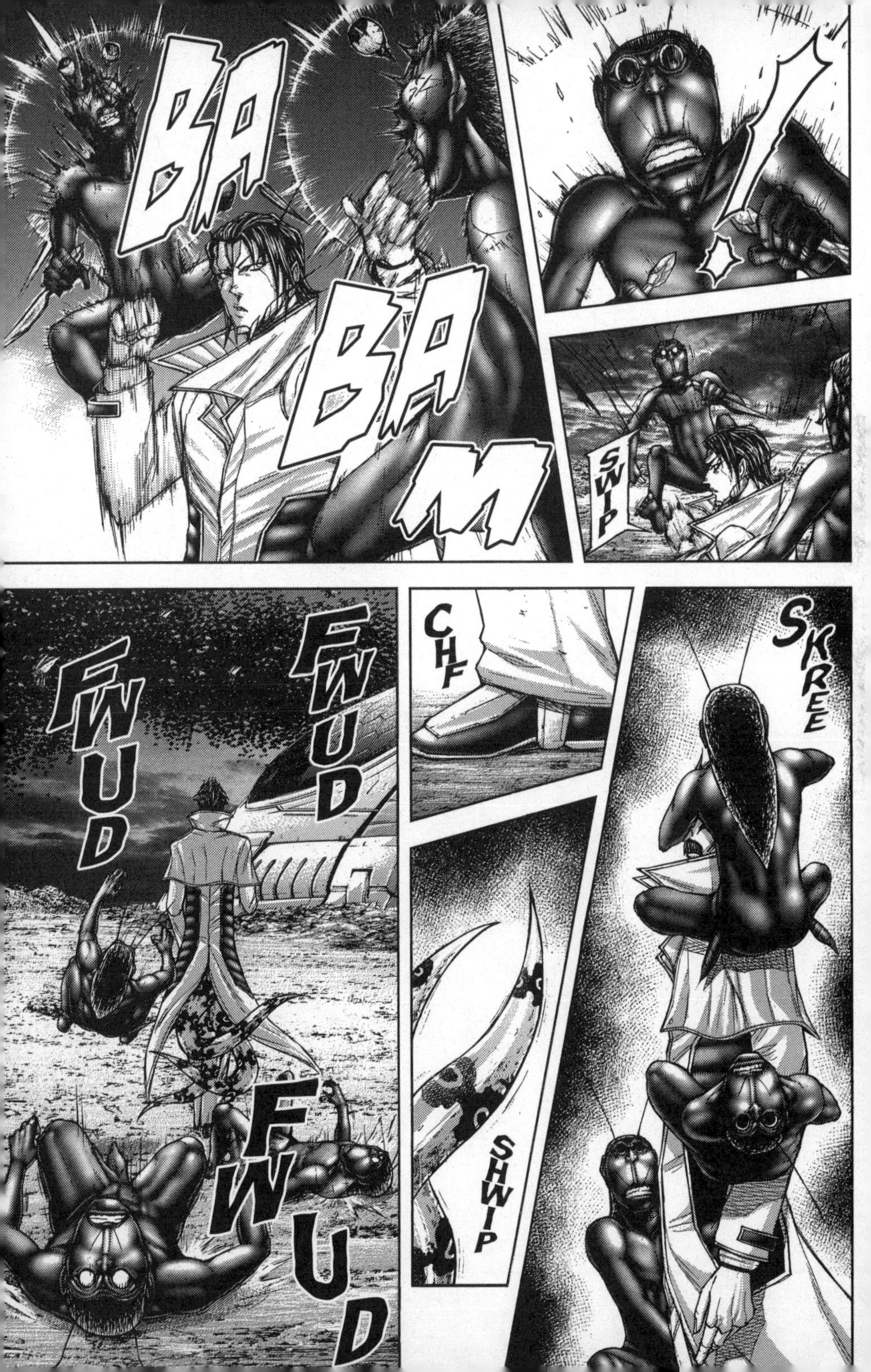
!
SWIP
BA
BA
BAM
SKREE
CHF
SHWIP
FWUD
FWUD
FWUD

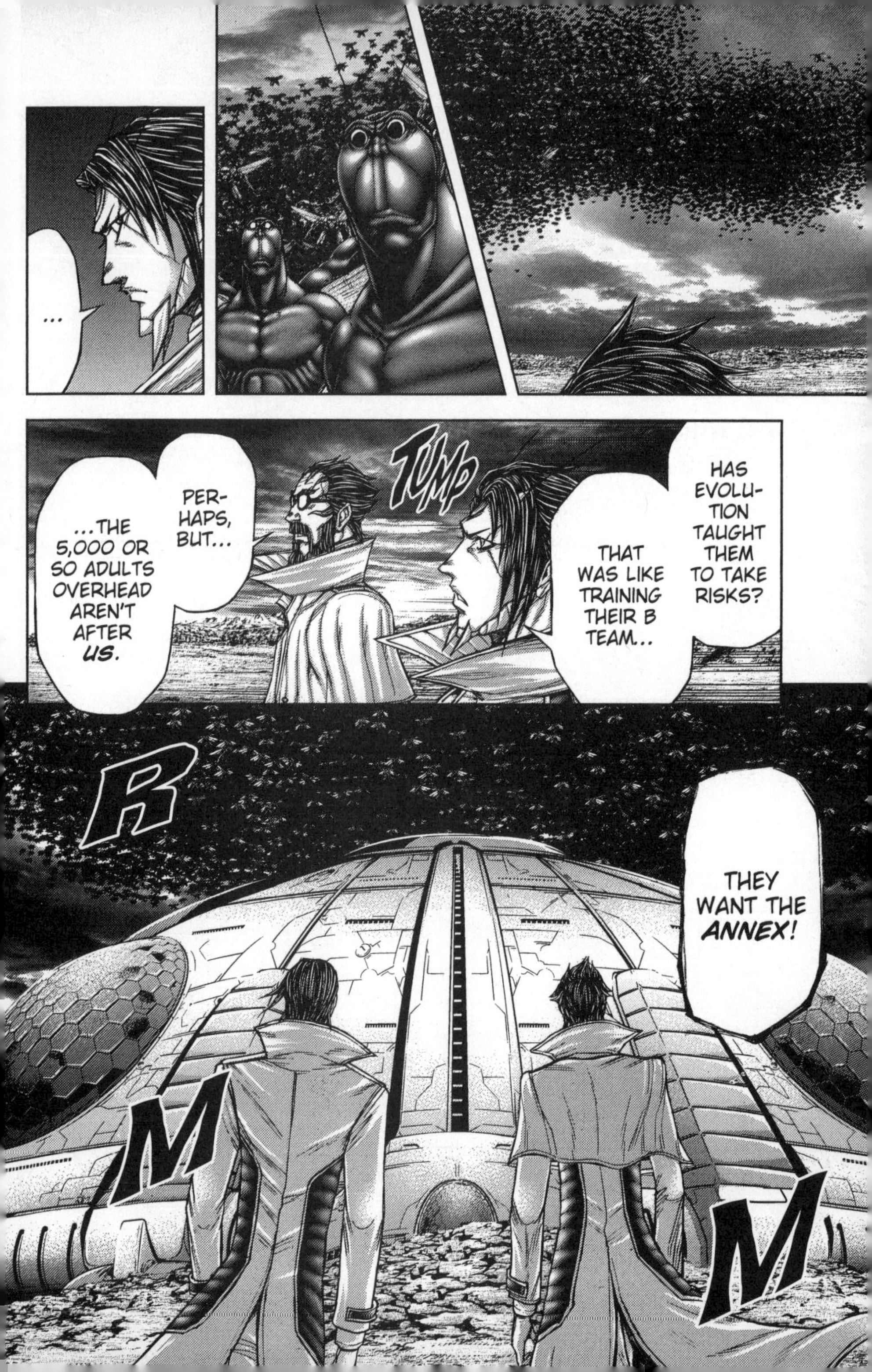
...
HAS EVOLUTION TAUGHT THEM TO TAKE RISKS?
THAT WAS LIKE TRAINING THEIR B TEAM...
TUMP
PERHAPS, BUT...
...THE 5,000 OR SO ADULTS OVERHEAD AREN'T AFTER *US*.
THEY WANT THE *ANNEX*!
R
M
M

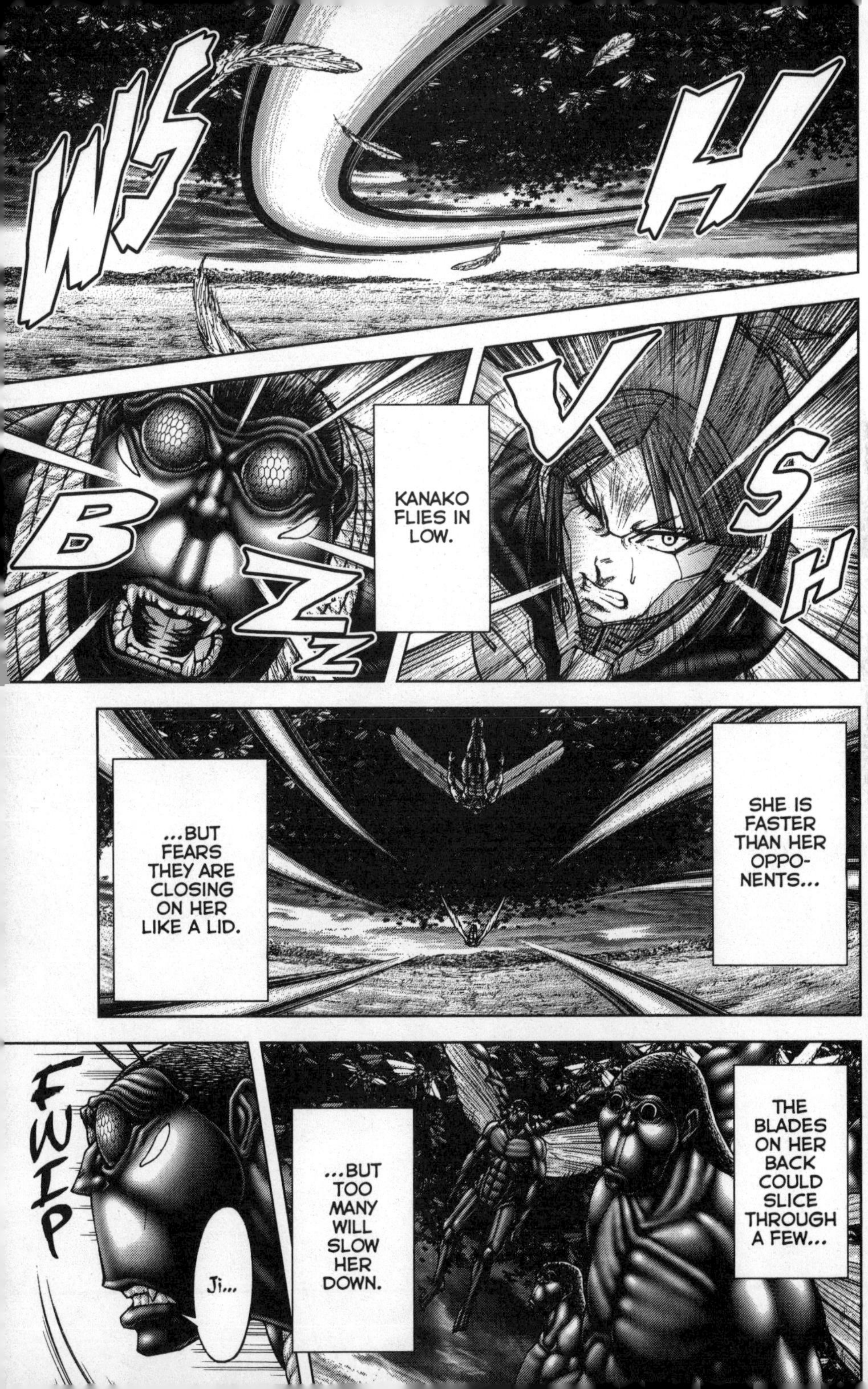
WSH
VSH
KANAKO FLIES IN LOW.
BZZ
SHE IS FASTER THAN HER OPPO-NENTS...
...BUT FEARS THEY ARE CLOSING ON HER LIKE A LID.
THE BLADES ON HER BACK COULD SLICE THROUGH A FEW...
...BUT TOO MANY WILL SLOW HER DOWN.
Ji...
FWIP

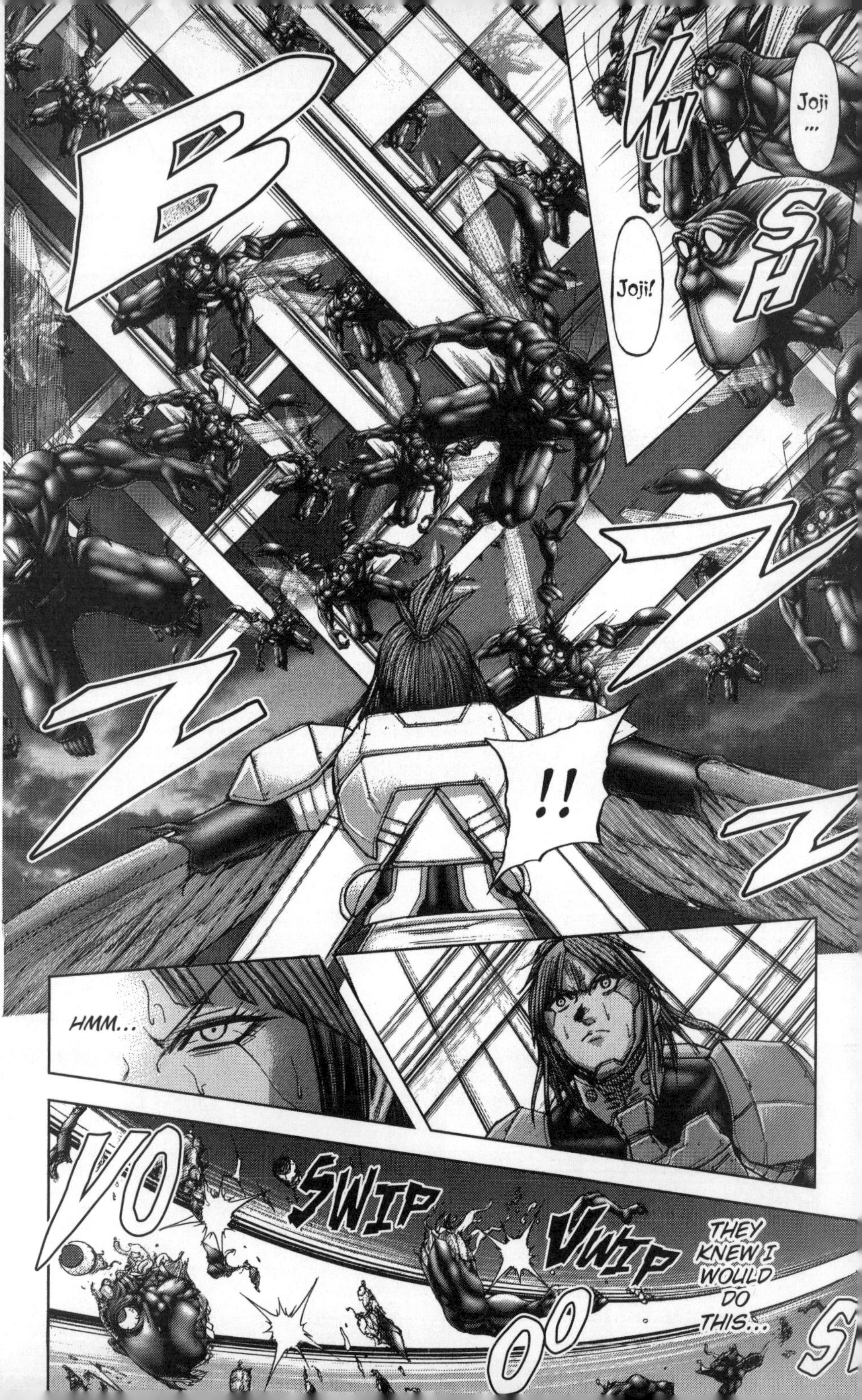
VW
Joji ...
SH
Joji!
B
Z
Z
Z
!!
HMM...
THEY KNEW I WOULD DO THIS...
VWIP
SWIP
VO
OO

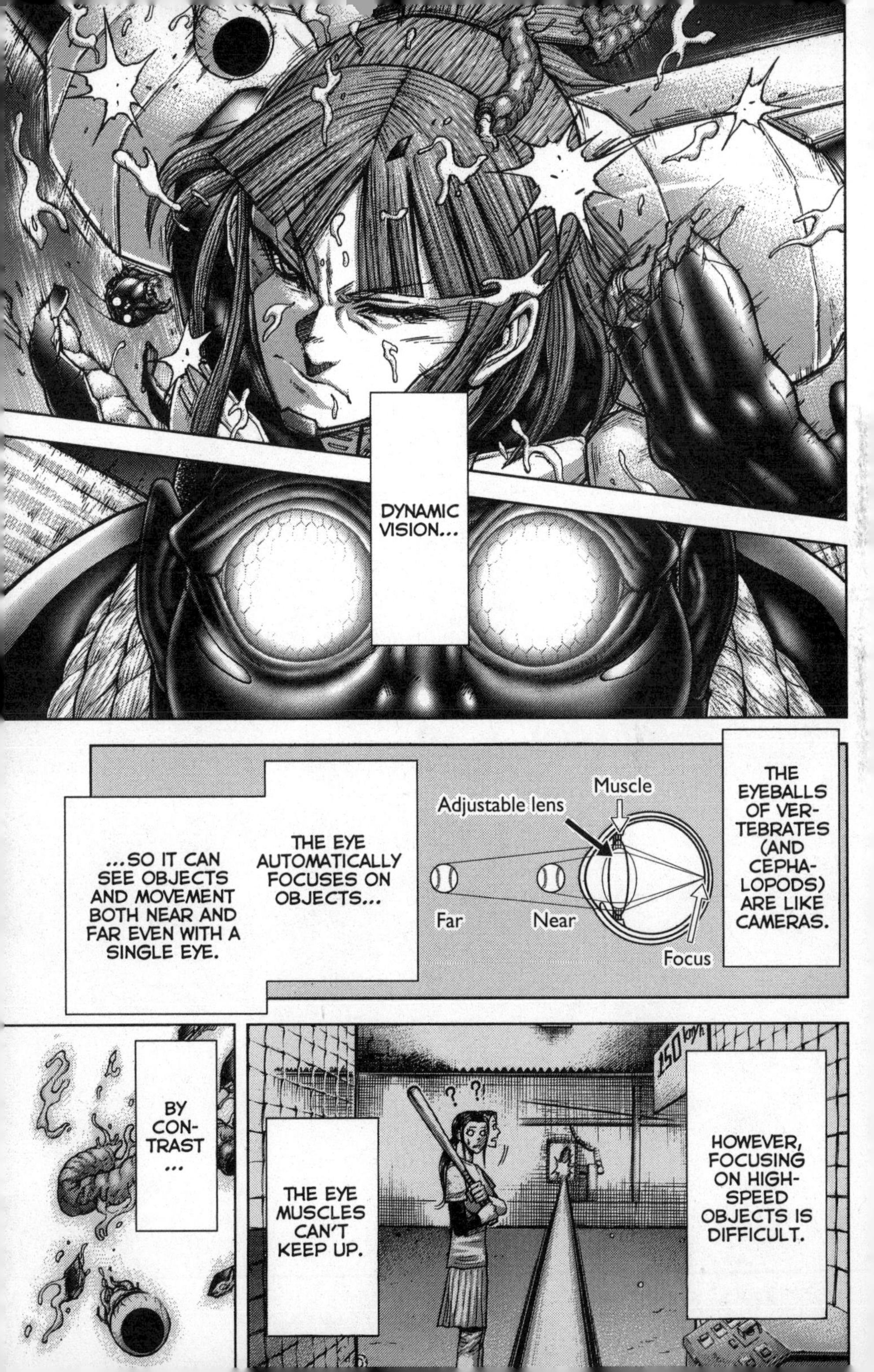
DYNAMIC VISION...
THE EYEBALLS OF VERTEBRATES (AND CEPHALOPODS) ARE LIKE CAMERAS.
Muscle
Adjustable lens
Far
Near
Focus
THE EYE AUTOMATICALLY FOCUSES ON OBJECTS...
...SO IT CAN SEE OBJECTS AND MOVEMENT BOTH NEAR AND FAR EVEN WITH A SINGLE EYE.
150 km/h
HOWEVER, FOCUSING ON HIGH-SPEED OBJECTS IS DIFFICULT.
THE EYE MUSCLES CAN'T KEEP UP.
BY CONTRAST...

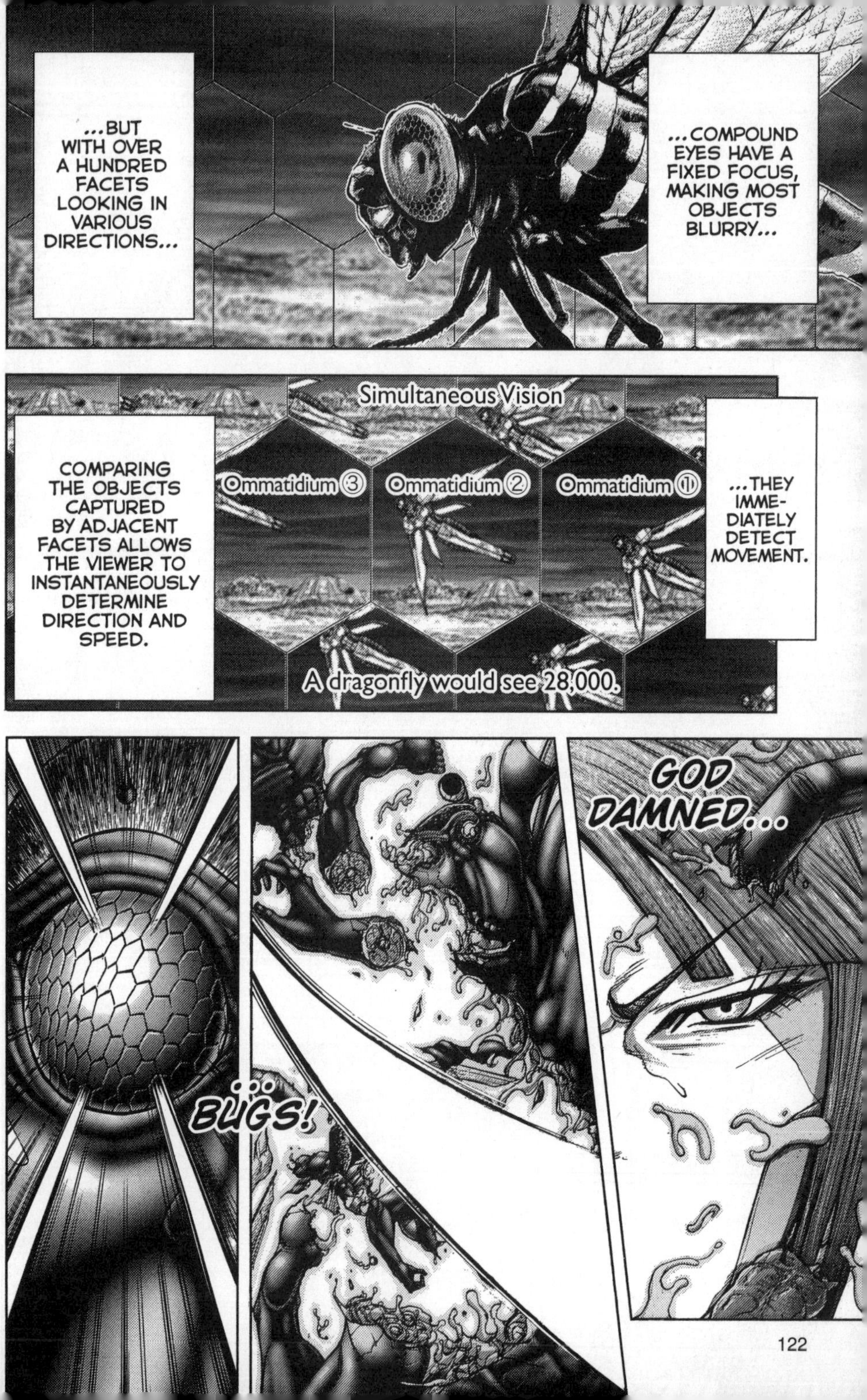
...COMPOUND EYES HAVE A FIXED FOCUS, MAKING MOST OBJECTS BLURRY...
...BUT WITH OVER A HUNDRED FACETS LOOKING IN VARIOUS DIRECTIONS...
Simultaneous Vision
...THEY IMME-DIATELY DETECT MOVEMENT.
Ommatidium ①
Ommatidium ②
Ommatidium ③
COMPARING THE OBJECTS CAPTURED BY ADJACENT FACETS ALLOWS THE VIEWER TO INSTANTANEOUSLY DETERMINE DIRECTION AND SPEED.
A dragonfly would see 28,000.
GOD DAMNED...
...BUGS!

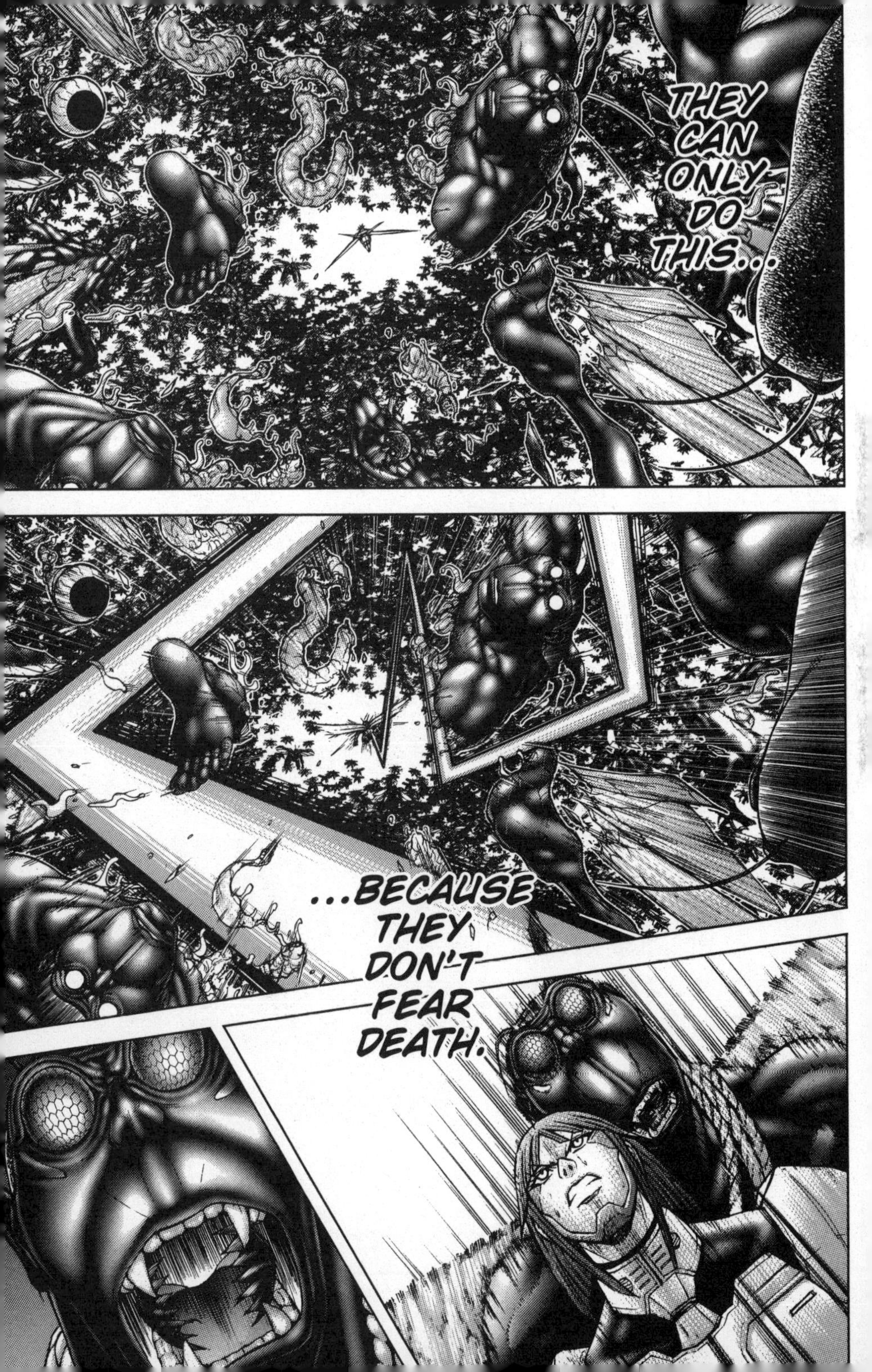
THEY CAN ONLY DO THIS...
...BECAUSE THEY DON'T FEAR DEATH.

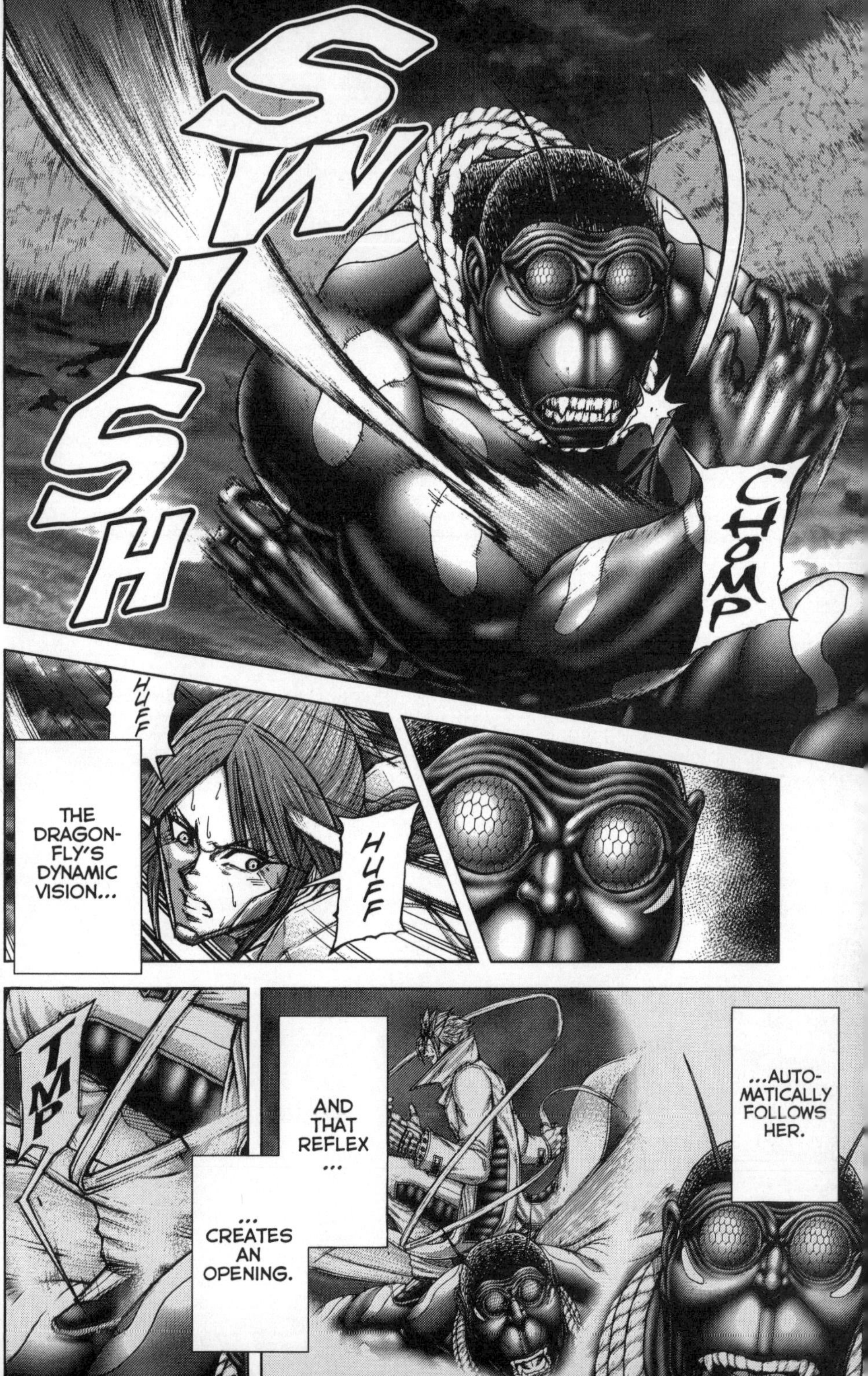
SWISH
CHOMP
HUFF
HUFF
THE DRAGON-FLY'S DYNAMIC VISION...
...AUTO-MATICALLY FOLLOWS HER.
AND THAT REFLEX ...
... CREATES AN OPENING.
TMP

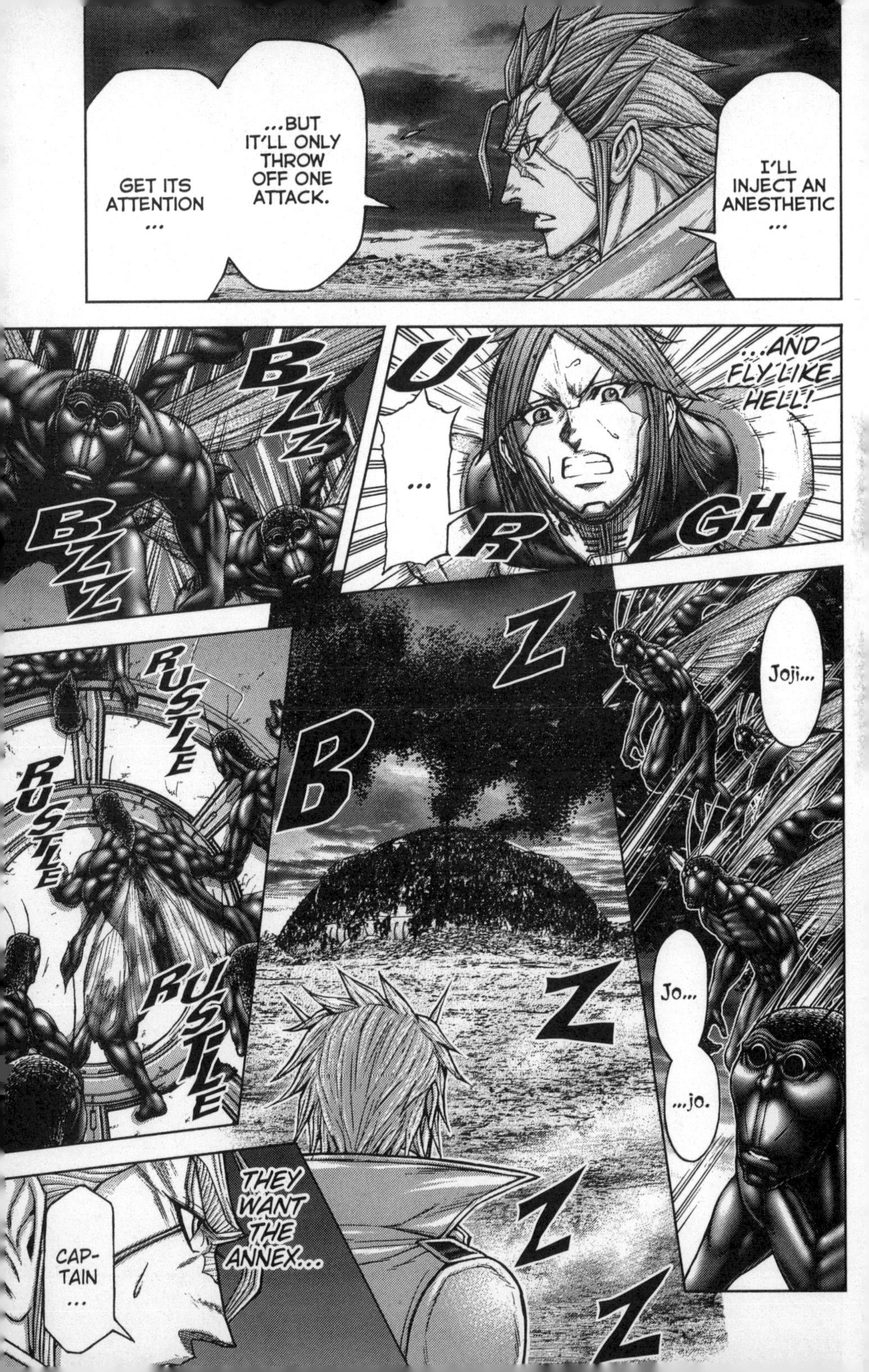

I'LL INJECT AN ANESTHETIC ...
...BUT IT'LL ONLY THROW OFF ONE ATTACK.
GET ITS ATTENTION ...
...AND FLY LIKE HELL!
URRGH
...
BZZ
BZZ
Joji...
Jo...
...jo.
BZZZZ
RUSTLE
RUSTLE
RUSTLE
THEY WANT THE ANNEX...
CAP-TAIN ...

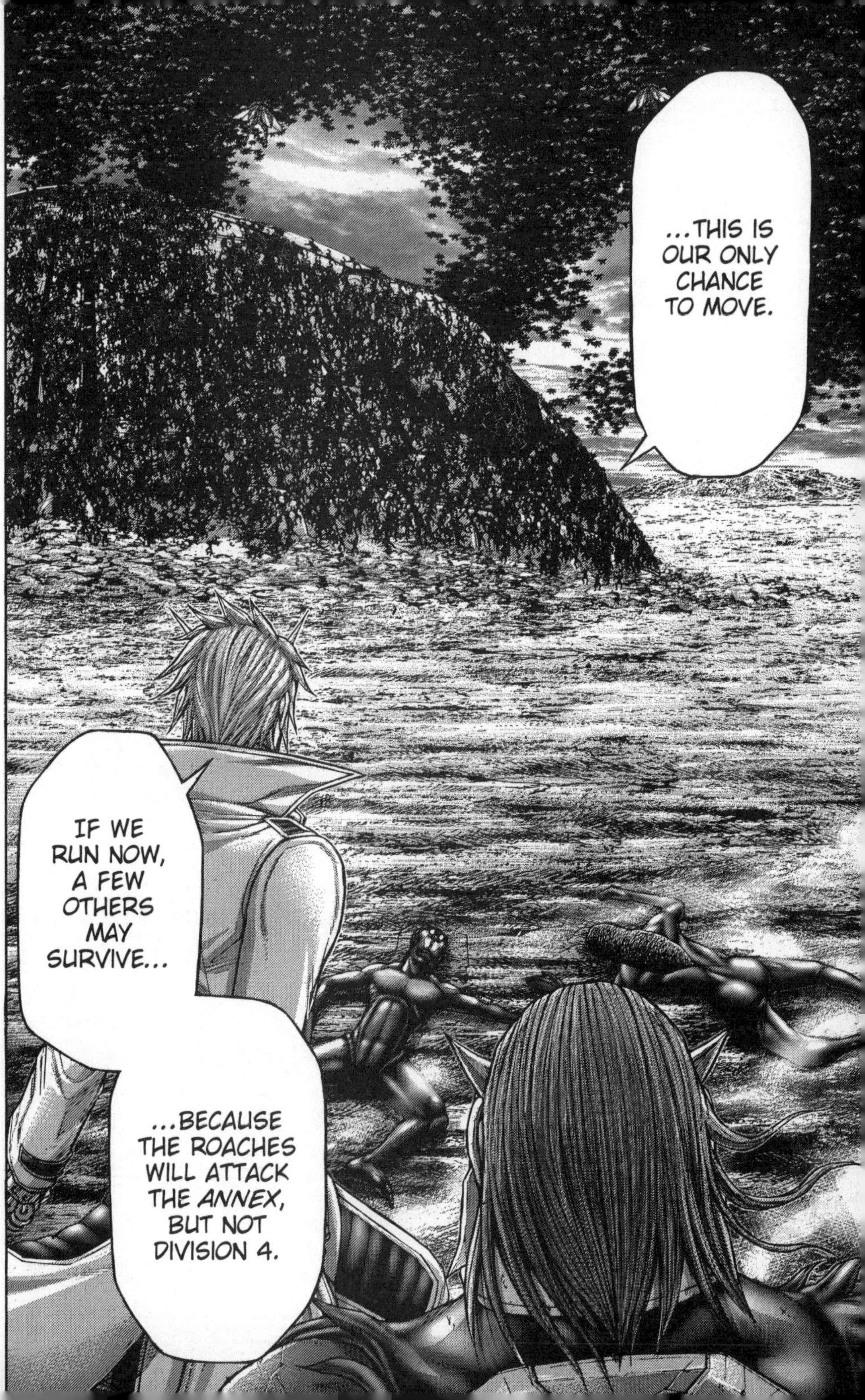
...THIS IS OUR ONLY CHANCE TO MOVE.
IF WE RUN NOW, A FEW OTHERS MAY SURVIVE...
...BECAUSE THE ROACHES WILL ATTACK THE *ANNEX*, BUT NOT DIVISION 4.

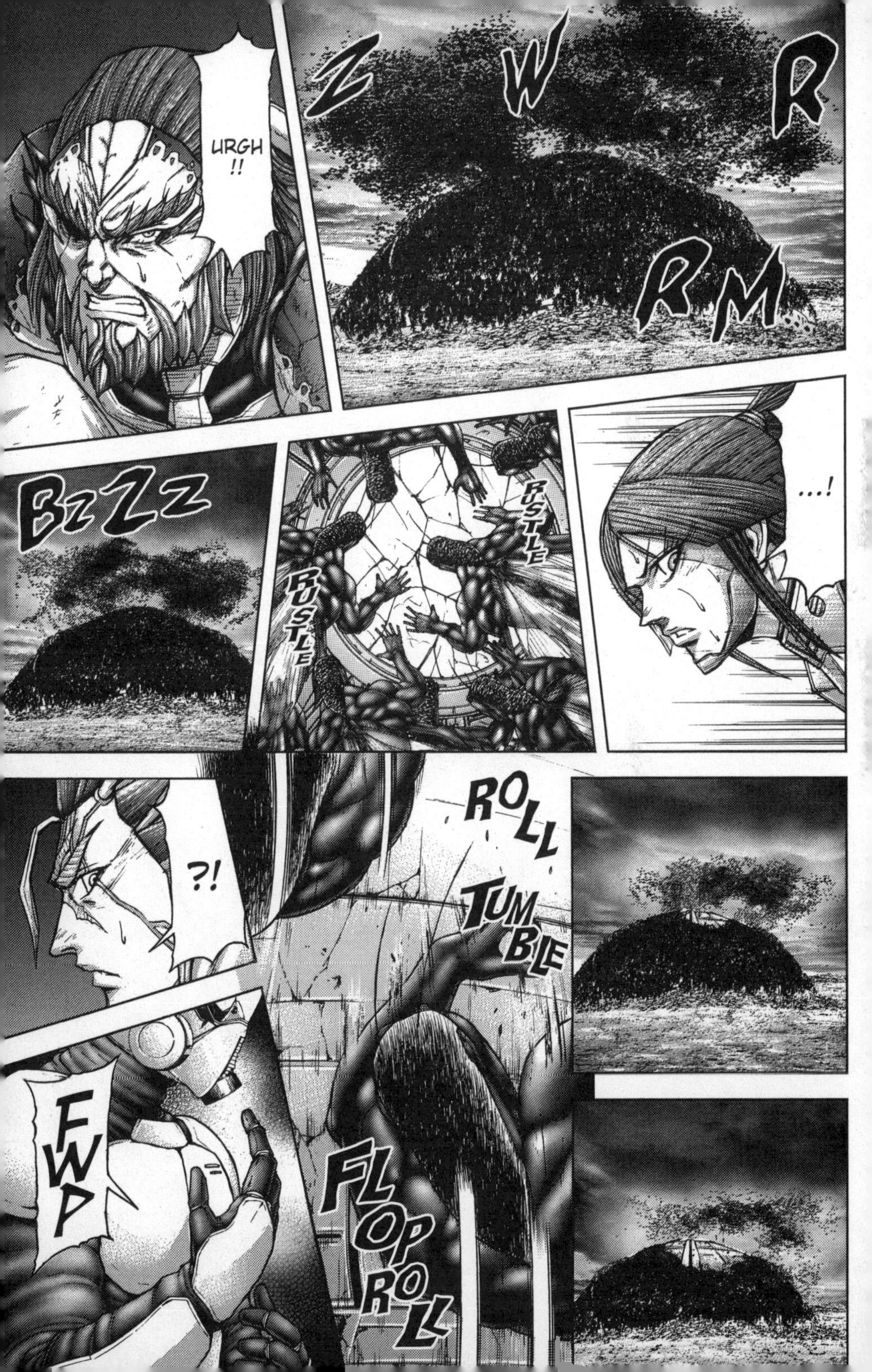
ZWRRM
URGH!!
...!
RUSTLE
RUSTLE
BZZZ
ROLL
TUMBLE
?!
FLOP ROLL
FWP

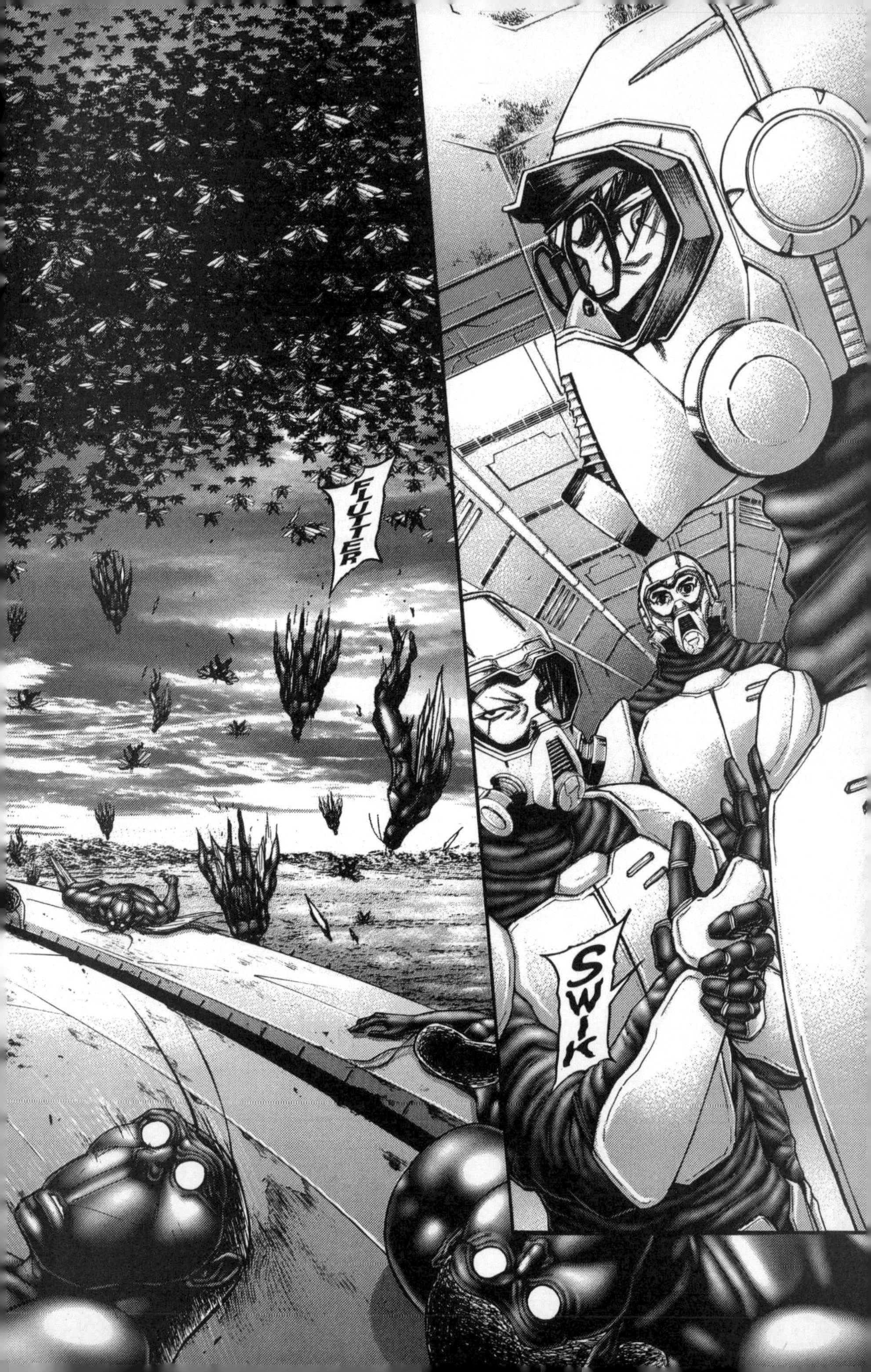
SWIK
FLUTTER

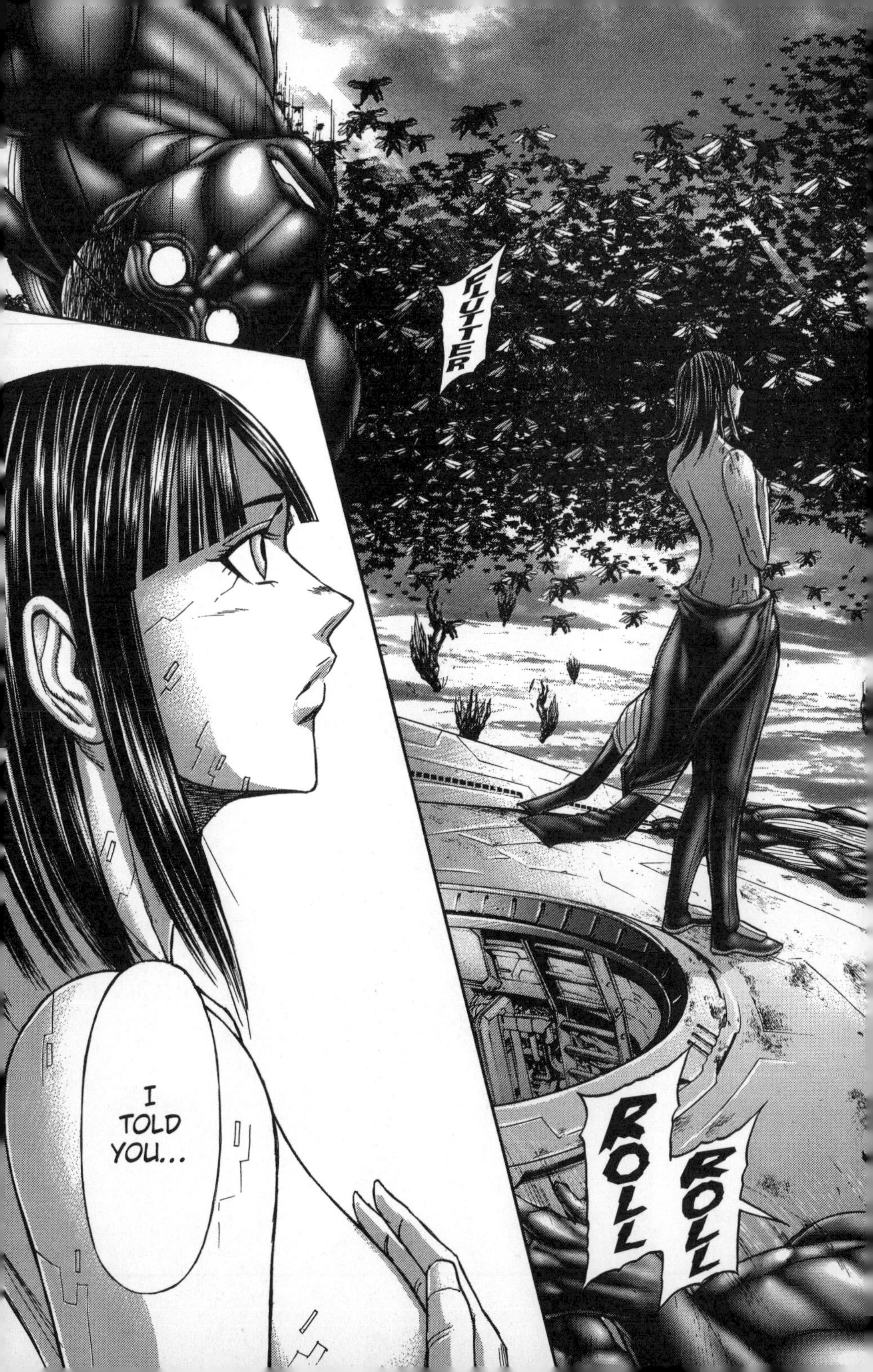
FLUTTER
ROLL ROLL
I TOLD YOU...

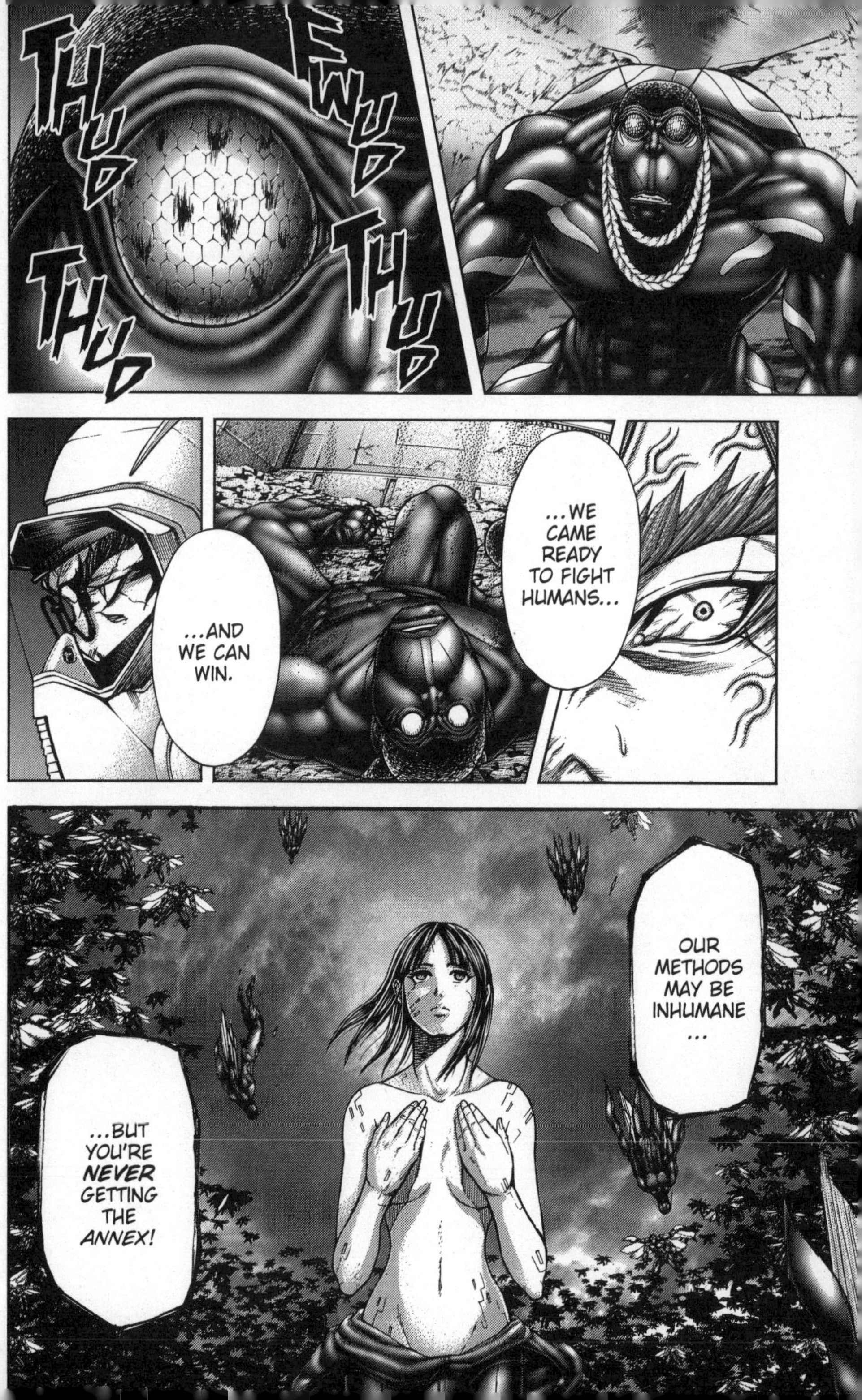
FWUD
THUD
THUD
THUD
...WE CAME READY TO FIGHT HUMANS...
...AND WE CAN WIN.
OUR METHODS MAY BE INHUMANE ...
...BUT YOU'RE *NEVER* GETTING THE *ANNEX*!

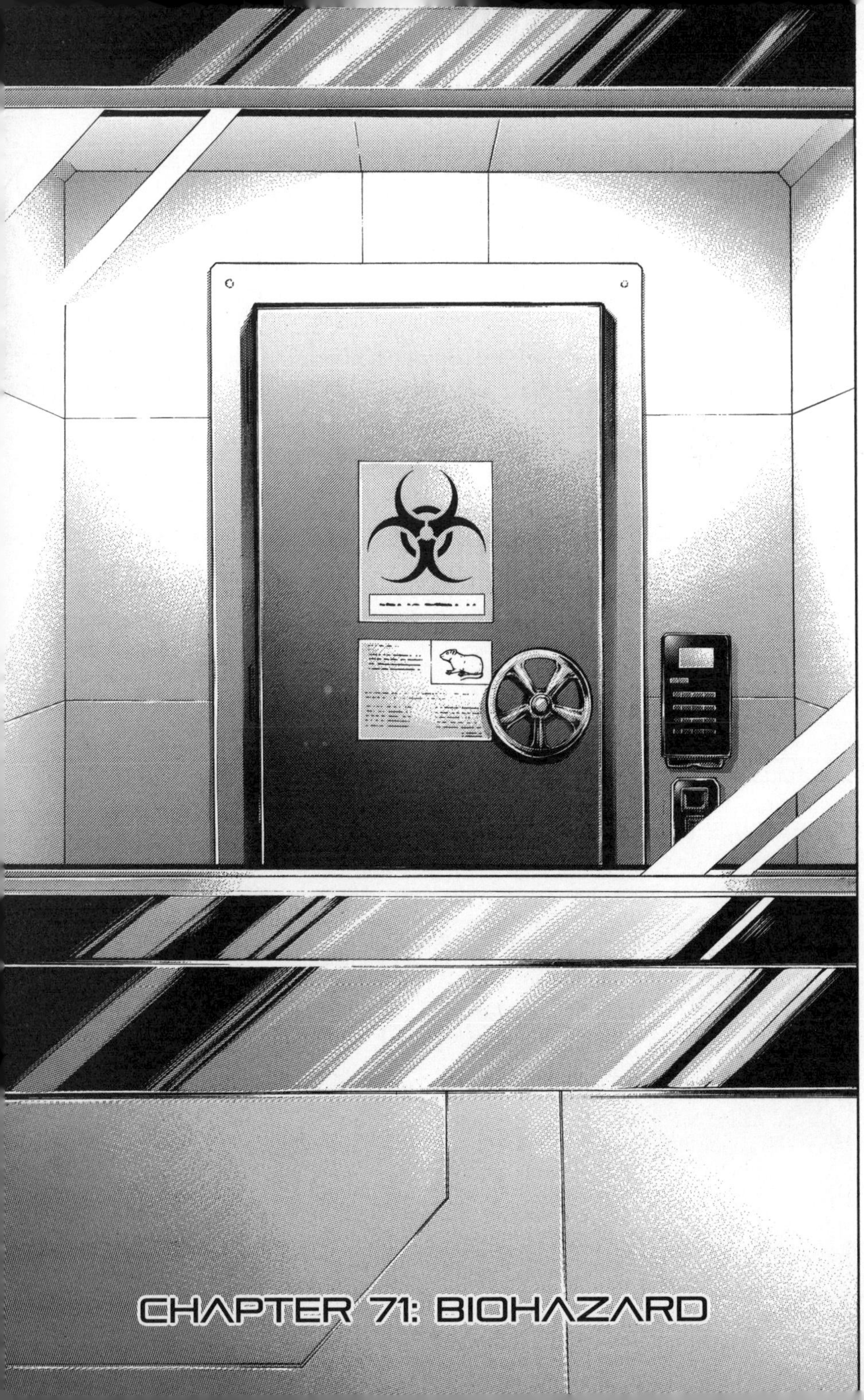
CHAPTER 71: BIOHAZARD

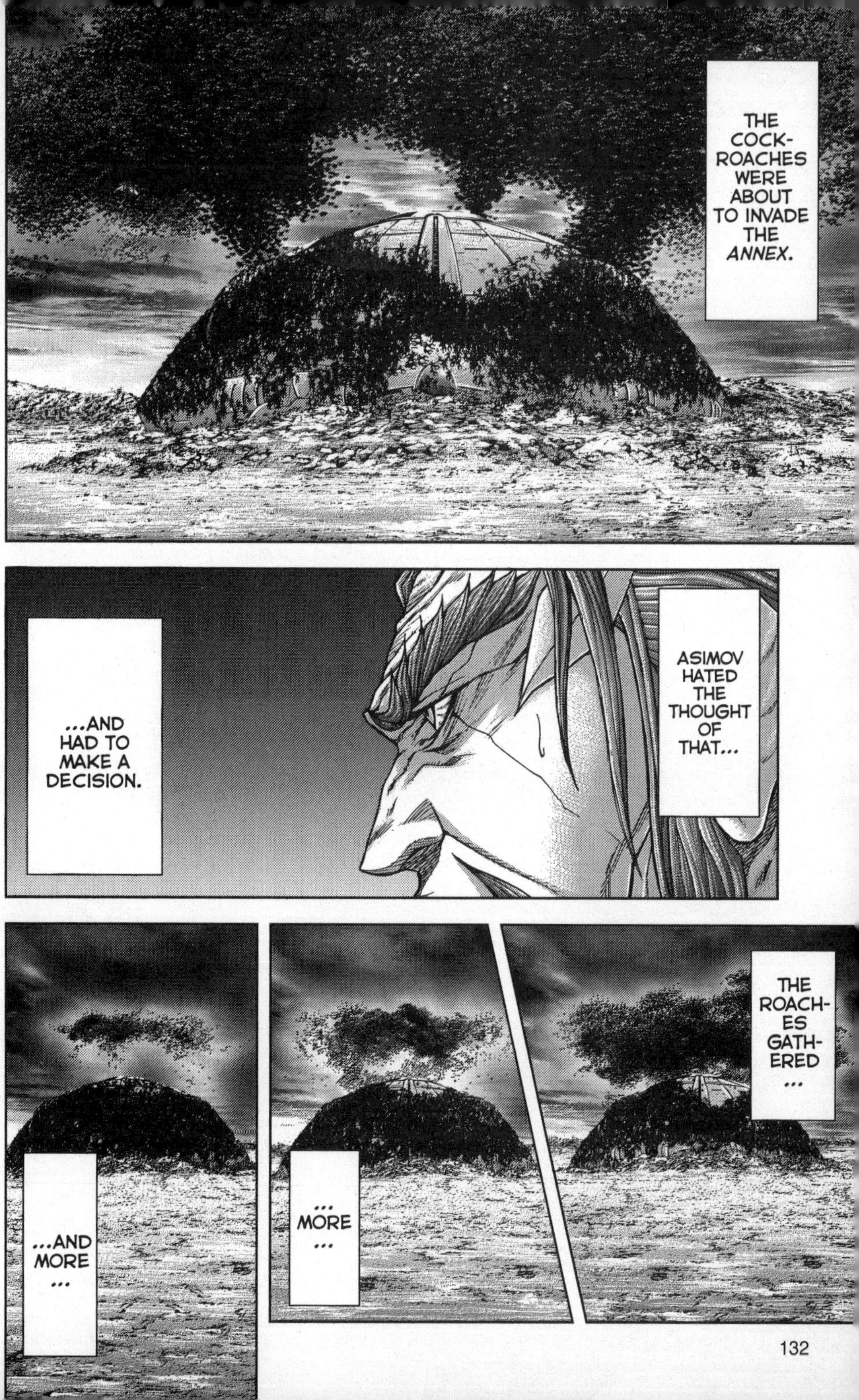
THE COCKROACHES WERE ABOUT TO INVADE THE *ANNEX*.
ASIMOV HATED THE THOUGHT OF THAT...
...AND HAD TO MAKE A DECISION.
THE ROACHES GATHERED...
...MORE...
...AND MORE...

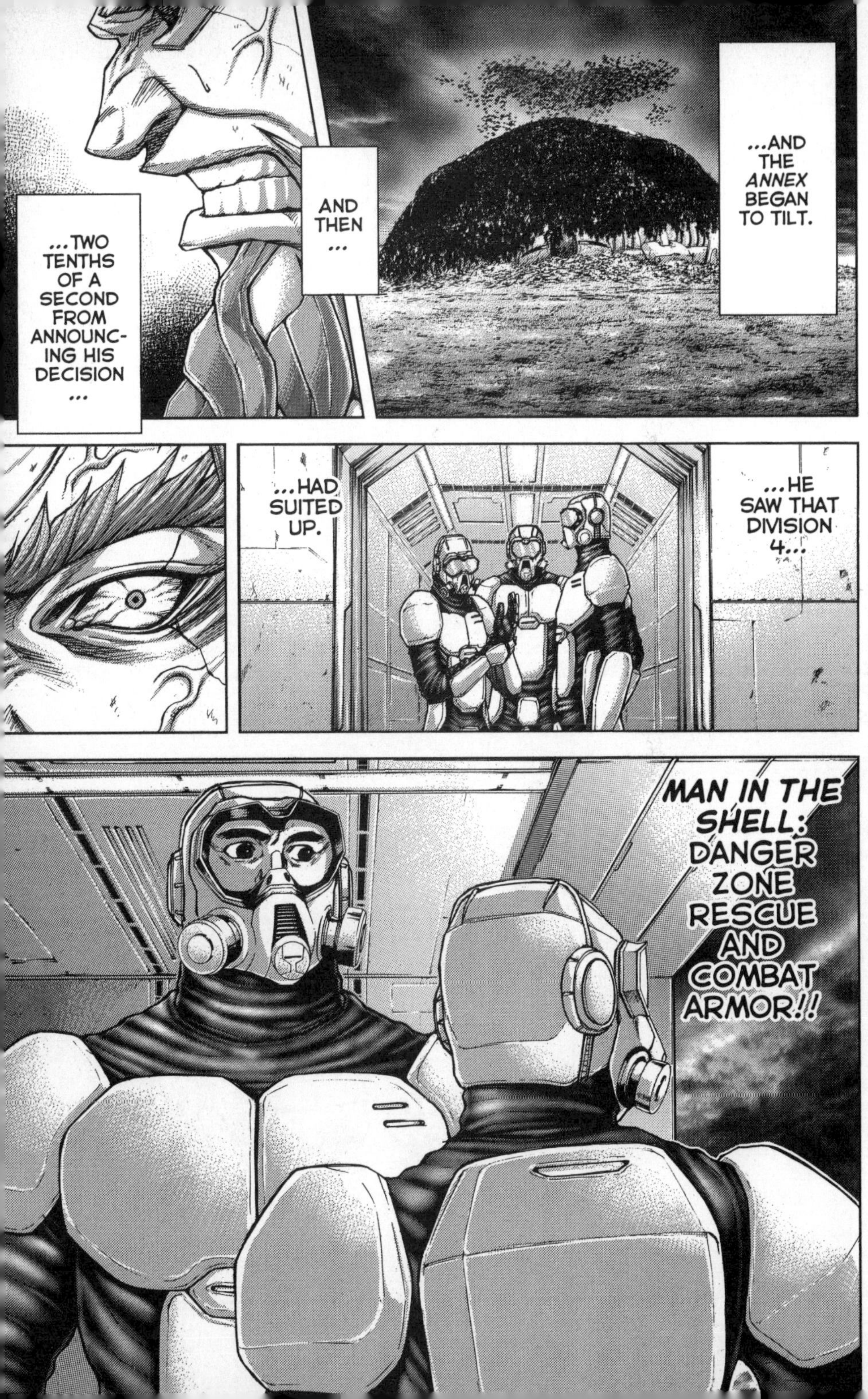
...AND THE ANNEX BEGAN TO TILT.
AND THEN ...
...TWO TENTHS OF A SECOND FROM ANNOUNCING HIS DECISION ...
...HE SAW THAT DIVISION 4...
...HAD SUITED UP.
MAN IN THE SHELL: DANGER ZONE RESCUE AND COMBAT ARMOR!!

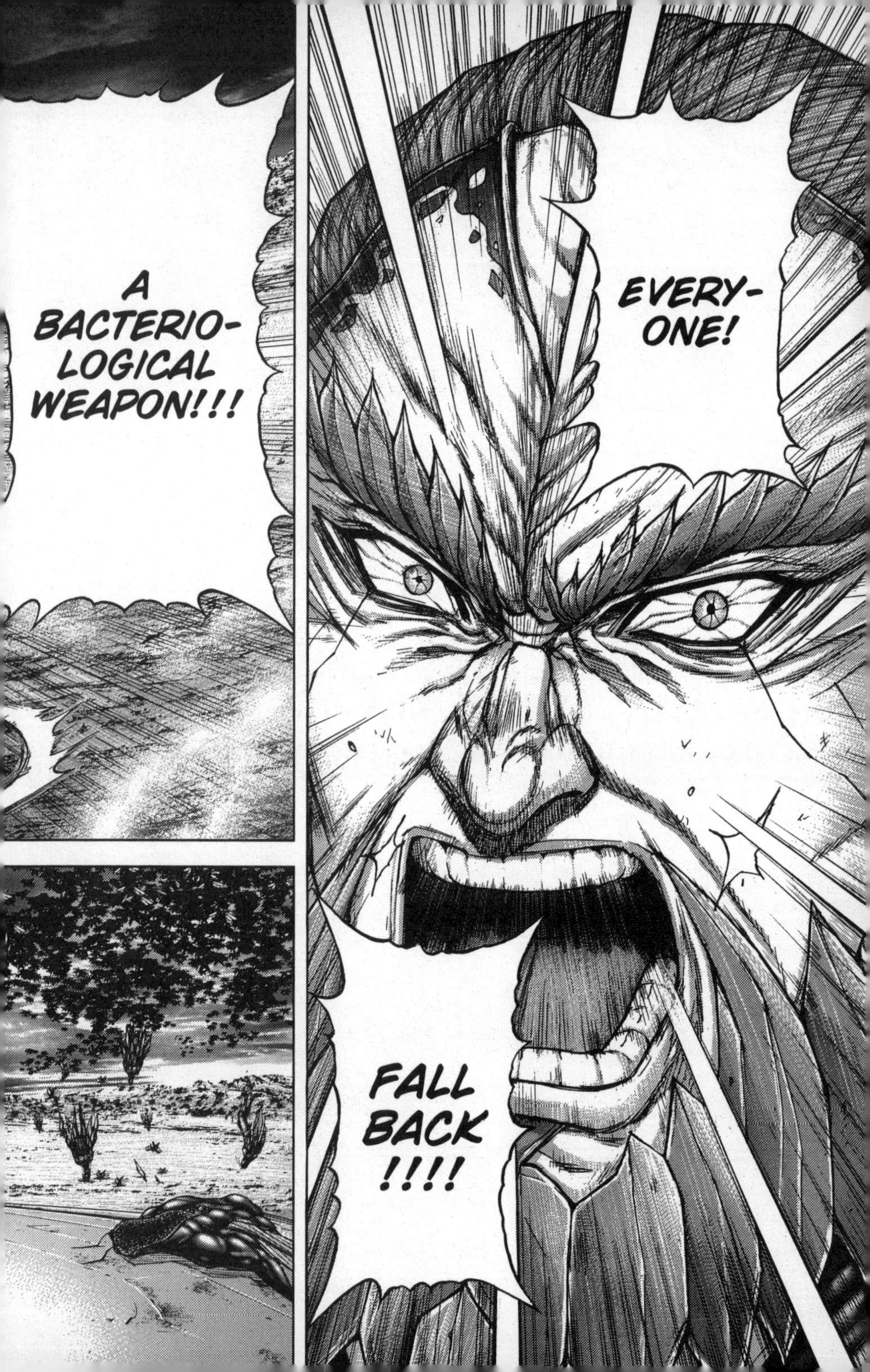
EVERY-ONE!
FALL BACK!!!!
A BACTERIO-LOGICAL WEAPON!!!

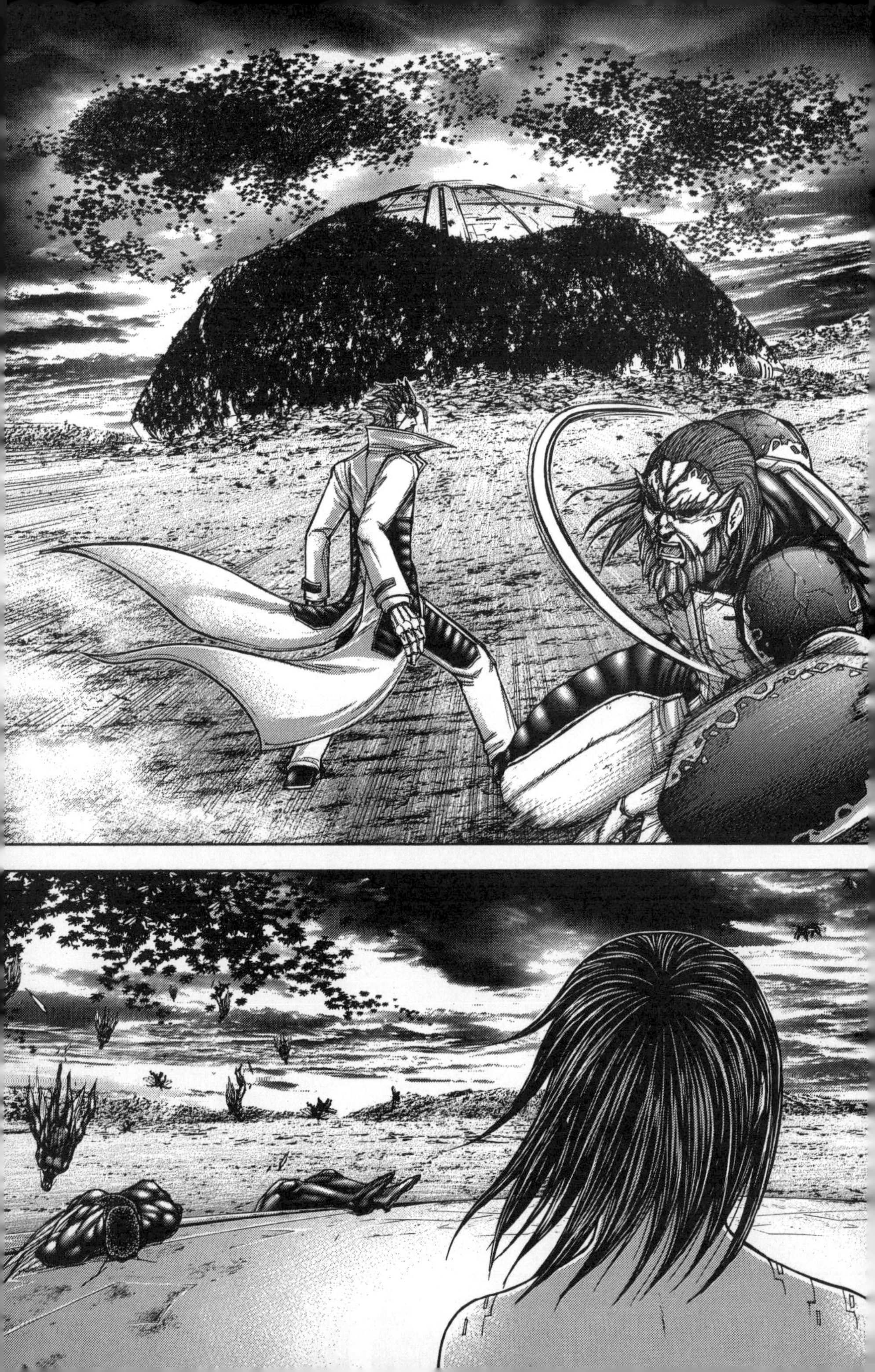

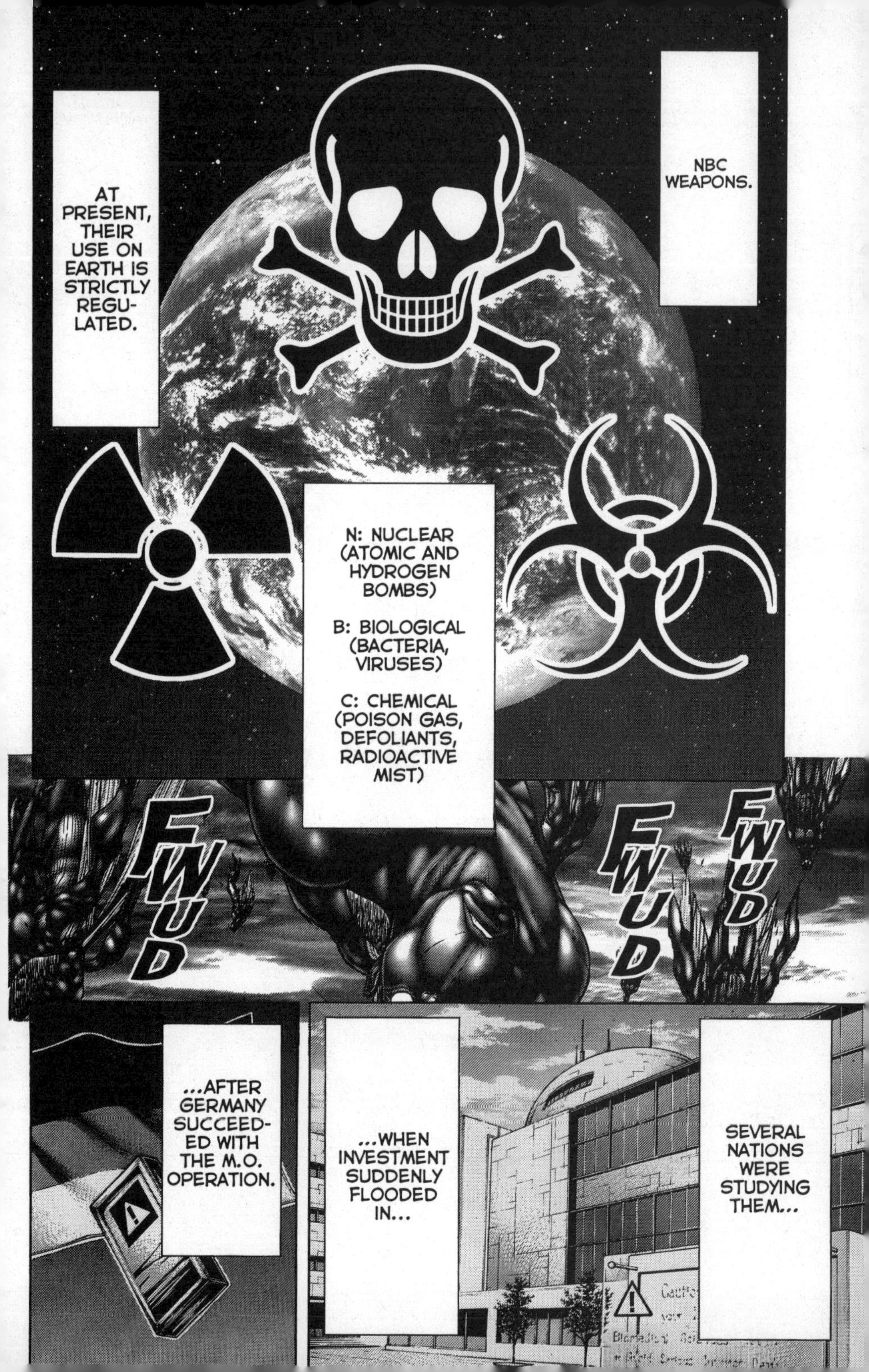
NBC WEAPONS.
AT PRESENT, THEIR USE ON EARTH IS STRICTLY REGU-LATED.
N: NUCLEAR (ATOMIC AND HYDROGEN BOMBS)
B: BIOLOGICAL (BACTERIA, VIRUSES)
C: CHEMICAL (POISON GAS, DEFOLIANTS, RADIOACTIVE MIST)
FWUD
FWUD
FWUD
SEVERAL NATIONS WERE STUDYING THEM...
...WHEN INVESTMENT SUDDENLY FLOODED IN...
...AFTER GERMANY SUCCEED-ED WITH THE M.O. OPERATION.

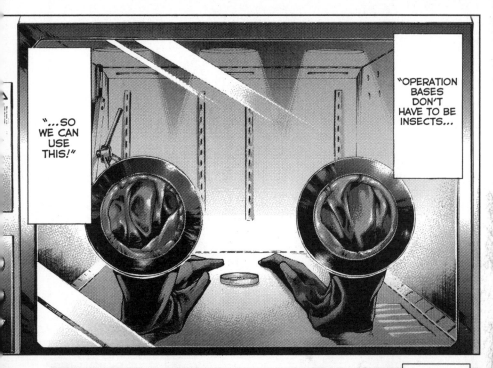

"OPERATION BASES DON'T HAVE TO BE INSECTS...
"...SO WE CAN USE THIS!"
THEY STOLE THE M.O. TECHNO-LOGY FROM GERMANY...
...JUST LIKE THEY ALL DID...
...AND EVERYONE DREAMED OF TURNING IT INTO A WEAPON...
...BUT THE COUNTRY TO APPLY IT *EFFECTIVELY* WAS *CHINA*.
"IT HAS TO BE YOU."

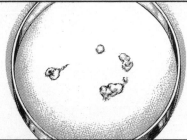

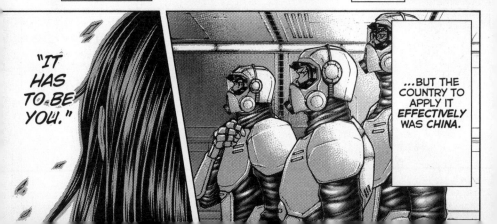

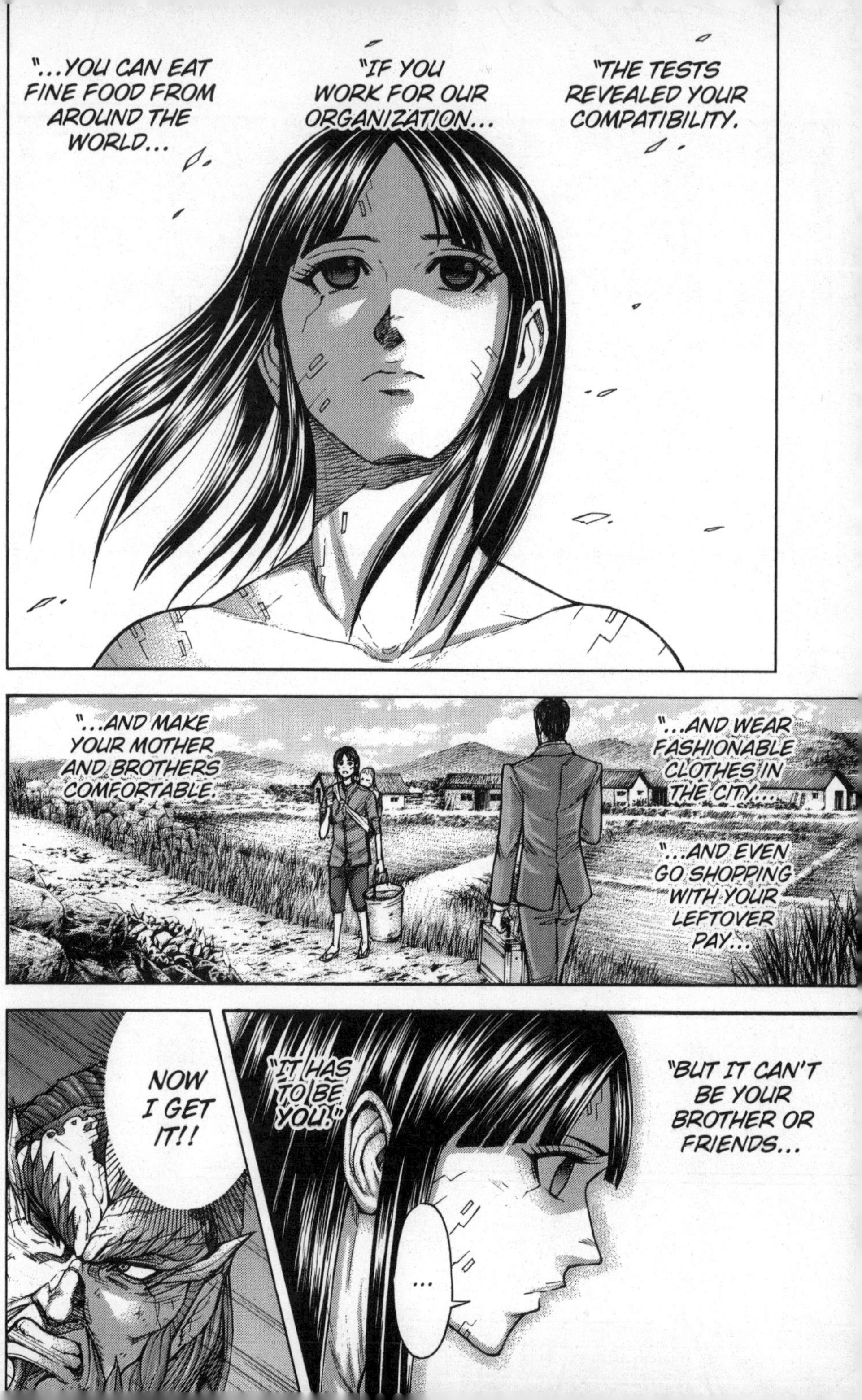
"THE TESTS REVEALED YOUR COMPATIBILITY.
"IF YOU WORK FOR OUR ORGANIZATION...
"...YOU CAN EAT FINE FOOD FROM AROUND THE WORLD...
"...AND WEAR FASHIONABLE CLOTHES IN THE CITY...
"...AND EVEN GO SHOPPING WITH YOUR LEFTOVER PAY...
"...AND MAKE YOUR MOTHER AND BROTHERS COMFORTABLE.
"BUT IT CAN'T BE YOUR BROTHER OR FRIENDS...
"IT HAS TO BE YOU."
...
NOW I GET IT!!

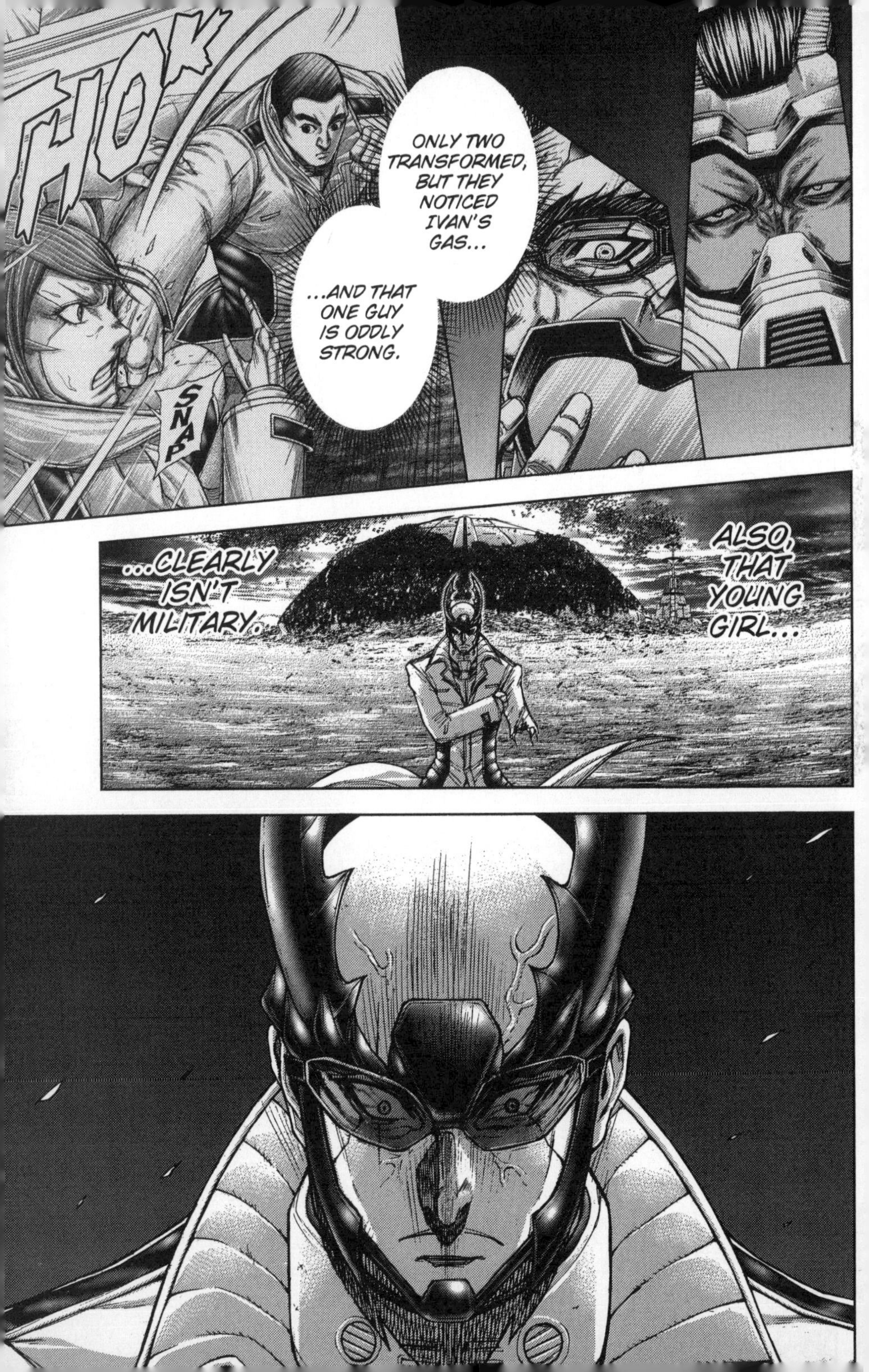
ONLY TWO TRANSFORMED, BUT THEY NOTICED IVAN'S GAS...
...AND THAT ONE GUY IS ODDLY STRONG.
THOK
SNAP
ALSO, THAT YOUNG GIRL...
...CLEARLY ISN'T MILITARY.

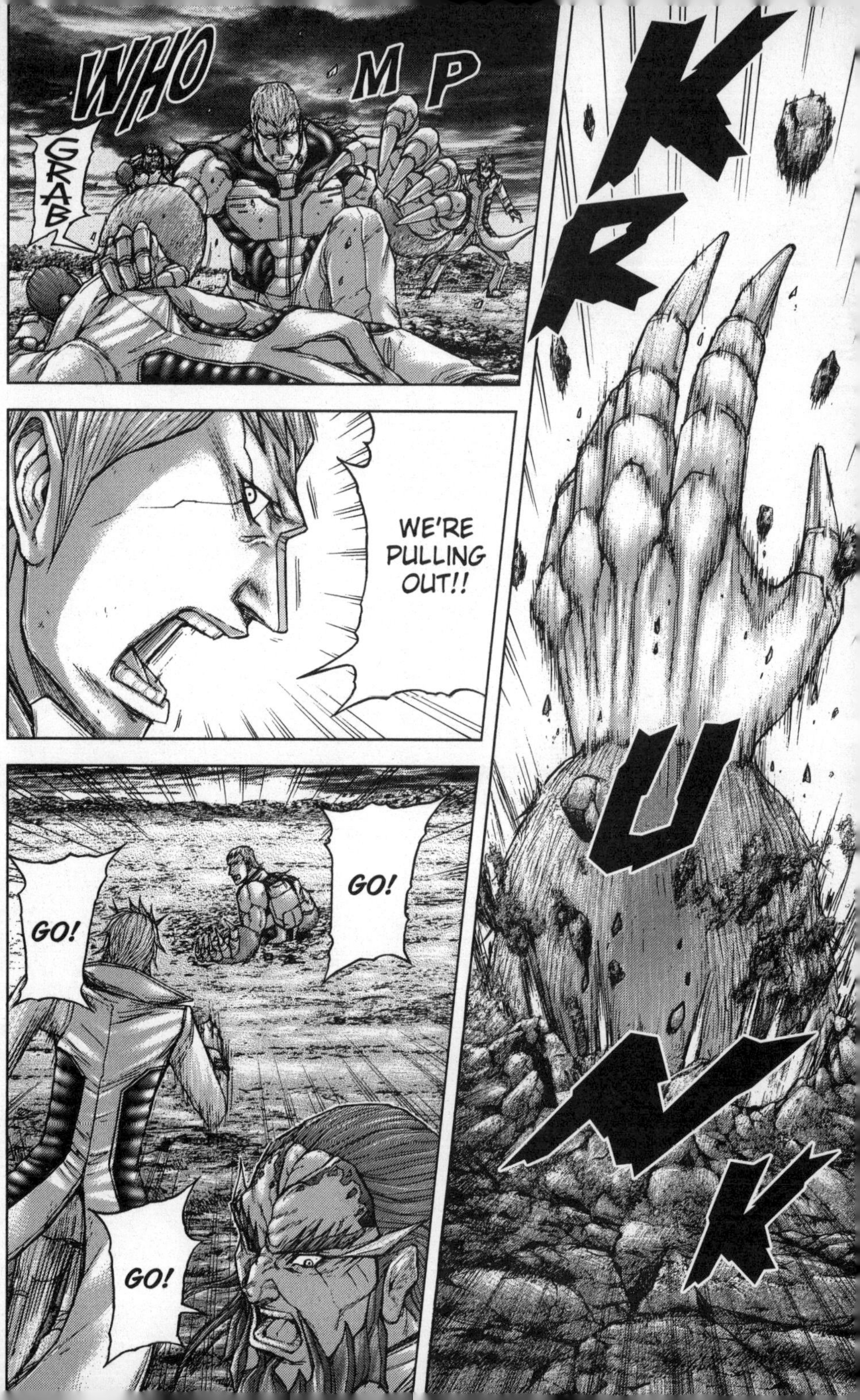
KRUNK
WHOMP
GRAB
WE'RE PULLING OUT!!
GO!
GO!
GO!

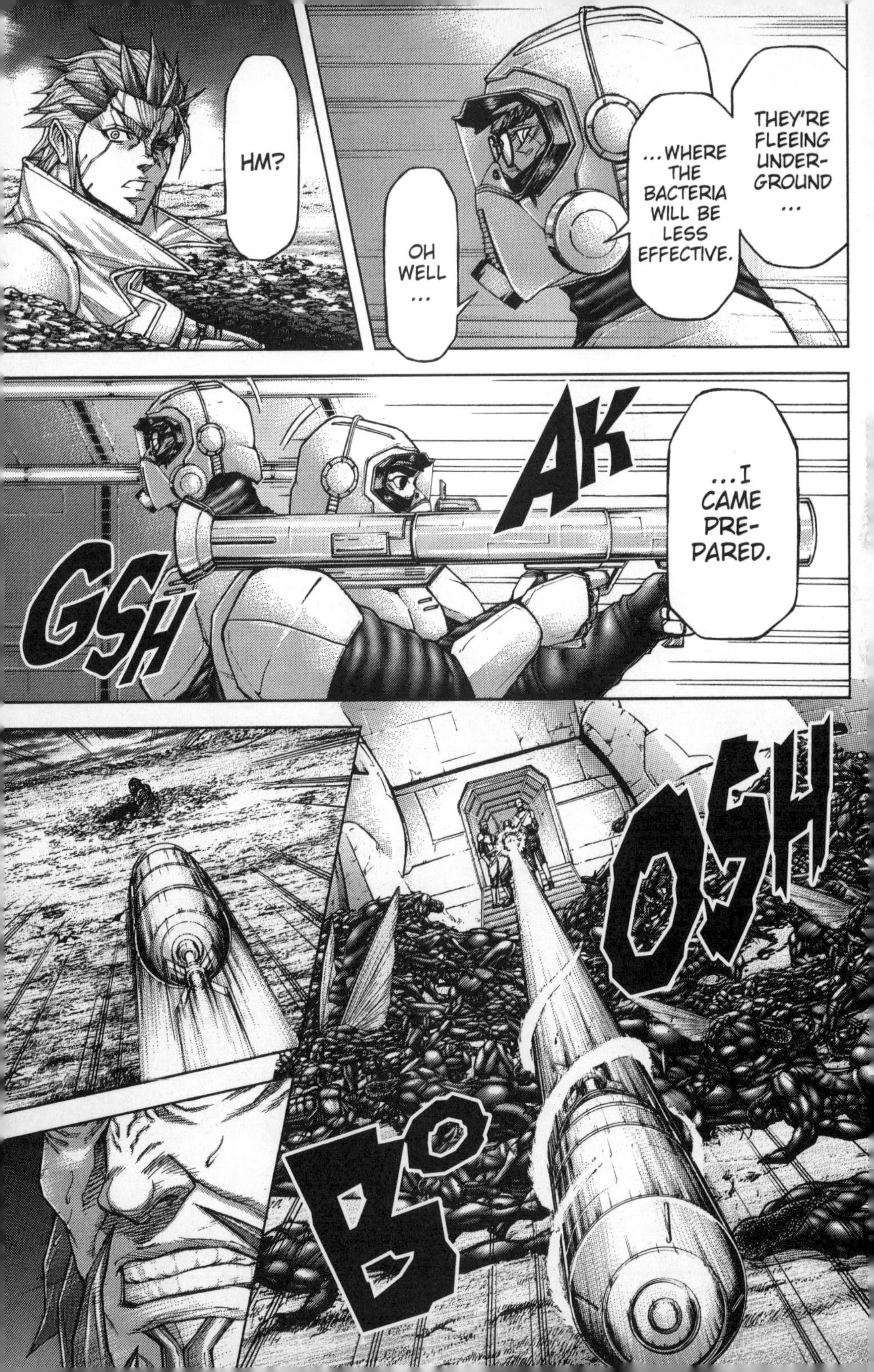

THEY'RE FLEEING UNDER-GROUND...
...WHERE THE BACTERIA WILL BE LESS EFFECTIVE.
OH WELL...
HM?
...I CAME PRE-PARED.
AK
GSH
OSH
BO

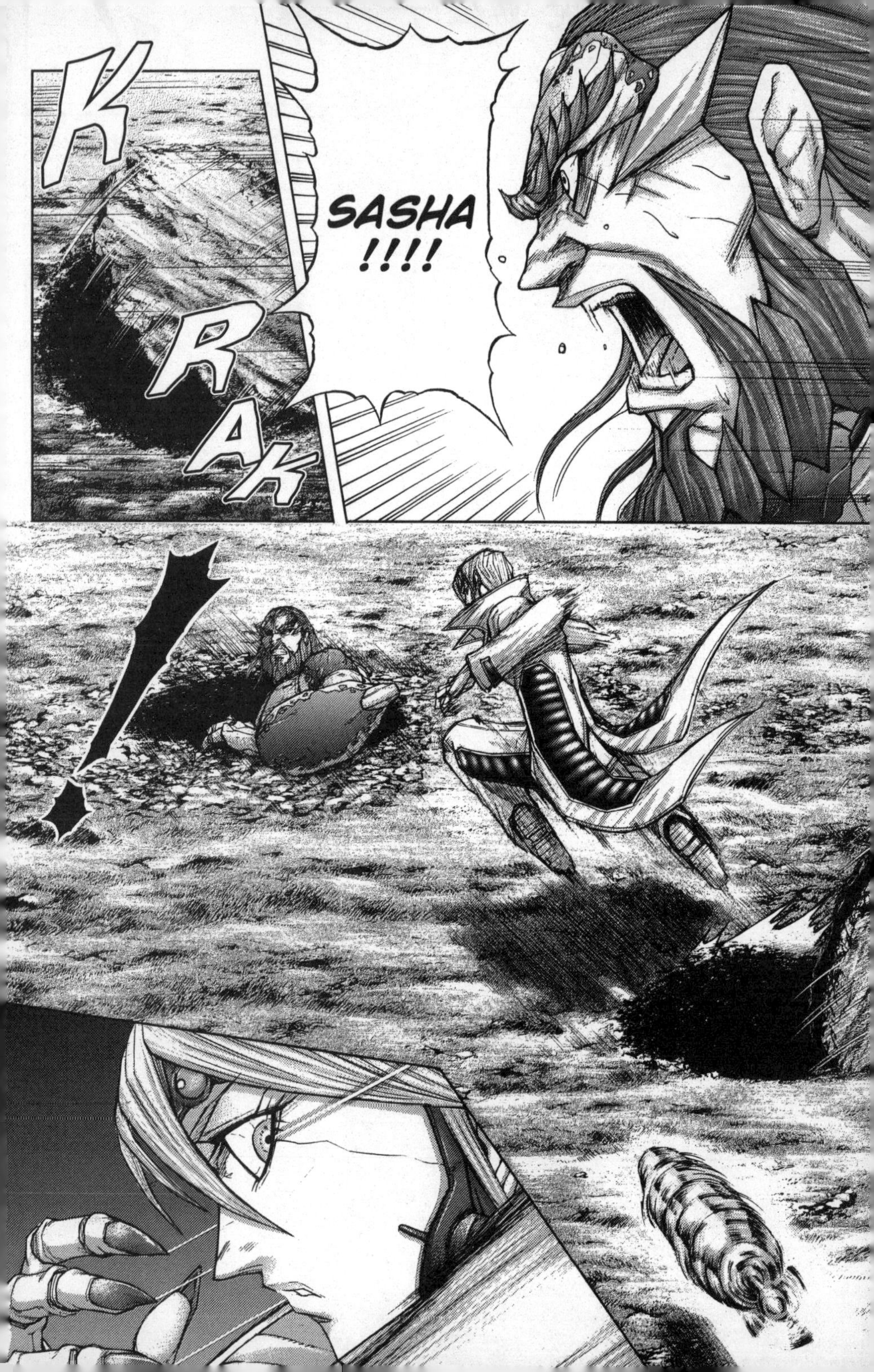
SASHA !!!!
KRAK
!

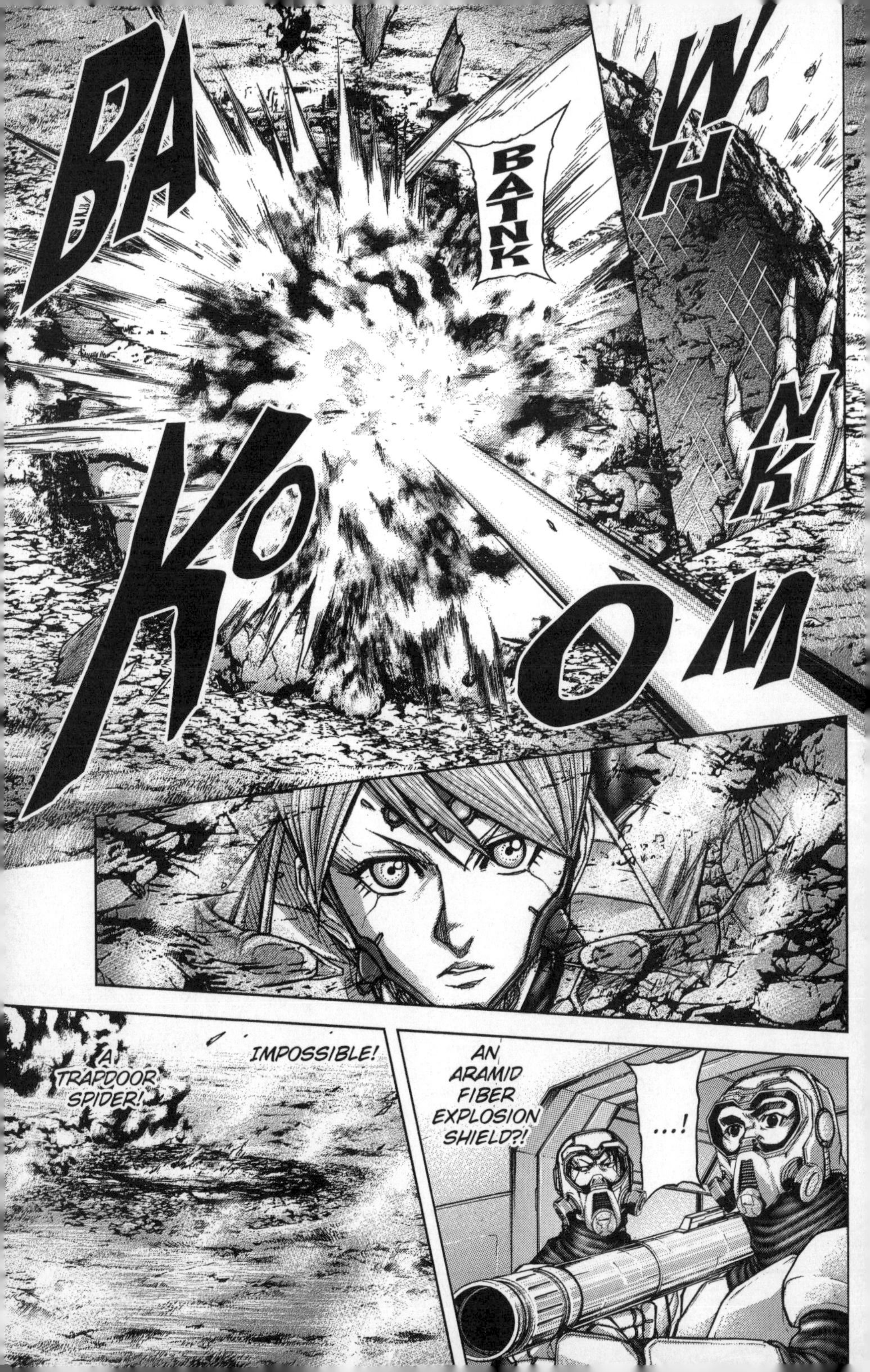
WHANK
BATINK
BAKOOM
AN ARAMID FIBER EXPLOSION SHIELD?!
...!
IMPOSSIBLE!
A TRAPDOOR SPIDER!

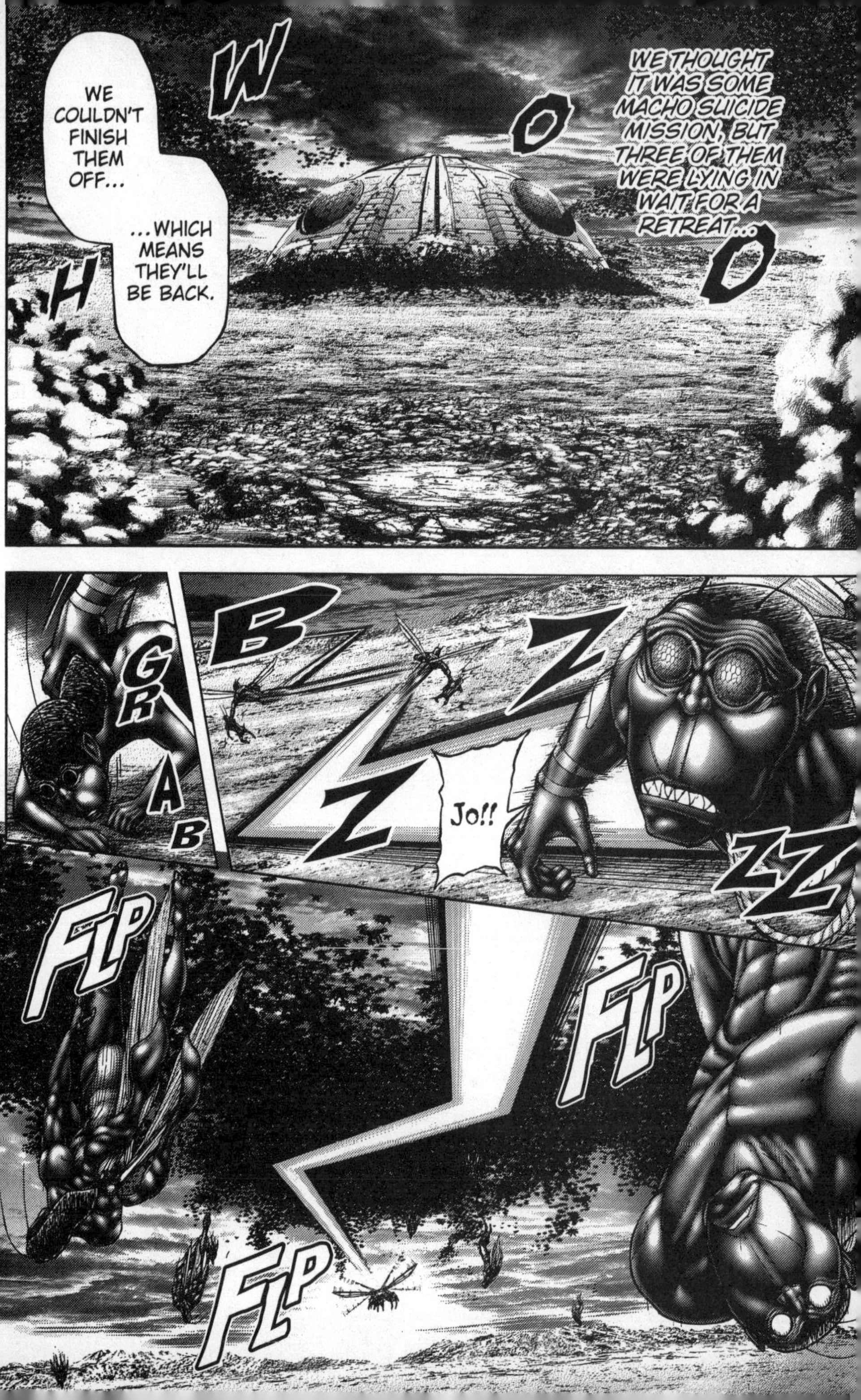
WHOOO
WE THOUGHT IT WAS SOME MACHO SUICIDE MISSION, BUT THREE OF THEM WERE LYING IN WAIT FOR A RETREAT...
WE COULDN'T FINISH THEM OFF...
...WHICH MEANS THEY'LL BE BACK.
ZZZ
Jo!!
BZZZ
GRAB
FLP
FLP
FLP

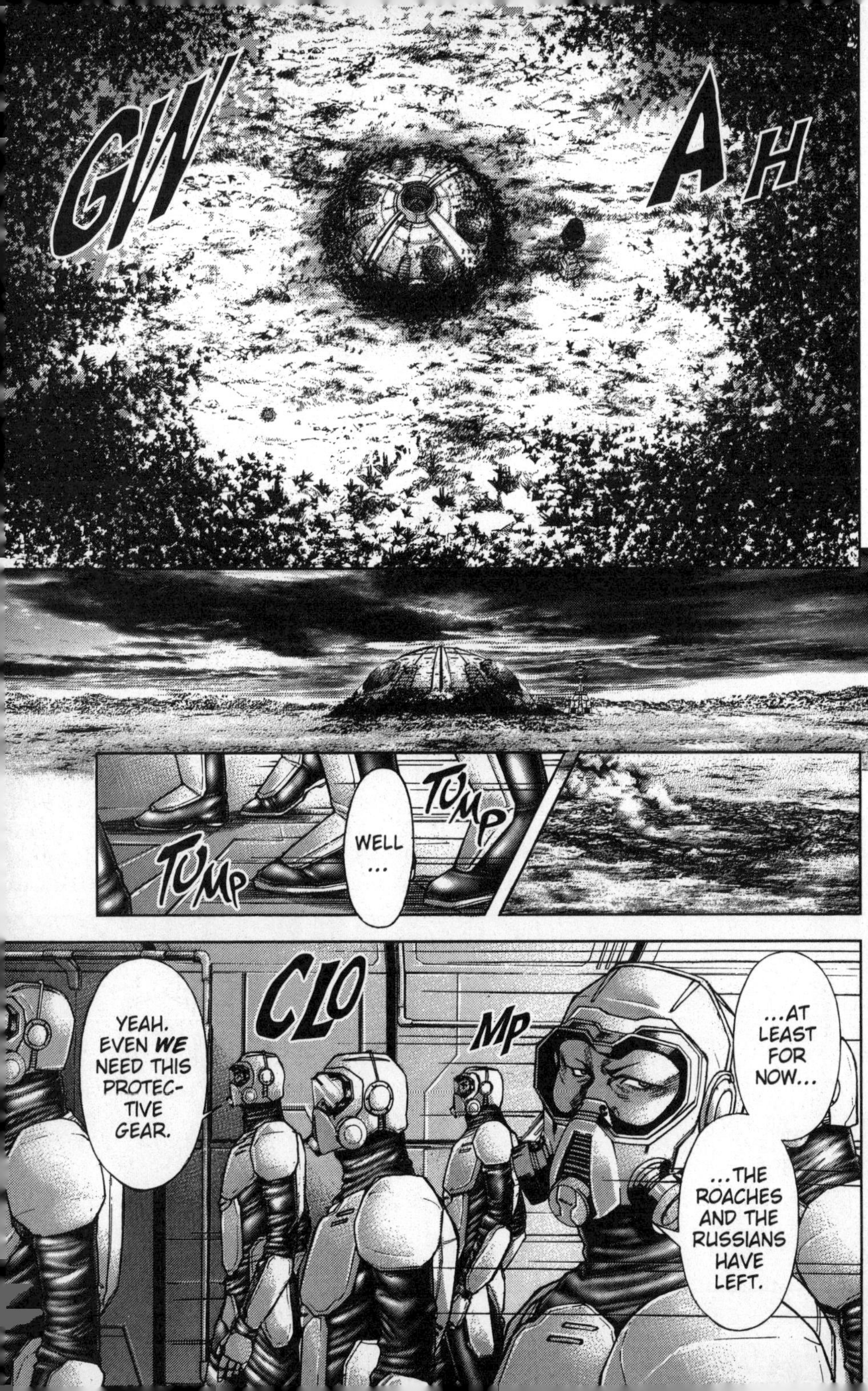
GW AH
TUMP
WELL ...
TUMP
...AT LEAST FOR NOW...
...THE ROACHES AND THE RUSSIANS HAVE LEFT.
CLOMP
YEAH. EVEN *WE* NEED THIS PROTEC-TIVE GEAR.

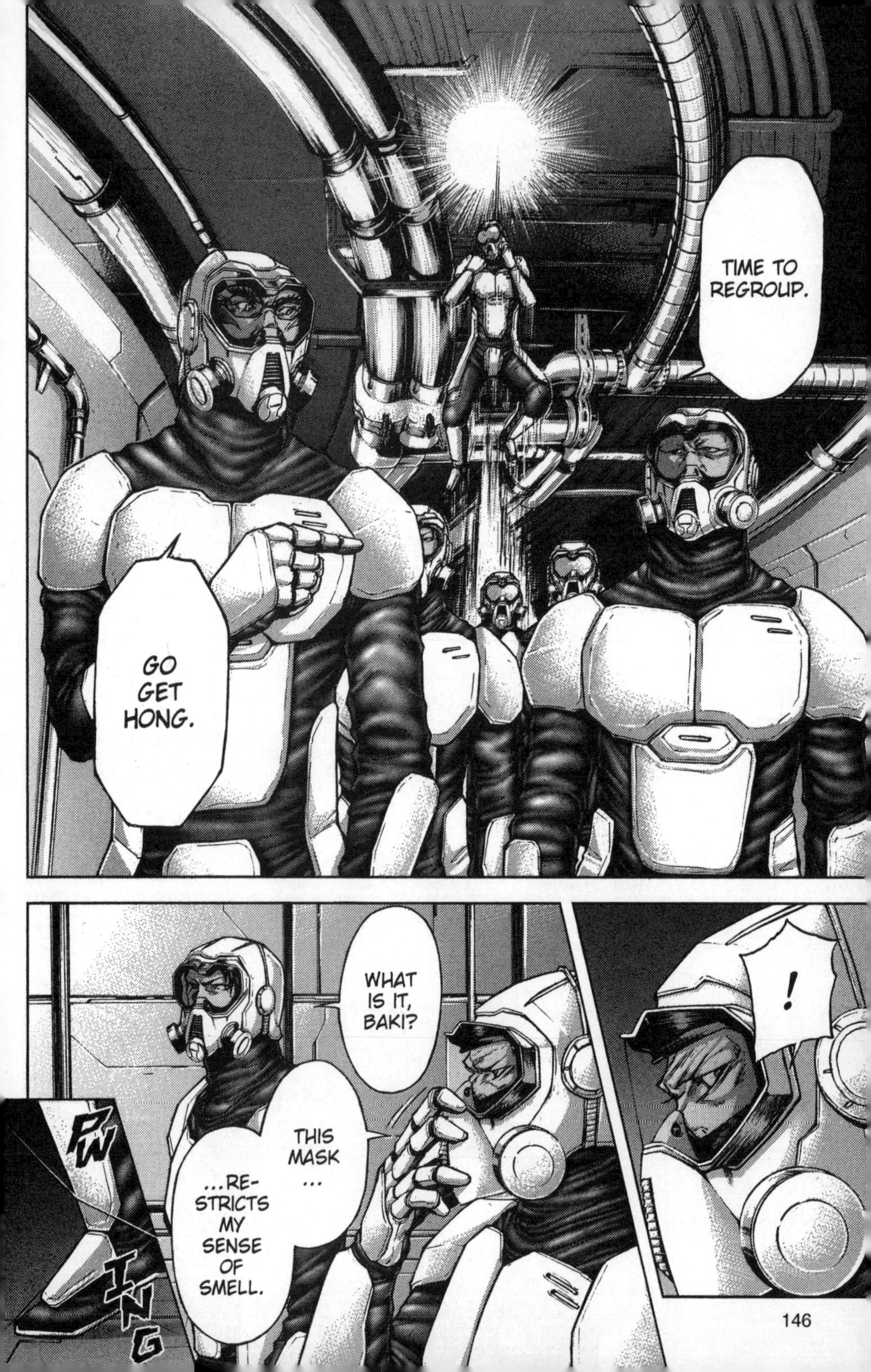
TIME TO REGROUP.
GO GET HONG.
!
WHAT IS IT, BAKI?
THIS MASK ...
...RE-STRICTS MY SENSE OF SMELL.
PWING

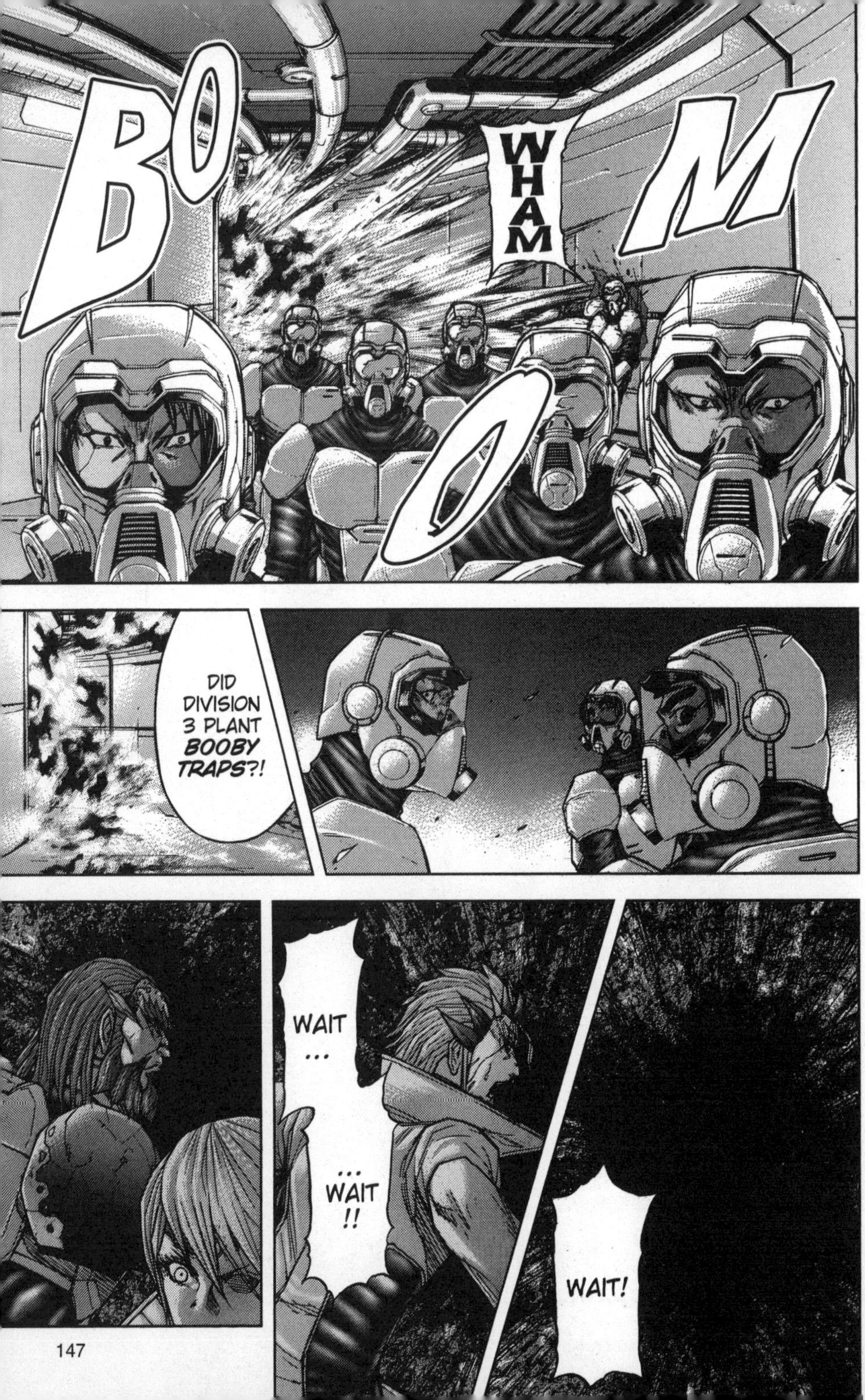
BOOM
WHAM
DID DIVISION 3 PLANT BOOBY TRAPS?!
WAIT!
WAIT ...
... WAIT !!

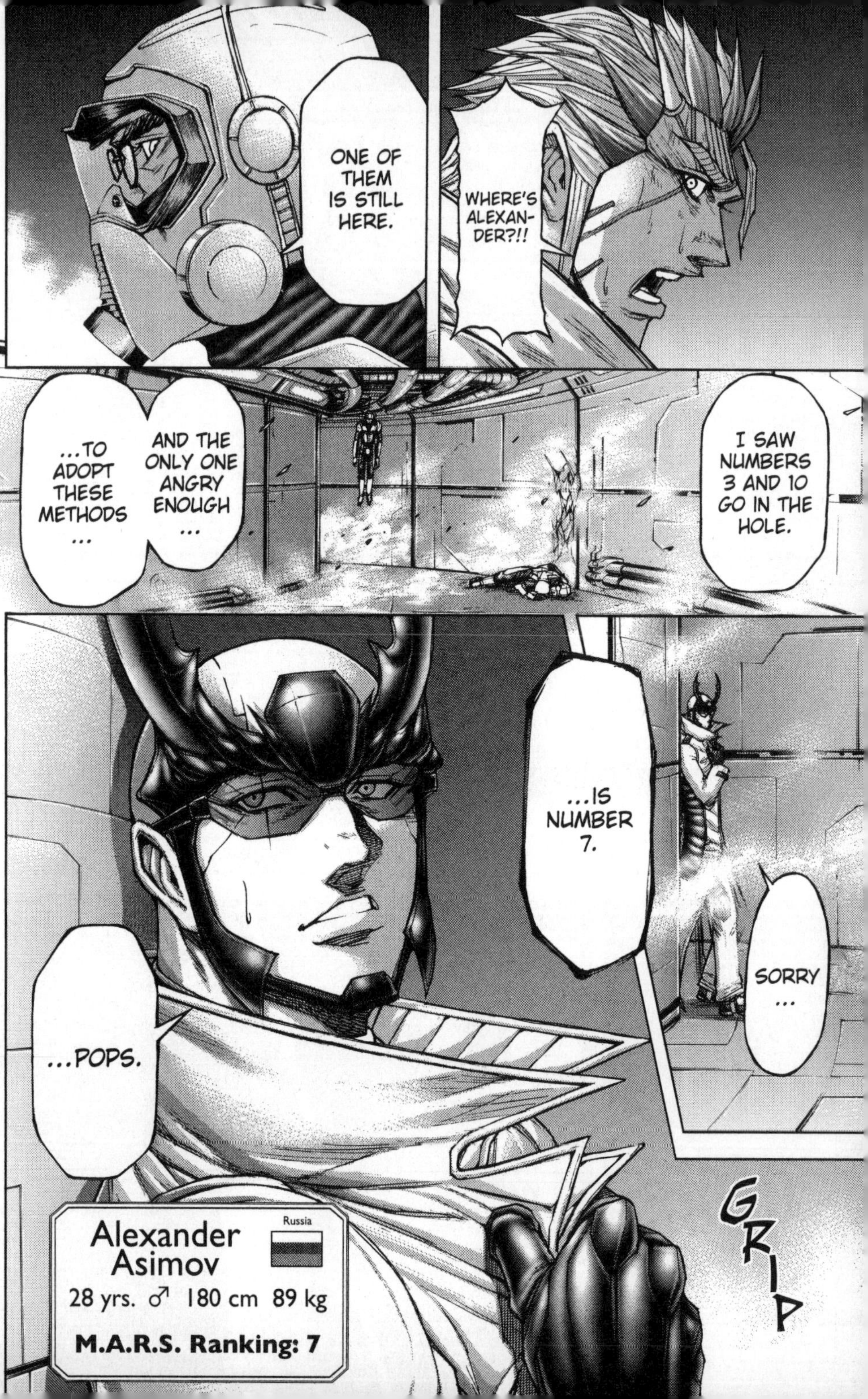
WHERE'S ALEXANDER?!!
ONE OF THEM IS STILL HERE.
I SAW NUMBERS 3 AND 10 GO IN THE HOLE.
AND THE ONLY ONE ANGRY ENOUGH...
...TO ADOPT THESE METHODS...
...IS NUMBER 7.
SORRY...
...POPS.
GRIP
Alexander Asimov
Russia
28 yrs. ♂ 180 cm 89 kg
M.A.R.S. Ranking: 7

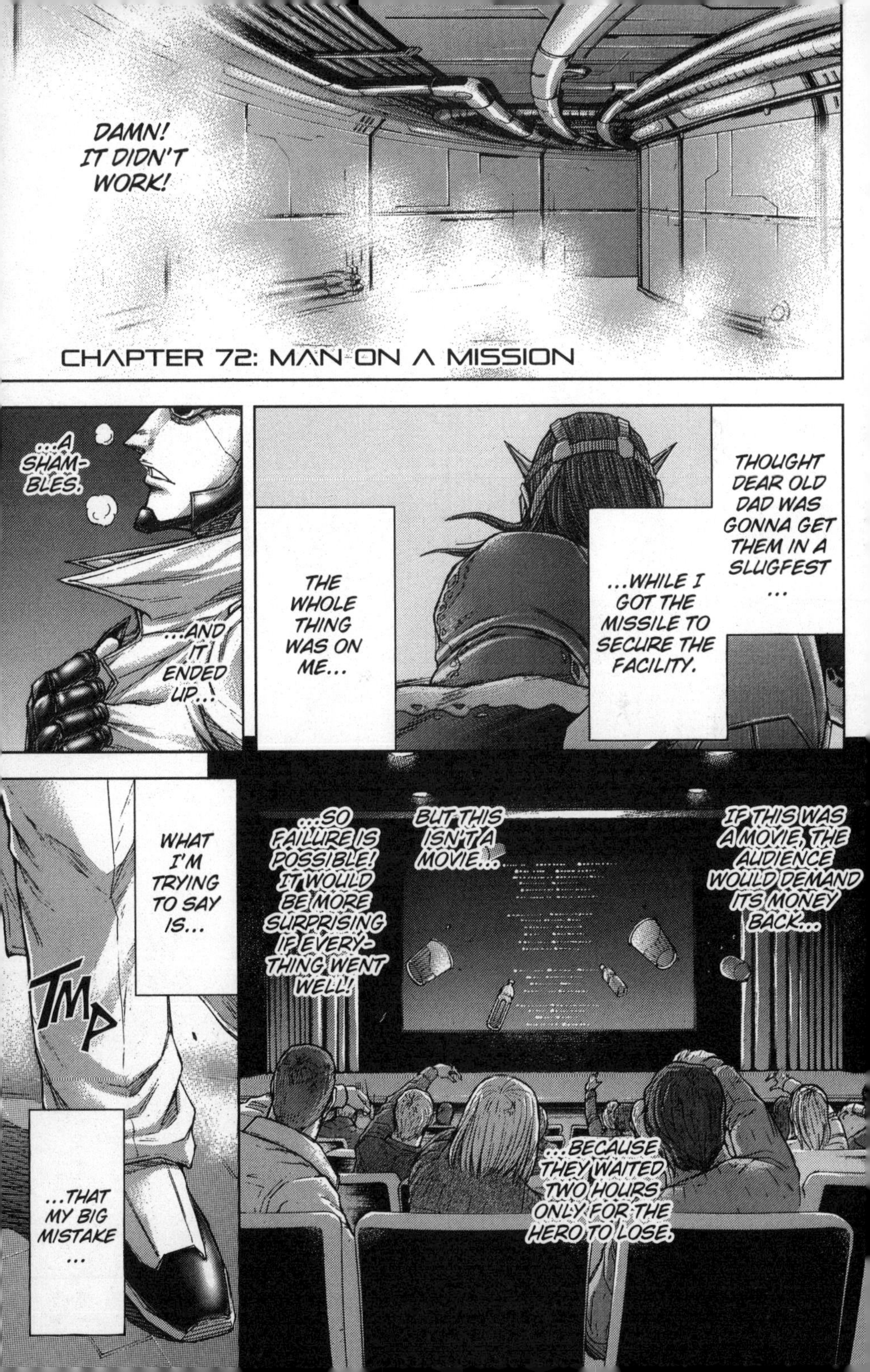

DAMN! IT DIDN'T WORK!
CHAPTER 72: MAN ON A MISSION
THOUGHT DEAR OLD DAD WAS GONNA GET THEM IN A SLUGFEST...
...WHILE I GOT THE MISSILE TO SECURE THE FACILITY.
THE WHOLE THING WAS ON ME...
...AND IT ENDED UP...
...A SHAMBLES.
IF THIS WAS A MOVIE, THE AUDIENCE WOULD DEMAND ITS MONEY BACK...
...BECAUSE THEY WAITED TWO HOURS ONLY FOR THE HERO TO LOSE.
BUT THIS ISN'T A MOVIE...
...SO FAILURE IS POSSIBLE! IT WOULD BE MORE SURPRISING IF EVERYTHING WENT WELL!
WHAT I'M TRYING TO SAY IS...
TMP
...THAT MY BIG MISTAKE...

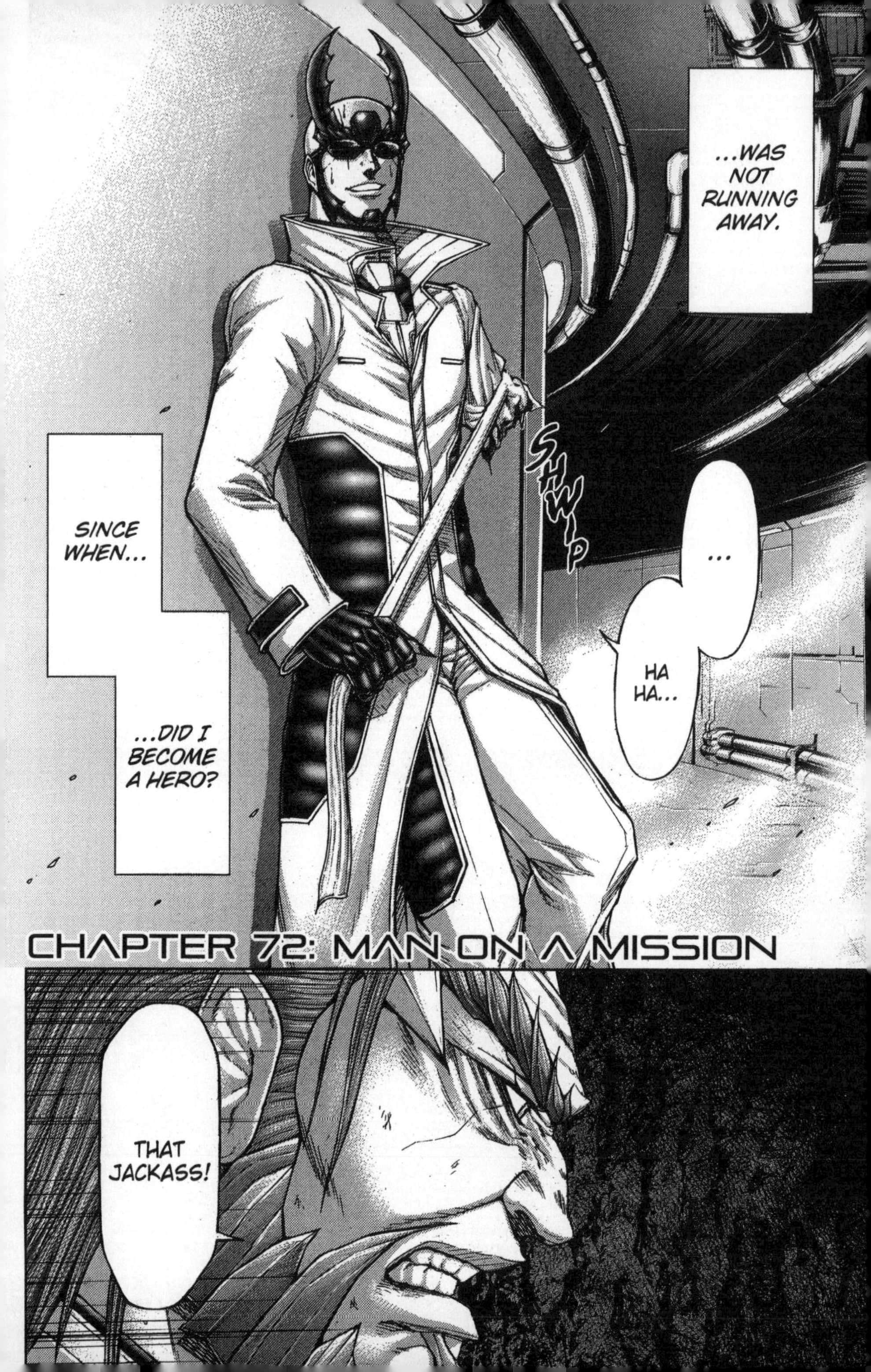
...WAS NOT RUNNING AWAY.
SINCE WHEN...
...DID I BECOME A HERO?
SHWIP
...
HA HA...
CHAPTER 72: MAN ON A MISSION
THAT JACKASS!

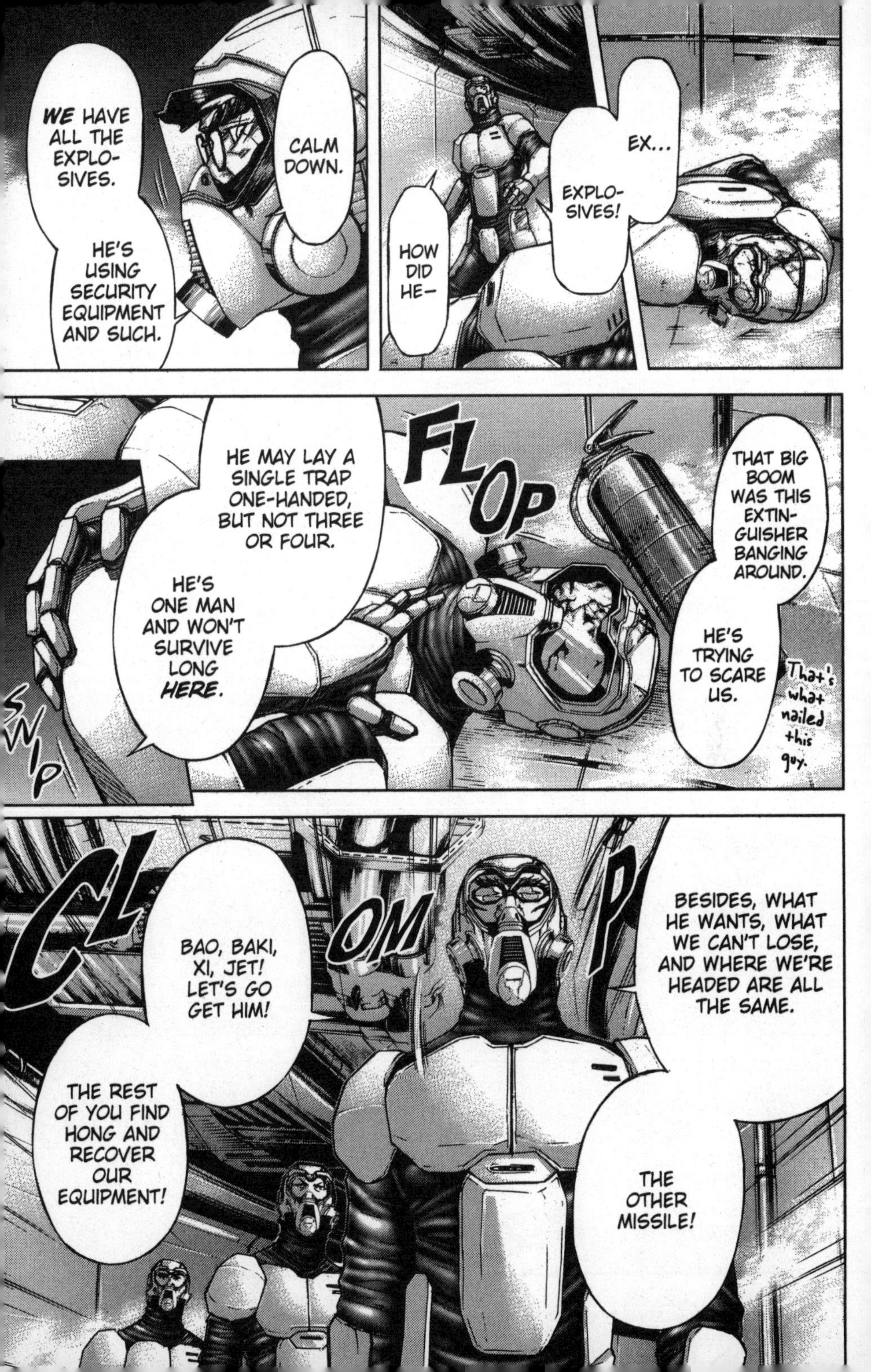
EX...
EXPLO-SIVES!
HOW DID HE—
CALM DOWN.
WE HAVE ALL THE EXPLO-SIVES.
HE'S USING SECURITY EQUIPMENT AND SUCH.
That's what nailed this guy.
THAT BIG BOOM WAS THIS EXTIN-GUISHER BANGING AROUND.
HE'S TRYING TO SCARE US.
FLOP
HE MAY LAY A SINGLE TRAP ONE-HANDED, BUT NOT THREE OR FOUR.
HE'S ONE MAN AND WON'T SURVIVE LONG HERE.
SNIP
BESIDES, WHAT HE WANTS, WHAT WE CAN'T LOSE, AND WHERE WE'RE HEADED ARE ALL THE SAME.
THE OTHER MISSILE!
CLOMP
BAO, BAKI, XI, JET! LET'S GO GET HIM!
THE REST OF YOU FIND HONG AND RECOVER OUR EQUIPMENT!

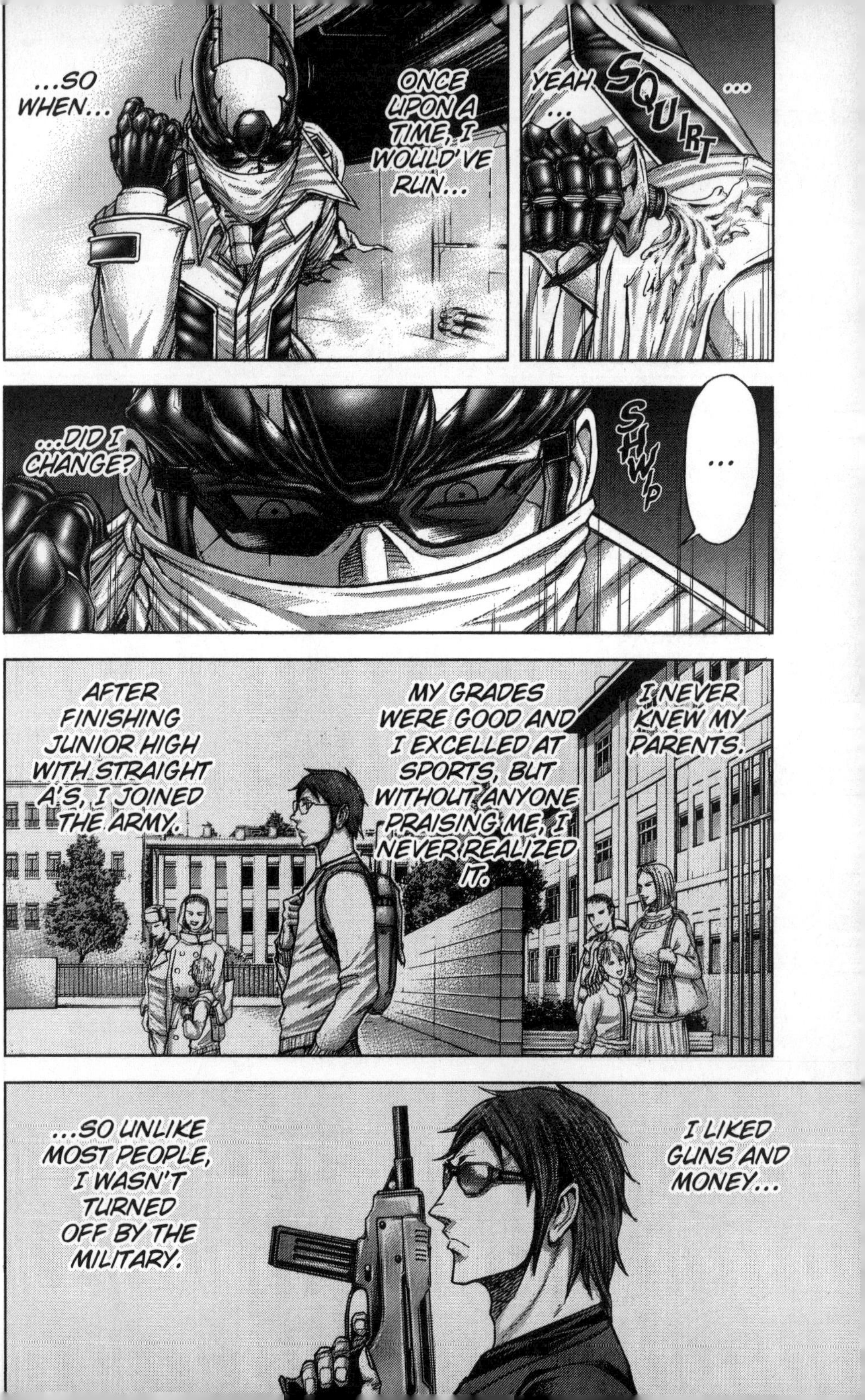
...
SQUIRT
YEAH ...
ONCE UPON A TIME, I WOULD'VE RUN...
...SO WHEN...
...
SHWIP
...DID I CHANGE?
I NEVER KNEW MY PARENTS.
MY GRADES WERE GOOD AND I EXCELLED AT SPORTS, BUT WITHOUT ANYONE PRAISING ME, I NEVER REALIZED IT.
AFTER FINISHING JUNIOR HIGH WITH STRAIGHT A'S, I JOINED THE ARMY.
I LIKED GUNS AND MONEY...
...SO UNLIKE MOST PEOPLE, I WASN'T TURNED OFF BY THE MILITARY.

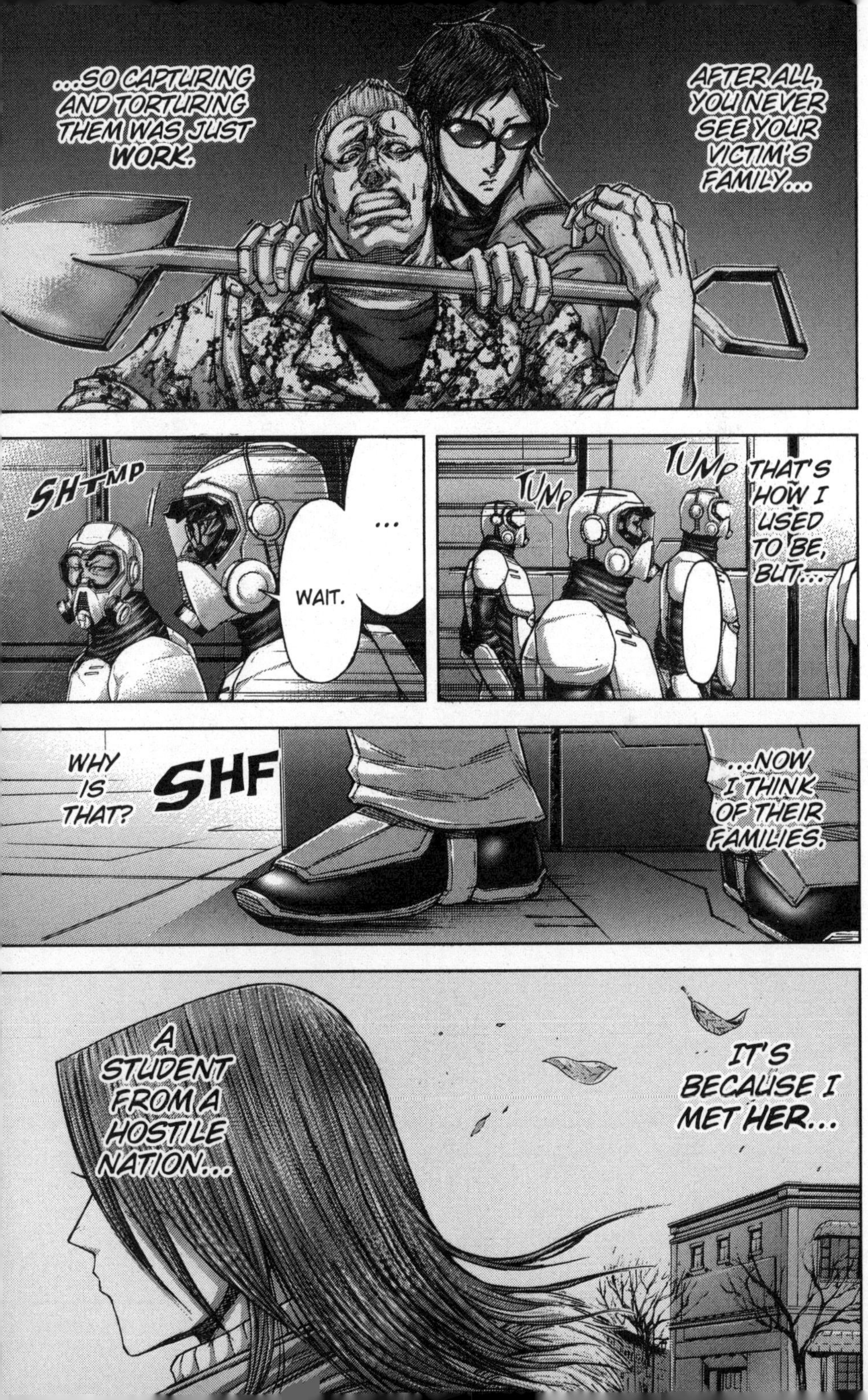
AFTER ALL, YOU NEVER SEE YOUR VICTIM'S FAMILY...
...SO CAPTURING AND TORTURING THEM WAS JUST WORK.
TUMP
TUMP
THAT'S HOW I USED TO BE, BUT...
...
WAIT.
SHTMP
...NOW I THINK OF THEIR FAMILIES.
SHF
WHY IS THAT?
IT'S BECAUSE I MET HER...
A STUDENT FROM A HOSTILE NATION...

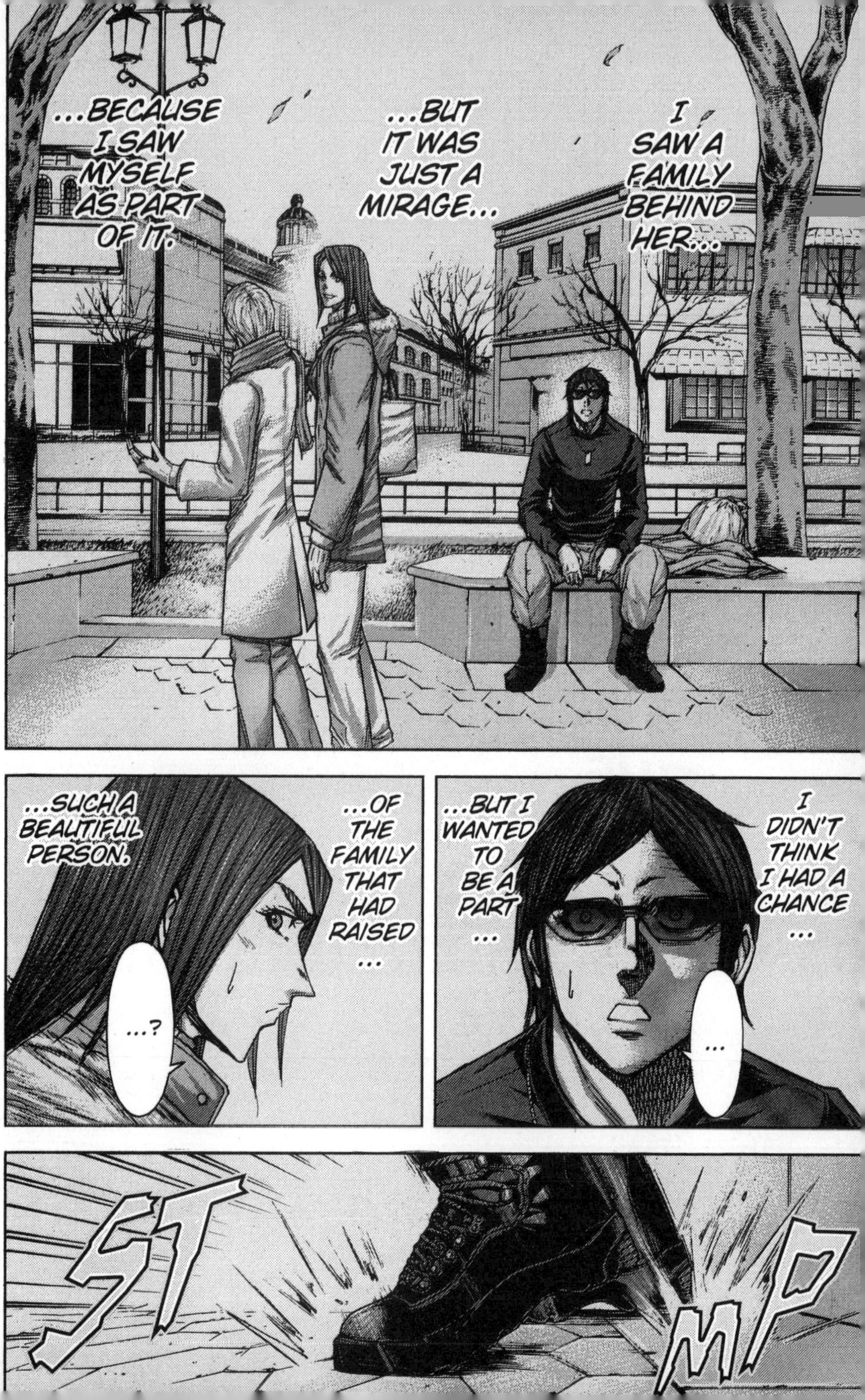
I SAW A FAMILY BEHIND HER...
...BUT IT WAS JUST A MIRAGE...
...BECAUSE I SAW MYSELF AS PART OF IT.
I DIDN'T THINK I HAD A CHANCE...
...BUT I WANTED TO BE A PART...
...
...OF THE FAMILY THAT HAD RAISED...
...SUCH A BEAUTIFUL PERSON.
...?
ST
MP

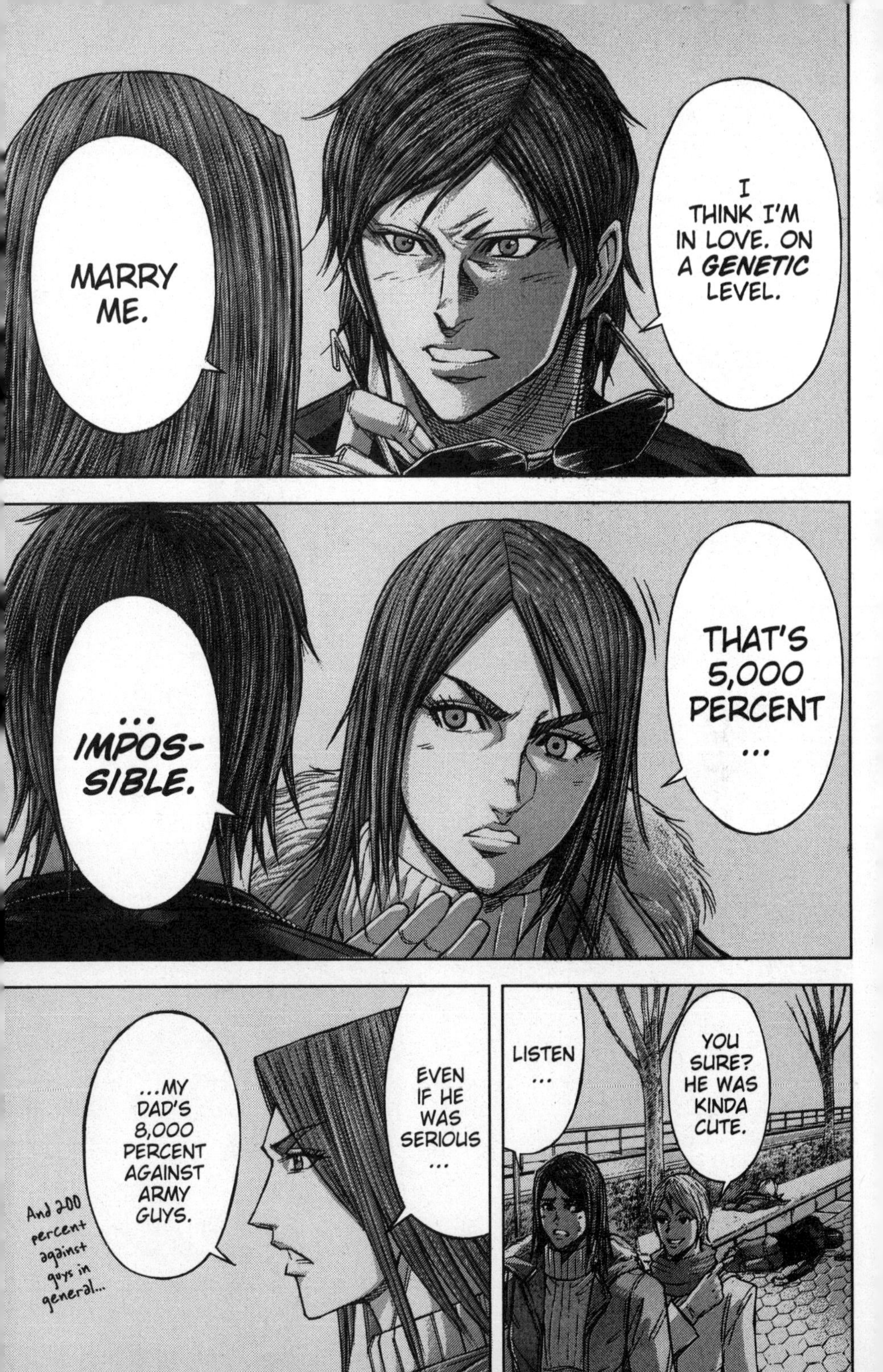
I THINK I'M IN LOVE. ON A GENETIC LEVEL.
MARRY ME.
THAT'S 5,000 PERCENT ...
... IMPOS-SIBLE.
YOU SURE? HE WAS KINDA CUTE.
LISTEN ...
EVEN IF HE WAS SERIOUS ...
...MY DAD'S 8,000 PERCENT AGAINST ARMY GUYS.
And 200 percent against guys in general...

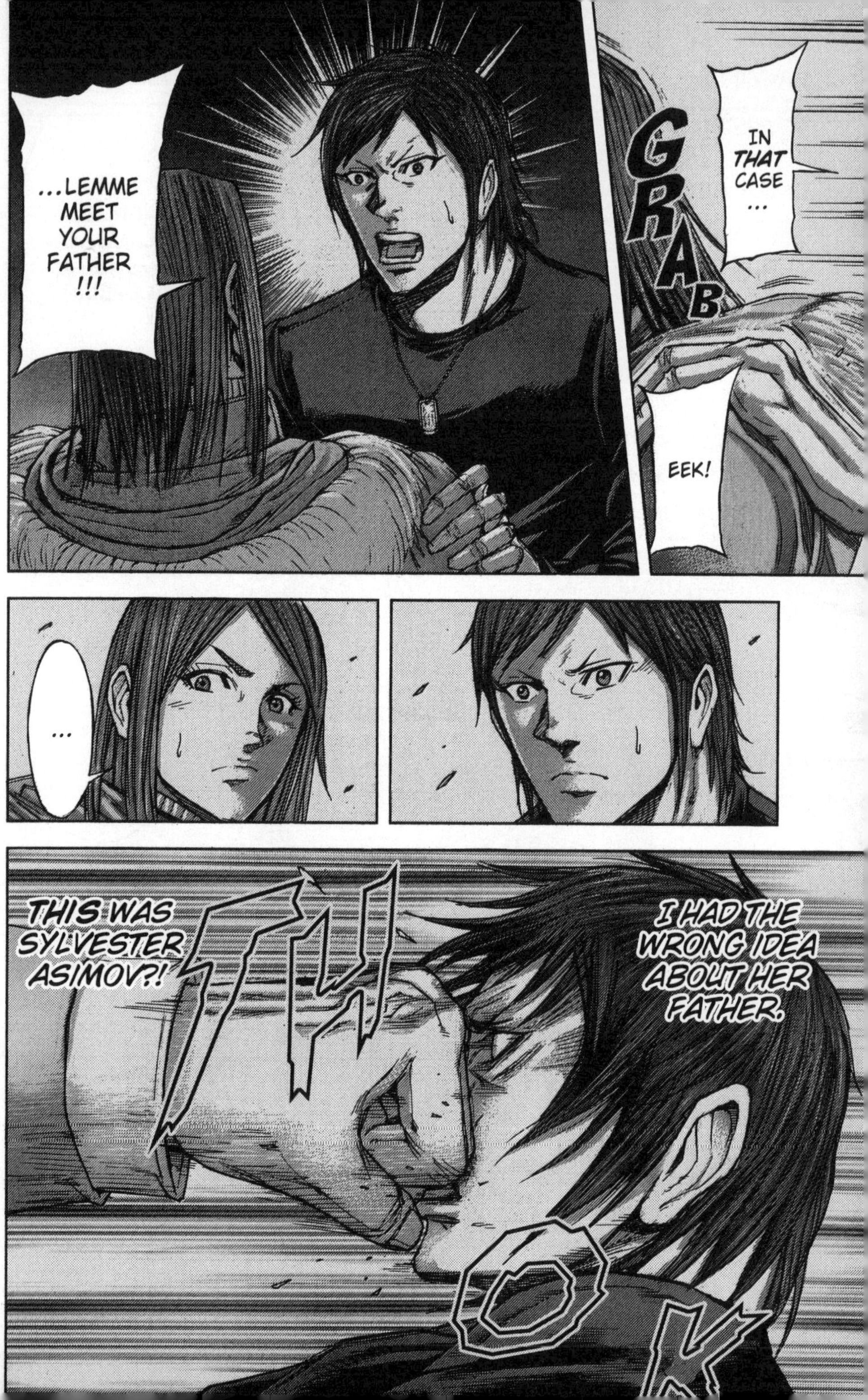
IN THAT CASE...
GRAB
EEK!
...LEMME MEET YOUR FATHER!!!
...
I HAD THE WRONG IDEA ABOUT HER FATHER.
THIS WAS SYLVESTER ASIMOV?!

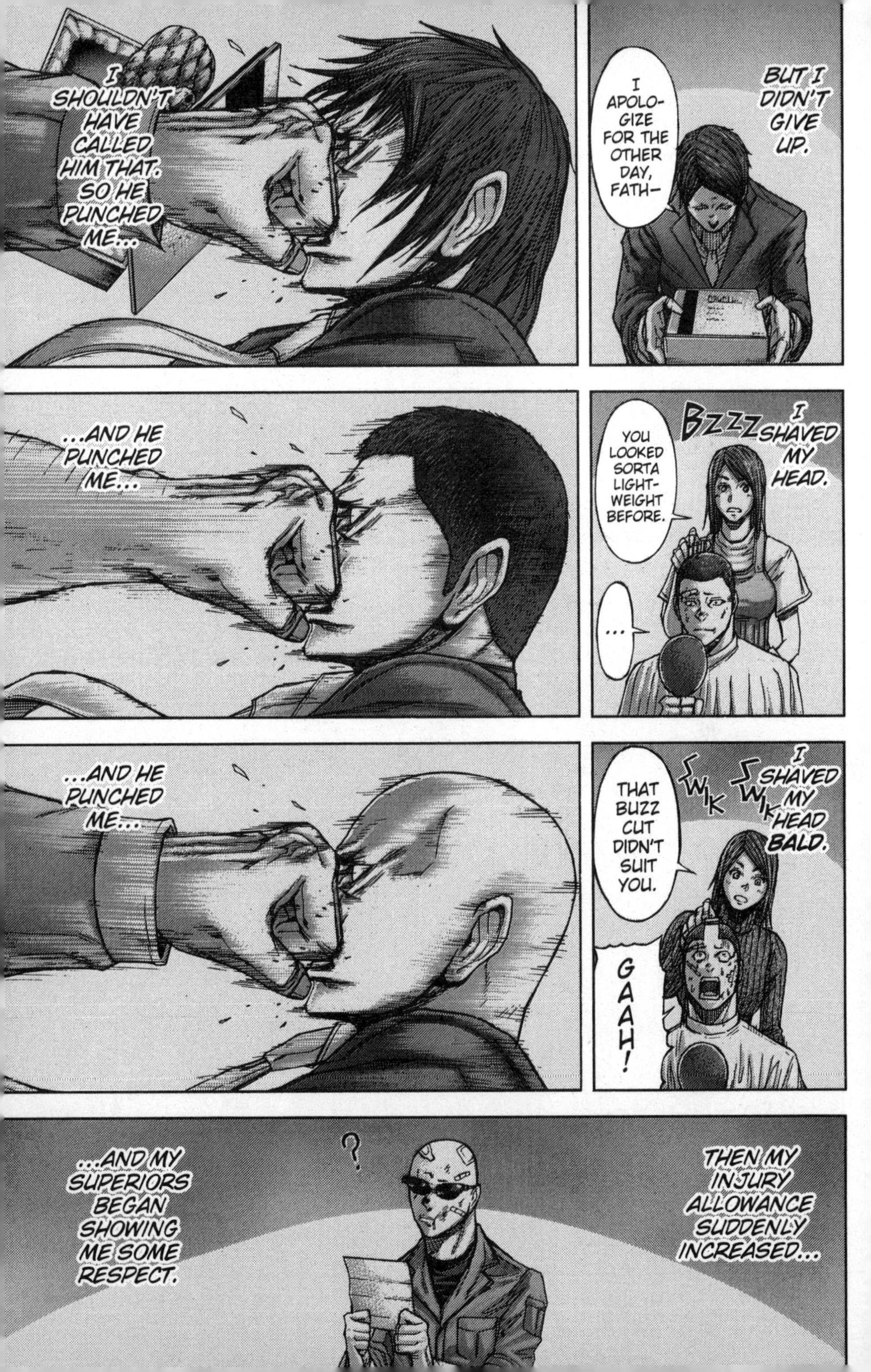
BUT I DIDN'T GIVE UP.
I APOLOGIZE FOR THE OTHER DAY, FATH—
I SHOULDN'T HAVE CALLED HIM THAT. SO HE PUNCHED ME...
BZZZ
I SHAVED MY HEAD.
YOU LOOKED SORTA LIGHTWEIGHT BEFORE.
...
...AND HE PUNCHED ME...
SWIK
SWIK
I SHAVED MY HEAD BALD.
THAT BUZZ CUT DIDN'T SUIT YOU.
GAAH!
...AND HE PUNCHED ME...
THEN MY INJURY ALLOWANCE SUDDENLY INCREASED...
?
...AND MY SUPERIORS BEGAN SHOWING ME SOME RESPECT.

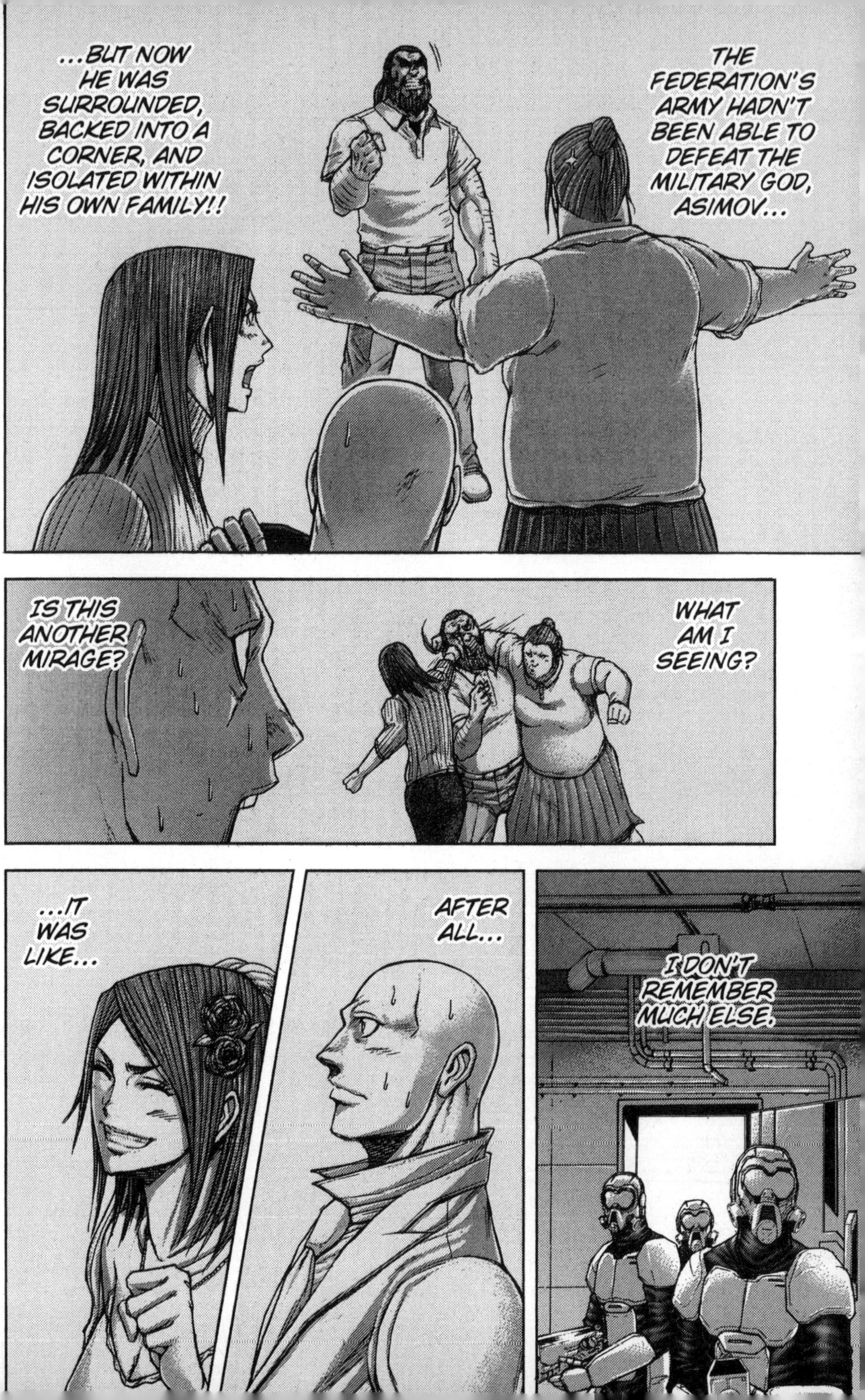
THE FEDERATION'S ARMY HADN'T BEEN ABLE TO DEFEAT THE MILITARY GOD, ASIMOV...
...BUT NOW HE WAS SURROUNDED, BACKED INTO A CORNER, AND ISOLATED WITHIN HIS OWN FAMILY!!
WHAT AM I SEEING?
IS THIS ANOTHER MIRAGE?
I DON'T REMEMBER MUCH ELSE.
AFTER ALL...
...IT WAS LIKE...

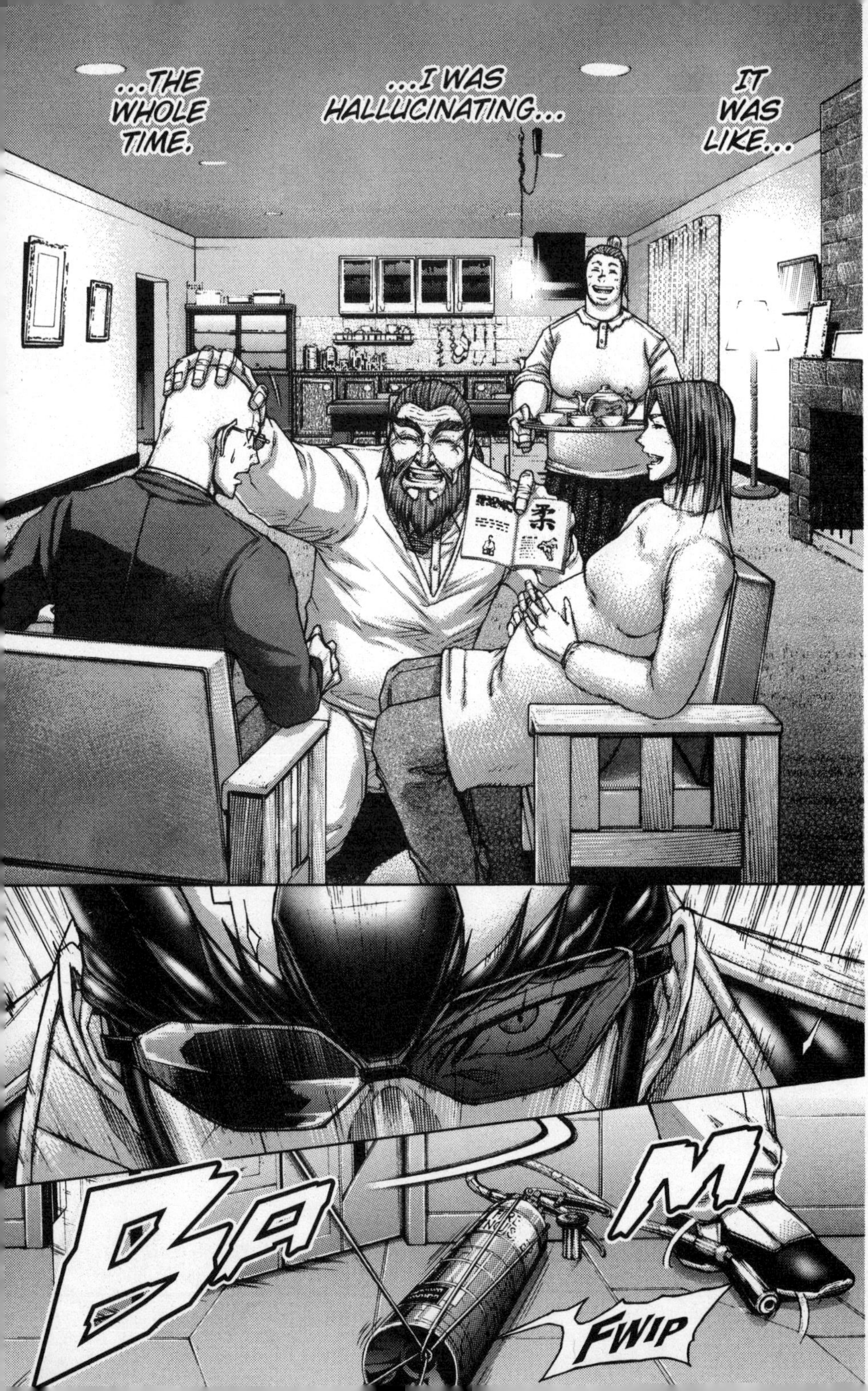
IT WAS LIKE...
...I WAS HALLUCINATING...
...THE WHOLE TIME.
柔
BAM
FWIP

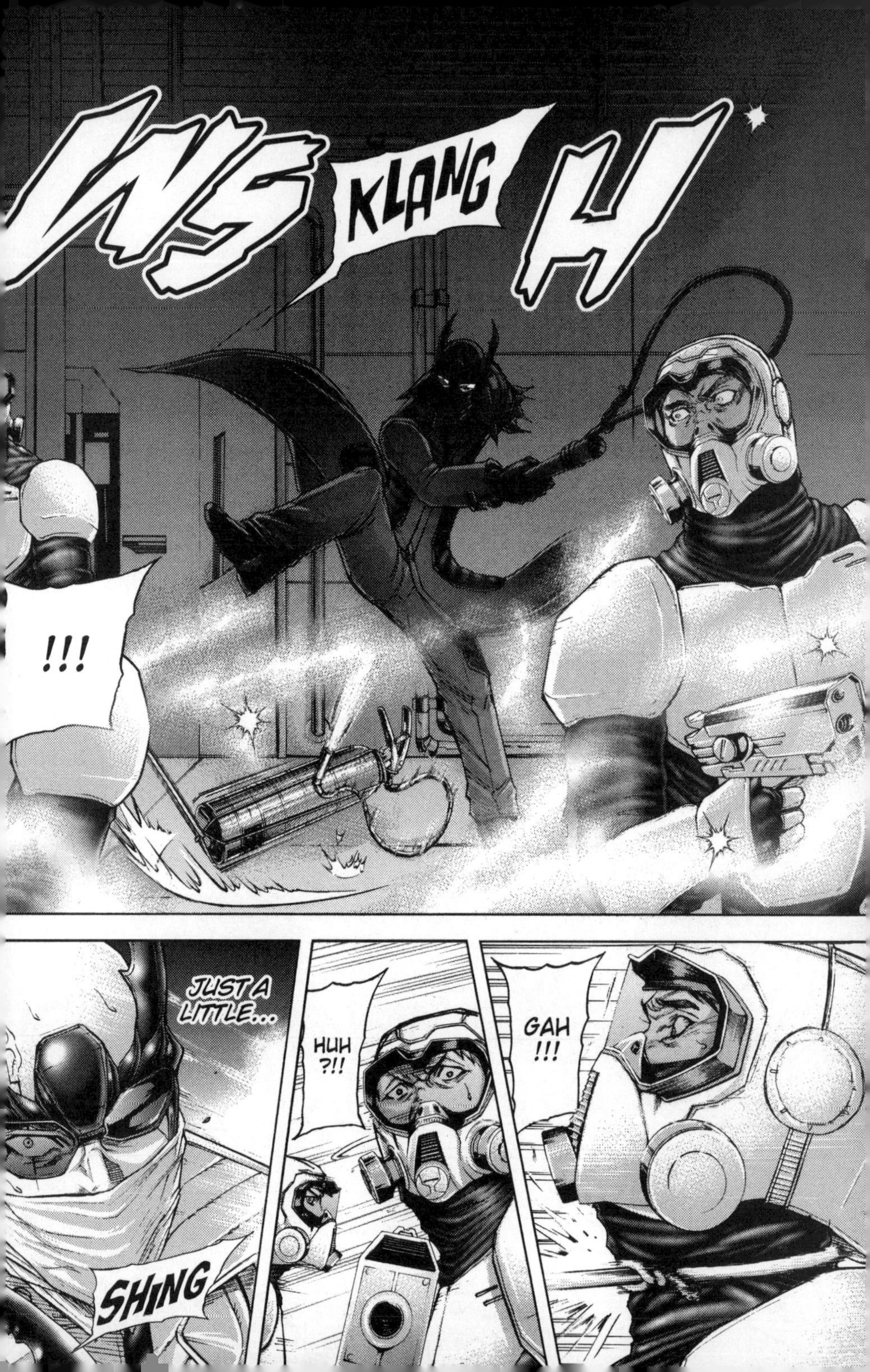
KLANG
!!!
GAH !!!
HUH ?!!
JUST A LITTLE...
SHING

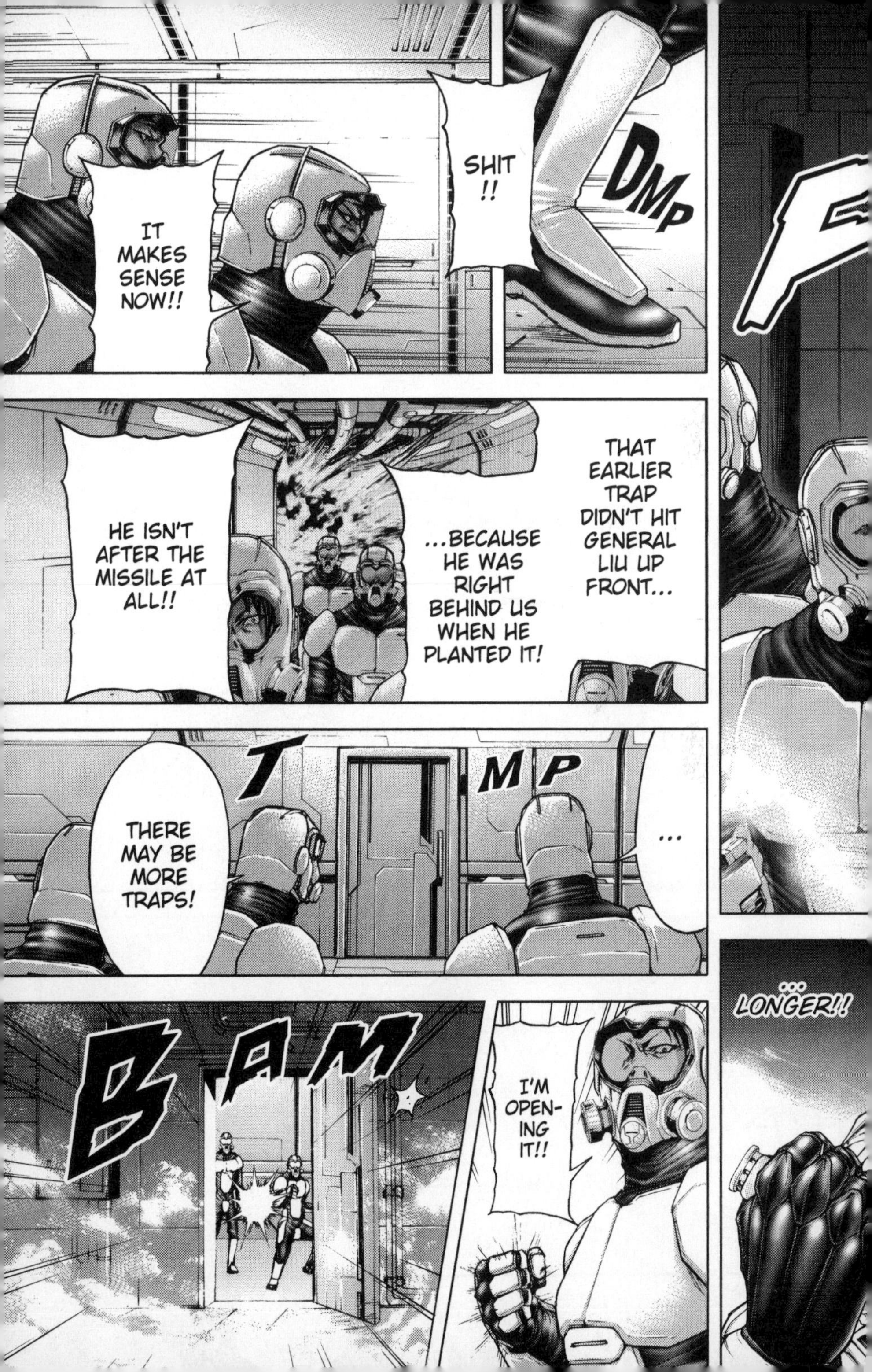
F
SHIT!!
DMP
IT MAKES SENSE NOW!!
THAT EARLIER TRAP DIDN'T HIT GENERAL LIU UP FRONT...
...BECAUSE HE WAS RIGHT BEHIND US WHEN HE PLANTED IT!
HE ISN'T AFTER THE MISSILE AT ALL!!
...
T MP
THERE MAY BE MORE TRAPS!
...LONGER!!
I'M OPEN-ING IT!!
BAM

...!!

NO
WAY
...

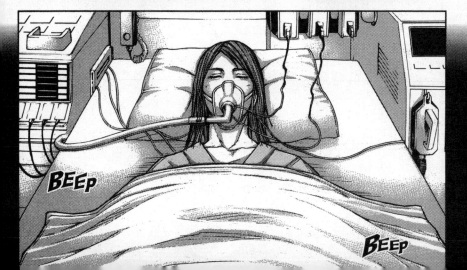

BEEp

BEEp

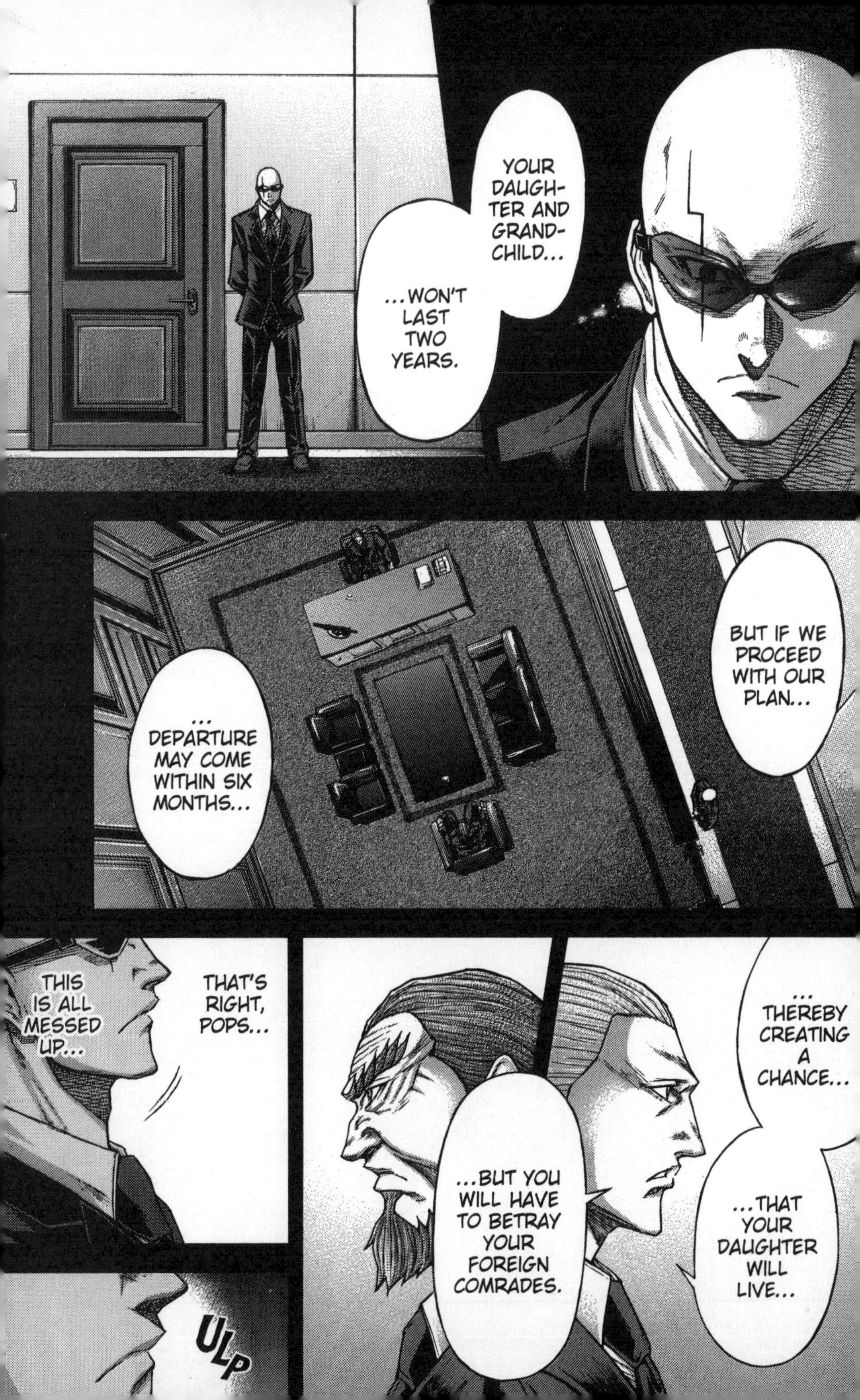
YOUR DAUGHTER AND GRANDCHILD…
…WON'T LAST TWO YEARS.
BUT IF WE PROCEED WITH OUR PLAN…
…DEPARTURE MAY COME WITHIN SIX MONTHS…
…THEREBY CREATING A CHANCE…
…THAT YOUR DAUGHTER WILL LIVE…
…BUT YOU WILL HAVE TO BETRAY YOUR FOREIGN COMRADES.
THAT'S RIGHT, POPS…
THIS IS ALL MESSED UP…
ULP

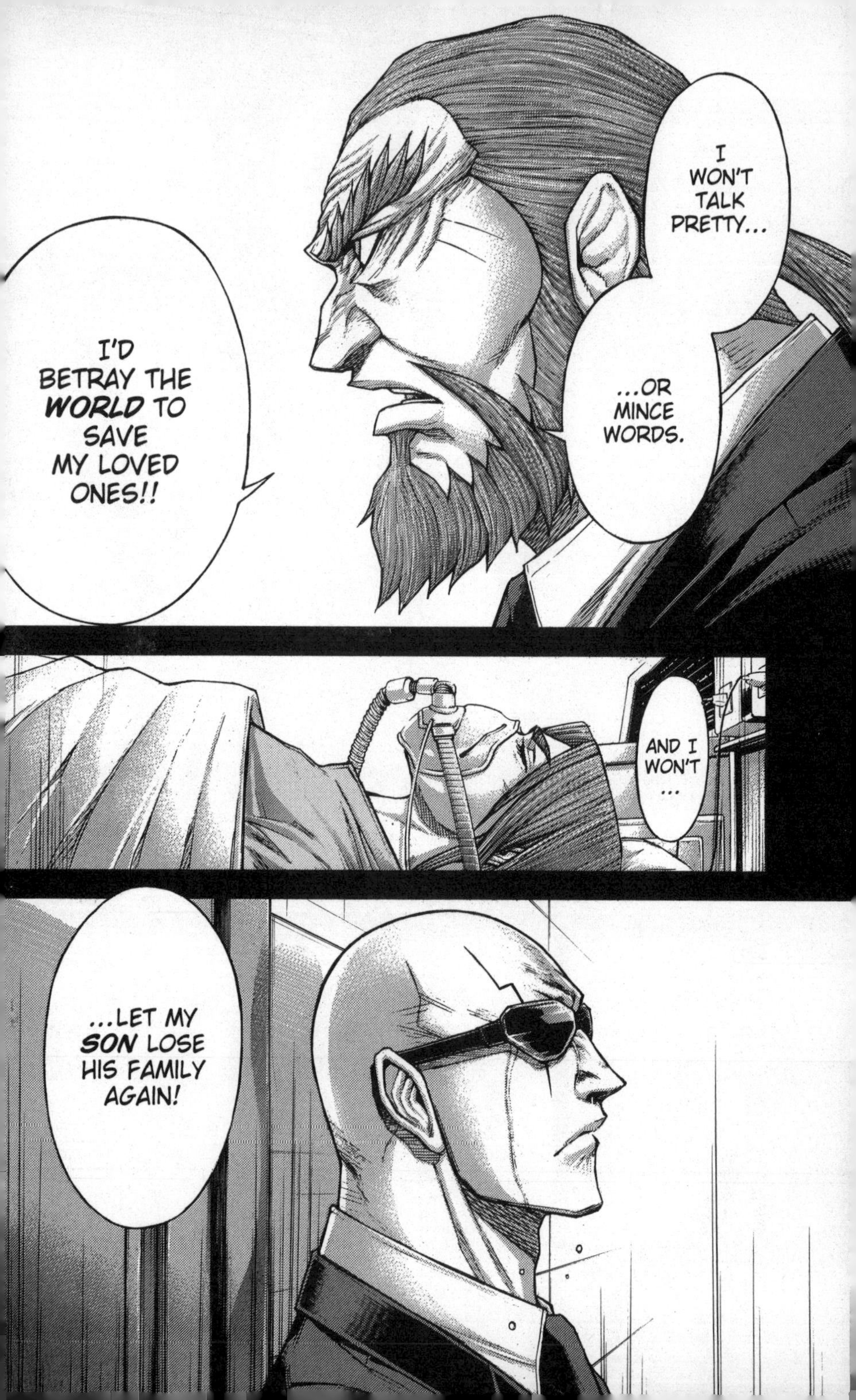
I WON'T TALK PRETTY...
...OR MINCE WORDS.
I'D BETRAY THE WORLD TO SAVE MY LOVED ONES!!
AND I WON'T ...
...LET MY SON LOSE HIS FAMILY AGAIN!

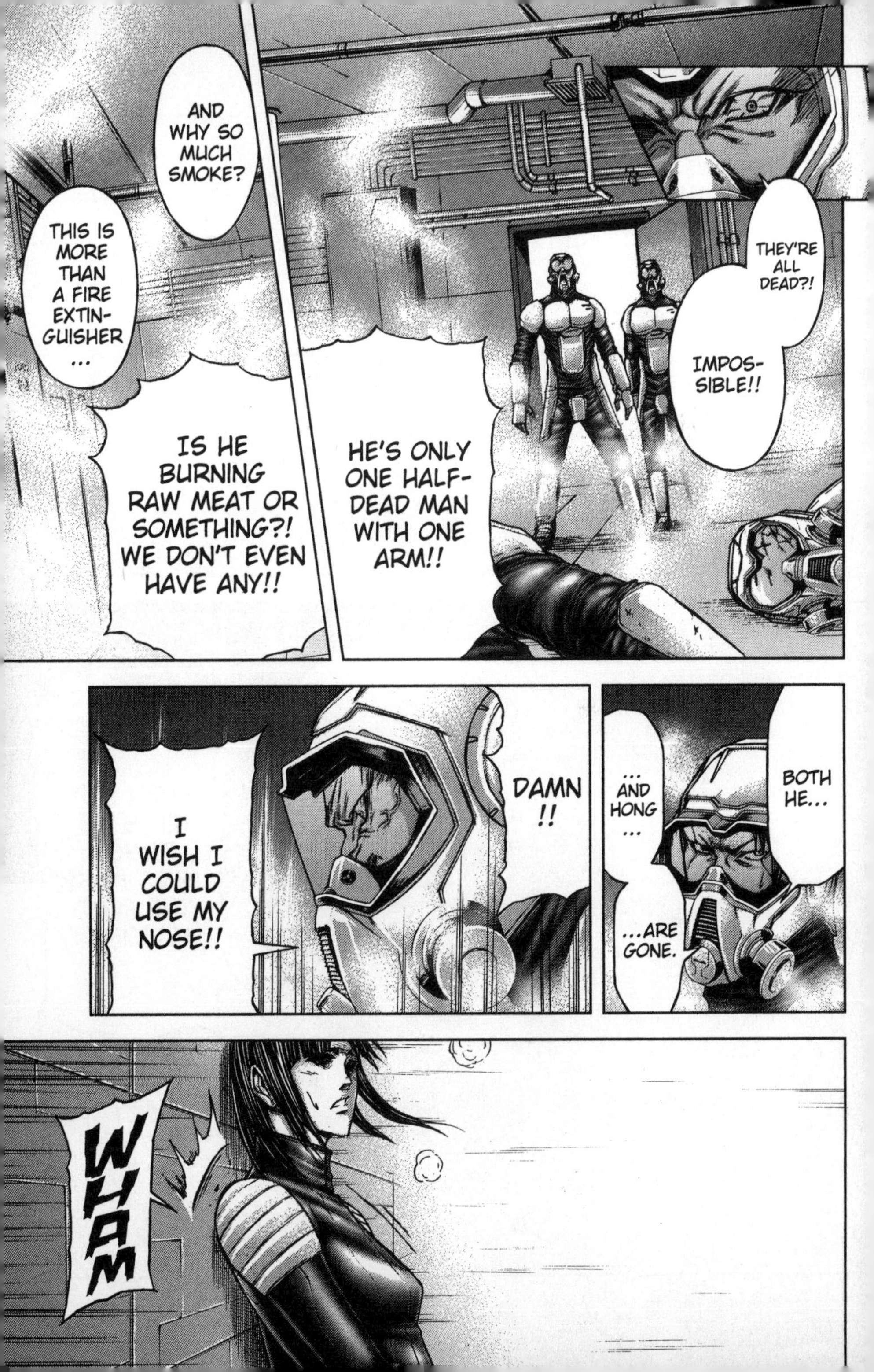
THEY'RE ALL DEAD?!
IMPOSSIBLE!!
HE'S ONLY ONE HALF-DEAD MAN WITH ONE ARM!!
AND WHY SO MUCH SMOKE?
THIS IS MORE THAN A FIRE EXTINGUISHER...
IS HE BURNING RAW MEAT OR SOMETHING?! WE DON'T EVEN HAVE ANY!!
BOTH HE...
...AND HONG...
...ARE GONE.
DAMN!!
I WISH I COULD USE MY NOSE!!
WHAM

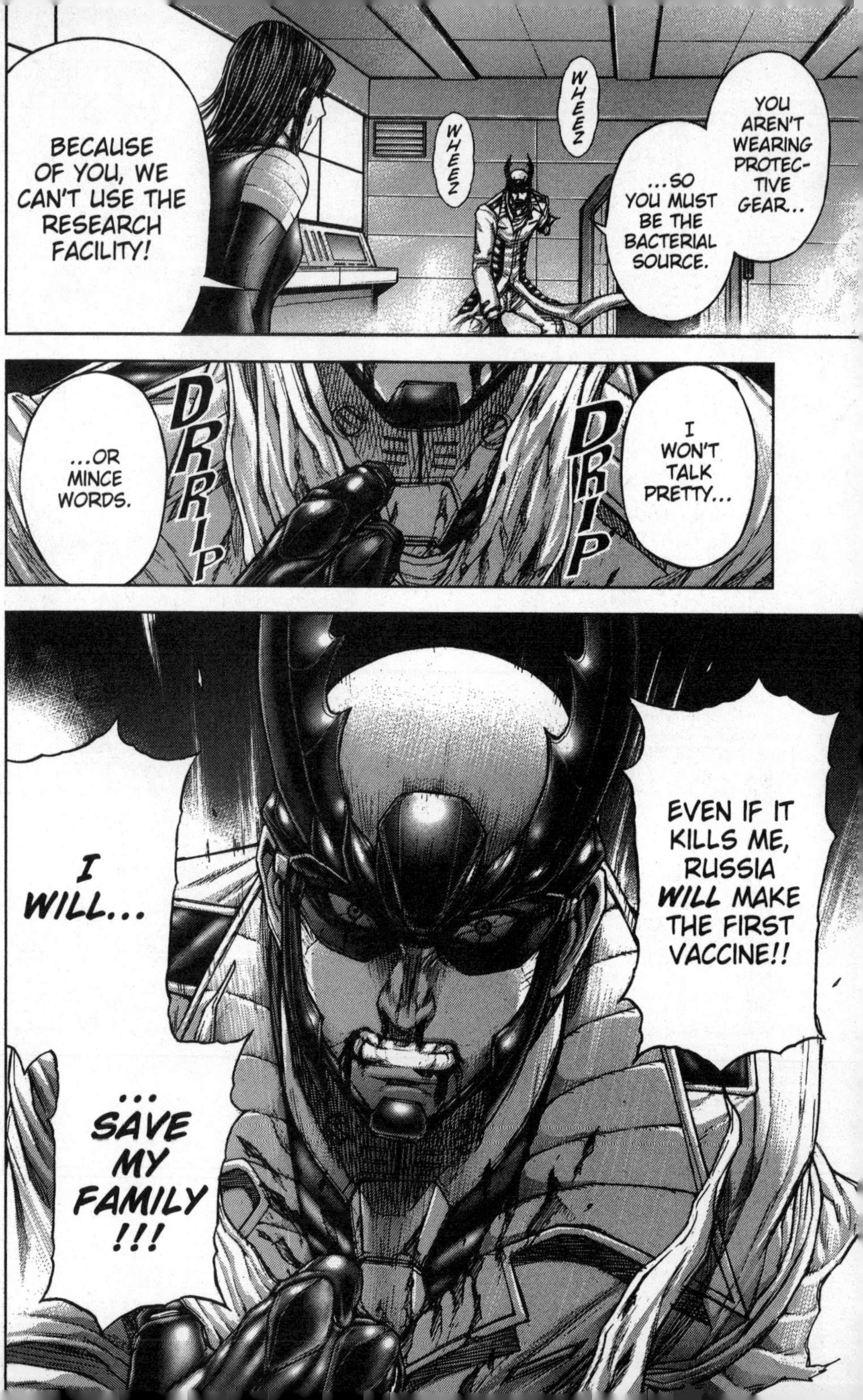
YOU AREN'T WEARING PROTECTIVE GEAR...
...SO YOU MUST BE THE BACTERIAL SOURCE.
WHEEZ
WHEEZ
BECAUSE OF YOU, WE CAN'T USE THE RESEARCH FACILITY!
I WON'T TALK PRETTY...
DRIP
DRRIP
...OR MINCE WORDS.
EVEN IF IT KILLS ME, RUSSIA WILL MAKE THE FIRST VACCINE!!
I WILL...
...SAVE MY FAMILY!!!

TERRA FORMARS
Character

Alexander Asimov ♂

Russia   28 yrs.   180 cm   89 kg

M.A.R.S. Ranking: 7

Favorite Foods: Cottage cheese, black tea
Dislikes: Nudes with body paint
Eye Color: Brown   Blood Type: O
DOB: January 26 (Aquarius)
Hobbies: Retro video games

Lost both parents to a terrorist attack soon after birth, then his grandmother died when he was four. After that, he grew up in an orphanage, but it wasn't a good environment.

On Asimov's team, he serves as just another soldier to avoid the appearance of a conflict between work and family. Also, he uses the name Alexander because a woman soldier on the team has a similar name.

For a few months recently, he tried to regrow his hair, but it wasn't coming in well, so he got worried and went back to a chrome dome while on the *Annex*.

Aaron Yuzik ♂

Russia   25 yrs.   190 cm   101 kg

Operation Base: Scolopendra subspinipes japonica [a type of centipede]

Favorite Foods: Gratin, red wine
Dislikes: Business hotels with showers whose
            temperature is difficult to control
Eye Color: Gray   Blood Type: AB
DOB: July 15 (Cancer)
Hobbies: Blending tea, reading

Wanted to be a designer but couldn't make a living off it and ran into opposition from his parents, so he decided to join the military for a while.

In part thanks to his natural physique, he soon advanced, and then he married a woman in the military, so now it's hard to quit. However, he likes his job in the military well enough.

He doesn't have any children. The Russian army usually asks for volunteers for the *Annex Project*, but isn't entirely above coercion. Aaron accepted this job in place of soldiers who have children.

CHAPTER 73: I LOVE YOU

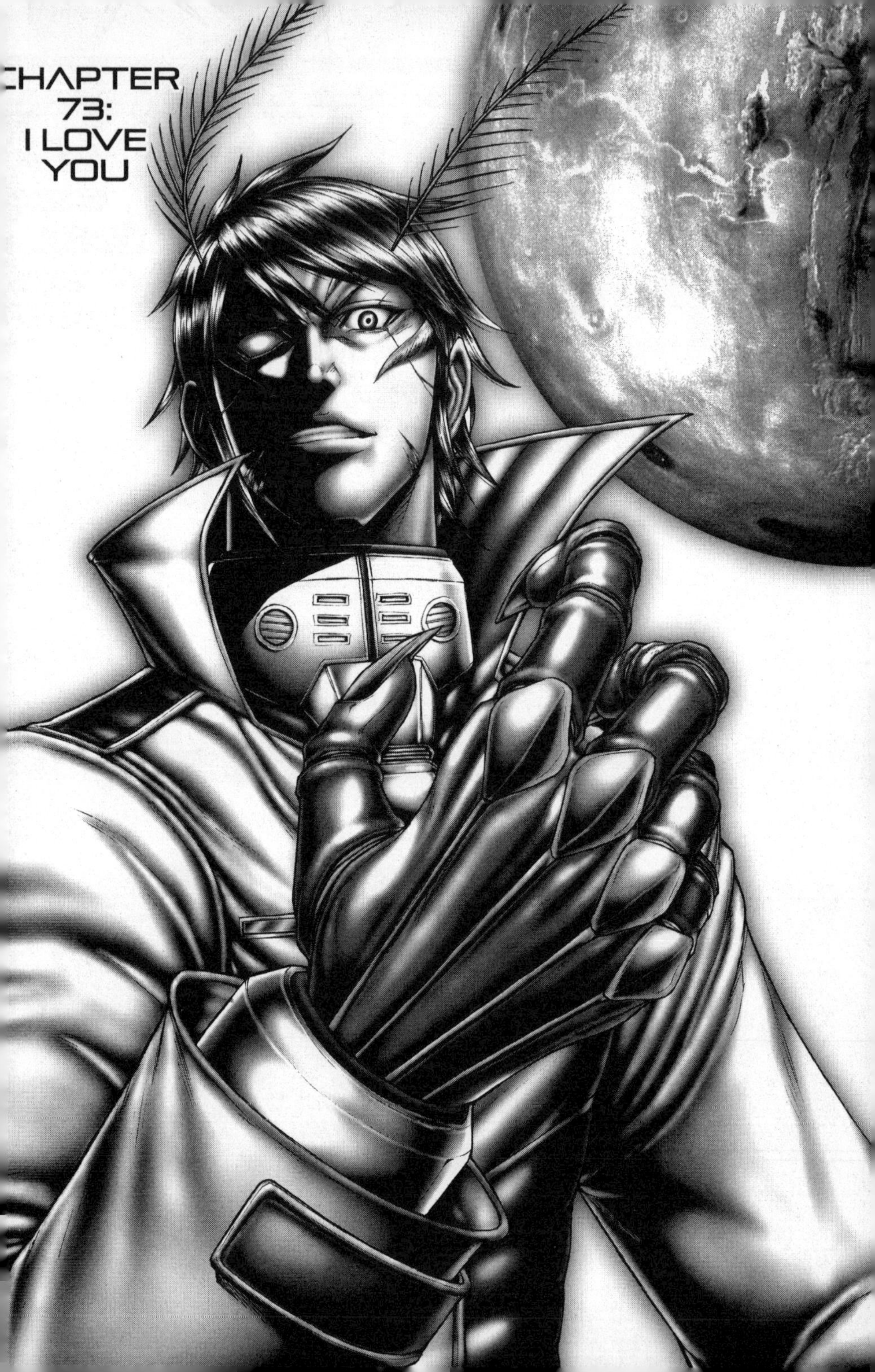

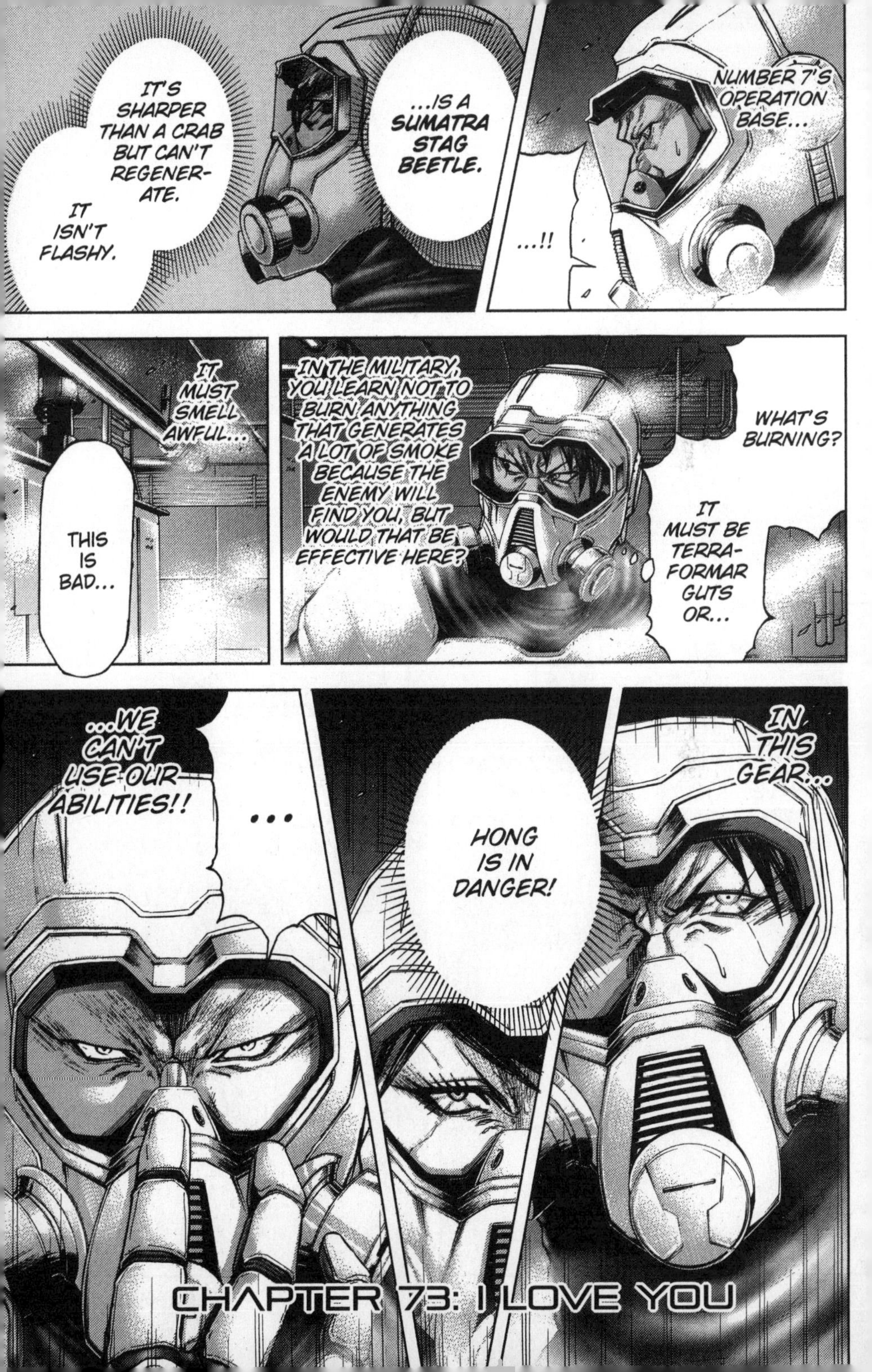
NUMBER 7'S OPERATION BASE...
...!!
...IS A SUMATRA STAG BEETLE.
IT'S SHARPER THAN A CRAB BUT CAN'T REGENERATE.
IT ISN'T FLASHY.
WHAT'S BURNING?
IT MUST BE TERRA-FORMAR GUTS OR...
IN THE MILITARY, YOU LEARN NOT TO BURN ANYTHING THAT GENERATES A LOT OF SMOKE BECAUSE THE ENEMY WILL FIND YOU, BUT WOULD THAT BE EFFECTIVE HERE?
IT MUST SMELL AWFUL...
THIS IS BAD...
IN THIS GEAR...
HONG IS IN DANGER!
...WE CAN'T USE OUR ABILITIES!!
...
CHAPTER 73: I LOVE YOU

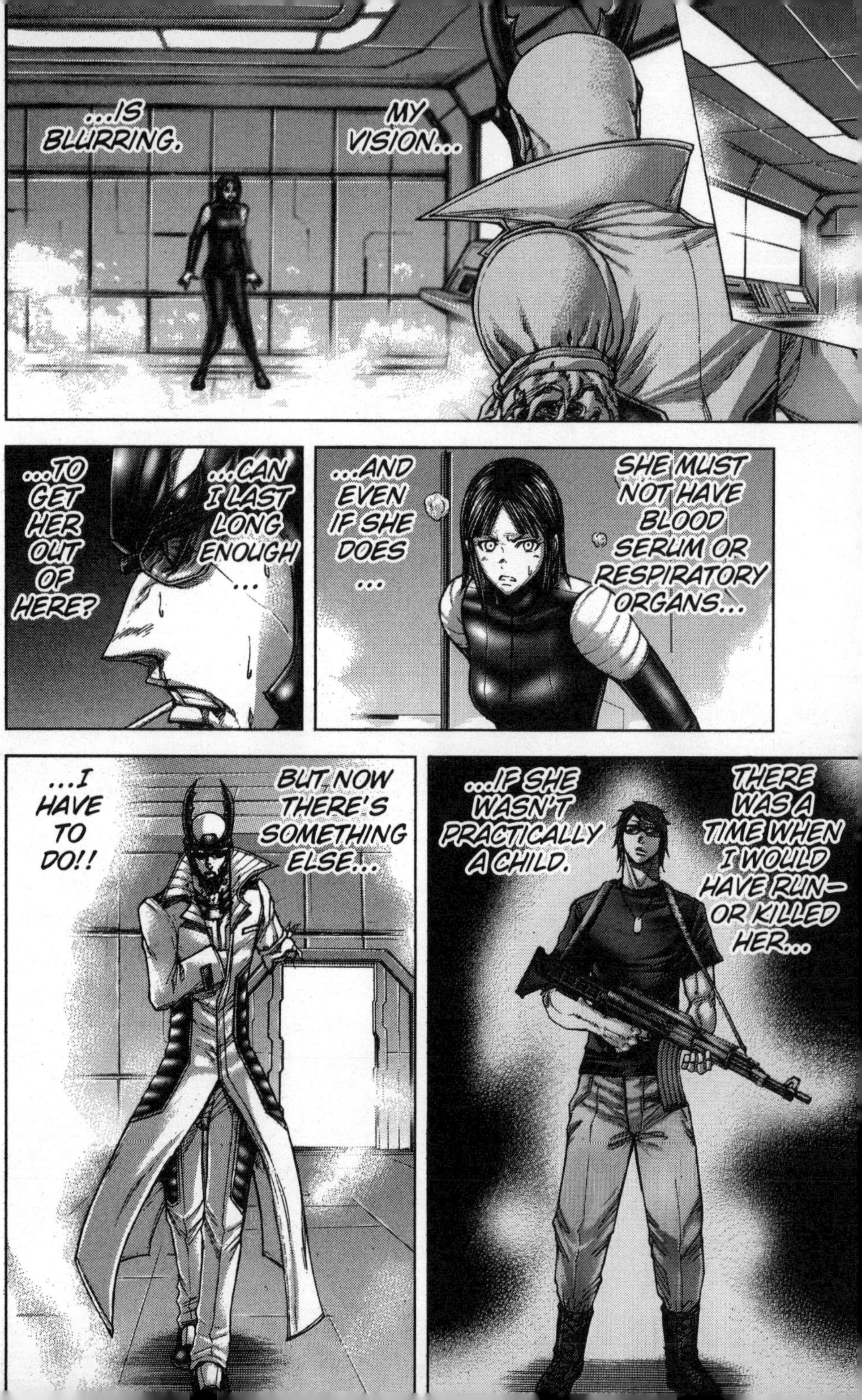
MY VISION...
...IS BLURRING.
SHE MUST NOT HAVE BLOOD SERUM OR RESPIRATORY ORGANS...
...AND EVEN IF SHE DOES...
...CAN I LAST LONG ENOUGH...
...TO GET HER OUT OF HERE?
THERE WAS A TIME WHEN I WOULD HAVE RUN—OR KILLED HER...
...IF SHE WASN'T PRACTICALLY A CHILD.
BUT NOW THERE'S SOMETHING ELSE...
...I HAVE TO DO!!

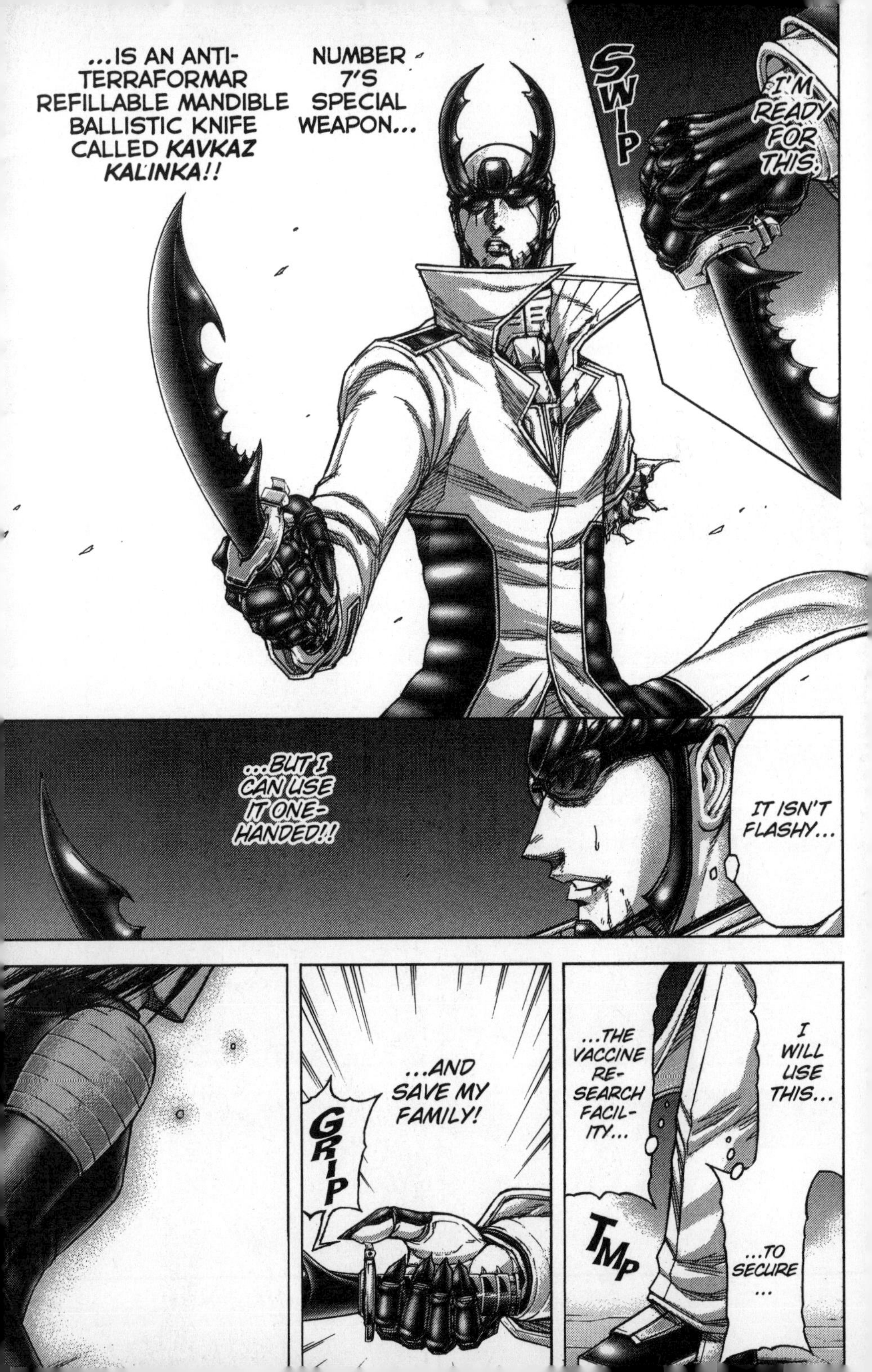

SWIP
I'M READY FOR THIS.
NUMBER 7'S SPECIAL WEAPON...
...IS AN ANTI-TERRAFORMAR REFILLABLE MANDIBLE BALLISTIC KNIFE CALLED KAVKAZ KALINKA!!
IT ISN'T FLASHY...
...BUT I CAN USE IT ONE-HANDED!!
I WILL USE THIS...
...TO SECURE...
...THE VACCINE RE-SEARCH FACIL-ITY...
TMP
GRIP
...AND SAVE MY FAMILY!

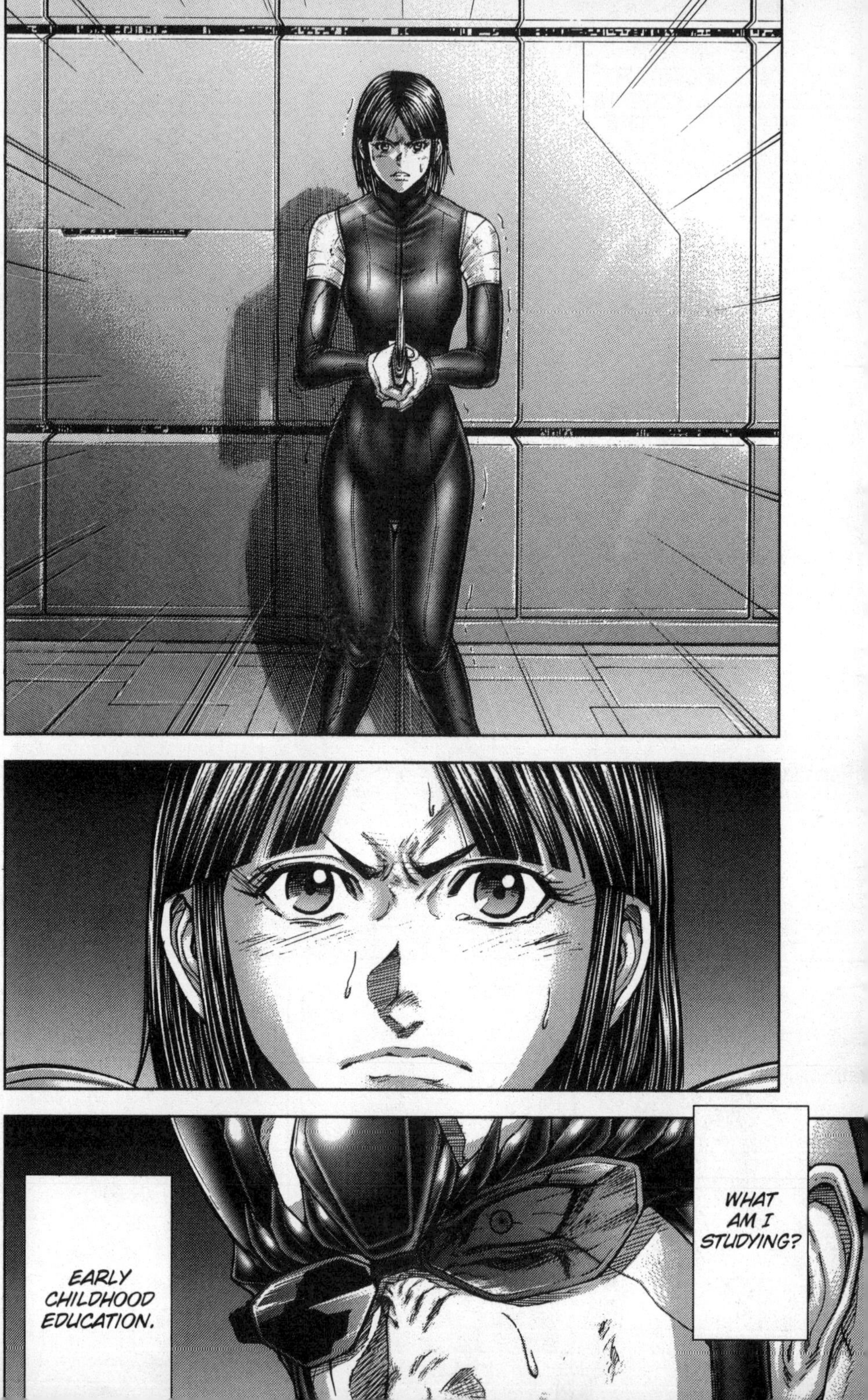
WHAT AM I STUDYING?
EARLY CHILDHOOD EDUCATION.

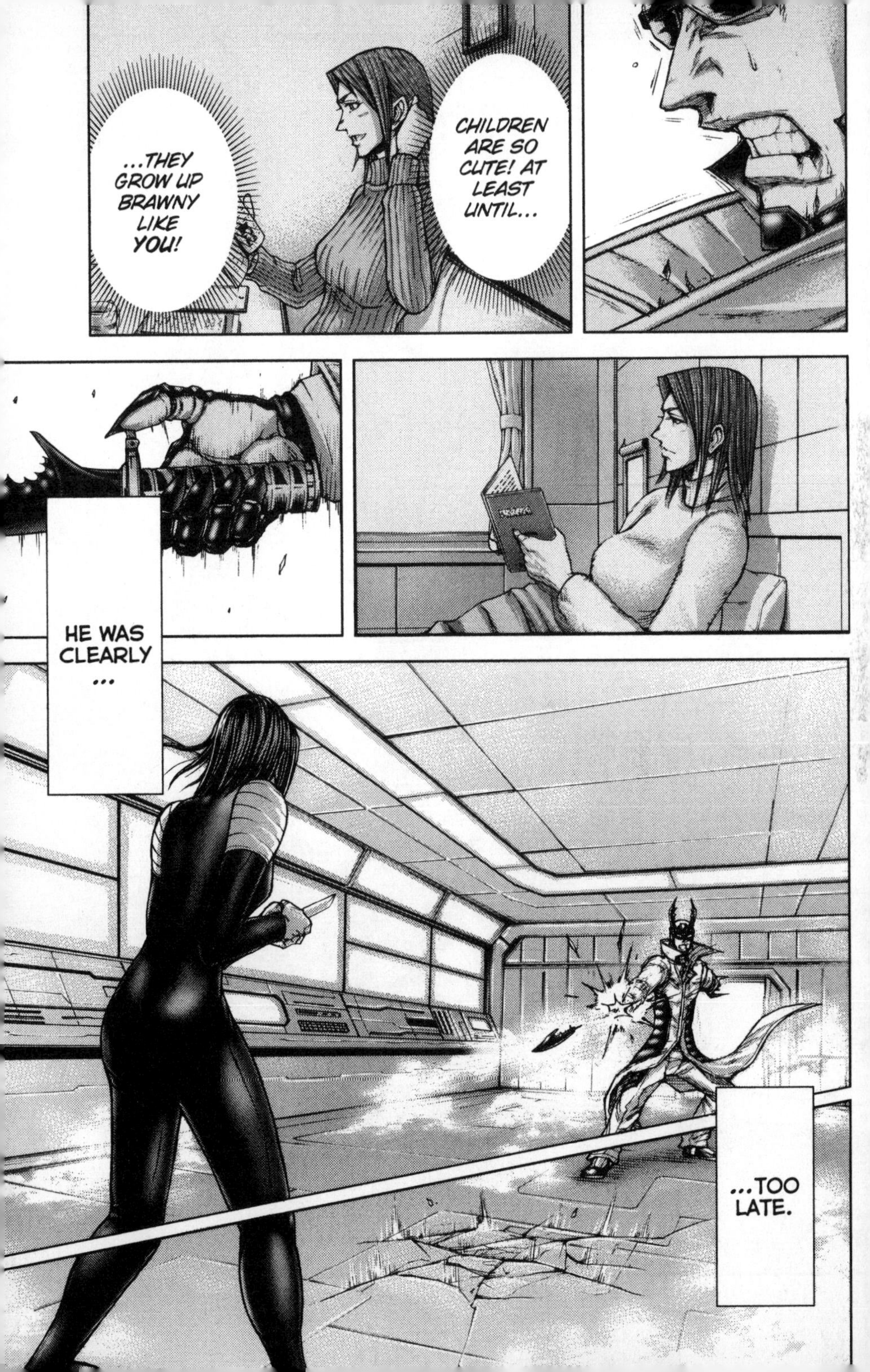
CHILDREN ARE SO CUTE! AT LEAST UNTIL...
...THEY GROW UP BRAWNY LIKE YOU!
HE WAS CLEARLY ...
...TOO LATE.

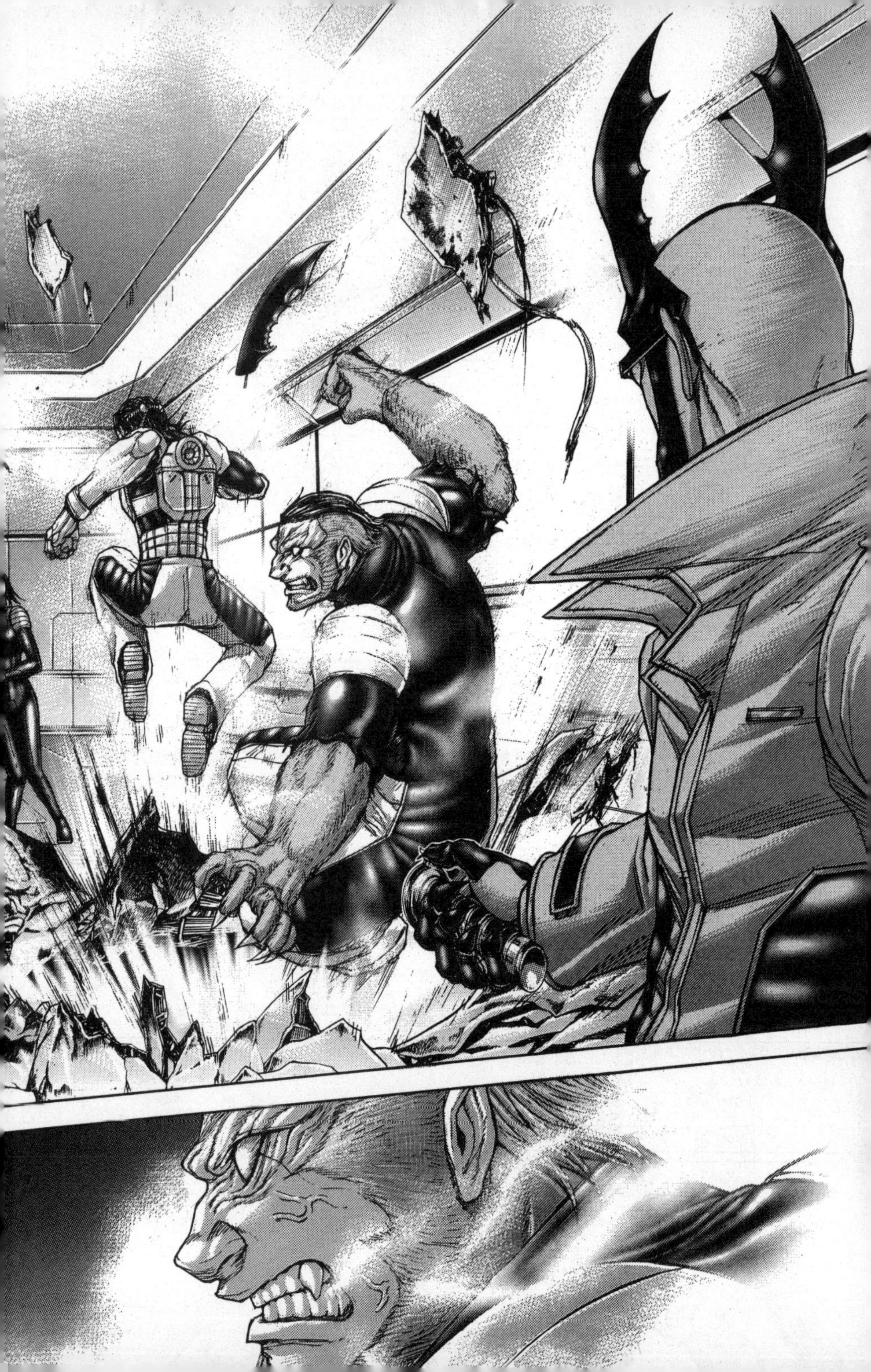

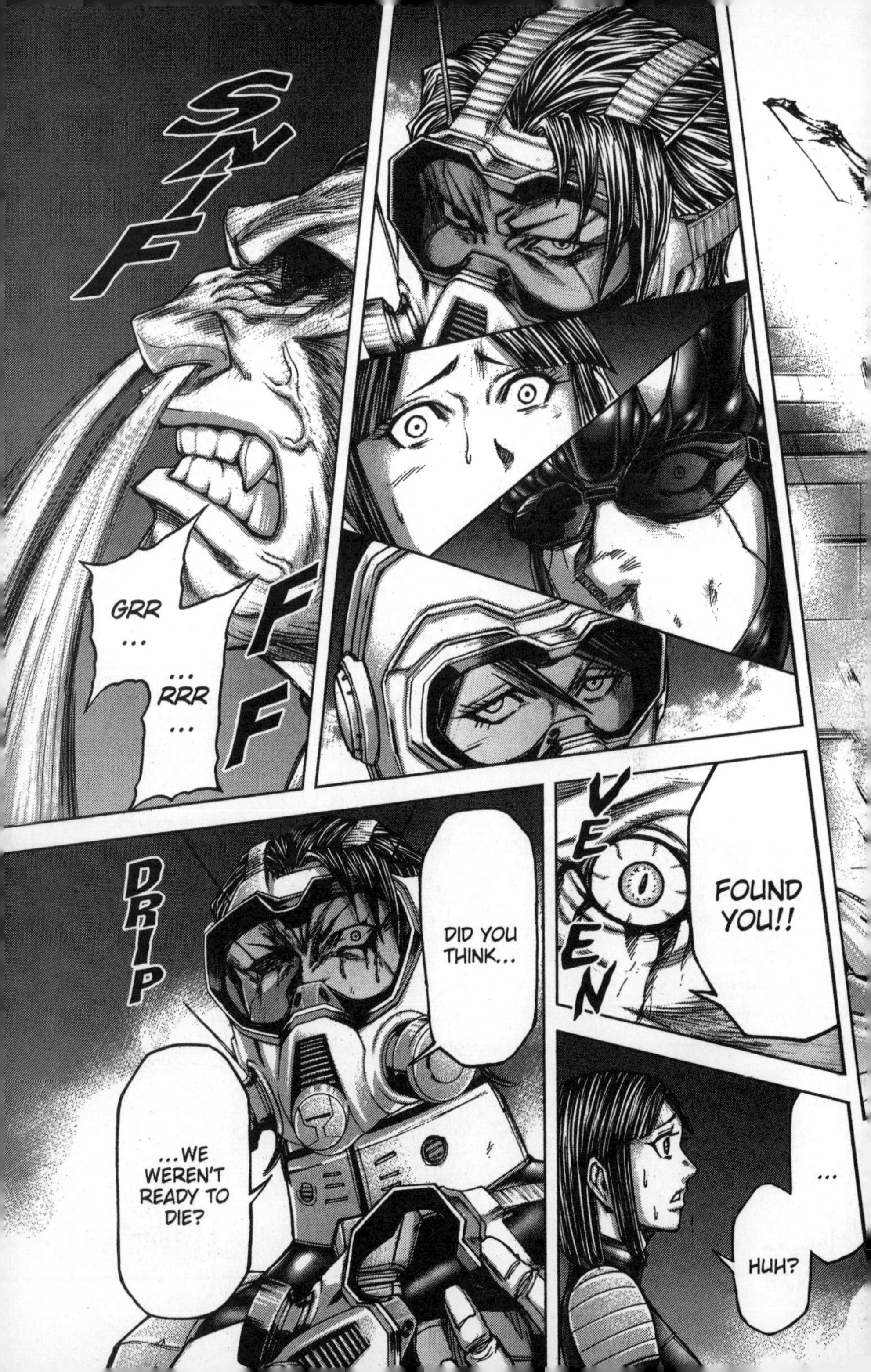
SNIFF
GRR... ...RRR...
FF
VEEEN
FOUND YOU!!
...
HUH?
DRIP
DID YOU THINK...
...WE WEREN'T READY TO DIE?

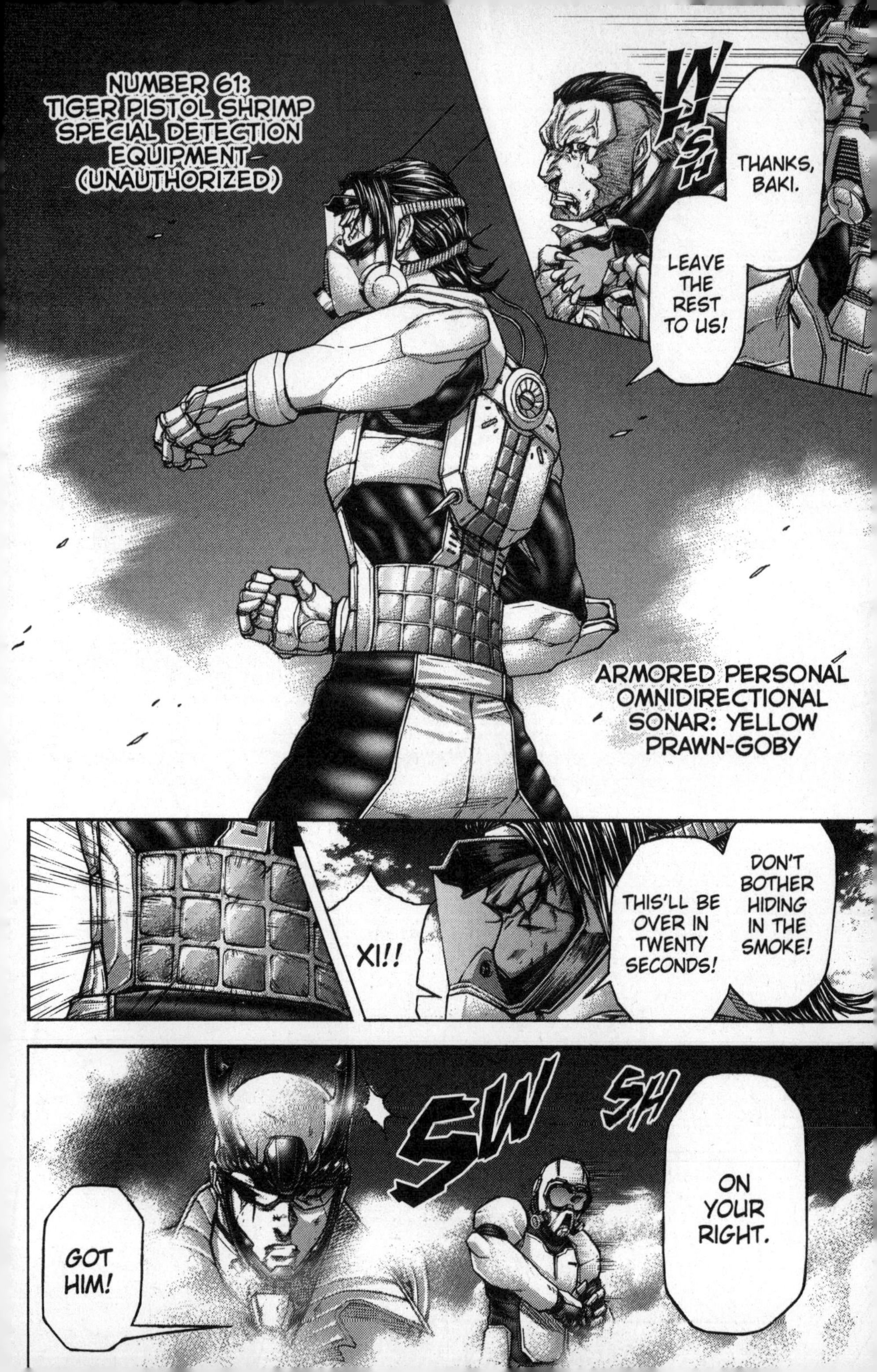
WHSH
THANKS, BAKI.
LEAVE THE REST TO US!
NUMBER 61: TIGER PISTOL SHRIMP SPECIAL DETECTION EQUIPMENT (UNAUTHORIZED)
ARMORED PERSONAL OMNIDIRECTIONAL SONAR: YELLOW PRAWN-GOBY
DON'T BOTHER HIDING IN THE SMOKE!
THIS'LL BE OVER IN TWENTY SECONDS!
XI!!
SW SH
ON YOUR RIGHT.
GOT HIM!

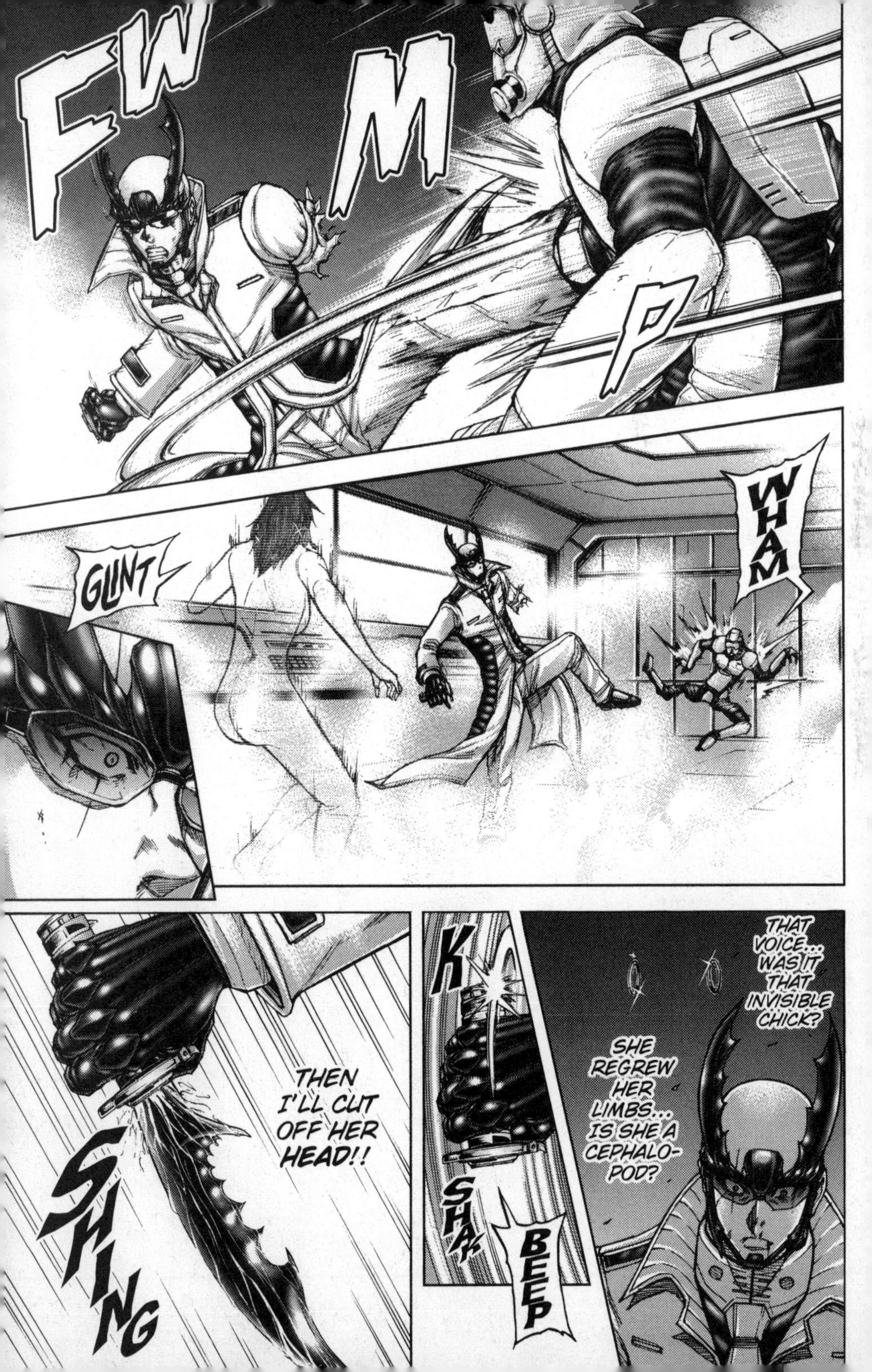
FWMP
WHAM
GLINT
THAT VOICE... WAS IT THAT INVISIBLE CHICK?
SHE REGREW HER LIMBS... IS SHE A CEPHALO-POD?
K
SHAK
BEEP
THEN I'LL CUT OFF HER HEAD!!
SHING

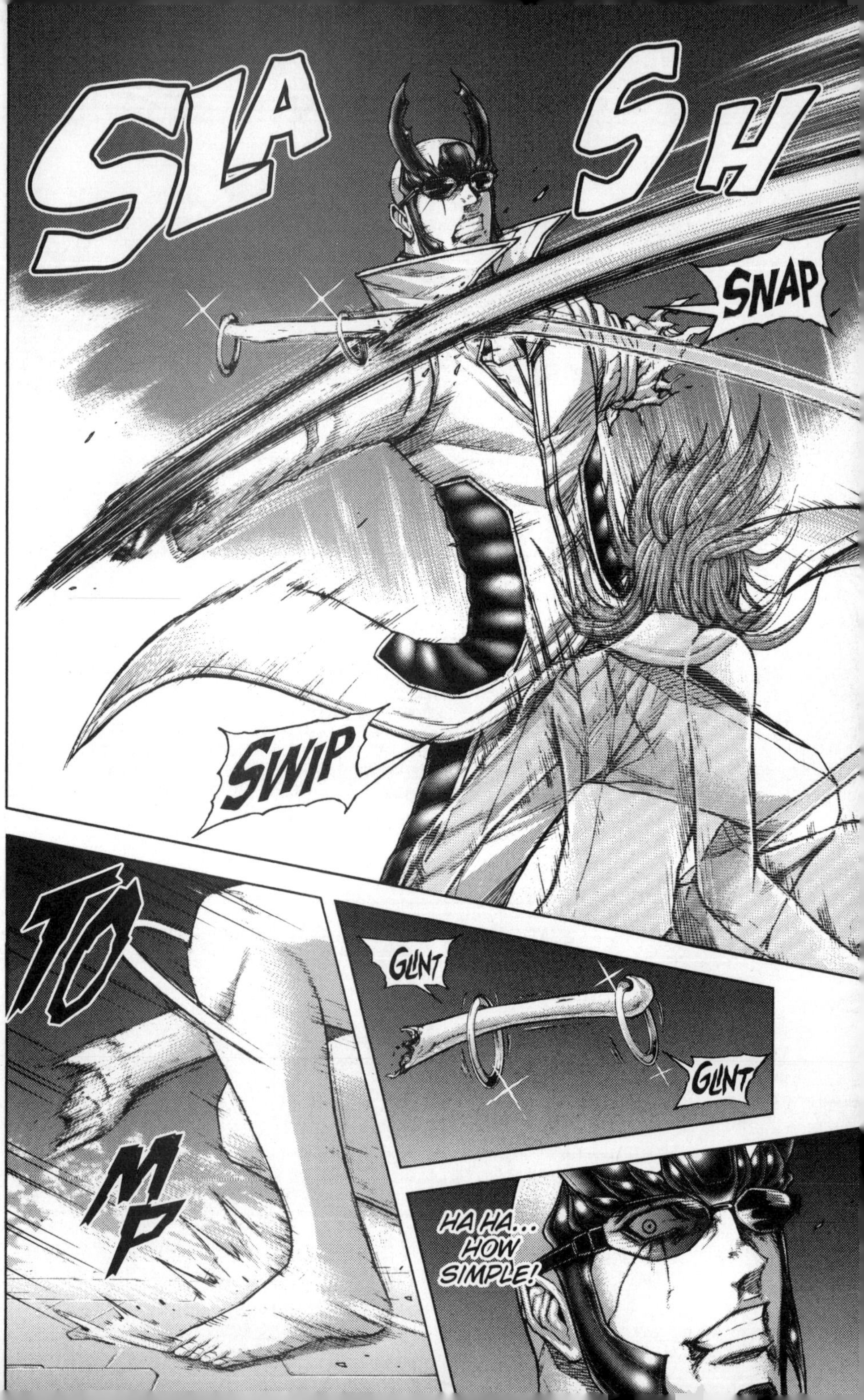
SLASH
SNAP
SWIP
GLINT
GLINT
HA HA... HOW SIMPLE!
TOMP

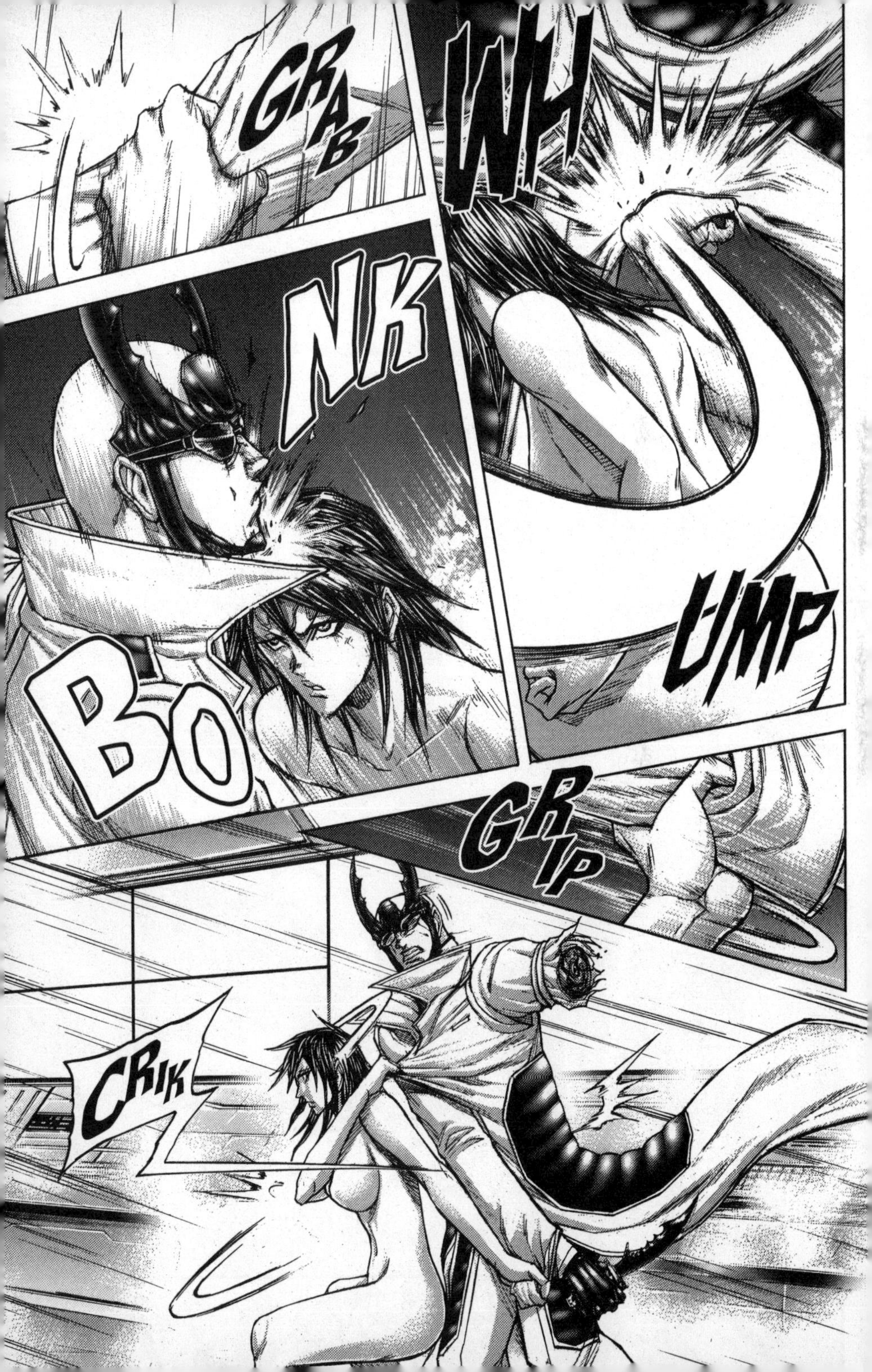
WH
UMP
GRAB
BO
NK
GRIP
CRIK

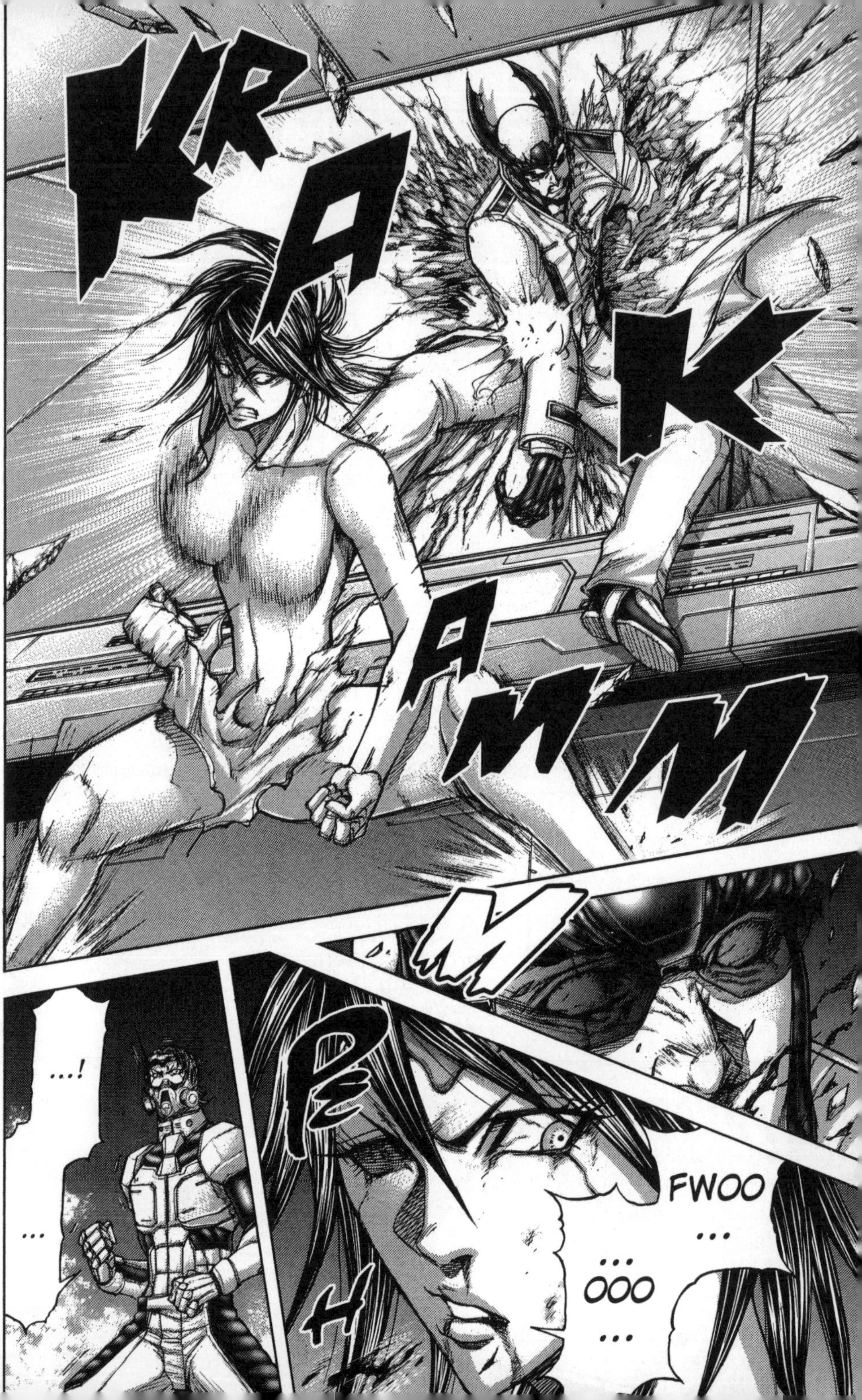
KRAK
AMMM
FWOO
...
...
OOO
...
...!
...

SHUF

SWOOO

NUMBER 99 CAN BEAT HIM? WHAT A JOKE!

FWUD

STAGGER

HOW MANY SECONDS HAS IT BEEN?

I NEED A SUIT! AND *FAST!*

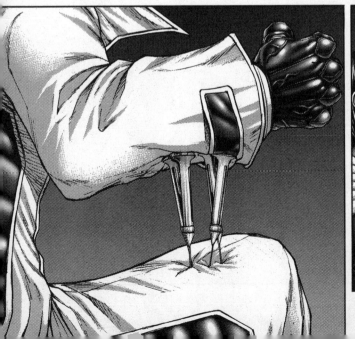

...

UM...

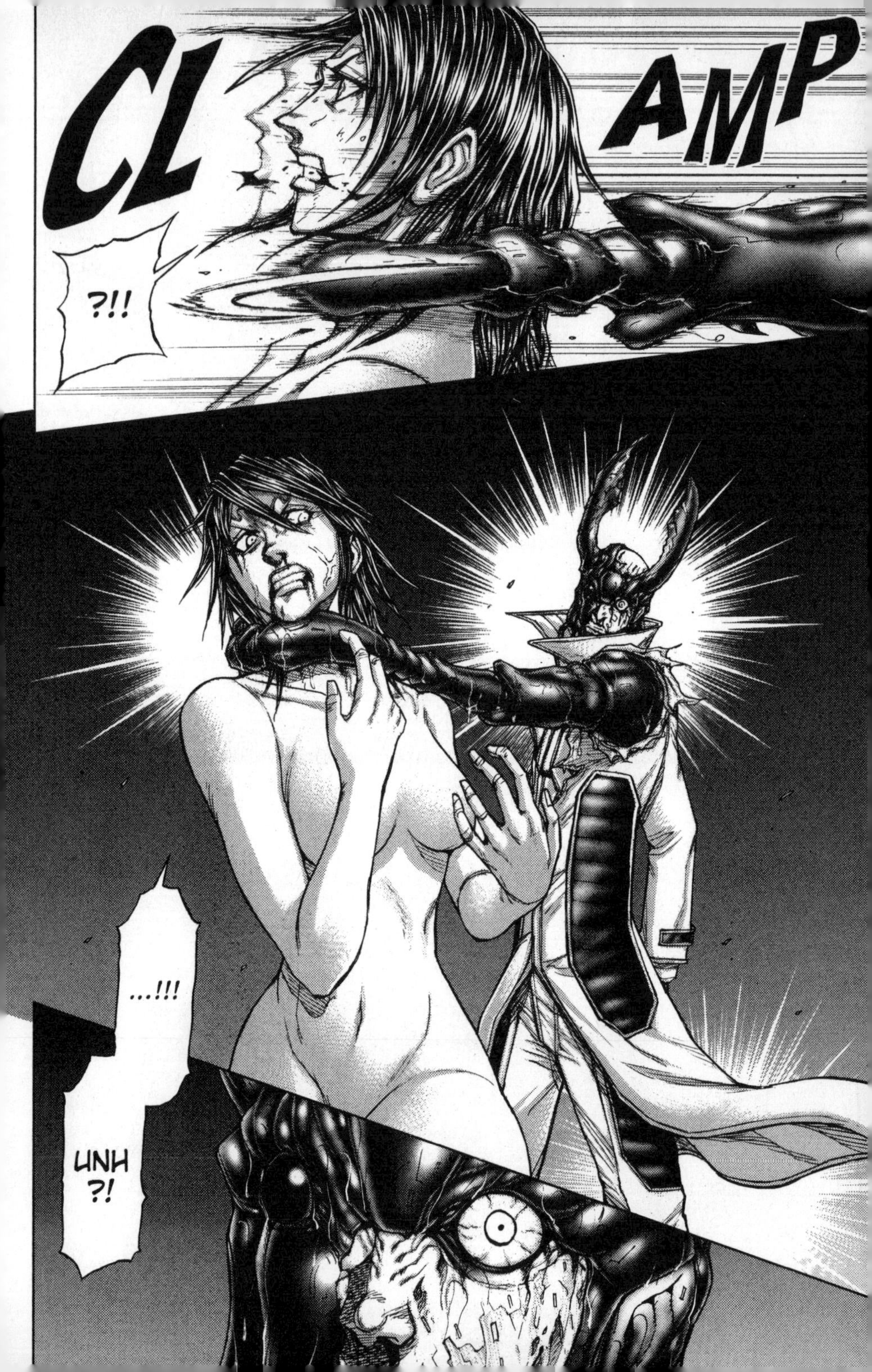
CLAMP
?!!
...!!!
UNH ?!

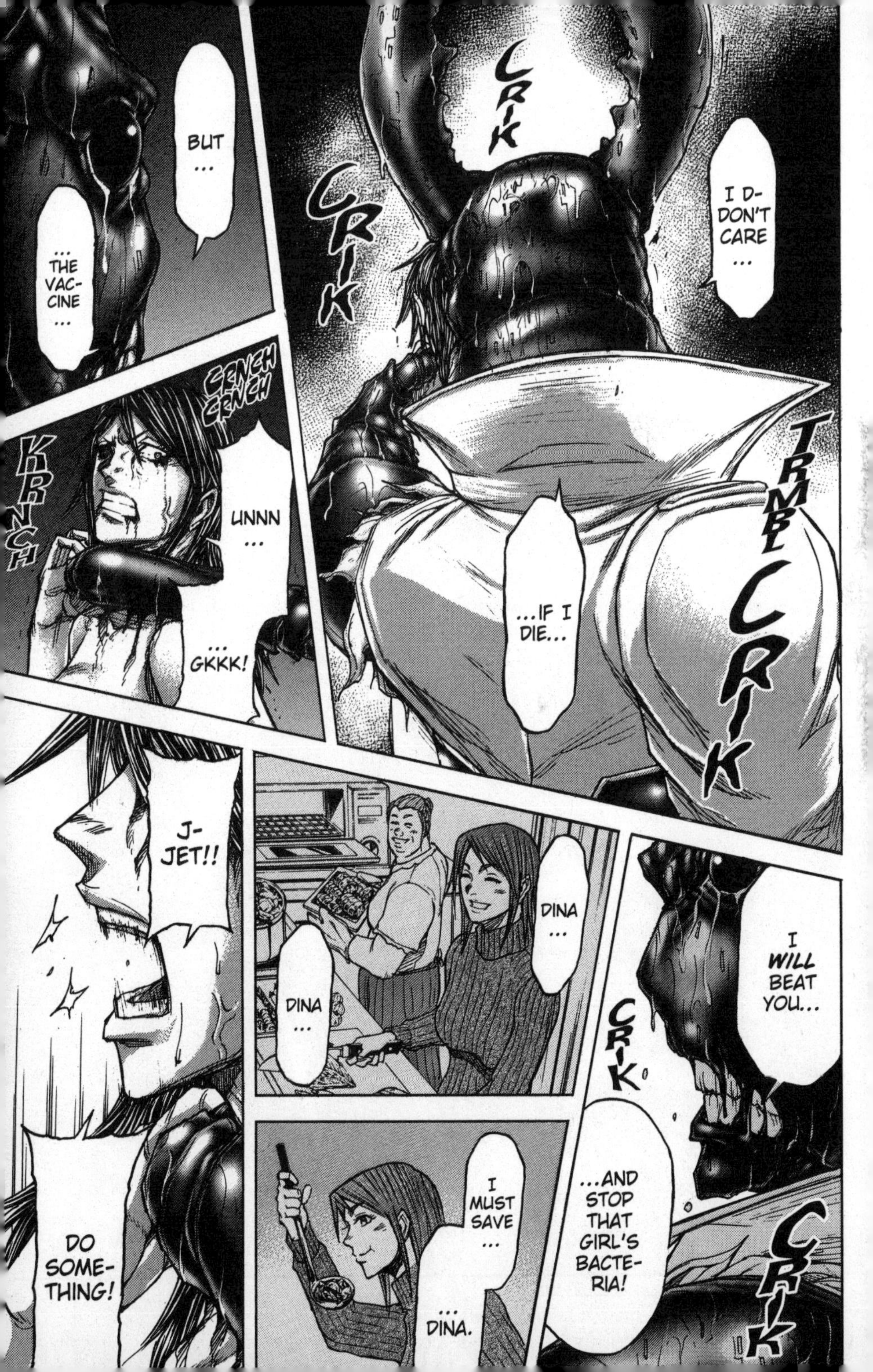
CRIK
I D-DON'T CARE...
CRIK
TRMBL
CRIK
...IF I DIE...
BUT...
...THE VACCINE...
CRNCH CRNCH
UNNN...
KRRNCH
...GKKK!
I WILL BEAT YOU...
CRIK
...AND STOP THAT GIRL'S BACTERIA!
CRIK
DINA...
DINA...
I MUST SAVE...
...DINA.
J-JET!!
DO SOMETHING!

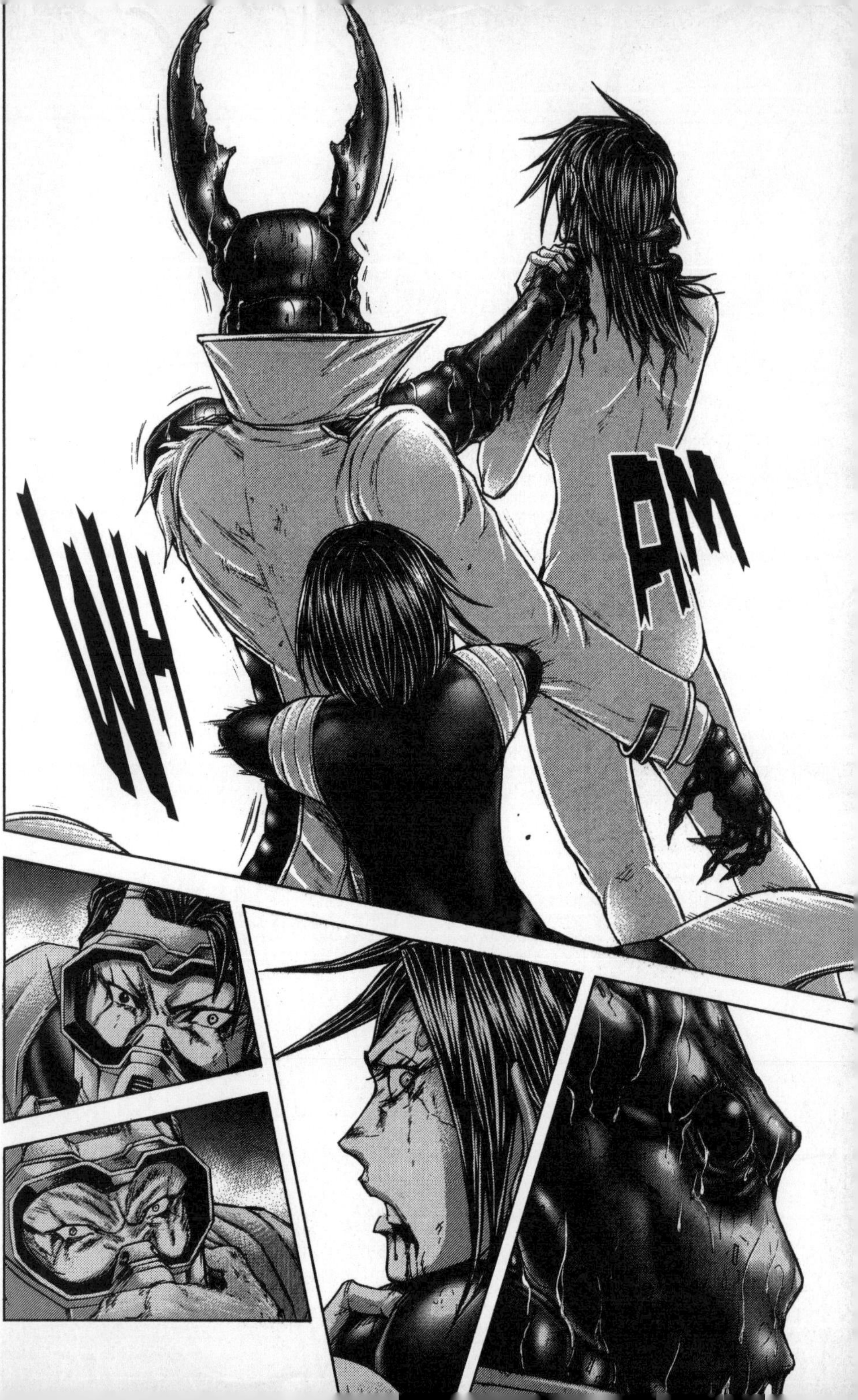
WHAM

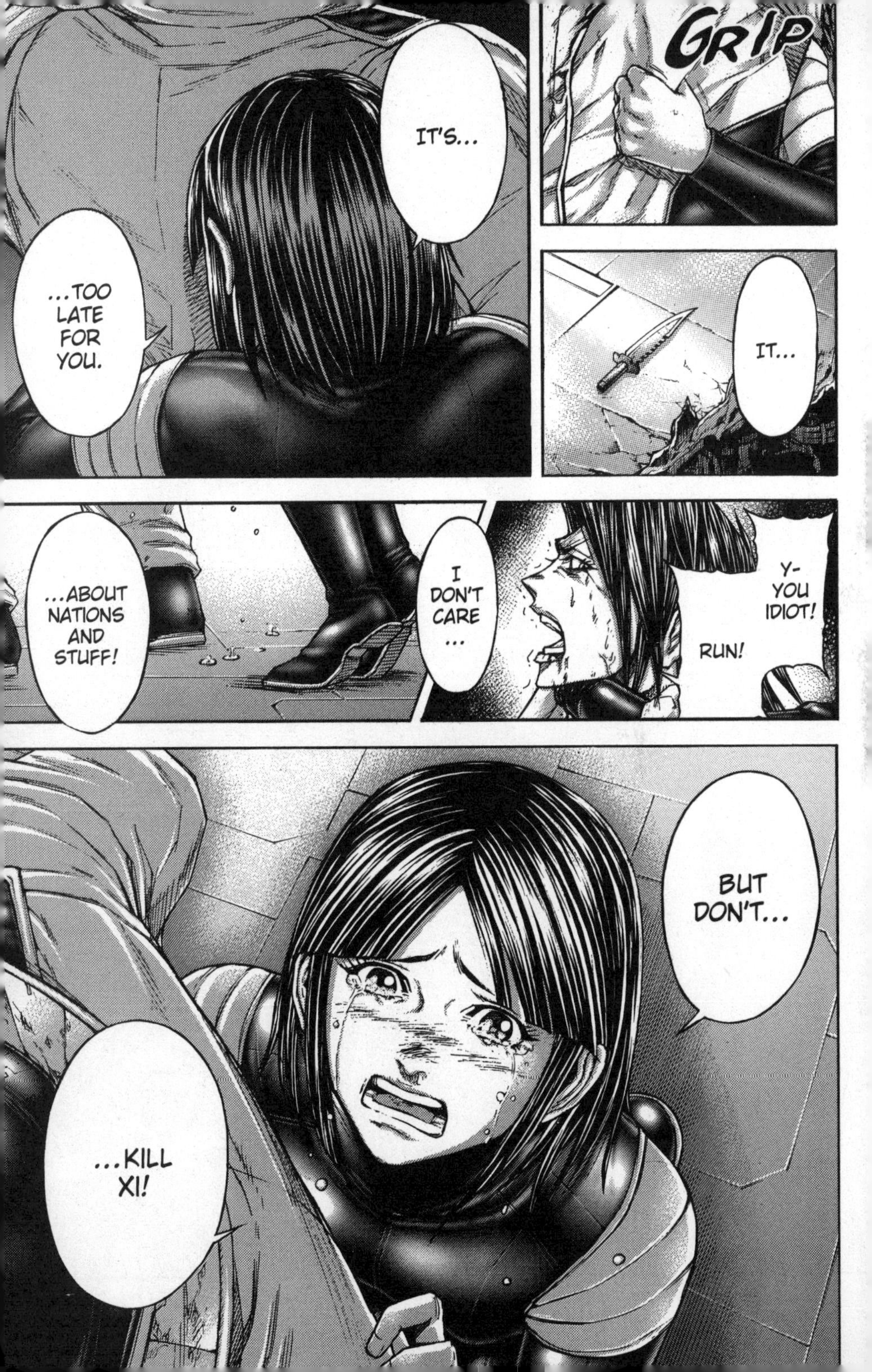
GRIP
IT...
IT'S...
...TOO LATE FOR YOU.
Y-YOU IDIOT!
RUN!
I DON'T CARE...
...ABOUT NATIONS AND STUFF!
BUT DON'T...
...KILL XI!

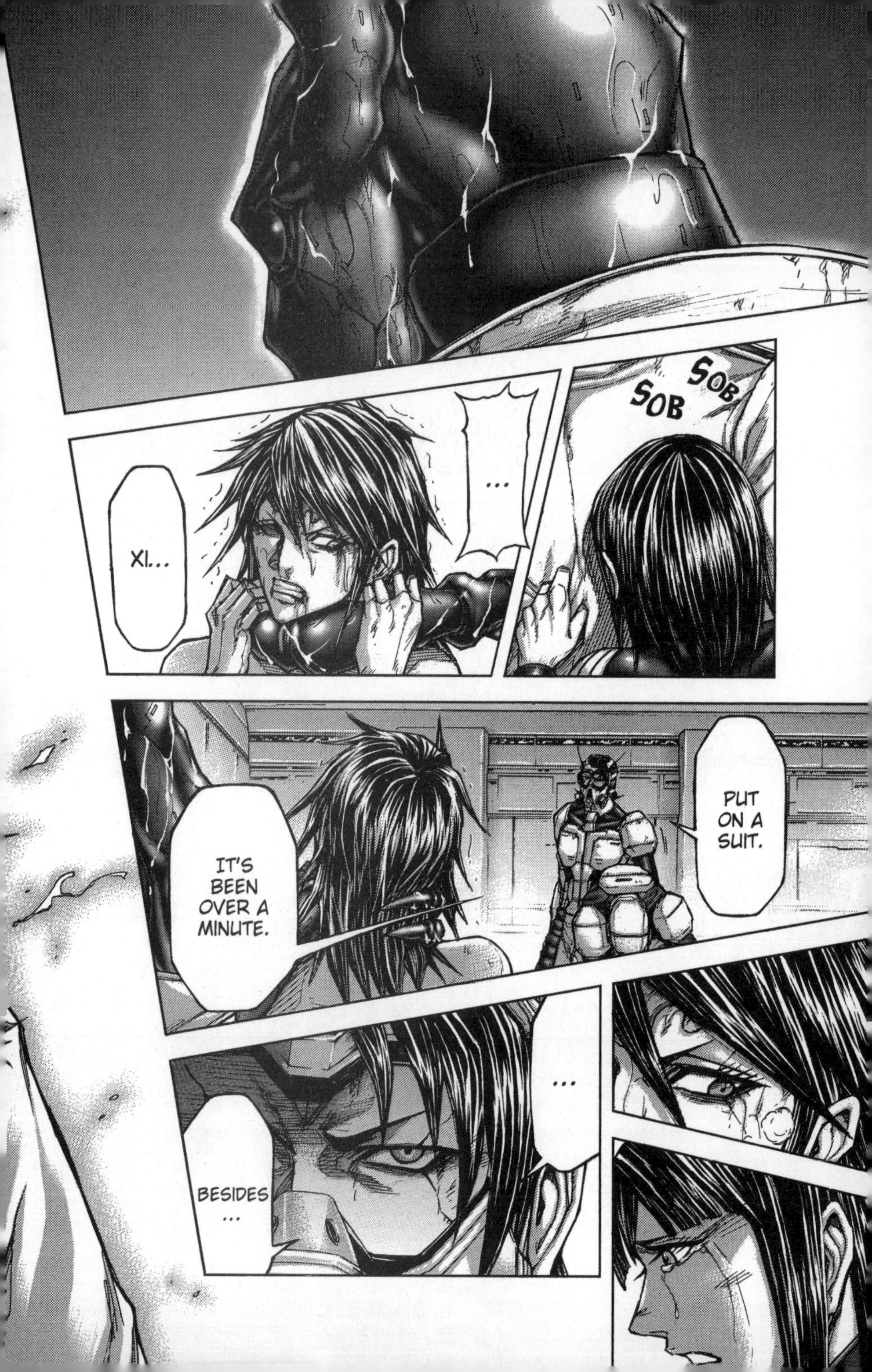
SOB
SOB
...
XI...
PUT ON A SUIT.
IT'S BEEN OVER A MINUTE.
...
BESIDES ...

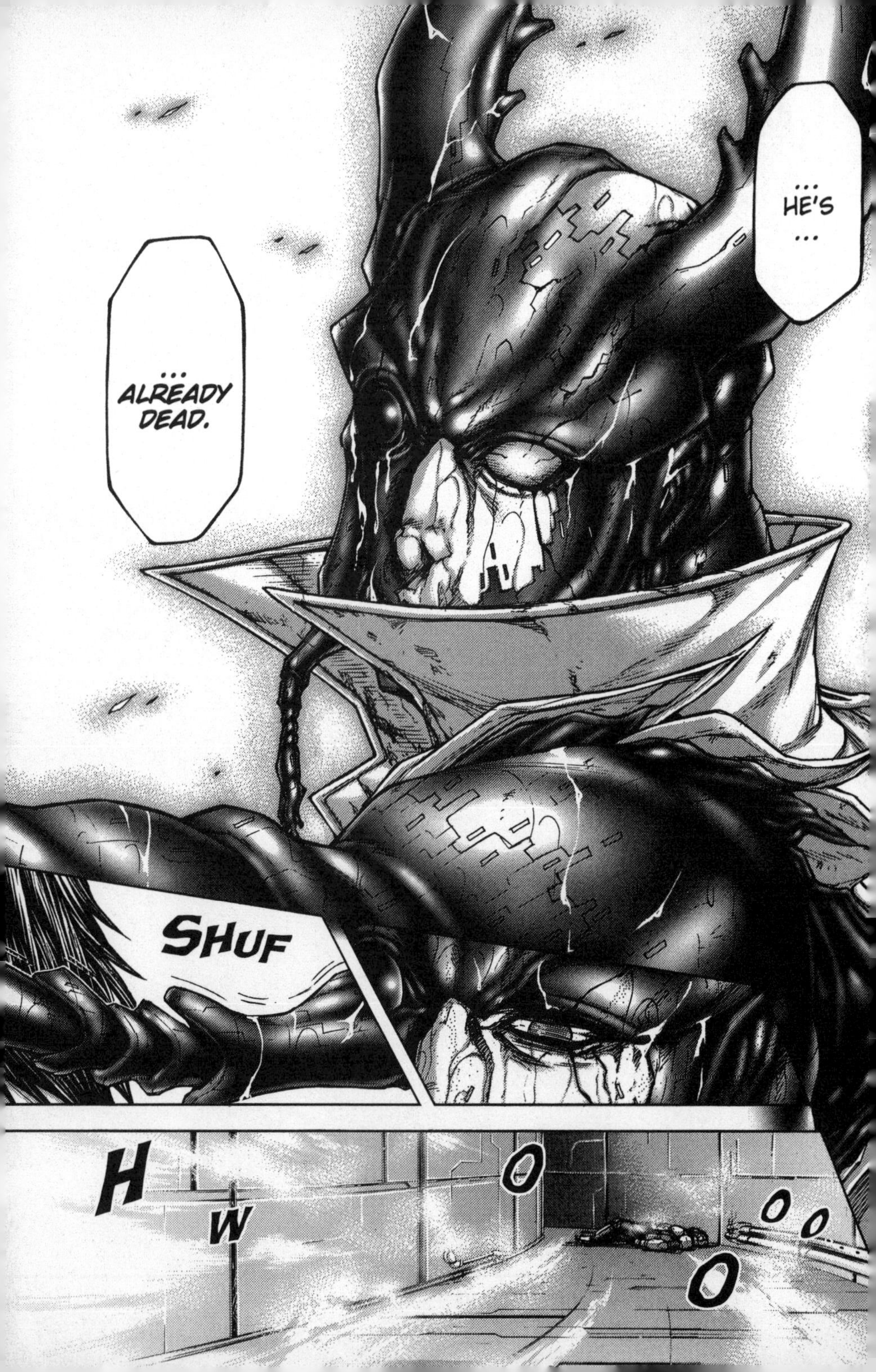
... HE'S ...
... ALREADY DEAD.
SHUF
HWOOOOO

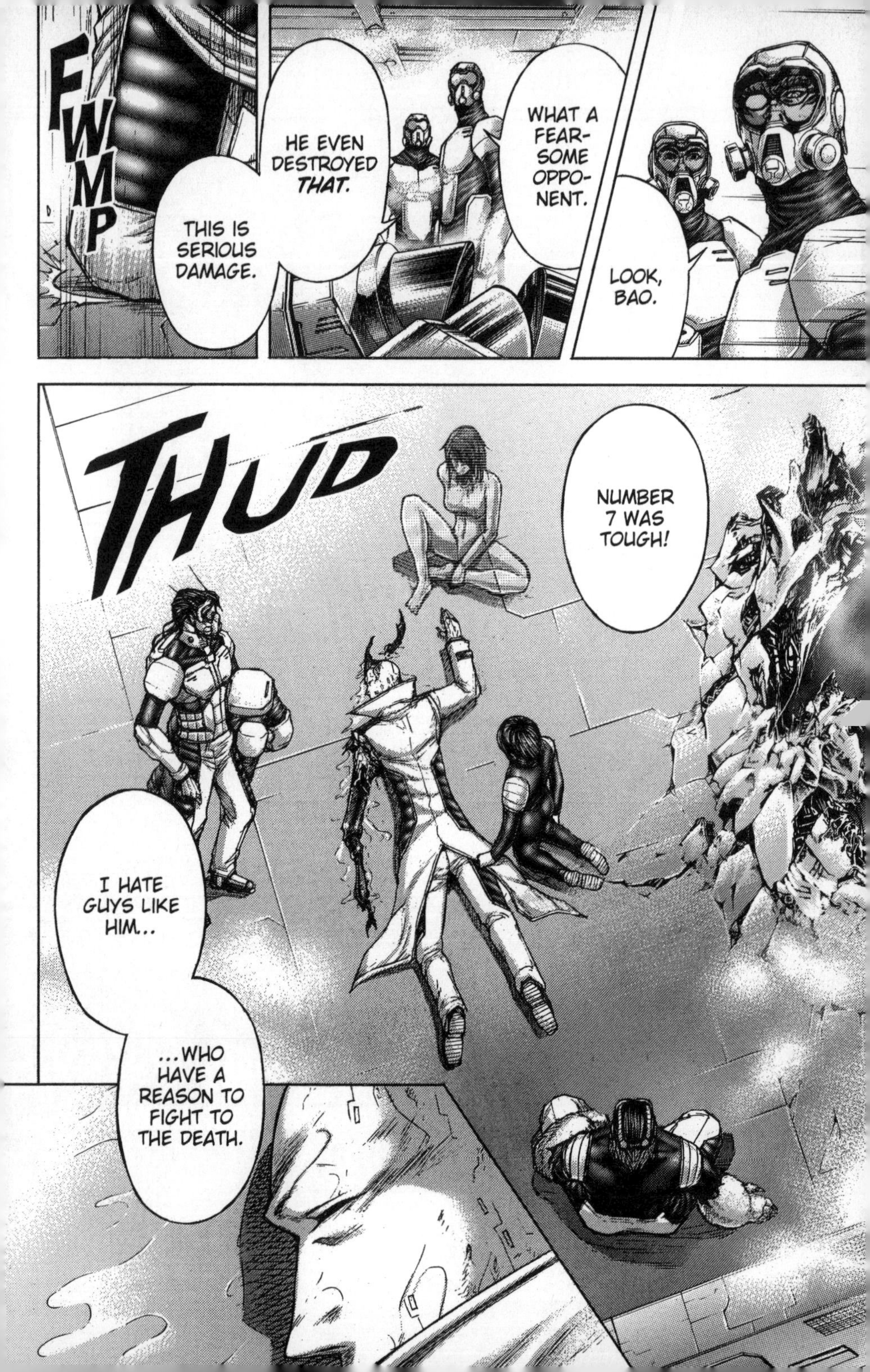
WHAT A FEAR-SOME OPPO-NENT.
LOOK, BAO.
HE EVEN DESTROYED *THAT*.
THIS IS SERIOUS DAMAGE.
FWMP
THUD
NUMBER 7 WAS TOUGH!
I HATE GUYS LIKE HIM...
...WHO HAVE A REASON TO FIGHT TO THE DEATH.

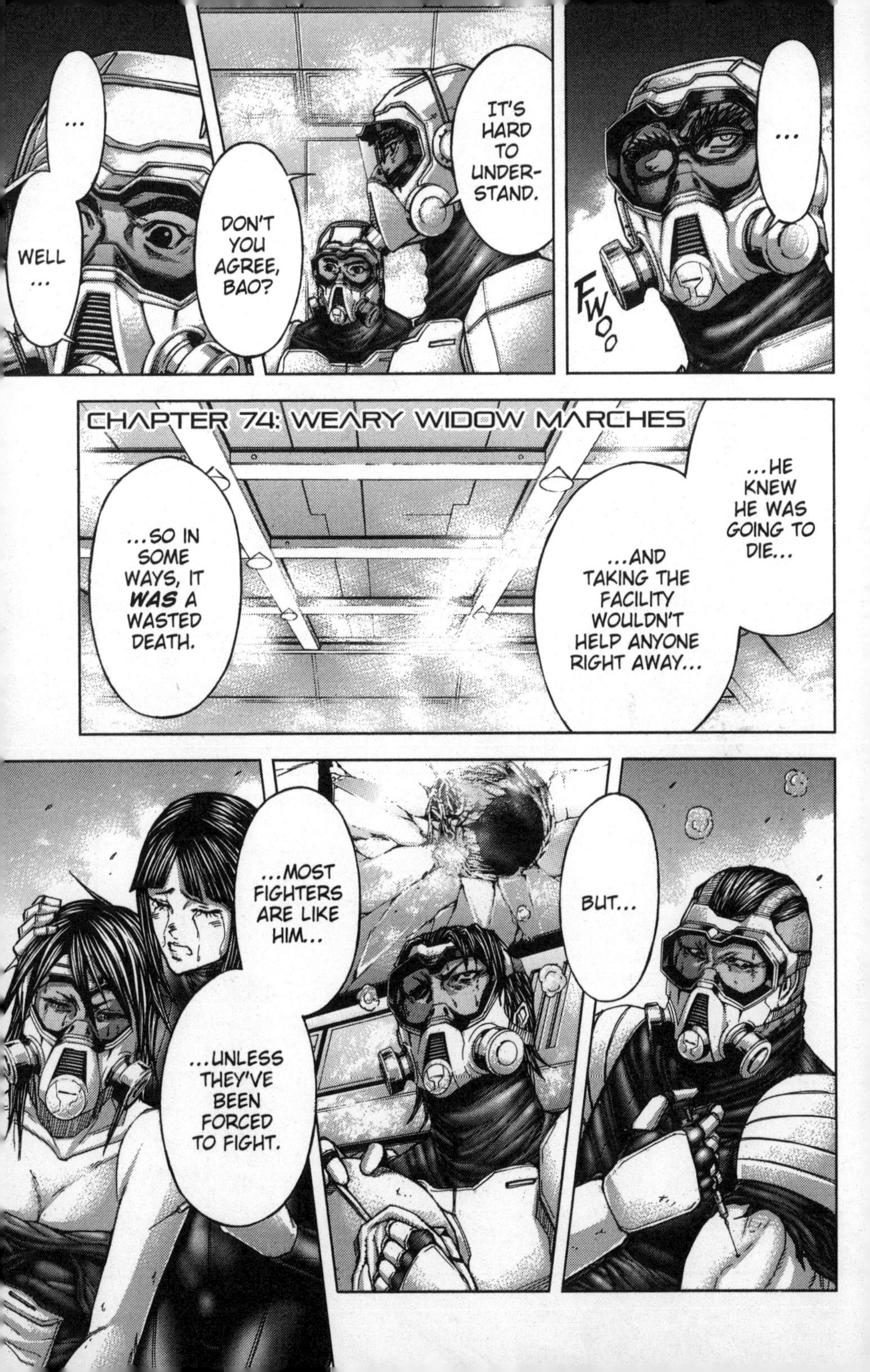
...
FWOO
IT'S HARD TO UNDERSTAND.
DON'T YOU AGREE, BAO?
...
WELL ...
CHAPTER 74: WEARY WIDOW MARCHES
...HE KNEW HE WAS GOING TO DIE...
...AND TAKING THE FACILITY WOULDN'T HELP ANYONE RIGHT AWAY...
...SO IN SOME WAYS, IT ***WAS*** A WASTED DEATH.
BUT...
...MOST FIGHTERS ARE LIKE HIM...
...UNLESS THEY'VE BEEN FORCED TO FIGHT.

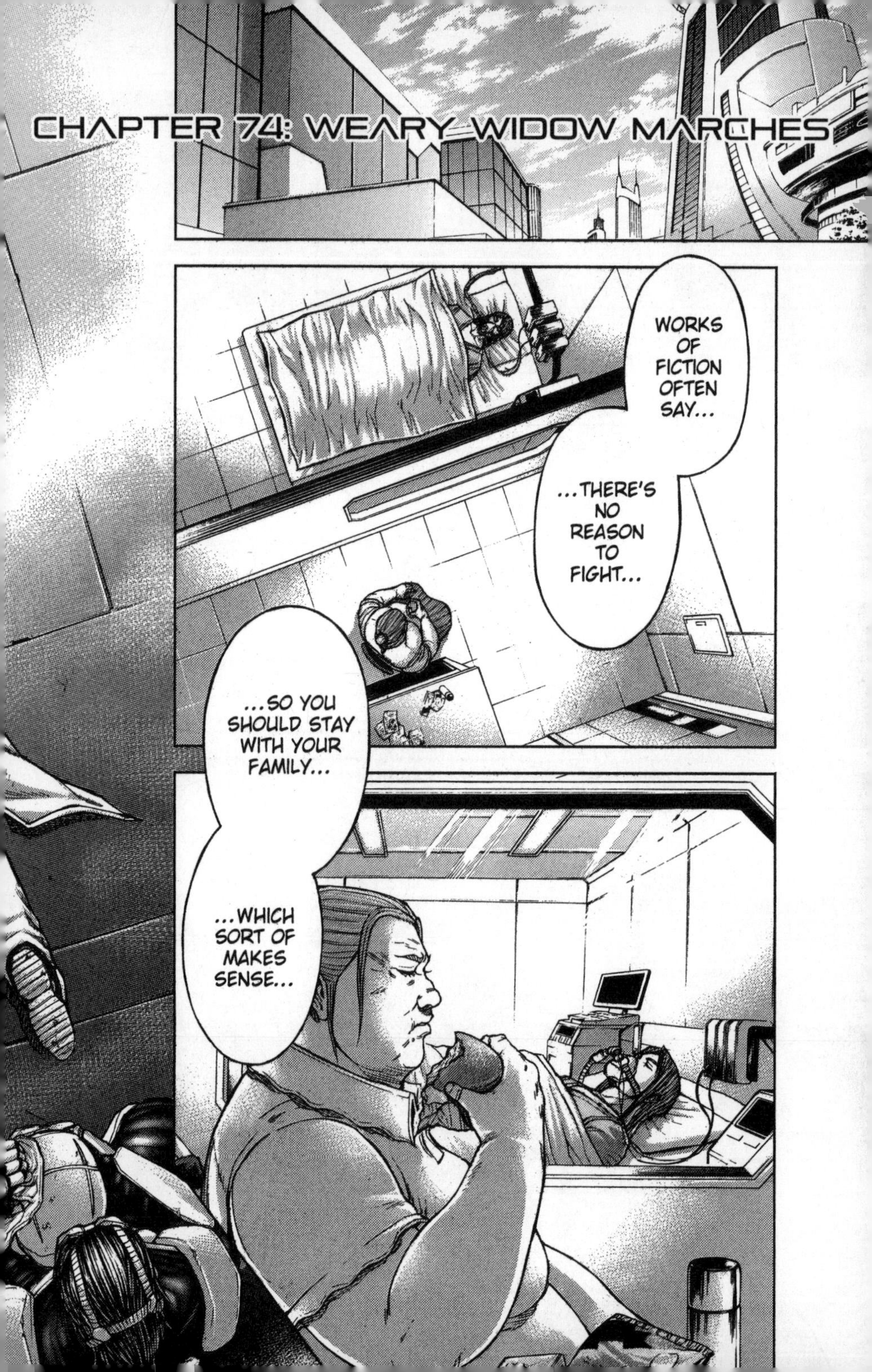
CHAPTER 74: WEARY WIDOW MARCHES
WORKS OF FICTION OFTEN SAY...
...THERE'S NO REASON TO FIGHT...
...SO YOU SHOULD STAY WITH YOUR FAMILY...
...WHICH SORT OF MAKES SENSE...

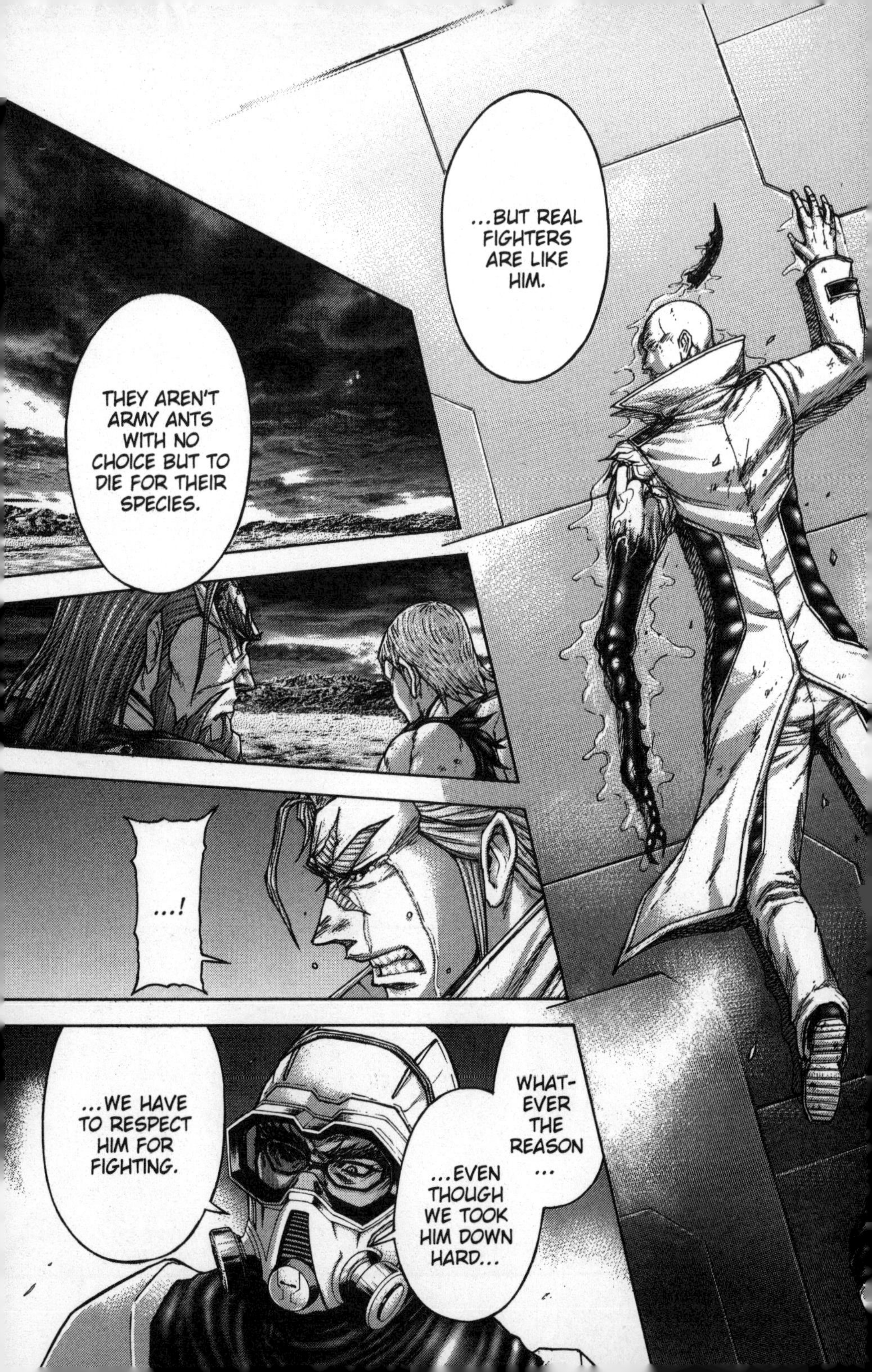
...BUT REAL FIGHTERS ARE LIKE HIM.
THEY AREN'T ARMY ANTS WITH NO CHOICE BUT TO DIE FOR THEIR SPECIES.
...!
WHAT-EVER THE REASON...
...EVEN THOUGH WE TOOK HIM DOWN HARD...
...WE HAVE TO RESPECT HIM FOR FIGHTING.

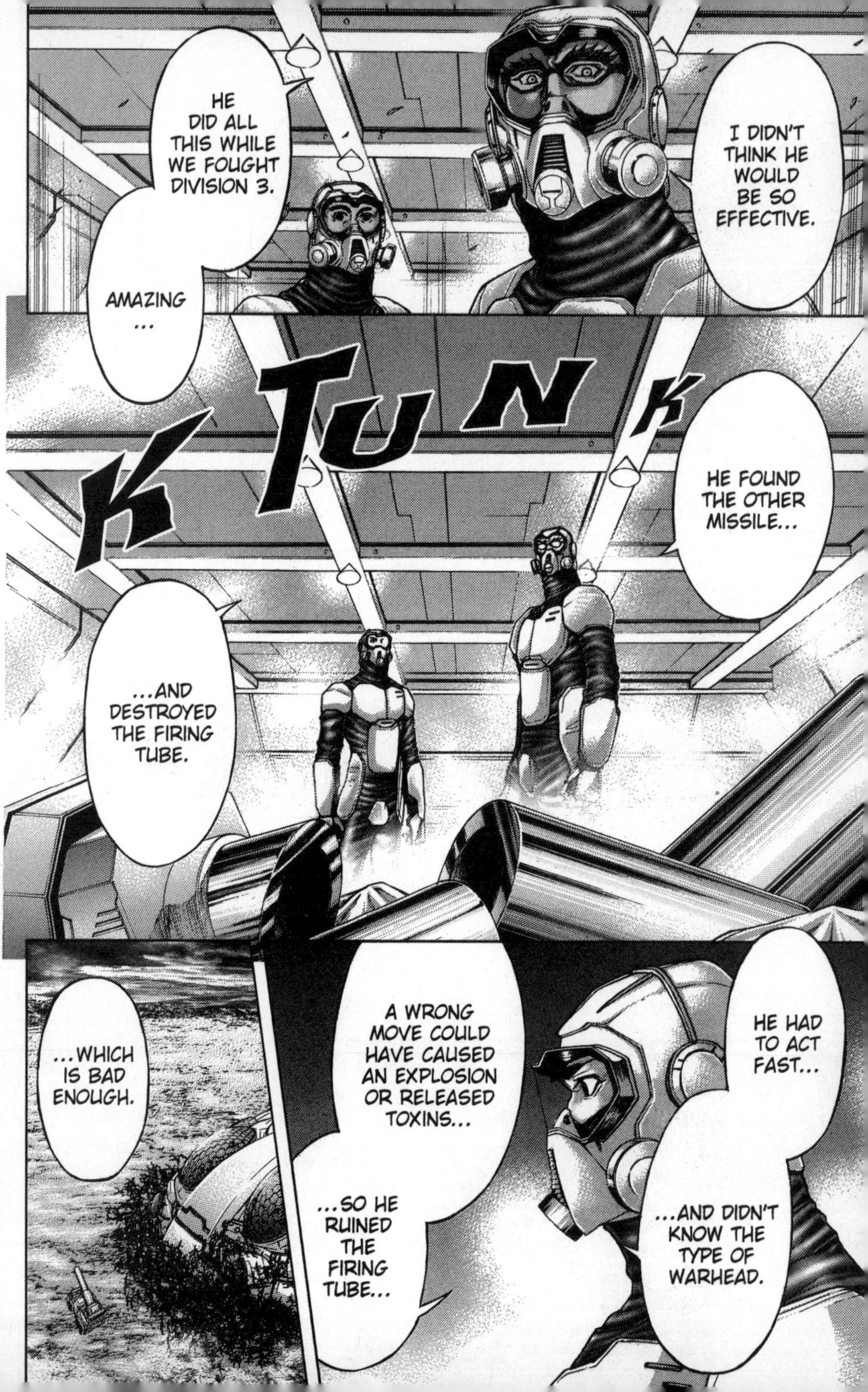
I DIDN'T THINK HE WOULD BE SO EFFECTIVE.
HE DID ALL THIS WHILE WE FOUGHT DIVISION 3.
AMAZING ...
KTUNK
HE FOUND THE OTHER MISSILE...
...AND DESTROYED THE FIRING TUBE.
HE HAD TO ACT FAST...
...AND DIDN'T KNOW THE TYPE OF WARHEAD.
A WRONG MOVE COULD HAVE CAUSED AN EXPLOSION OR RELEASED TOXINS...
...SO HE RUINED THE FIRING TUBE...
...WHICH IS BAD ENOUGH.

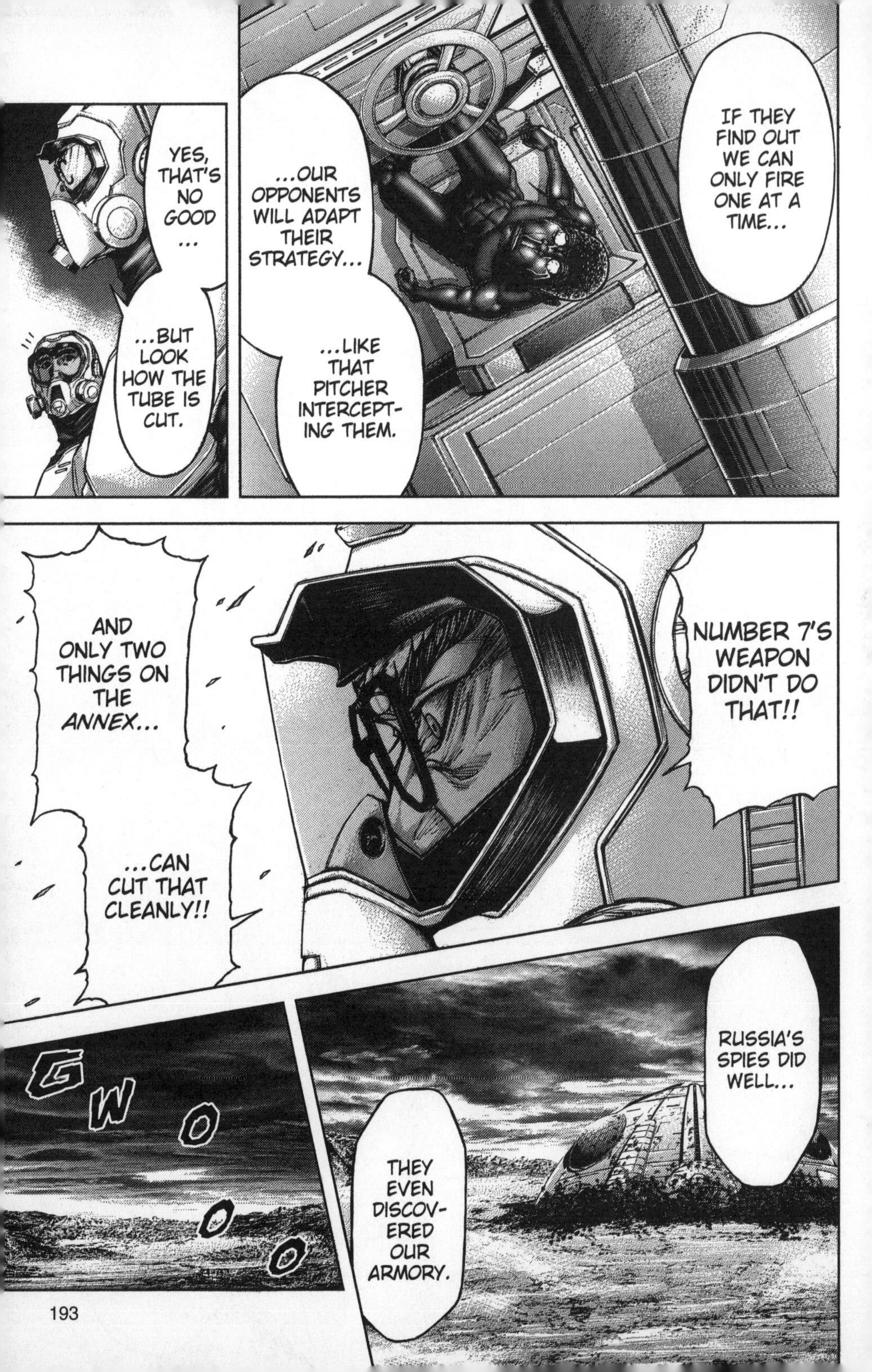
IF THEY FIND OUT WE CAN ONLY FIRE ONE AT A TIME...
...OUR OPPONENTS WILL ADAPT THEIR STRATEGY...
...LIKE THAT PITCHER INTERCEPTING THEM.
YES, THAT'S NO GOOD...
...BUT LOOK HOW THE TUBE IS CUT.
NUMBER 7'S WEAPON DIDN'T DO THAT!!
AND ONLY TWO THINGS ON THE *ANNEX*...
...CAN CUT THAT CLEANLY!!
RUSSIA'S SPIES DID WELL...
THEY EVEN DISCOVERED OUR ARMORY.
GWOOOO

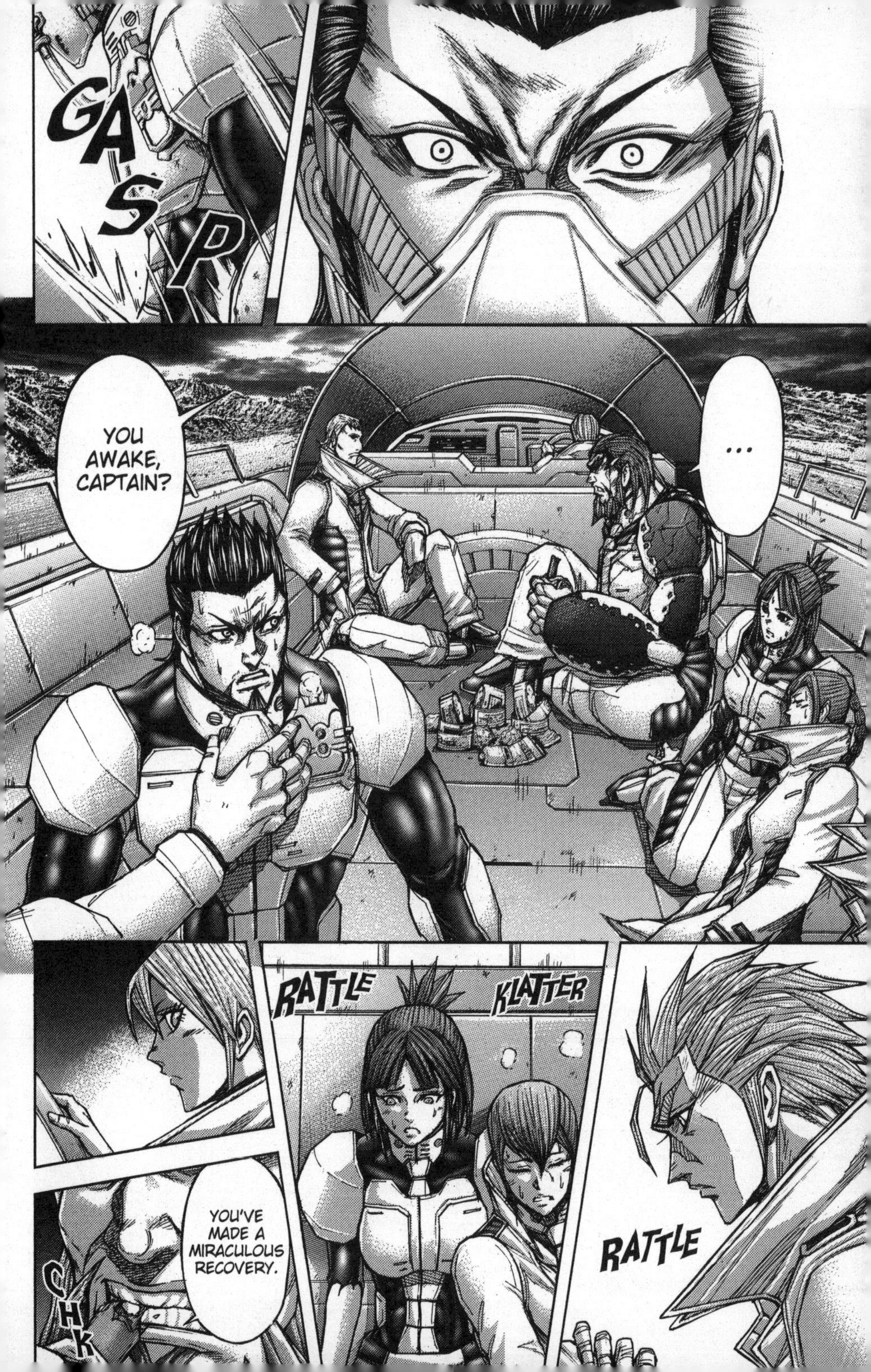
GASP
...
YOU AWAKE, CAPTAIN?
RATTLE
KLATTER
RATTLE
YOU'VE MADE A MIRACULOUS RECOVERY.
CHK

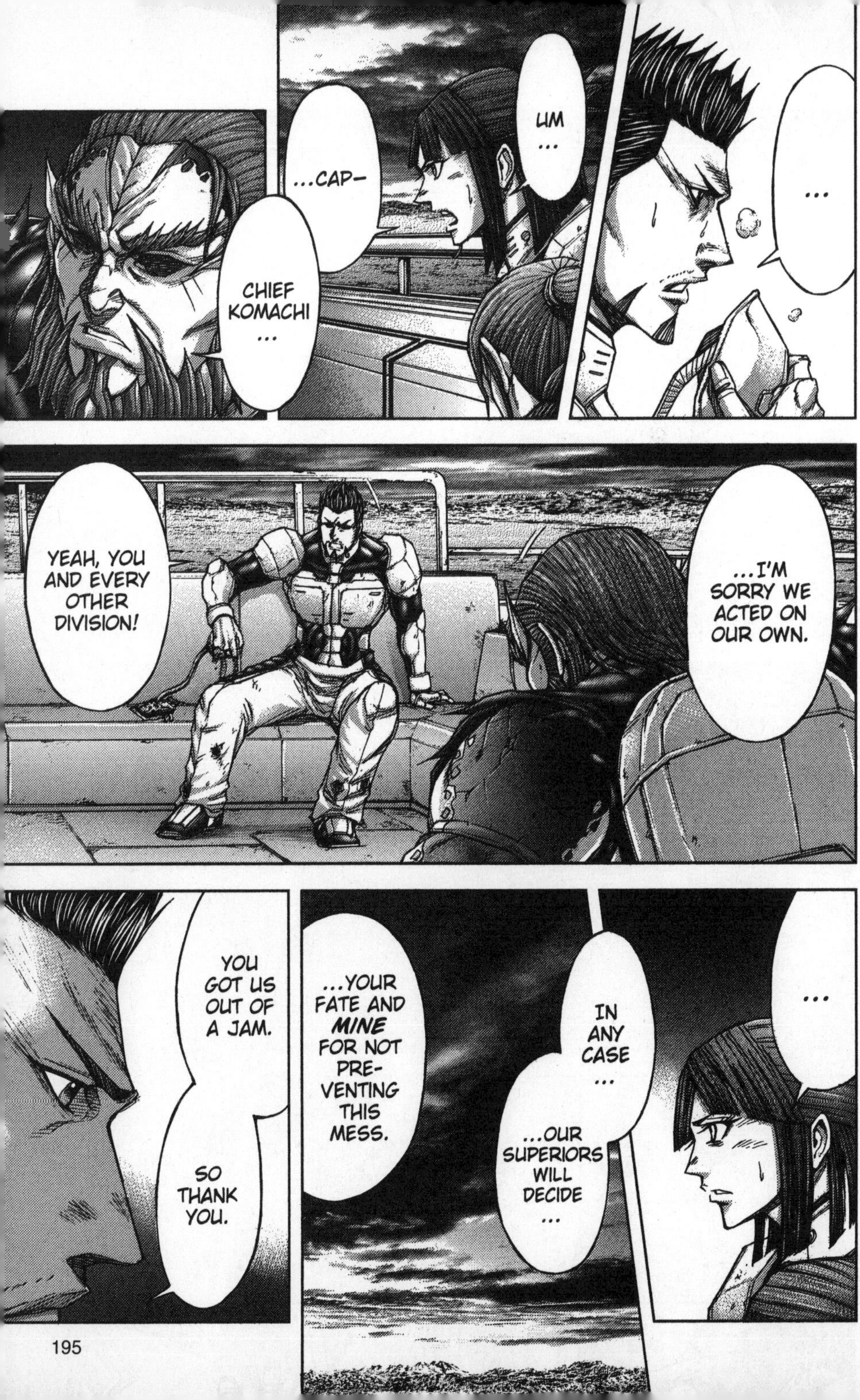
...
UM ...
...CAP—
CHIEF KOMACHI ...
...I'M SORRY WE ACTED ON OUR OWN.
YEAH, YOU AND EVERY OTHER DIVISION!
...
IN ANY CASE ...
...OUR SUPERIORS WILL DECIDE ...
...YOUR FATE AND *MINE* FOR NOT PRE-VENTING THIS MESS.
YOU GOT US OUT OF A JAM.
SO THANK YOU.

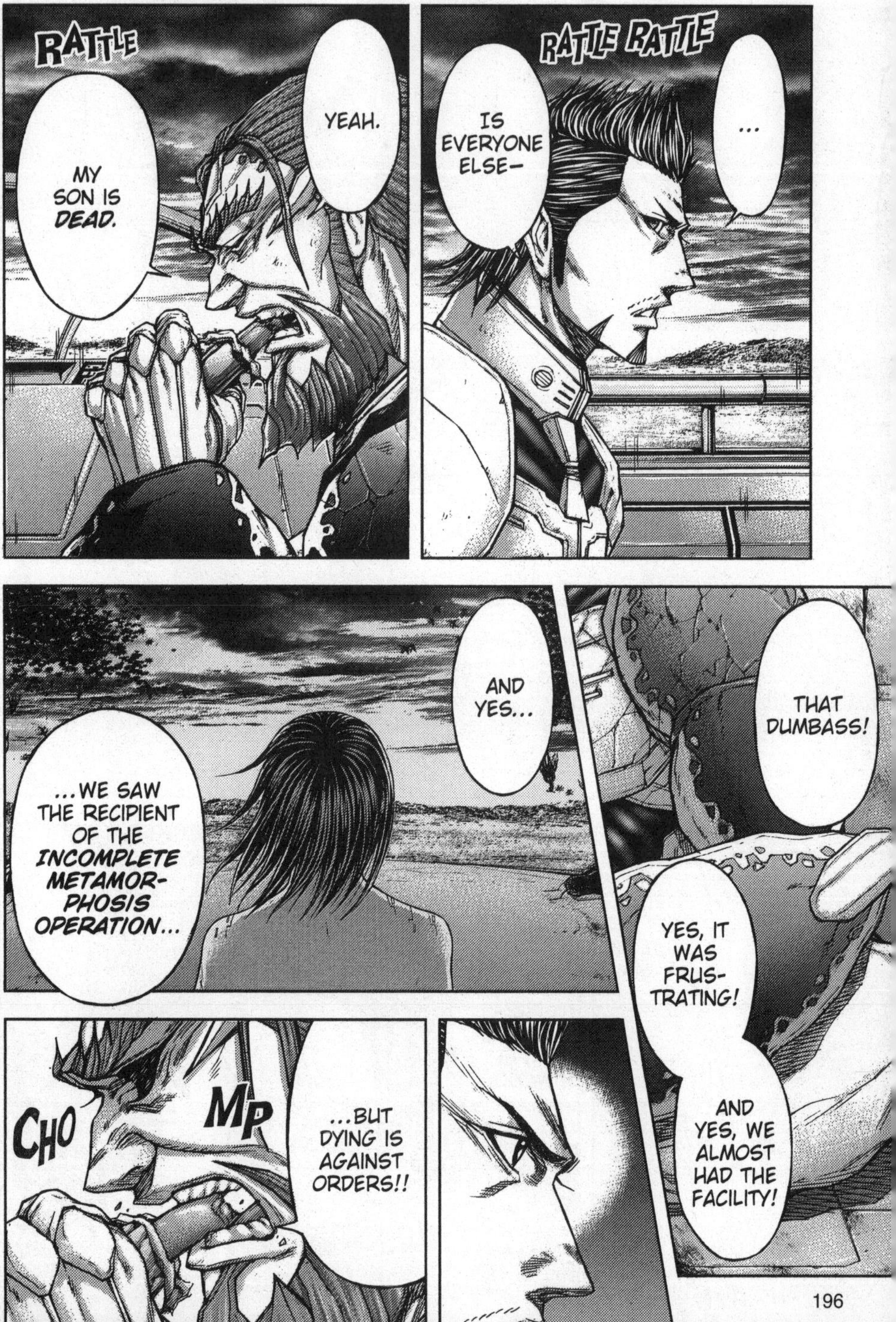

RATTLE RATTLE
...
IS EVERYONE ELSE—
RATTLE
YEAH.
MY SON IS DEAD.
THAT DUMBASS!
YES, IT WAS FRUS-TRATING!
AND YES, WE ALMOST HAD THE FACILITY!
AND YES...
...WE SAW THE RECIPIENT OF THE INCOMPLETE METAMOR-PHOSIS OPERATION...
CHOMP
...BUT DYING IS AGAINST ORDERS!!

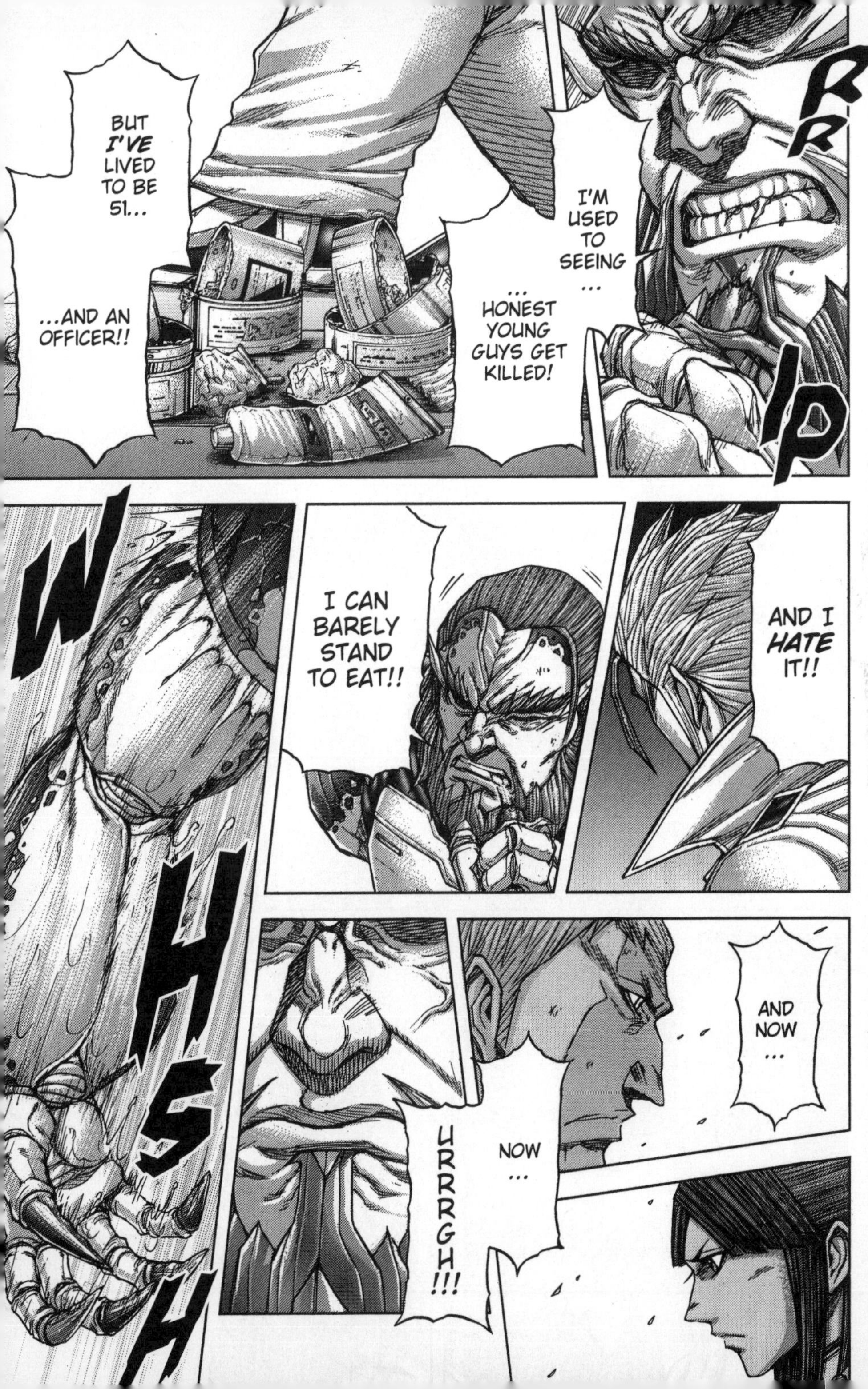
RRIP
I'M USED TO SEEING ...
... HONEST YOUNG GUYS GET KILLED!
BUT *I'VE* LIVED TO BE 51...
...AND AN OFFICER!!
AND I *HATE* IT!!
I CAN BARELY STAND TO EAT!!
AND NOW ...
NOW ...
URRRGH!!!
WHHSH

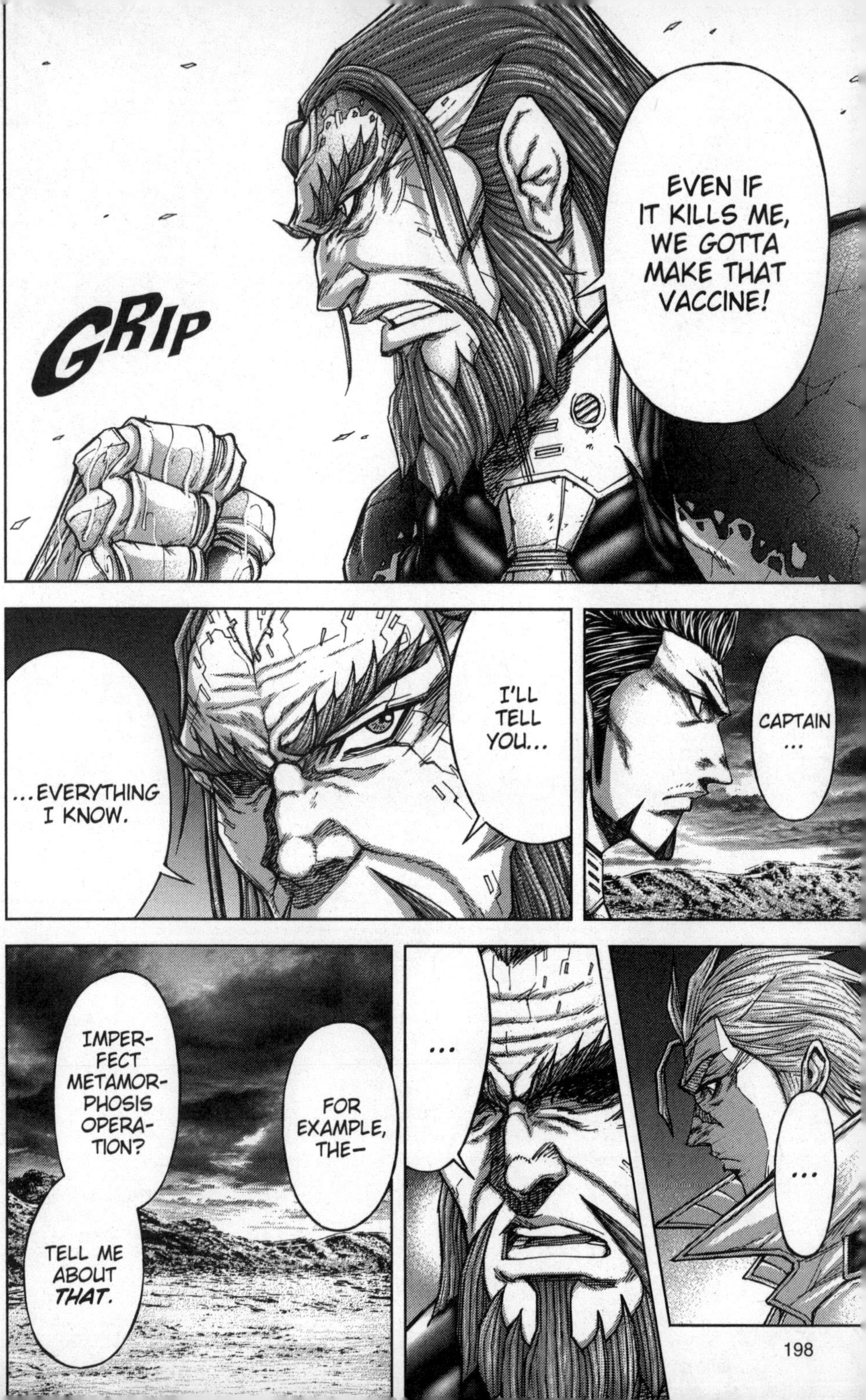

GRIP
EVEN IF IT KILLS ME, WE GOTTA MAKE THAT VACCINE!
CAPTAIN ...
I'LL TELL YOU...
...EVERYTHING I KNOW.
...
...
FOR EXAMPLE, THE—
IMPERFECT METAMORPHOSIS OPERATION?
TELL ME ABOUT *THAT*.

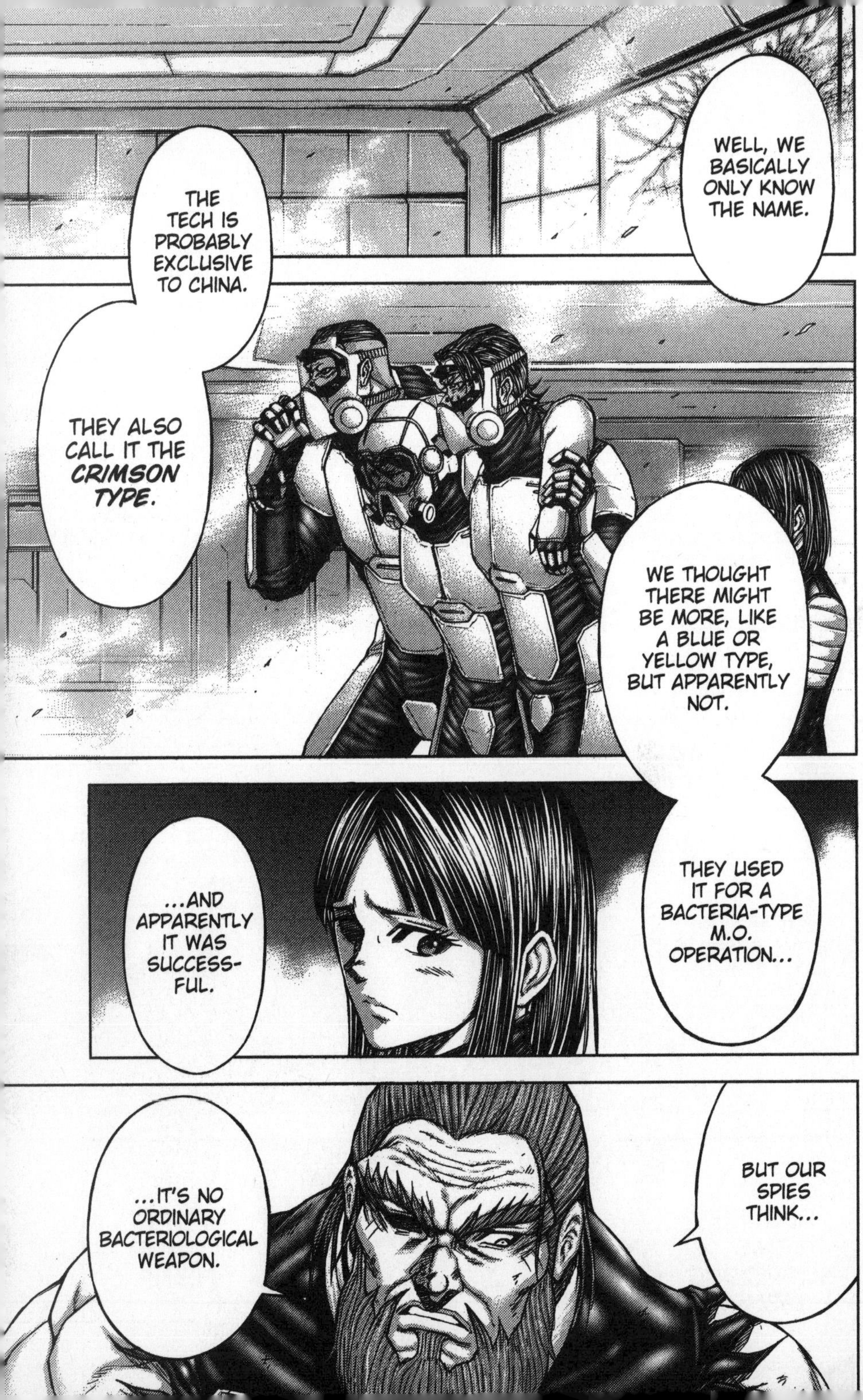
WELL, WE BASICALLY ONLY KNOW THE NAME.
THE TECH IS PROBABLY EXCLUSIVE TO CHINA.
THEY ALSO CALL IT THE *CRIMSON TYPE*.
WE THOUGHT THERE MIGHT BE MORE, LIKE A BLUE OR YELLOW TYPE, BUT APPARENTLY NOT.
THEY USED IT FOR A BACTERIA-TYPE M.O. OPERATION...
...AND APPARENTLY IT WAS SUCCESS-FUL.
BUT OUR SPIES THINK...
...IT'S NO ORDINARY BACTERIOLOGICAL WEAPON.

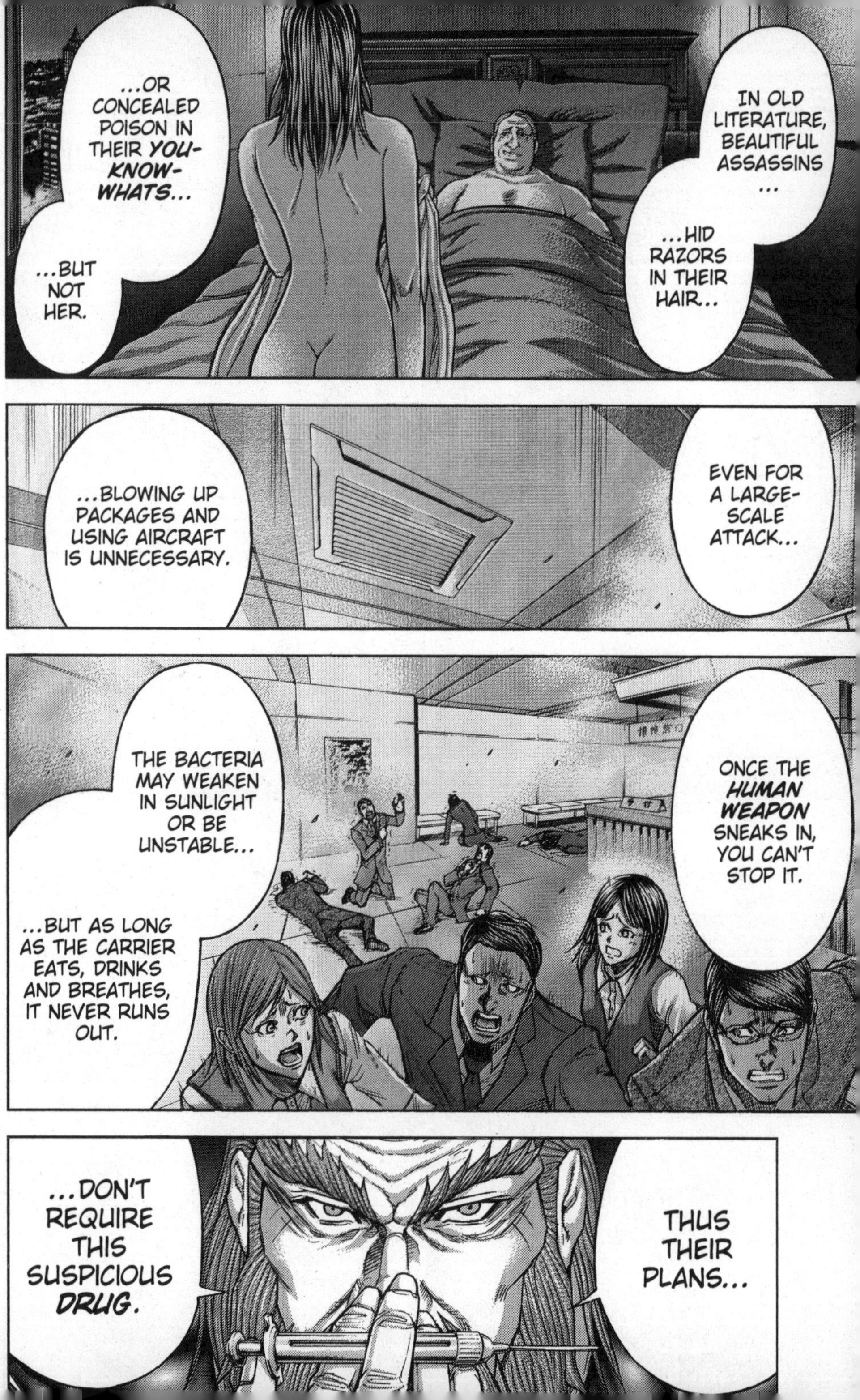
IN OLD LITERATURE, BEAUTIFUL ASSASSINS ...
...HID RAZORS IN THEIR HAIR...
...OR CONCEALED POISON IN THEIR ***YOU-KNOW-WHATS***...
...BUT NOT HER.
EVEN FOR A LARGE-SCALE ATTACK...
...BLOWING UP PACKAGES AND USING AIRCRAFT IS UNNECESSARY.
ONCE THE ***HUMAN WEAPON*** SNEAKS IN, YOU CAN'T STOP IT.
THE BACTERIA MAY WEAKEN IN SUNLIGHT OR BE UNSTABLE...
...BUT AS LONG AS THE CARRIER EATS, DRINKS AND BREATHES, IT NEVER RUNS OUT.
THUS THEIR PLANS...
...DON'T REQUIRE THIS SUSPICIOUS ***DRUG***.

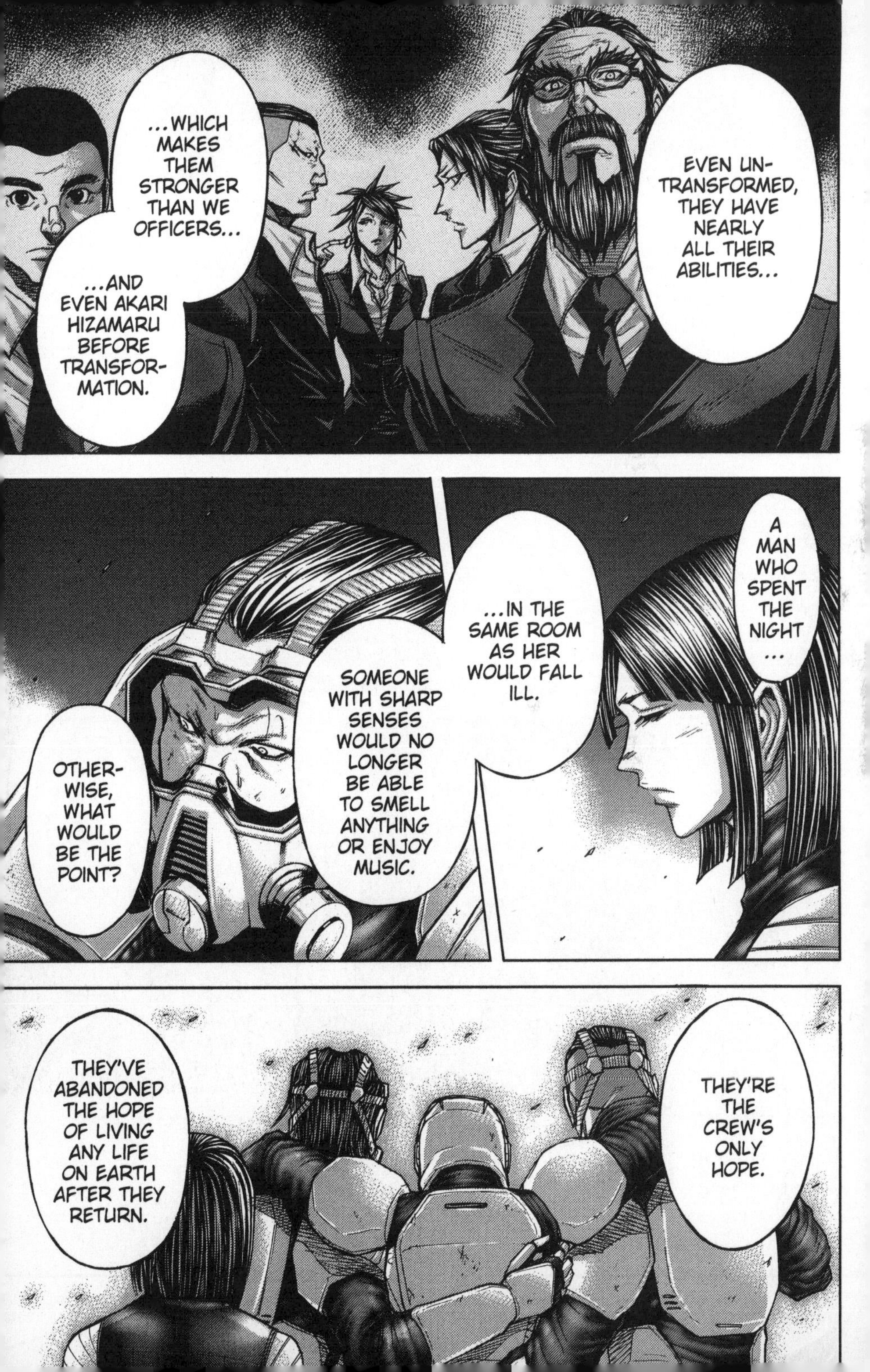
EVEN UN-TRANSFORMED, THEY HAVE NEARLY ALL THEIR ABILITIES...
...WHICH MAKES THEM STRONGER THAN WE OFFICERS...
...AND EVEN AKARI HIZAMARU BEFORE TRANSFOR-MATION.
A MAN WHO SPENT THE NIGHT ...
...IN THE SAME ROOM AS HER WOULD FALL ILL.
SOMEONE WITH SHARP SENSES WOULD NO LONGER BE ABLE TO SMELL ANYTHING OR ENJOY MUSIC.
OTHER-WISE, WHAT WOULD BE THE POINT?
THEY'RE THE CREW'S ONLY HOPE.
THEY'VE ABANDONED THE HOPE OF LIVING ANY LIFE ON EARTH AFTER THEY RETURN.

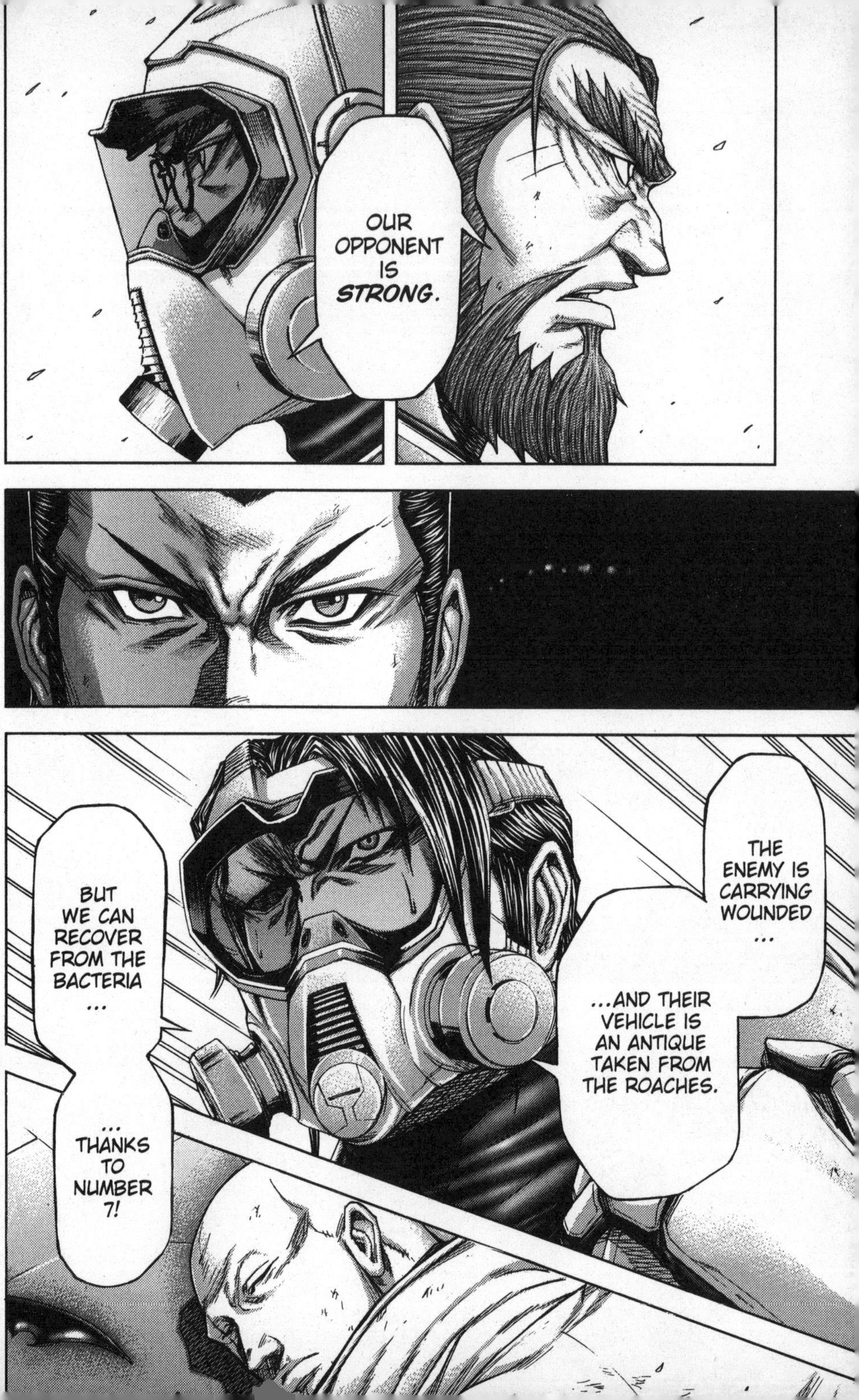
OUR OPPONENT IS STRONG.
THE ENEMY IS CARRYING WOUNDED...
...AND THEIR VEHICLE IS AN ANTIQUE TAKEN FROM THE ROACHES.
BUT WE CAN RECOVER FROM THE BACTERIA...
...THANKS TO NUMBER 7!

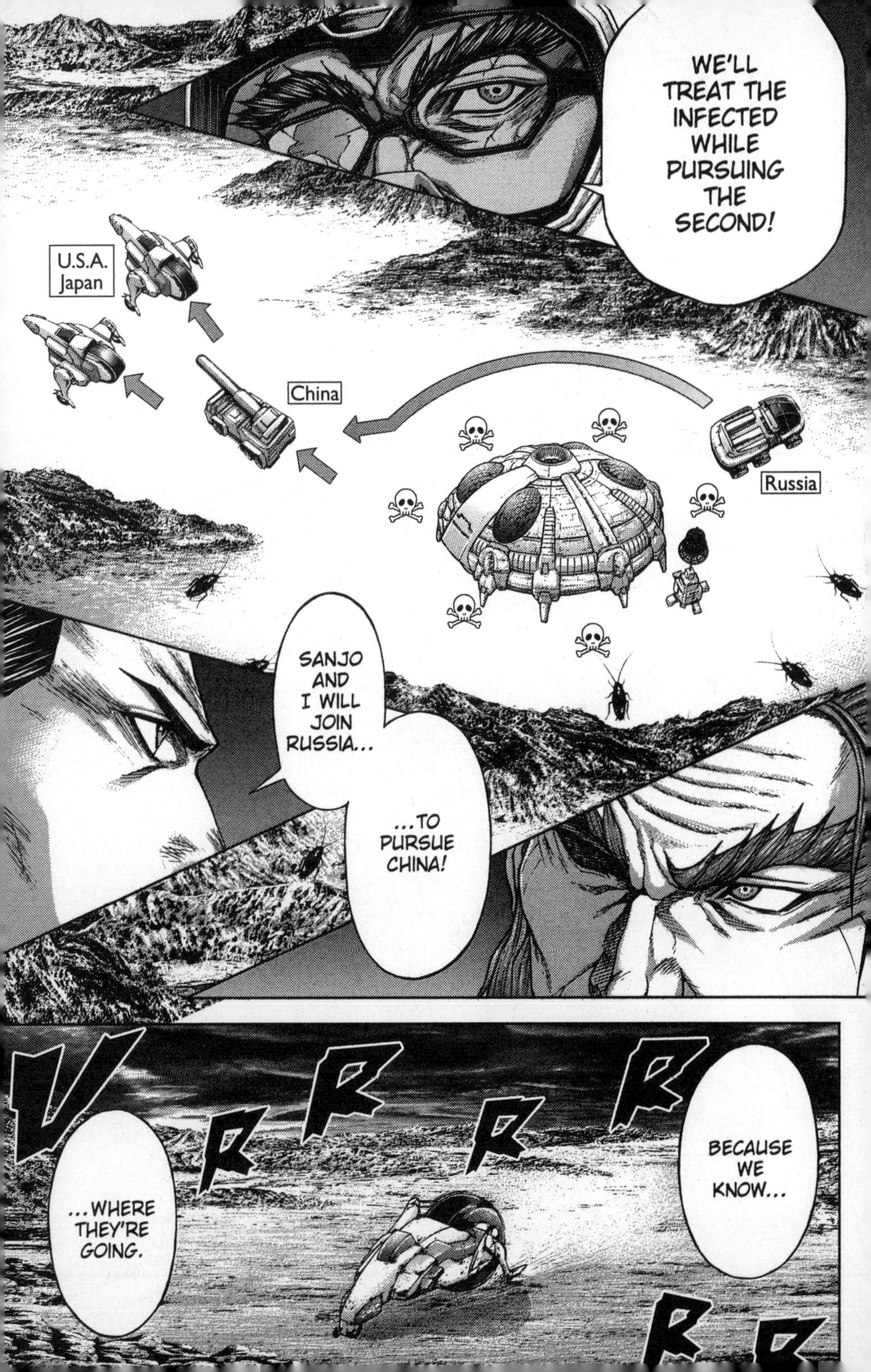
WE'LL TREAT THE INFECTED WHILE PURSUING THE SECOND!
Russia
China
U.S.A.
Japan
SANJO AND I WILL JOIN RUSSIA...
...TO PURSUE CHINA!
VRRRRRR
BECAUSE WE KNOW...
...WHERE THEY'RE GOING.

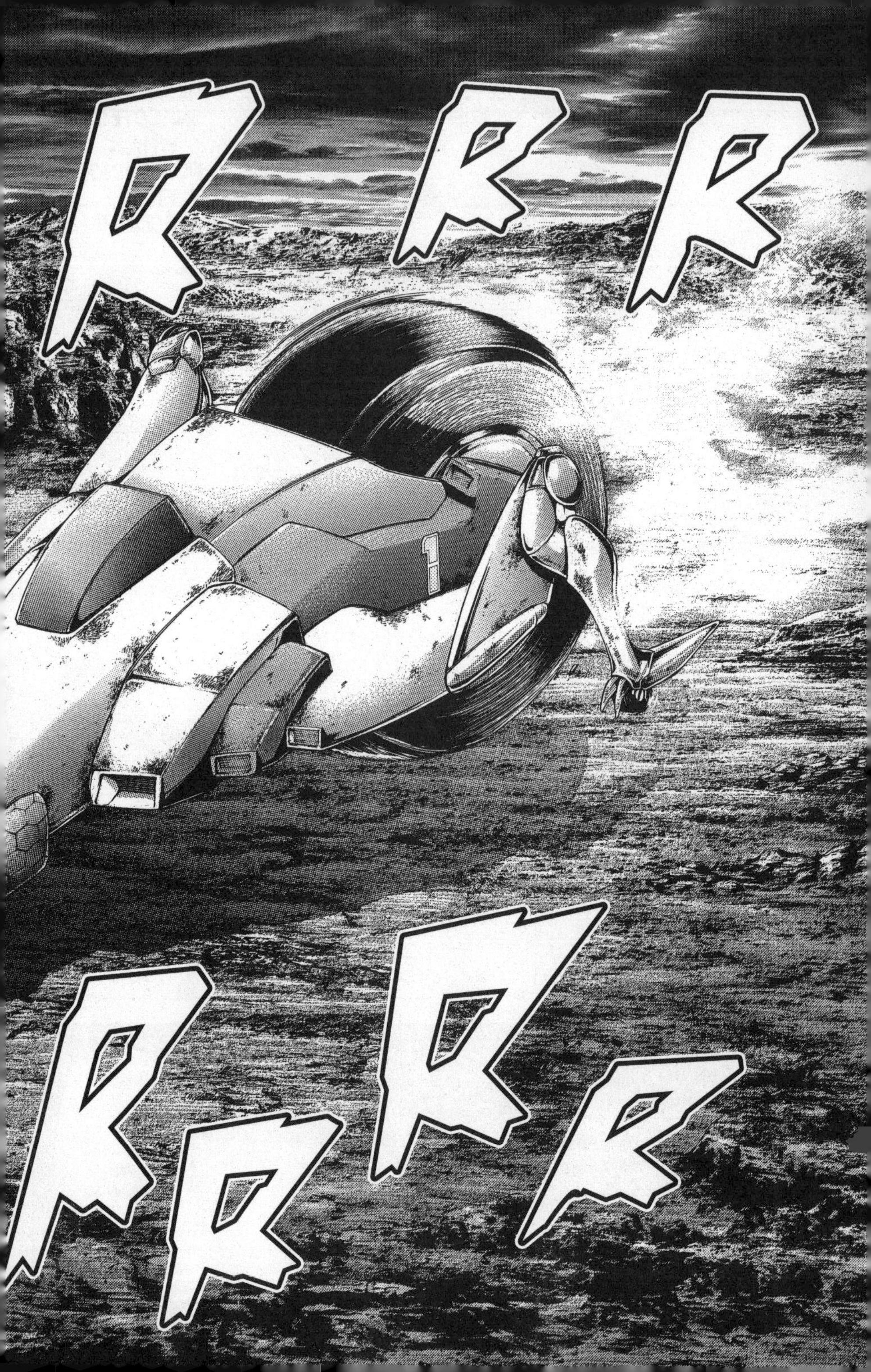
RRR
RRRR

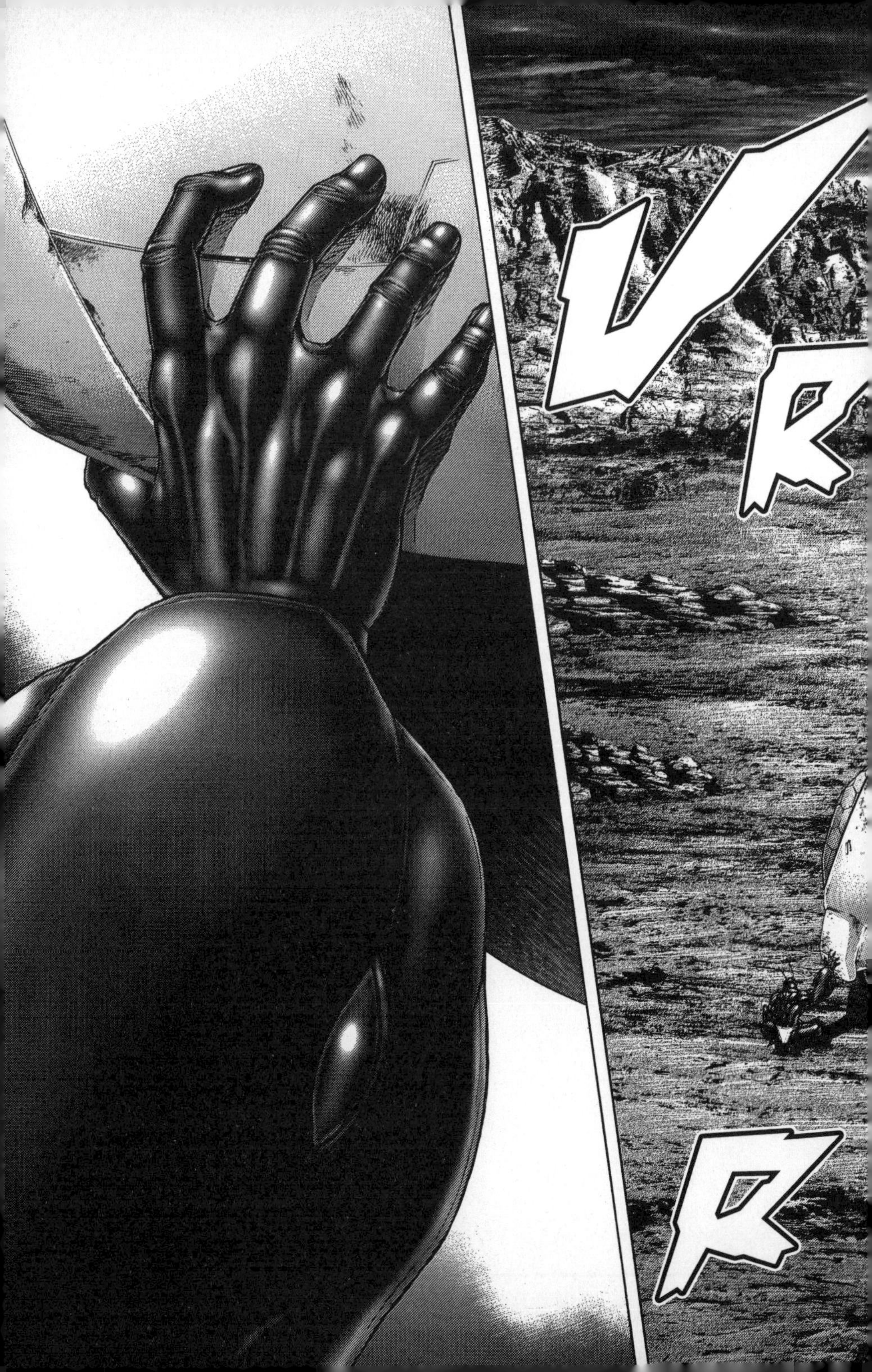
VRR

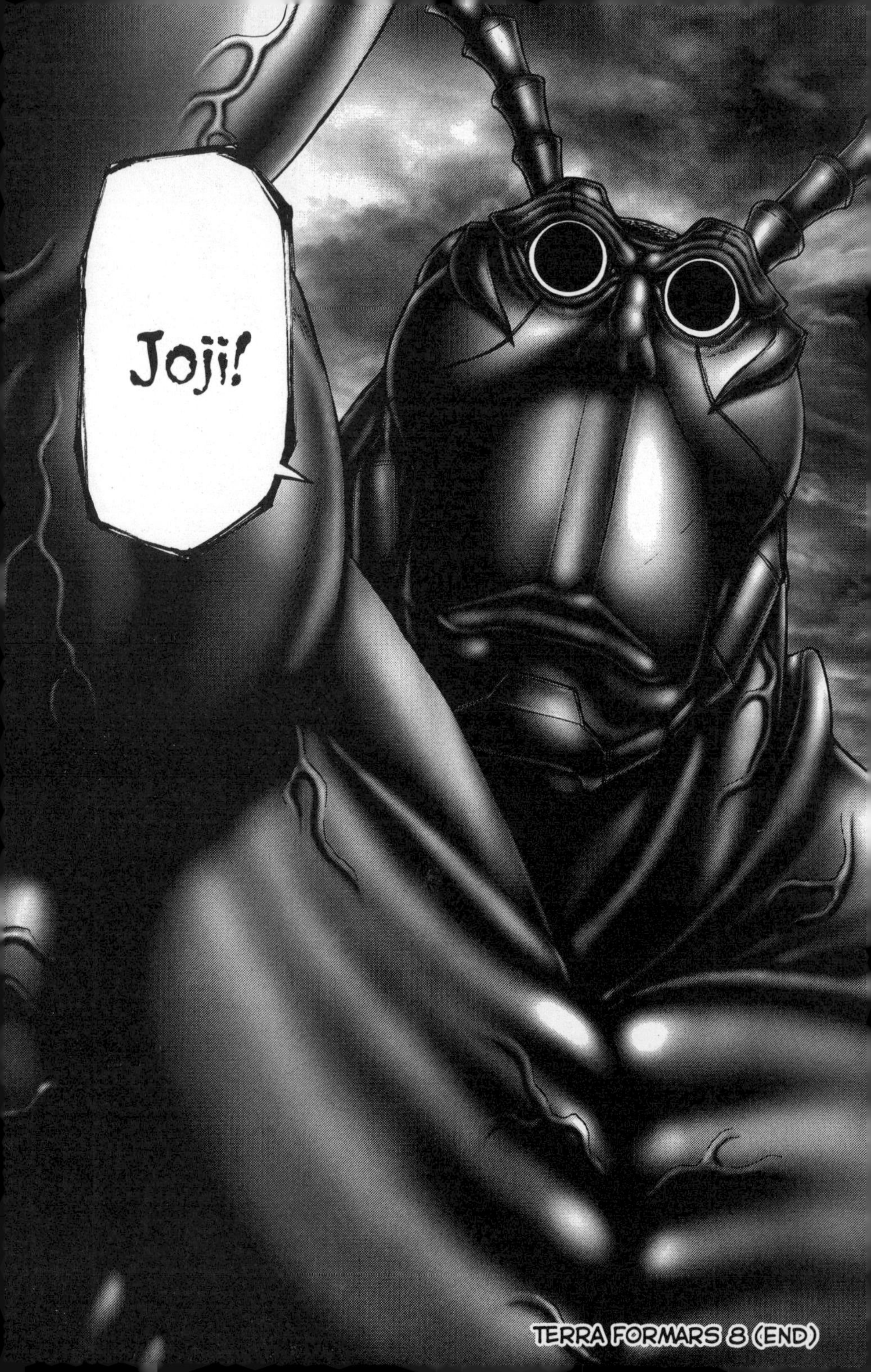
Joji!
TERRA FORMARS 8 (END)

TERRA FORMARS
Volume 8
VIZ Signature Edition

Story by YU SASUGA
Art by KENICHI TACHIBANA

TERRA FORMARS © 2011 by Ken-ichi Tachibana,Yu Sasuga/SHUEISHA Inc.
All rights reserved.
First published in Japan in 2011 by SHUEISHA Inc., Tokyo.
English translation rights arranged by SHUEISHA Inc.

Translation & English Adaptation/John Werry
Touch-up Art & Lettering/Annaliese Christman
Design/Izumi Evers
Editor/Mike Montesa

Printed in the U.S.A.

Published by VIZ Media, LLC
P.O. Box 77010
San Francisco, CA 94107

10 9 8 7 6 5 4 3 2 1
First printing, September 2015

Hey! You're Reading in the Wrong Direction!

This is the **end** of this graphic novel!

To properly enjoy this VIZ graphic novel, please turn it around and begin reading from **right to left.** Unlike English, Japanese is read right to left, so Japanese comics are read in reverse order from the way English comics are typically read.

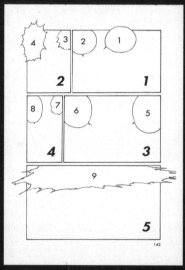

Follow the action this way

This book has been printed in the original Japanese format in order to preserve the orientation of the original artwork. Have fun with it!